THE ROSE-TINTED MENAGERIE

THE
ROSE-TINTED
MENAGERIE

William Johnson

Introduction by Desmond Morris
Preface by Prince Sadruddin Aga Khan

First published 1990 by Heretic Books Ltd, P O Box 247, London N17 9QR
World copyright © 1990 William M. Johnson
Copyright on illustrations as credited

Distributed in North America by
Inland Book Co.
140 Commerce St.
East Haven CT 06512, USA.

Distributed in Australia by
Bulldog Books,
PO Box 155, Broadway,
NSW 2007, Australia.

British Library Cataloguing in Publication Data

Johnson, William
    The rose-tinted menagerie.
    1. Illegal trade in animals
    I. Title
    382.43

ISBN 0-946097-28-3

Printed and bound in the E C. by
Norhaven A/S, Viborg, Denmark.

Typeset by Artset Graphics, London N17 (081-365 1013)

CONTENTS

ACKNOWLEDGEMENTS

The author gratefully acknowledges financial assistance from The Bellerive Foundation and Care for the Wild that has enabled him to research and write this book.

The Bellerive Foundation was established in 1977 by Prince Sadruddin Aga Khan. It implements a series of programmes addressing a wide range of interrelated issues.

In developing countries, *Bellerive Rural Technology* operates grass-roots fuelwood conservation programmes, notably through the promotion of efficient cooking systems and agroforestry. The emphasis is on practical assistance which actively involves communities in deciding their own future.

The Groupe de Bellerive is a group of independent experts committed to promoting widespread public debate on diverse problems of science and society. Particular attention is given to publicising the real or potential repercussions of technological innovation on peace and the environment.

Alp Action is a new international initiative supporting practical solutions to Alpine degradation and promoting the sustainable development of mountain regions. It is co-ordinated by Bellerive and links industry, business, the financial community and science with conservation.

Bellerive is committed not only to the protection of the environment but also to the conservation of fauna and flora. *Bellerive Conservation and Animal Welfare* stimulates public awareness of these issues and takes part in international efforts to preserve endangered species. Recent examples include far-reaching campaigns, involving celebrities and the media, to save the African elephant from extinction and to highlight the conservation and humane implications of the fur industry.

In recognition of its work, Bellerive has been elected to the Global 500 Honour Roll of the United Nations Environment Programme for "outstanding practical achievements in the protection and improvement of the environment."

The Bellerive Foundation can be contacted at P.O. Box 6, 1211 Geneva 3, Switzerland. Tel. (022) 46 88 66.

Care for the Wild: In 1984 a group of men and women, after many years of working for wildlife, came together to form a new charity — one whose sole purpose was the protection of wild animals and their habitat. The founders of *Care for the Wild* were aware that many animal charities were including a few wildlife issues in their activities, but none were working exclusively on the urgent need to protect all wildlife from killing for profit and sport, cruelty, and destruction of habitat. Today, *Care for the Wild is one of the very few organisations working* to prevent cruelty that also addresses the vital issue of destruction of habitat. In recent years, *Care for the Wild* has provided funds for the re-introduction of the British Otter; a wildlife rehabilitation centre caring for injured owls; anti-poaching teams in the national parks of Rwanda and sanctuaries for the Black Rhino in Africa. It continues to campaign to end the commercial killing of kangaroos in Australia; to end the trade in wildcats from South America for the fashion fur industry, and the continuing hunt of baby seals in Canada.

Care for the Wild can be contacted at 1 Ashfords, Horsham Road, Rusper, West Sussex RH12 4QX, England. Tel. (0293) 871596.

Additional Research and Photographic Work
by Matthias Schnellmann

INTRODUCTION

As a professional zoologist I have become increasingly uneasy about the way our species has been treating the other animals with which we share this small planet. Despite our greater understanding of the behaviour and needs of animals, there are many areas in which there has been remarkably little reduction in their exploitation and persecution. One such area is that of the performing animal, and it is this topic that William Johnson has been investigating with painstaking attention to detail. His report on the modern menagerie should be read by anyone who cares about the welfare of animals.

Recently I felt compelled to outline a new Bill of Rights for animals and formulated ten commandments that we must obey if we are to show true respect for other species. Two of those commandments are relevant here. One states that 'No animal should be dominated or degraded to entertain us,' and another adds that 'No animal should be kept in captivity unless it can be provided with an adequate physical and social environment.'

It is hard to think of a performing animal act that does not break at least one of these two rules and it is high time that we re-examined this whole subject with a more critical eye.

In carrying out this re-examination there can be no better guide than William Johnson. After you have read his words you will find it difficult to rest easy until major improvements have been made in this area.

I have long argued that if wild animals are to be confined in captivity as a means of keeping the human population in close touch with nature, then their conditions must, of necessity, be as natural as possible. Unless they can perform their usual behaviour patterns, their captive state provides a distorting mirror that is of little use to anybody. It tells us nothing about nature because it is so artificial. And nothing could be more artificial than the performing animal carrying out silly tricks in the ring, on the stage, or in the dolphinarium.

A great deal has been written about the cruelty involved in the training of performing animals, but in my view cruelty is not the central issue. Of course, when it occurs, it is an abomination, but even if it can be shown that only kindness is involved in the preparation of a particular act, that still does not excuse it if the result is a ridiculously unnatural routine for the species concerned.

To see a magnificent wild creature wearing a comic hat and carrying out quasi-human actions is demeaning to the animal, even if it can be proved that it is enjoying the process. It degrades it because it makes it into something it is not. It reduces it to a caricature of humanity.

I have met many circus people and some of them have impressed me by the concern they have shown for their animals. Not all of them are cruel, by any means. But in the end all of them are involved in presenting a spectacle that is completely outdated in its central concept. The idea that it is funny to see wild animals coerced into acting like clumsy humans, or thrilling to see powerful beasts reduced to cringing cowards by a whip-cracking trainer is primitive and medieval. It stems from the old idea that we are superior to other species and have the right to hold dominion over them. The first flowering of this concept was to be seen in the slaughters of the Roman circus and it has since been kept alive by religious teachings that have insisted on setting mankind above and apart from all the rest of creation.

We must rid ourselves of that earlier arrogance and recognise that we, too, are part of nature and must respect it in all its forms. If we fail to do this, our own future on this planet is seriously at risk. A start must be made by trying to change the way people think about animals, and per-suading them to look at each species form its own point of view. One of the first steps will be to turn our backs on the travesty of nature that is the performing animal. Let the human circus survive and flourish with its thrills, spills and excitements, and its colourful traditions. But let the animal circus join bear-baiting, bull-baiting and cock-fighting in the dustbin of antique abuses that no longer entertain us.

DESMOND MORRIS

Oxford, 1990.

PREFACE
by Prince Sadruddin Aga Khan

For those who have always felt an instinctive revulsion for the travelling menagerie, it might not seem altogether surprising that cruelty and deprivation lurks behind all the razzmatazz and glitter of the circus world. But I'm pleased to say that this book is not merely content with recounting in abstract the suffering that these animals must endure in order to provide their human audience with a short-lived thrill. Here, we also see the animals as individuals, and in graphic detail, the shadowy enterprises, dealers and showmen who profit from their exploitation.

A pair of baby elephants straining feverishly at the heavy chains which shackle them to the ground in a circus tent; ice-skating polar bears that must live most of their lives confined to boxes no more than a metre square; a giant panda — that most famous endangered species of all — trained to blow a trumpet and ride a motorbike. Haunting images such as these abound in William Johnson's book, *The Rose-Tinted Menagerie*.

As he so lucidly reveals, the true nature of those unfortunate creatures that must snarl, dance or mimic their human masters under the big top is as mocked today as it was when the circus first sprang to life in the amphitheatres of ancient Rome.

Epitomised by that endless tale of misfortune that lies behind the clown-like smile of the captive dolphin, we see how illusion has been crafted meticulously in order to convince the public that the performing circus animal is happy and content in its deprived surroundings. That deprivation, as William Johnson points out, is far more fundamental than is first suggested by the bare, cramped and squalid pools and cages to be seen in virtually every menagerie and oceanarium. The species they contain have been estranged from the myriad influences which shaped their natures and existence in the wild.

As a philosophical work that should become of major importance to the conservation movement, *The Rose-Tinted Menagerie* puts the exploitation of animals in circuses and oceanaria into the much broader context of global environmental destruction and humankind's ailing relationship with the planet.

On a journey through history, we see the evolution of that fearful anthropocentrism which afflicts the human race in our species' futile quest for supremacy over the Earth. As William Johnson suggests, it is perhaps inevitable that the fragmentation so evident in human society today is the direct legacy of our separation from Mother Nature. Indeed, it may well be surmised that speciesism, coupled with humanity's unwillingness to perceive the vital inter-relationships which compose a global ecology, has done more damage to the environment than any other single factor. By the same token, encouraging a holistic or all-embracing perception of the living Earth must be at the heart of humanity's awakening ecological awareness. In many respects, we must sweep away the outmoded ideas and institutions that still bind us to an environmentally-damaging past. That endangered species should still inhabit the beast wagons of travelling shows, that dolphins and whales should still be captured and carted around the world for exhibition is not only unconscionable in itself, but also serves to perpetuate an insidious utilitarian view of creation.

The Rose-Tinted Menagerie is an impressive contribution to the cause of conservation and animal welfare. I very much hope that it will play, as it deserves, a fundamental role in shaping a new ecological awareness.

PREFACE

> *"The exhibiting of trained animals I abhor. What an amount of suffering and cruel punishment the poor creatures have to endure in order to give a few moments of pleasure to men devoid of all thought and feeling."*
> — Albert Schweitzer

Depicting lions and elephants roaming free in an almost pristine wilderness, a brightly-coloured facade acts as the public entrance to Knie's circus menagerie. Paradoxically, it also conceals from first view, cramped and barred animal wagons. It is here perhaps, in this vivid gateway of naive and exotic scenery, that one can perceive the very quintessence of the circus and its customary appendage, the travelling zoo.

The fascination that the circus evokes is, after all, part of an age-old tradition of sensation, stirring showmanship, and above all, *illusion*. There is the big top with its flying banners and flags, the arena where lion-tamers, conjurers, acrobats, clowns and jugglers test their skills before a spellbound and often rapturous audience. And there is the circus menagerie where visitors can come face to face with some of the most exotic and endangered animals in the world, from snow leopards to elephants, from rhinos to chimpanzees and orang-utans.

Realising that many of these animals will never be released from their cages — except perhaps to enter the circus ring — does the facade of the menagerie represent a Potemkin-like front of deliberate deceit or merely an innocuous juggling of reality to entrance the public? Are the animals as happy in their captivity as the circus would have us believe, or is this too no more than a conjuring trick, part of its professional vocation as being the grand master of illusion? What lies beyond this radiant facade, which seems to confer upon the menagerie a sublime sense of innocence, a bond of human empathy and friendship with the animal kingdom?

A visit to the zoo, it has been said, can tell us more about ourselves than about the animals we encounter locked into cages. In its essence perhaps, this idea sees the cage bars as representing the great divide between humanity and nature, a two-way mirror reflecting mutual imprisonment. Wandering casually around the typical circus menagerie, one can observe humans reacting to the animals beyond the bars in a multitude of different ways. Streaked with sweat, there are fathers who have come equipped with video cameras to record their family outing for posterity, encouraging the children to pose before a cage of fluffy and mischievous tiger cubs.

There is a group of young girls taking an elephant ride, squealing in nervous excitement as the friendly lumbering giant lurches around the compound ringed by circus caravans. Standing on her pushchair with bright, excited eyes there is a toddler dangling a plush monkey toy in front of a cage of rhesus monkeys, trying to evoke some response from the nervously indifferent animals. Nearby, there's a gang of unruly schoolboys mocking the animals through the bars, pulling faces and mimicking the noises of the jungle. But at the other end of the menagerie, under the strong noonday sun, two young children are looking pensively into a cage of panthers and leopards that are panting from thirst and heat exhaustion as they lie on the aluminium floors of their barred wagons. Plaintively, and with devastating innocence, one of the children complains to his mother: "But they don't have any room to live!" Such disparate and often starkly polarised reactions are symptomatic of the controversy which is beginning to rock the very foundations of what the circus claims to be one of its oldest traditions: the travelling animal show. It is for this reason alone that circus illusion has become an ever more precious commodity, ingeniously employed to blunt and deflect burgeoning public criticism over animal abuse in the menagerie.

Writes circus historian Marian Murray: "Exaggeration is the very spirit of the circus, and certain circus men seem to have tried to outdo each other in mendacity." From the notorious dolphin dealer who claims to have "lost the least dolphins in the country" to the Italian circus whose menagerie features "the biggest and most ferocious gorilla in the world"; from "The Greatest Show on Earth" to "the most modern dolphinarium in Europe," it is in this passion for rhetoric, hyperbole, and superlatives that one can perceive something altogether more sinister and contrived than mere showmanship. It is not only that the steel bars of the cages emphasise and even reinforce the separation between human and animal, or that the whip-wielding animal tamer serves to perpetuate the myth of human supremacy over nature. Lurking behind all the tinsel and glitter is a deliberate and systematic attempt to camouflage the cruelty and deprivation that the wild circus animal and dolphin must face in captivity. Yet the illusion of the circus and dolphinarium is today nowhere more evident than in their much-vaunted claim to be playing a vital role in education. Ice-skating polar bears, dolphins singing a squeaky rendition of "Happy Birthday", a snow leopard frozen into a begging posture while balancing on a revolving discotheque ball under multi-coloured spotlights; given the brashness and gall that is an inherent part of the circus tradition, perhaps one shouldn't be overly astonished that such degrading spectacles are now routinely portrayed as "natural behaviour". In this respect, there could hardly be a better motto for today's circus impresario than a line found in Lewis Carroll's *Alice Through the Looking Glass:* "It's as large as life and twice as natural!"

Though little more than an elaborate conjuring trick, the educational justification for the circus menagerie's continuing existence not only turns reality on its head, but also turns a spellbound and gullible audience into clowns. Even some respected scientists insist that there is "a certain something" in seeing a wild animal in the flesh that allegedly cannot be reproduced by any other means, a rather vague and decidedly unscientific term coined by Dr Margaret Klinowska to justify the continuing exploitation of dolphins in captivity in her review of the industry on behalf of the British government in 1985.

Yet not content with merely depicting itself as educational, the circus menagerie has also jumped on the conservation bandwagon, claiming that its efforts in captive breeding will ultimately help save endangered species from extinction. But like all circus illusions, this one too is both tenuous and contradictory and does not bear up to further scrutiny. Indeed, wary of potential public interest in the release of their animals into the wild, circus owners and their animal trainers are the first to admit to the impracticalities of re-introduction, partly on the grounds that their animals have lost their natural instincts — though they hasten to add that the creatures retain enough of their innate wildness to be "educational" in the ring. Rather, the circus seems to be idly mimicking the current fad of the world's high-tech zoos which, while paying only lip service to the cause of protecting natural habitats, have devised a kind of Thousand Year Reich of animal conservation, intending to "keep species on ice" for the millenium it will take until the Earth's human population declines and pressure eases on the environment. With characteristic opportunism, the circus gratefully shadows the footsteps of such consummate futility, their beast wagons holding some of the most endangered species in the world, ostensibly to be conserved for the dim and distant future. For the most part, they will be only too literally conserved, like vacuum-packed meat in the supermarket or pickled organs in the laboratory. Deprived of their natural instincts and the habitat which, teeming with influences, shaped their very character and existence both as unique species and unique individuals, many are destined to become no more than bizarre parodies of their former selves, spiritually dead, tamed, broken, their wild knowledge lost forever.

Asian elephants, Bengal tigers, lowland gorillas, Himalayan bears, Pygmy hippos — these are just some of the creatures who must endure a life-time of captivity in chains or behind bars, inhabiting an environment characterised by deprivation, starkness, emptiness. Small wonder then, that many creatures are driven to insanity in this "Noah's Ark" of the circus. Though showmen and impresarios prefer to term them the "ambassadors of the animal kingdom", sadly, they are often no more than ailing, unwilling emissaries of a dying world. Indeed, the whips, muzzles, chains, electric prods, and other tools used in the circus are constant reminders that these animals are being forced to perform for their human audience. And in this respect the performing circus animal is at the mercy not only of the master who wields the whip but also of the public who, distracted by the glittering show, either overlooks or ignores its plight.

Though every sub-species tiger is on the endangered species list, in the circus, bred to excess, they are often worth more dead than alive. Those cuddly and delightfully mischievous newborn cubs, star attractions of the menagerie, all too soon grow up and become an unwanted burden that must somehow be disposed of — to a disreputable animal dealer perhaps, some down-at-heel travelling show, a research laboratory or even restaurants or food wholesalers who specialise in exotic meats. Other species may often fare little better: the elephants of the Chipperfield circus dynasty, for example, which in 1986 were chained in a pitch-black container in the hold of a ship for several months, while on a problem-plagued 40,000 km journey around the world; or the Russian performing bears who must spend most of their lives confined to a cage a metre square, their psychological terror and aggression blunted by the habitual use of drugs. use of drugs. These are the bitter realities of today's animal ghettoes, and although some children still dream of running away to the circus, perhaps many of the animals forced to perform in the arena dream of running away from the big top. Yet in all this misery there are vast profits at stake, not only at the circus and dolphinarium turnstile, but also in animal dealing. Dealers like the notorious Walter Sensen of West Germany, for instance, continue to line their own pockets by trafficking in endangered species such as Asian elephants, gorillas, chimpanzees and Commerson dolphins.

Notwithstanding the subterfuge that the industry has constructed out of education and conservation, the exploitation of animals in the circus menagerie and dolphinarium is actually characterised by a profound human ignorance of wildlife and ecology, not to mention the same chronic human psychosis which is inexorably turning a green planet into a desert — our belief in our own supremacy as a species, and the conviction that all of creation has been put exclusively at our disposal. "What has the elephant done, what crime has the elephant committed that it should be kept in chains?" asks elephant specialist Dr Fred Kurt, yet few scientists dare to ask such ultimately pertinent questions. Steeped as it is in utilitarian anthropocentrism, the law does little to prevent the systematic abuse of the performing animal. In its own circus-like contortions to marry off economic pragmatism with "ethical considerations" it has unwittingly contrived to further the myth of the content and happy animal prisoner. It is thus that under the existing legal regime, those vested with a responsibility to ensure the protection of menagerie animals are more likely to give the circus manager the benefit of the doubt rather than the animals themselves. Furthermore, a legislative process that does little more than legitimise the crime also reduces us to bicker about pool sizes and what constitutes authentic education under the big top or valid conservation in the beast wagon, when in actual fact we should be agreeing on a fundamental bill of rights for the animal nation.

A tropical paradise, pristine beaches of white coral sands, palm trees, crystal waters, a blue infinite horizon, and a school of jumping, playing dolphins. Alluring and iridescent scenes like this act as the backdrop to many a concrete dolphin pool reeking of chlorine. Much has been said, written and sung of the relationship between two of the most highly evolved life forms on the planet, one inhabiting land, the other sea. Yet today, in a society where nothing is sacred, this also includes the dolphin which in countless marine circuses around the world has been reduced to a perpetually-smiling clown coerced to perform a tedious repertoire of stunts to entertain the public. For the oceanarium manager the frozen smile of the captive dolphin is a happy illusion. More than any other single contrived ruse in his own tedious repertoire of deceit, it is that endearing, irresistible dolphin smile which so conveniently serves to camouflage misery and pitiless exploitation. It camouflages the fact that once in human hands, even the bubbling ebullient dolphin can be turned into a suicidal manic depressive; it helps to conceal the brutal capture of the animals in the wild, where, for every individual destined to live in the "synthetic sea water" of the oceanarium tank, many others may perish, including mothers and nursing calves; finally, it also tends to allay the suspicion, felt by many, that the dolphin pool is actually nothing more than a bare, concrete jail. The harsh discipline and the relentless clockwork routine that the captives must face also seems to bear a striking resemblance to human prison camps designed to break, punish and degrade their inmates. As former whale and dolphin trainer Doug Cartlidge points out, "deprivation of food plus solitary confinement in reduced areas is still being used in the discipline and training of cetacea." Yet "Flipper Inc." is a billion-dollar enterprise; in recent years, notwithstanding greater public concern for animal rights, performing dolphins have been discovered languishing in hotel swimming pools, in primitive travelling circuses, and even in nightclubs to add — what should we say? — a certain exotic *something* to a strip-tease revue.

During the course of my investigation into the international dolphin trade, which I first embarked upon in 1985, the most incriminating and lurid evidence was provided by former dolphin trainers who once represented such enterprises as Conny Gasser's Travelling Flipper Show, Don Robinson's Flamingo Land in Yorkshire, Windsor Safari Park founded by circus baron Billy Smart, and the most infamous of all, Bruno Lienhardt's Liechtenstein-registered postbox company, the International Dolphin Show. In sixteen years, these few trainers alone have had first-hand knowledge of 62 dolphins dying in captivity.

One particular episode illustrates how the rose-tinted veil conceals such deaths and misery from the public. In 1972, Debbie Steele, who now works with the mentally-handicapped in London, was an assistant dolphin-trainer at Jean Tiebor's Porthcawl dolphinarium in South Wales. On the date in question, the 2.74m deep pool contained three dolphins, two large females and a younger, smaller individual named Baby Tara. With a packed house and Harlech Television cameras recording the show, image became of such paramount importance that not even a stricken, mortally-wounded dolphin was permitted to disrupt the happy, smiling illusion. "There were about 500 people in the audience and the television cameras were there," recounts Debbie Steele. "During the show, we suddenly realised that the two females had stopped performing and we saw them swimming very fast around the pool and both of them ramming the baby. The baby went to one side, all wobbly and obviously in distress, and I rushed towards the pool ready to dive in and pick her up but the boss stopped me and said 'no, we must make it look like it's part of the show.' So I got into a wet suit double-quick, came around the side of the pool, presented myself to the audience, dived in, and held up the baby to the surface of the water so she could breathe. She was still alive then, wiggling and twitching a bit and breathing in gasps. Then I swam her into the holding pen and there she died while the show went on. For the next 20 minutes I was treading water, holding her up and pretending she was still alive. When the last person in the audience had left and the television crew had dismantled their equipment, they finally fished me out, and then the body of Baby Tara which they laid out on the side of the pool. No one in the audience had realised a thing, and I was seething at the deceit of it all and the part that they'd made me play in it. I quit there and then."

No doubt today's impresario in the dolphin trade will describe such abuse as a thing of the past, but the public has been fobbed off with the same routine patter since cruelty was first condemned in the circus, menagerie and dolphinarium. Indeed, the "thing of the past" is perhaps the most enduring of all brightly-coloured circus illusions. Yet the figment of the happy performing animal in the circus is not quite as old as the much-cherished tradition itself. Indeed, when the circus menagerie began its life almost two thousand years ago, it was not rose-tinted at all, but blood-red.

WILLIAM JOHNSON, 1990

"We are fighting neither for ourselves nor for man. All of us, voluntarily or involuntarily, consciously or unconsciously — plants, animals human beings and ideas — are struggling for the salvation of God."

— Nikos Kazantzakis, Heraklion, Crete, 1924

Elephant trainer Louis Knie leads one of his elephants through the centre of Berne, in a publicity drive organized in conjunction with the department store, Jelmoli. (William Johnson.)

I. THE BLOOD - RED MENAGERIE

*"The people that once bestowed commands, consulships,
legions and all else, now meddles no more and eagerly longs
for just two things, 'panem et circenses'."*
— Juvenal (60-130 AD)

"From Rome to Ringling!" has long been the rallying cry of the world's
most ardent circus fans, proud of the pedigree genealogy which saw the
hippodromes and amphitheatres of ancient Rome evolve into the most
distinguished of today's circuses. They conveniently forget that the
cherished tradition of the performing animal in the circus came into being
and was nurtured during the cruellest and most sordid epoch of the
Roman Empire. Similarly, as the last failing emperors took on the mantle
of Christianity, imperial Rome's utilitarian attitude towards creation was
destined to become our own insidious and enduring legacy, with nature
regarded almost as something extraneous to human survival and spiritual
well-being. Under Roman law, animals, like slaves, were without rights;
they were regarded as having been created solely for human convenience,
a belief that persists to this very day. While this may not represent the
birth of the tyranny of anthropocentrism as such, it at least marked the
age which nourished it most and allowed it to grow rampant. Indeed, it
was probably here where civilisation first learned how to drive animals
systematically into extinction — and it was the ancestor of today's circus
and menagerie which played the fundamental role as master of that lesson.

In her definitive historical study *Circus!*, dedicated to "the men and
women, now and yesterday, who have created that timeless delight, that
imperishable fantasy," the American author Marian Murray points to the
indisputable link between contemporary animal trainers and those of
ancient Rome. "The trained animals," she wrote, "which delighted audiences then as now, form the closest link between the Roman amphitheatre
and the modern circus. Trainers of today can do little that was not done at
least as well by those in Rome." Yet from the very beginning, the performing arts and the tamed animal show had quite distinct roots. Along
the banks of the Nile, as long ago as 2500 BC, rich and poor alike were
entertained by jugglers, acrobats and jesters. Small bands of playes even
roamed from village to village, like the itinerant show poeple of the Middle Ages. But the "tradition" of the circus animal does not belong in this
more enlightened period of history. Though the Egyptian aristocracy
trained animals for hunting and kept them as pets — including such

species as hyenas, leopards and lions — and regarded many creaturs from the cat to the crocodile as sacred, there were no performing animals as such. It was necessary that a far more mechanistic culture, one almost contemptuous of nature, would invent the idea of the performing wild beast, quite simply because from its very inception, its basis was to ridicule and demean the innate character of the animal.

> *"It is recorded that Hanno, one of the most distinguished of the Carthaginians, was the first human being who dared to handle a lion and exhibit it as tamed, and that this supplied a reason for his impeachment, because it was felt that a man of such an artful character might persuade the public to anything, and that their liberty was ill entrusted to one to whom even ferocity had so completely submitted."*
> — Pliny the Elder

The circus is reputed to have begun its life in ancient Rome in 329 BC, when building began on the Circus Maximus situated in the long narrow valley between the Palatine and Aventine hills. According to legend this had been the site of horse racing even from the time that Romulus, the founder of Rome, was suckled by a she-wolf. Resembling an elongated "U" rather than what was later to become the traditional circle, Circus Maximus comprised a sand-covered course or arena, a platform or podium for more distinguished guests such as senators and knights, the imperial box reserved for the emperor and his immediate entourage, and to the rear of this, the familiar tiers of stadium-like seating and terraces for the rowdy Roman masses. From the arena they were entertained by chariot races and, in another striking parallel to the contemporary circus, daring displays of equestrian and acrobatic skills such as bareback racing, sometimes of two highly trained horses simultaneously by one rider who would leap continually from one to the other. Undoubtedly Maximus was the most famous of the many Roman circuses scattered throughout the empire, and in 7 BC, following elaborate renovations by Julius Caesar and Augustus, Dionysius of Helicarnassus declared it to be one of the "wonders of Rome". Testifying to the enduring popularity of the circus, in its final form under the Christian emperor Constantine in the 4th century AD, the edifice was about 610m long and 183m wide, and could seat 200,000 people.

Large numbers of citizens being entertained by chariot races and other exhibitions of dare-devil horsemanship might seem innocuous enough, but such was the ravenous public demand for sensation that, just to keep the crowds electrified, the spectacles presented in the circus were obliged to become ever more exotic, ever more cruel and ever more fatal. It was thus that all too soon the chariot races were purposely designed to end in death for either man or beast. Collisions and spectacular crashes became so frequent that charioteers were even equipped with knives to cut themselves free from the mangled machines, men and beasts sprawled over the arena, and it is said that the ritual mayhem brought raucous cheers of appreciation from the crowd. A death or maiming was of little consequence — after all, most of these charioteers were slaves and so regarded as non-persons under Roman law, just like animals. But how did virtually an entire civilisation fall under a collective spell of debilitating illusion, one which could beguile so insidiously, all the while masquerading as hard-headed reality? It was an illusion which feasted upon them, silently, malignantly, gradually devouring not only their empire, but their very souls. It was an illusion which seemed to give reassurance and potency to their society and the foundations of its philosophy while at the same time draining its vitality and life blood. It was an illusion which could soothe and appease the masses, inducing them to trade so gratefully their individuality for the comforting anonymity of the crowd. And as with any crowd syndrome, the illusion offered self-assurance and complacency as the empire unravelled at the seams, and later, stupor and paralysis as Rome burned. In its essence it was a conviction of god-like infallibility, a chosen people whose civilisation had been endowed with divinely inspired supremacy over the forces of nature. Perhaps it was not the first civilisation to be seduced by this, the most addictive and perfidious of drugs, but it certainly wouldn't be the last.

> *"Africa captures elephants by means of pitfalls; when an elephant straying from the herd falls into one of these all the rest at once collect branches of trees and roll down rocks and construct ramps, exerting every effort in an attempt to get it out. Previously for the purpose of taming them the kings used to round them up with horsemen into a trench made by hand so as to deceive them by its length, and when they were enclosed within its banks and ditches they were starved into submission."*
> — Pliny the Elder

This flamboyant display of human power over nature was not only evident within the circus arena of course, but was practised with a vengeance against the wilderness itself. Entire forests were razed to feed Rome's ravenous economy and war machine, turning a green landscape into desert and dust throughout the occupied territories; it pursued a scorched earth policy in battle, leached the earth of its nutrients in careless farming, left little more than maquis scrub or bare rock throughout the Mediterranean basin, butchered wildlife en masse for no other reason than an obsessive need to prove the supremacy and virility of the Empire, and established a massive animal trade to supply the circuses, amphitheatres and menageries, a never-ending demand which brought many species to the brink of extinction. Even a new trend towards mass urbanisation was encouraging human separation from the living Earth. Supreme self-confidence in this domination over nature was epitomised by the orator and philosopher Cicero (106-43 BC) who wrote: "We are the absolute masters of what the earth produces... by our hands we endeavour, by our various operations on this world, to make, as it were, another nature." It could just as well have been an ironic inscription on the future headstone of the Empire. Religious beliefs, which were both abstract and utilitarian, bolstered the Romans' mechanistic view of creation. "Roman mythology seems poor when compared with the poetic and spiritual richness of Greek and Oriental mythologies," writes F. Guirand in the *Larousse Encyclopedia of Mythology*. "The Romans were practical people with little imagination and they sought to form a religion which corresponded to their needs. It was important to them to feel sheltered from the perils which threatened the group or the individual; but they experienced no mystic necessity to love and worship the superhuman powers to whom they had recourse. Their gods were protectors for whose services they paid; and in case of failure their wages were withheld. *Do ut des*: I give to thee so that thou givest to me; such was the cynical profession of faith that one might inscribe above the entrance of the Roman Pantheon."

But perhaps especially symbolic of the Roman psychosis was the fact that military victories and religious festivals would be celebrated by an orgy of killing in the circus arena. Wildcats, bears, elephants, hippopotami, the largest and most exotic species that the animal-catchers could supply were all butchered for the sake of entertainment, with the conquering audience ecstatic, worked up into a frenzy of blood-lust. While officials at the inauguration of Pompey had offered 500 lions, 410 leopards and 17 elephants, the dedication of the Colosseum saw 9,000 wild animals sacrificed in a spectacle lasting a hundred days. On another occasion, to celebrate a military triumph, 11,000 animals were brutally destroyed. In one great festival, notes Marian Murray, enough animals were killed to stock all the zoos of modern Europe.

Taking into account our own war against wildlife, the reasons for such madness are as pertinent today as ever — and just as elusive. Can it be that Roman society, male-dominated and increasingly aggressive, experienced some entrenched psychological terror towards the femininity of the ancient Mother Earth which once used to inspire reverence? Or deeper still, an atavistic terror of the capriciousness of the elements, of evasive, intimidating spirit as opposed to solid dependable matter, even a jealousy of the gods? Perhaps such questions may never be answered and yet they remain as vital as the first time they were ever asked because they reveal one of the few saving graces of this species that has so devastated the Earth that gave it birth — a sign not only that our conscience is still intact but also that our humanity, our part of natural Earth, our authentic human *nature* has not entirely been obliterated within us. If there is a lesson that can be learnt from the downfall of ancient Rome it is one of deep ecology: how, as landscapes and wildlife were devastated, so too was their reflection within the human identity. As the earth turned to dust, so did the inner soul and so did the will to survive as a civilisation.

For Imperial Rome, the circus, symbolised in later years by the epic entertainment presented in the Colosseum, would become the quintessence of this war against the Earth. A perfect illustration of the Roman psychosis, their terror of nature despite their avowed supremacy over it, was the digging of a huge moat, 3m wide and 3m deep, as protection against the doomed wild beasts of the circus arena. It was as though the superstitious Romans believed that escaping animals might come to take revenge for their fallen and imprisoned brethren, almost as though the condemned were engaged in some bizarre conspiracy to conquer Rome. It is here that one can perceive traits peculiar to any anthropocentric society, the conceit which induces humans to confuse size with quality and military and economic might with invincibility, as though gigantism as a guiding principle could even defeat the gods themselves. But despite elevating their emperors to the rank of gods, convincing themselves that brawn alone could tame the capricious forces of nature which so intimidated them, ironically it was precisely these natural powers which in the end brought the civilisation to its knees. On a purely material level it was the ecological holocaust that the Romans wreaked which enfeebled the Empire's entire system, rendering it far more susceptible to other threats, including the onslaughts of the barbarians. On a spiritual level, it was nature's subtlety of paradox and its perpetual striving for balance which in the end outfoxed the Romans with all their might and armour. For the more they prided themselves as cool-headed realists, their society emphasising an avowed supremacy by suppressing the Earth's innate personality within them, its untamed wildness, its femininity — all those qualities that became abhorrent to the Romans in their quest for order and power — the more apparent became their lethal weakness for pastime and fantasy. Nowhere was this more evident than in the Roman circus-amphitheatre, the first of which was built to serve the capital in 29 BC. The desperate need to satisfy this craving for entertainment and escapism led to different kinds of extravaganza — gladiatorial contests, animal baiting and the wholesale carnage of both man and beast under the thin guise of "hunting" and "sport". The resulting crowd frenzy only led to insatiable demands for more, demands that even an emperor-god would have been foolhardy to deny. This vicious circle was destined to spin relentlessly, and would not cease until the Empire had crumbled. First, however, for more than six hundred years, nature would be ridiculed, condemned, tortured and slaughtered in the arena.

It is recorded that during the reign of Augustus (27 BC-AD 14), 3500 wild animals were put to death at the Circus Maximus alone. All in all, literally hundreds of thousands of animals were destined to be sacrificed to Roman vanity in the Empire's many circuses and amphitheatres. Add to this the systematic destruction of habitat, animals killed during capture and transport, animals killed for sport or from that irrational lust for killing anything wild, and the death toll must have soared into the millions. But still the thirst for ever-intensifying sensation could not be slaked. Under Nero in the 1st century AD, even the torture of Christians became a star attraction at the Circus Caligulas. There were few protests against such marketable massacres. Remarks H. H. Scullard with pungent irony in his history of Rome, *From the Gracchi to Nero*:

> "An age which was apparently unmoved when 6000 of Spartacus' followers were crucified along the Appian Way is not likely to have been affected by the sufferings of animals, but it is good to know that at least once some qualms were felt. When at the games which celebrated the dedication of Pompey's gift to Rome of her first stone theatre in 55 BC, 500 lions and 17 elephants were slaughtered, Cicero wrote, 'What pleasure can it give to a cultured man to see weak human beings mangled by a powerful wild beast or a splendid animal transfixed by a hunting-spear?' Pliny the Elder records that the spectators were so moved by the pitiful sight of the dying elephants in the arena that they rose as one man and damned Pompey: 'But Pompey's elephants when they had lost all hope of escape tried to gain the compassion of the crowd by indescribable gestures of entreaty, deploring their fate with a sort of wailing, so much to the distress of the public that they forgot the general and his munificence carefully devised for their honour, and bursting into tears rose in a body and invoked curses on the head of Pompey for which he soon afterwards paid the penalty.'"

In earlier days, the games had been held in observance of fixed religious festivals or to celebrate military triumphs, but such was the public demand that successive emperors were ever more loathe to deny the people the staple, state-supplied doses of their narcotic entertainment. In response to this public clamouring for "bread and circuses", the numbers of official commemoration days set aside for public indulgence in the games became increasingly preposterous. As the satirist Juvenal wrote of his fellow countrymen, with acid sarcasm: "The people that once bestowed commands, consulships, legions and all else, now meddles no more and eagerly longs for just two things, *panem et circenses*." By Claudius' reign nearly half of the year was allotted to official holidays, though this benefited only the affluent and idle. There were 159 commemoration days a year, and on 93 of them games were held at public expense. To further placate the demands of the masses, admission to the circus was free of charge, though wine vendors and the Roman equivalent of fast-food merchants, bookmakers, and prostitutes plied a lively trade amongst the crowds. "The cry for *Panem et Circenses*, for free food and entertainment," writes Scullard, "that rose so loudly during the Empire, was already heard in the late Republic... In addition to the regular festivals, individuals, especially candidates for office, staged gladiatorial combats and won votes by pandering to the cruelty and blood-lust of the mob."

Even as Rome became mired in stultifying corruption, threats of incipient revolution in the colonies, and the first waves of barbarians massing across the borders, nothing could quench the public's thirst for illusion and pastime. Possibly, to those few who somehow remained immune to the Roman disease, that endless refrain of *"bread and circuses!"* might well have represented the curse which foreshadowed the civilisation's inevitable demise. Moreover, such extravaganzas were not only billed in the nerve-centre of Rome, but could be found in the provinces at such influential cities as Milan, Pompeii and Verona. Ensuring that the moral cancer would spread throughout the system, they were also scattered through the Empire's far-flung colonies — from Arles, Lyon and Nimes in the French "provincia", to Dorchester and Caerleon in Britain, Carthage in North Africa, Tarragona, Sagunto and Merida in Spain, and Constantinople in present-day Turkey. Only the Greek East, says Scullard, was "less receptive to this barbarous practice", perhaps because of that culture's intimate spiritual relationship with nature.

It was in the Colosseum, dedicated in 80 AD, the largest of the Empire's amphitheatres, that this Roman decadence was most apparent. Indeed, this most imposing edifice of all might also be seen as a monument to the civilisation's pitiful hubris in striving so ostentatiously to display its presumed supremacy over all creation. Here, a succession of emperors, mad either with incest, the paranoia of conspiracy, or lust for their own glory and deification, could indulge their wildest fantasies by playing god and presiding over the fate of both man and animal, incited by the rapturous adoration and blood-lust of the mob. It is recorded that the emperor Commodus even killed elephants, hippos, rhinos, tigers, bears and lions with his own hand in the Colosseum. In the space of just one day he supposedly massacred 100 bears, and on another afternoon's sport finished off, using different weapons, 100 lions that he had ordered be turned loose against him. Although regarded as an architectural masterpiece, the Colosseum also reveals the Roman mania for the grandiose, where rudimentary technology, such as it was, encouraged power over nature. The machine, after all, is viewed as yet another testament to human superiority over animals, and in the amphitheatre machines were used specifically to belittle the condemned creatures. One such ingenious device was the cochlea, or revolving door, a Roman invention which prolonged the humiliation of the animal. These, writes Marian Murray, "became the feature of a lively game. Several were set up in the floor of the Colosseum, and the crowds roared with delight to see an athlete adroitly evade a pursuing beast, leaping into the angle between the panels, and whirling to safety just as the animal thought it had cornered his prey." A similar invention, guaranteed to evoke uproarious laughter, was a kind of see-saw with two men suspended in baskets from each end of a pole. Just before a taunted lion or tiger pounced on one of the men, he would be launched into the air out of harm's way. The animal would then rush to the basket on the opposite end of the pivot, and so the game continued. Despite more than 1,600 years of human development, the same kind of degrading treatment is still very much in evidence in the contemporary circus. Betraying their mania for the grandiose and vulgar were other, more impressive, mechanical special effects. "In the time of Septimius Severus," says Murray, "a ship was drawn up from the Colosseum underground, and 'wrecked' in view of the populace, spewing forth lions, leopards, bison, wild asses and ostriches. During the same reign, after a dead whale had been picked up on a beach, a model whale was constructed for the amphitheatre, and became a dramatic container for fifty bears, from which they rushed out to meet swords and javelins." Trap doors in the floor of the arena led to great, high-arched cellars connected by an intricate network of tunnels. Besides housing lifts and winching machinery, scenery and other "stage-props" were stored here, as well as animals fated for imminent slaughter which would have been transported to the Colosseum the night before from the huge menagerie outside the Praenestine Gate. When their turn came, they would be winched up through the trap doors, suddenly appearing, no doubt bewildered and terrified, before the bellowing and shrieking masses in the grandstands. Otherwise the instinctively cowering animals would be driven out of their cages and through the tunnels to the arena by setting straw alight behind them or goading them with red-hot irons. Under the *loges* occupied by the ruling elite stood the massive Doors of the Dead, through which the carcasses or the mortally wounded were removed.

It was here in the Colosseum's massive sand-filled arena that gladiators recruited from prisoners of war and condemned criminals became part of a ritual slaughter which was supervised by magistrates. As this was billed as sport it naturally followed that in at least some of these spectacles there had to be an element of sporting chance involved, and so depending on his classification, a gladiator might be equipped with net, trident or sword to win his battle against the ferocious beasts. Half-starved to make them hungry enough to "perform", some will point out that this is another similarity with today's circus animal.

For consistently good displays, surviving gladiators could expect fame and fortune from an appreciative crowd. But as Scullard remarks, "his hour of fame was likely to be brief and he would have to survive many a further combat before he could hope for his *rudis*, the wooden sword that symbolised his discharge. Courage and skill might occasionally save a man, but even more pitiful and degrading for the spectators were the *munera sine missione*, butcheries from which no one might survive, and also the practice of exposing unarmed victims *ad bestias*, to the mercy of the lions." It is said that 2,000 gladiators and about 230 wild animals were billed to die in one celebration alone during the Colosseum's hey-days. So popular were these extravaganzas with the crowds that later such *bestiarii*, men who pitted themselves against wild animals in the arena, were specially trained for the task and, says Scullard, survivors often "prided themselves on their scars and bites." In turn, some of the beasts too, rather than being butchered immediately, would be trained to perform tricks, and it is interesting to note that most of these were specifically designed to ridicule and degrade the animal. It provided relief for the audience from the usual fare of undiluted blood and gore, and they rocked with laughter at seeing elephants that danced, and — to the evident delight of Tiberius who watched from the imperial box of the Circus Maximus — walked the tightrope. Recounts Pliny in his *Natural History*: "It is known that one elephant which was rather slow-witted in understanding instructions given to it and had been punished with repeated beatings, was found at night practising the same." However much they would prefer a more respectable heritage, today's wild animal tamer is the direct descendant of such human mockery of nature. Yet even this gruesome heritage can, for those who perpetually see the circus and its animal acts through rose-tinted glasses, appear relatively innocuous. The Romans gradually became "skilful and ingenious trainers", wrote Marian Murray, as if somehow to soften the indescribable horror of it all. The animals, she added, "fought like gladiators" in the arena, "bears fought or danced on command," elephants "could walk through crowded rooms and sit neatly at table," and "lions, leopards, tigers, even boars and wolves went through the same kind of turns we see in the ring today."

Another spectacular attraction was animal baiting, known as *venationes*, and in typical Roman fashion this too was done on a grand scale, encouraging elephants and rhinos to attack and maul each other, or even gentle antelopes to butt each other to death. That such stunts were in direct contradiction to the animals' inherent natures is yet another aspect of the animal training legacy bequeathed to the modern circus. Like the peep shows which were later to become an important feature of the modern circus, the Romans also collected human freaks whenever and wherever they could. Objects of unabashed curiosity, dwarfs, giants, hermaphrodites, men and women with three eyes or pointed heads were exhibited under the broad genre of *miracula* and were sold as slaves in Rome's monstrosity market.

Bringing prestige to this or that emperor who introduced them to the civilised world, were exotic species never seen before, eliciting gasps of wonder from the audience, animals to inspire dread, freaks of species, the larger the better, giant snakes, crocodiles, rhinos and hippopotami. Already in the third century BC, it is recorded that the consul Metellus, wishing to highlight his military victory, displayed 142 elephants that he had captured in Carthage. Following the celebrations and pageantry, the strange, unknown beasts were simply put to death because no one had any idea what to do with them. In much the same way as the circus procession in the twentieth century marches through the town to rouse the people and entice them towards the show ground and big top, so the Roman parade first of all marched around the circus amphitheatre, displaying rare and wonderful animal curiosities, followed by acrobats and tumblers. Species mentioned as displayed by various emperors included Indian rhinos, a white elephant from Siam, and even a polar bear under Nero. In the parade, traditionally held at dawn for the premiere of a *venatio* advertised throughout the city by criers and posters, the animals would often be inexplicably painted in bright colours. "Occasionally," wrote Murray, "a touch of unkind humour was introduced by covering the bears with glue, so that when they rolled in the arena they picked up sand, leaves, feathers, and straw."

It became fashionable for the rich and influential to keep their own menageries of exotic species for the sake of prestige. Octavius Augustus, during a fifteen-year reign as emperor, collected 3,500 animals, including 420 trained tigers, 260 lions, 600 African leopards and cheetahs, a rhinoceros and a hippopotamus — the first to be seen in Rome — crocodiles, elephants, bears and Mediterranean monk seals, now one of the most endangered and forgotten species on Earth. It is recorded that Mark Anthony, with the actress Cytheris beside him, drove from Brindisi to Rome in a chariot drawn by lions. Similarly, the infamous Heliogabalus, who owned a menagerie containing several hippopotami and a rhinoceros, liked to show off around town with lions, tigers or stags drawing his chariot. "He also loved practical jokes," notes Marian Murray. "He would put lions and tigers, whose teeth and claws had been extracted, into the bedrooms of his drunken guests — several of whom, on awakening, died of fright." Says Scullard: "The vast numbers of animals, such as elephants, lions, tigers, leopards, panthers and hippopotami, that had to be shipped to Rome to gratify Roman cruelty gave rise to a large-scale trade in wild beasts."

Almost the same could be said today of course, with the proviso that the trade has somehow been sanitised by being "regulated" and subject to law. But as we shall see later, this is another similarity which our own civilisation seems to share with the Romans — an entirely inordinate faith that the reality of a situation can somehow be immediately rectified simply through issuing an executive order or proclamation, the comforting delusion that a species protected on paper is also protected in reality.

Significantly, it was neither any moral enlightenment nor the impact of Christianity which finally put a stop to the genocide of nature in the circus amphitheatre, but simply a chronic shortage of victims. "These ghastly displays, with their degrading influence on spectators, lasted for centuries," writes Scullard, and indeed it was virtually inevitable that such moral decadence should have helped bring once mighty Rome to its knees. Even the Christian emperors were reluctant to move against the circus amphitheatre, for fear of inflaming an already restless populace. Only in AD 326 did Constantine repeal the law which decreed that an unarmed man could be condemned to meet wild beasts in the arena, though the "hunting" of wild animals in the Colosseum continued until the sixth century because no emperor, whether Christian or pagan, dared to deprive the public of their favourite pastime. As the seventeenth-century philosopher Thomas Hobbes remarked acidly: "The Papacy is not other than the Ghost of the deceased Roman Empire, sitting crowned upon the grave thereof."

The Circus of Gaius and Nero, seating about 100,000 avid spectators, was built on land near the Vatican. Nero had had no qualms about seeing the fledgling Christian sect persecuted for entertainment there. Writes Scullard: "Their punishment was terrible: some were thrown to the beasts in the amphitheatre, and others were smeared with pitch and used by Nero as living torches to light the games he held by night in the imperial gardens and the Vatican circus; the victims included, according to tradition, Saints Peter and Paul." Destroyed during the latter years of the Empire, the foundations of the Basilica of St Peter were built upon its ruins. But like the Romans that had come before them, the Christians and their Church were to prove no friend of the animal kingdom. Indeed, they were soon to turn upon what was left of the Roman menageries scattered throughout the Mediterranean lands, the ritual killing eventually falling into myth and legend as the Crusaders and other dragon-slayers hunted down and eliminated the creatures.

Perhaps anthropocentrism, like some kind of species-patriotism or even racism, could be described as a latent human condition, thriving only in environments of greed, materialism and narrow-mindedness. To search for the source of the disease is probably as futile as those intrepid jungle-slashing scientists trying to find the first green monkey to contract simian AIDS, only to discover that the virus, like the jungle path and planetary destiny itself, splits into myriad possibilities. Yet reflecting creation's untameable relativity, perhaps this is the most daunting phenomenon of all for a species which cannot quite decide whether to cherish or to frustrate freedom. Indeed, it is in humanity's war against planetary diversity, its subconscious aversion towards what it myopically perceives as chaos and anarchy, that we can perceive our species' chronic "fear of freedom" as described by Erich Fromm. In essence, this is what humanity so stubbornly rebels against — the capriciousness of creation which we must somehow develop, "civilise" and destroy to find concrete certainty. In the process, freedom is destroyed — and ultimately perhaps, even life itself. As Jean-Jacques Rousseau pointed out: "Man was born free, and everywhere he is in chains." One could also add, so almost invariably are animals after coming in contact with *homo sapiens*. All forms of exploitation — from the menagerie to the modern factory farm — embody an imprisonment for the animal. Most passionate defenders of the zoo, circus or animal farm excuse all of this on the grounds that the creatures know nothing else and are actually afraid to leave the cage which has become their entire world. But perhaps it is humanity that is afraid to leave its cage — the prison of our prejudices and intellectual preconceptions, our hectic schedules and appointments, all the things that bind us to our hermetically sealed reality, the security of our nine-to-five existence, our consumer goods, our insurances and pensions, our television sets, our locked houses...

In any event, what is beyond dispute is that the acute anthropocentrism that afflicted the Romans did not perish as that civilisation finally crumbled. The belief that animals were created solely for human convenience still persists to this very day, whether that exploitation manifests itself in the wild, on the factory farm, in the laboratory, or in the zoo or circus. Indeed, this chronic human disease seems to outlive any generation, any religion, any form of government. Is it then, merely human nature, the innate primordial instincts of species survival and self-preservation? Despite the obvious temptation to pass it off as such with a complacent shrug of the shoulders, it is a conclusion obviously contradicted by the very fact that behaviour of this kind manifests itself in distinctly unnatural ways, from concreting the jungle to constructing cities of monolithic skyscrapers. Moreover, such conduct, as the Earth gradually succumbs to destruction, must be regarded as indisputably suicidal. Whatever the root cause of this human condition, it may be safely surmised that its chronic and self-perpetuating course has been bolstered immeasurably by the character of human society and its inexorable weakness for conformism, regulation and standardisation. Perhaps this factor alone has, over the centuries, managed to boost, magnify and distort the coveted human role as master of creation out of all proportion, a self-imposed exile from Mother Earth and her natural laws inflamed into barely disguised contempt, scorn and condescension. Human religion, human philosophy and human science — perhaps in centuries to come it will be these proud institutions which will be found guilty of reinforcing, if not sometimes inciting the artificial borders between two distinct realities with two increasingly distinct values, that of nature and that of *homo sapiens*. Just how the innate complementary paradoxes of the universe have become interpreted as antagonistic dualities should never be underestimated, quite simply because this view of creation has permeated the very fabric of human society, a phenomenon so ubiquitous that it bears more than a passing resemblance to the harrowing disease of schizophrenia. In a sense, the acute disassociation of thoughts, words and actions that characterises schizophrenia might be thought of as the extreme effect of a more general and diluted fragmentation that afflicts the human race as a whole, a condition rooted in our divorce from nature since it was through that separation that we became deprived of the intuitive guidance of natural law. Though it is true that we have belatedly discovered ecology, it must be said that ecology is not a science, nor even a way of life, but merely the inadequate description of universal relativity, an art form perhaps that tries to portray the wonderful myriad interrelationships of worlds within worlds. More often than not — and revealing just how all-pervasive the disease is — ecology which by implication presupposes wholeness and interdependence, is reduced today to an archetypal museum science of separate, interchangeable building blocks of categorised species and habitats. Indeed, what better example could there be of this kind of fragmentary thinking than a zoo or menagerie that ostensibly imports an endangered species for "conservation", "captive breeding", and ultimately, "re-introduction", while at the same time the animal's natural habitat, the environment that gave it birth, moulded its character and spirit, is being irrevocably destroyed? Such examples are legion in almost every category, division and subsection of human society. In many cases they are the legacy of earlier and more fundamental separations fostered by religion — heaven from earth, god from nature, human from animal, the animate from the inanimate, the spiritual from the material. The chronic bigotry of religion in particular, whose patriarchs typically believe they can fit the consciousness of God into their own narrow minds, has played a leading role in fostering a diametric view of creation.

In God's Image

It has been said that one of the root causes of today's ecological crisis lies in the Judaeo-Christian tradition that humanity is separate from and superior to the natural world. Yet this dualistic view of creation actually contradicts many references to the sanctity and oneness of nature found in the scriptures of all the world's major religions, including Christianity.

Such injunctions to respect the Earth, however, were destined to be sacrificed to expedient re-interpretation, with influential theologians portraying creation as "man's" exclusive domain to exploit, dominate and control. Clashing human values — on one hand, a spiritually holistic perception which links humanity intimately with nature, and on the other, a more expedient and utilitarian view of the Earth — have disfigured all of the world's major religions. Undoubtedly, the legacy which the Christian Church has bequeathed to the world in regard to respect for nature and compassion towards animals has been bleak. As for utilitarianism, it may even be said that this philosophy has conquered the entire world, because the global economy, based on mass consumption — and by implication exploitation and destruction of nature — has been controlled since its inception by rich developed nations which possess a Christian heritage. Unfortunately, the profound ecological aspects of that heritage have long been suppressed to meet the demands of an egocentric theology.

> "Nothing is apt to mask the face of God so much as religion."
> — Martin Büber

It is in the first chapter of Genesis that God tells "man" to be fruitful and multiply, subdue the Earth and have dominion over it. How the Church has interpreted this Biblical version of Creation has long been a contentious issue, but in recent years the controversy has grown in tandem with the world's multiplying ecological crises. While more conservative theologians continue to believe that humanity was given not only the right but the duty to exploit the natural environment in order to civilise the Earth according to God's specific wishes, more reform-minded academics are convinced that God merely intended human beings to be respectful guardians and stewards of the Earth rather than exclusive owners. More outspoken, secular critics on the other hand interpret even the idea of "dominion" as cultivating the notion of human supremacy and believe that the Judaeo-Christian tradition has played a fundamental, if inadvertent role in leading the world to ecological devastation. In this view, it was not so much the scriptures themselves, but the fathers of the early Christian Church, who fostered the separation of humanity from nature. In terms of sheer expediency there was undoubtedly a dual benefit in embracing this concept. Not only was it used to justify the Church's war for influence against diverse pantheistic faiths which still believed in the sanctity and oneness of Mother Earth, but at the same time it also served to clear away inconvenient moral obstacles to the plundering of the Earth's natural wealth.

Moreover, the idea of separateness was bolstered by scriptural references to the unique Creation of "man" in God's image, and ironically there can be little doubt that this notion appealed to the same human vanity which, in Genesis, results in Adam and Eve's expulsion from the Garden of Eden. Indeed, that expulsion can in itself be regarded as symbolic of humanity's self-imposed separation from nature. But whatever diverse conclusions individuals may draw from the scriptures, it is virtually undeniable that the destruction of nature, and perhaps the vast majority of society's woes, can be blamed on the disease of fragmentation. As we have already seen, at the root of this condition is the tendency to perceive the world either in implacable black and white extremes or in unrelated categories — not only an antithesis to ecology which is inherently holistic, but also to the creed of oneness, regarded as sacred in numerous faiths and religions, including Christianity.

In the *Hexaemeron* Homily VIII of St Basil for example we find the following: "Our God has created nothing unnecessarily and has omitted nothing that is necessary." And in Hinduism's *Upanishads*: "Even by the mind this truth is to be learned: there are not many but only One. Who sees variety and not the unity wanders from death to death." At the heart of this appreciation of oneness is the macrocosm-microcosm idea, also found in the contemporary concept of "deep ecology". Again in the Upanishads we find written: "The little space within the heart is as great as this vast universe. The heavens and the earth are there, and the sun, and the moon, and the stars; fire and lightning and winds are there; and all that now is and all that is not: for the whole universe is in Him and He dwells within our heart." Similar sentiments are expressed by Jesus in a papyrus scripture of the second century AD, discovered in Egypt early this century: "Ye ask — Who are they which draw us to the kingdom, if the kingdom is in heaven?... the fowls of the air, and all beasts that are under the earth or upon the earth, and the fishes of the sea, these are they that draw you, and the kingdom of heaven is within you."

The fundamentally ecological idea that inter-relating diversity also leads to harmonious oneness is also found in the Great Catechism: "In the sensible world itself, though there is considerable mutual opposition of its various elements, yet a certain harmony maintained in those opposites has been devised by the wisdom that rules the universe, and thus there is produced a concord of the whole Creation with itself, and the natural contrariety does not break the chain of agreement..."

Similar sentiments are expressed by the world's religions with respect to humanity's relationship with other living species. Although it is written that Allah created "man" as His "vicegerent on earth", and animals to serve his needs — precepts which might have unintentionally encouraged some of the terrible cruelty inflicted upon animals in the Muslim world — the Qur'an also emphasises the equality between human and animal: "There is no beast on Earth, nor bird which flieth with its wings, but the same is a people like unto you." Furthermore, the scriptures of many religions specifically forbid the mistreatment of animals, whether or not those creatures have any economic usefulness to human beings. Islam's Mishkat al Masabih declares that "doing good to beasts is like the doing of good to human beings, a deed of charity; while cruelty to animals is forbidden just like cruelty to human beings." In Hinduism's Srimad-Bhagavatam we find the following: "One should treat animals such as deer, camels, asses, monkeys, mice, snakes, birds and flies exactly like one's own son. How little difference there actually is between children and these innocent animals." And in the words of the Buddha: "One thing only do I teach: suffering and the cease of suffering. Kindness to all living creatures is the true religion." Similarly, the Prophet-founder of the Baha'i faith, 'Abdu'l Baha, wrote some 150 years ago: "It is not only their fellow human beings that the beloved of God must treat with mercy and compassion, rather must they show forth the utmost loving kindness to every living creature... The feelings are one and the same, whether ye inflict pain on man or beast."

But as always, even amongst the most unanthropocentric religions, selective interpretation of the scriptures by influential theologians has often been used to justify virtually any abuse of nature that seems expedient to serve human needs or desires. It is quite possible, for example, that the early fathers of the Christian Church decreed that animals have no souls not only as a useful weapon against animism, but also to bolster the notion of "man's" unique creation in the image of God. And yet this is a philosophy not to be found anywhere in the Bible. Indeed, we find in Job 12:7-10: "But ask now the beasts and they shall teach thee; and the fowls of the air, and they shall tell thee: Or speak to the earth, and it shall teach thee: and the fishes of the sea shall declare unto thee. Who knoweth not in all these that the hand of the Lord hath wrought this? In whose hand is the soul of every living thing, and the breath of all mankind."

Despite such references in the scriptures, for the fathers of the Church nature became increasingly equated with the Devil in that pantheistic faiths which worshipped the Mother Earth and her spirits were viewed as evil and depraved. Yet the Church's obsession with dichotomy was not only confined to Good versus Evil. In direct opposition to pantheistic beliefs, spirit was to become divorced from matter, Earth separated from heaven, and God promoted aloft into a purely metaphysical realm. The notion of separateness was part of a human intellectual weakness for reductionism, the peculiar conviction that any complex idea or system can be completely understood if it is simplified by breaking it down into separate component parts. Reductionism, later to become so evident in science, was the invasive tool, the scalpel and forceps, which would be used in understanding the world, for knowledge too was power — however transient, however illusory.

Living in the 13th century, Thomas Aquinas, a member of the Dominican order, was instrumental in encouraging the Church to embrace scientific rationalism — a legacy of Aristotle which emphasised the primacy of human intelligence. Despite its aversion to "paganism", the Church had actually been experiencing the influences of neoplatonic thought ever since St Augustine embraced its creed of spiritual monism in the 5th century. But in its conversion to Christianity, the neoplatonic belief in universal oneness suffered such disfigurement that to later theologians — including Aquinas — it was misconstrued to mean that there was only one, homogeneous reality — their own. To some extent, this might explain the Church's medieval crusade against "heretical" beliefs and its rabid intolerance partly fathered by Aquinas.

In this period of European history, technical progress was already requiring men and women to move from agrarian to urban society, reinforcing human alienation from nature. In his publication *The Status of Animals in the Christian Religion*, C. W. Hume quotes historian Rosalind Hill as saying that there was "a tendency, in towns and along trade routes, to develop a much more urban, mercantile economy, so that people lived away from their animals and regarded them as expendable. It is rather interesting to find that the worst period of cruelty to human beings (practised because of fear) coincides with this — e.g. much more torture, burning of heretics, and witch-hunting, none of which had been very common in the Middle Ages. Right through this period and until the 18th century you had extremely brutal sports with animals, coinciding with public brutality to humans, and as far as the evidence goes the populace enjoyed both."

Still influenced by earlier Christian beliefs in the depravity of nature, including the inherent sinfulness of the naked human body, new generations of men and women, including clerics, were beginning to strive for mastery over the forces of nature. Rationalism was to become a prime mover in this new trend and Aquinas, canonised a saint in 1323, is still recognised by the Roman Catholic Church as its foremost philosopher and theologian. Although all Christian philosophers taught the distinction between matter and spirit, Aquinas believed in an intrinsic separation between the two. In this sense Aquinas also denounced the Christian tendency to sacralise the forces of nature and to connect nature to the miraculous or to the providence of God. This amounted to an antithesis of the beliefs of St Francis, today often referred to as the patron saint of ecology. "Through our dear Mother Earth be praised, my Lord," runs St Francis' *Canticle of the Creatures*. "She feeds us, guides us, gives us plants, bright flowers, And all her fruits." But to the Dominicans of Aquinas, such sentiments were contemptible in that they were both inimical to rationalistic thought and betrayed a similarity to the animistic beliefs which the Church had for so long struggled against. "If in Holy Scripture there are found some injunctions forbidding the infliction of some cruelty towards brute animals," wrote Aquinas, "this is either for removing a man's mind from exercising cruelty towards other men... or because the injury inflicted on animals turns to a temporal loss for some man..." It has been postulated that Aquinas founded this belief upon the jurisprudence of ancient Rome. "Only a person, that is, a being possessed of reason and self-control, can be the subject of rights and duties," declares the Catholic Encyclopedia. The striking similarities between Roman and canon law in this respect are further elucidated by C. W. Hume: "In the jurisprudence of ancient Rome nobody could have rights unless he was legally a person, persona, and originally you could not be a person unless you were free (a slave was not a person), nor unless you were a citizen (foreigners were not persons), nor unless you were a paterfamilias (sons, daughters and wives were not persons, and had no rights; a father could put his son to death at pleasure). Gradually more and more new classes of human beings acquired personality and with it legal rights, but animals never did so." During medieval trials however, animals accused of crimes or misdeeds continued to be held accountable for their actions, the defendants having much the same rights as humans, being provided with legal counsel. Found guilty of committing capital crimes, animals such as dogs, horses and pigs were even sentenced to death by hanging. Today, such trials may well seem like a theatre of the absurd, yet the human attitudes which gave rise to them, reflecting the legacy of pantheism, also implicitly recognised the intelligence of animals, their individuality, and their free will. Writes Rosalind Hill, a specialist in medieval history, in her publication *Both Small and Great Beasts*: "In a society which accepted without question the fact that Balaam's ass showed a good deal more perception and good sense than Balaam himself, there was much less pitying condescension towards the animal world than there is today."

To Aquinas, animals were devoid of reason, free will and soul and in this respect his views bear a striking resemblance to those of the rationalist René Descartes, who, four centuries later, became the founding father of science's mechanistic view of creation. Not only were the views of the Franciscans swept aside in this increasingly intolerant onslaught, but also much older Christian traditions, not least of all the belief in one common Creation. As St Chrysostom wrote in the 4th century: "Surely we ought to show creatures great kindness and gentleness for many reasons, but, above all, because they are of the same origin as ourselves." But to dialectical rationalism, emotion too was to become regarded as inferior to impassive intellect. And as animals more evidently displayed similar emotions to *homo sapiens* than similar thoughts, this amounted to yet another convenient justification for the notion of separateness. To Aquinas and his followers, nature was hostile to the survival of humanity and could only be controlled through reason. The supernatural view of the world cast its shadow over human progress and inhibited man's rightful supremacy over nature. Indeed, whether by accident or design, regarding the natural world as soulless, inanimate matter, devoid of any connection with its Creator, removed the final moral obstacle to its exclusive ownership and exploitation by *homo sapiens*. Destined to conquer and prevail, this doctrine was to set the course for a brutal war against the supernatural. Under the increasingly powerful influence of the Dominicans, in 1484 Pope Innocent VIII gave the Church's formal assent to the Inquisition. The witch-hunts which were to follow served not only to wipe out both real and imaginary practitioners in the arts of the occult — whether black or white magic — but also, by sheer intimidation and mass hysteria, to discourage even the most innocent beliefs in the spirits of nature. Indeed, the witch-hunts were destined to destroy the last remnants of cultural pantheism in Europe. In the two centuries which followed, it is estimated that over nine million peasants were burnt or tortured to death after being accused of witchcraft, as well as countless animals which were suspected of being under their evil command as so-called "familiars". Cats, for example, reputed to be the witch's most preferred familiar, were killed in their tens of thousands, and even up until the last century, relates Swiss author Hans Ruesch in *Slaughter of the Innocent*, the Church still considered it quite normal to celebrate All Saints Day in Italy by burning barrels of live cats in the piazzas.

> "For a certain type of intellectual mediocrity characterised by enlightened rationalism, a scientific theory that simplifies matters is a very good means of defence because of the tremendous faith modern man has in anything which bears the label 'scientific'. Such a label sets your mind at rest immediately, almost as well as 'Roma locuta causa finita': Rome has spoken, the matter is settled."
> — C. G. Jung

The Dark Ages of Science

Several characteristics underlined the distinction between "civilised man" and "dumb brutes", not least of all the concepts of intelligence, thought and free will. The human being, ashamedly trying to bury his own animalness, often under ludicrously stilted social etiquette and fashion, nevertheless resorted to rather primitive ways to elevate his own self-esteem, the most obvious of which was to relegate his former relatives in the animal kingdom to the status of inferior beings possessing neither soul nor conscious thought. One need only recall the shock which greeted Darwin's theory of evolution in Victorian England — the preposterous idea that humanity, made in the image of God, could somehow be descended from the apes! Despite predictable outrage there was actually little reason for the Church to lead a song and dance over the Darwin affair, since almost any controversial theory could be assimilated into already established ways of thinking. As the Church was soon to discover once it recovered from its knee-jerk denunciations of the Darwinian heresy, science harboured no perverse intentions to knock humanity off the throne of creation, but in fact merely wished to confirm with rationalism the biological preeminence of *homo sapiens*. Indeed, Darwin's theory, expediently reinterpreted as the *survival of the slickest*, emphasising the competition rather than the cooperation between species, seemed to justify every kind of social injustice as entirely natural.

> "Until he extends the circle of his compassion to all living things, man will not himself find peace."
> — Albert Schweitzer

Perhaps the greatest separation between "man and beast" that could be reinforced through science was intelligence. More than any other characteristic, thought is still regarded as the border between human and animal, and time and again the alleged inferiority of animal consciousness is used to justify their commercial exploitation, whether in the circus, the factory farm or the laboratory.

Until very recently, evidence of animals displaying conscious thought was regarded by science as inadmissible. Although too numerous to catalogue, such reports were simply dismissed or filed away as unexplained phenomena. This was because the very idea of animal intelligence was incompatible with established theories which classified animals as virtual automata, driven entirely by instinct. It was as though instinct and intuition was something primitive and inferior which the "civilised" human had outgrown. The 17th century French scientist and philosopher René Descartes was the founding father of this doctrine. Science was then in the process of becoming a powerful new religion, and had embarked on its own crusade to reconstruct the very foundations of human concepts of creation: rather than being endowed with insubstantial, metaphysical spirit, life would instead be reduced to precise mathematical formulae, its mechanistic workings quantifiable and comfortingly predictable. So powerful was the influence of Descartes in promoting this new doctrine that even the suggestion of animal consciousness was regarded as anathema in scientific circles. There was little or no protest from religious circles since, within Christian dogma, animals were already regarded as soulless and nature as perverse. It was thus only one step away for animals to be deprived of their minds as well, reduced to mere clockwork mechanisms. "I think therefore I am," declared the visionary Descartes, so perhaps it was logical to assume that because animals didn't think, they were not. Certainly, following the lead of ancient Rome and the bigotry of Aquinas they were not deemed worthy of rights, any more than the savages who, during the process of colonialism, faced the choice of being converted or killed. Given science's contempt for superstition, it is ironic indeed that its proud new ethic was also a legacy of age-old religious beliefs which had somehow conspired with human arrogance to put *homo sapiens* on the throne of creation, separated from all other life through the unique possession of soul and consciousness. And although science claimed the search for truth as its highest principle, there can be little doubt that from its very inception, its view of creation was guided by sheer expedience. For without soul, without mind, nature and her animal offspring could be regarded as little more than exploitable matter, existing only to serve the needs of the human race.

It was thus that Descartes and his contemporaries unwittingly ushered in a litany of horrors in the name of their new religion. Laboratory research at the time bore more than a passing resemblance to the holy Inquisition that it supplanted, where animals — sometimes literally nailed to the operating table — were tortured for the information that their machine-bodies would reveal under the scalpel and forceps wielded by the white-robed priests of the laboratory. Wrote a contemporary of Descartes: "The scientists administered beatings to dogs with perfect indifference and made fun of those who pitied the creatures as if they felt pain. They said the animals were clocks; that the cries they emitted when struck were only the noise of a little spring that had been touched, but that the whole body was without feeling. They nailed the poor animals up on boards by their four paws to vivisect them, to see the circulation of blood which was a great subject of controversy." Descartes and his colleagues marvelled that these "mechanical robots", as they called them, "could give such a realistic illusion of agony." Indeed, because they were machines, incapable of suffering, to Descartes the cries of the tortured animals amounted to no more than the creaking of a wheel. But then "why not whip the cart instead of the horse?" as Hans Ruesch suggests in his book *Slaughter of the Innocent*. "Descartes never troubled to explain that."

The Big Top and the Beast Wagon

Not surprisingly, performing animal shows thrived under such moral imperfections and the prevailing religious and scientific philosophy of reductionism. The issue of cruelty was irrelevant, the notion of animal rights plain madness. After the fall of Rome in 476 AD, itinerant animal trainers and performers exploited the nostalgia for the ruined Roman circus, travelling from town to town with bears, monkeys, lions and other exotic animals, as well as horses and dogs. There were no organised circuses as such, though jugglers, acrobats, dancers, sword swallowers, fire eaters, stilt walkers, fortune tellers and animal tamers, together with pick-pockets and other tricksters, wandered individually or in small groups through Europe, Asia and Africa. Small bands of Gypsies would roam the countryside with a performing bear or two, as they still do today in Yugoslavia, Romania and Turkey. With roads narrow, pitted and dangerous — alive with fugitive serfs, vagrants and thieves, quack medicine men, vagabond monks, and pedlars hawking their wares — most of Europe never dared to venture very far from home; when the travelling show people arrived in a town or village, they would be greeted with awe and wonder. Performing in exchange for food and sometimes lodging, their life was characterised — as it frequently still is today despite the romantic image — by chronic poverty and insecurity, a wretched existence which their animals could not help but share. They played wherever large groups of people gathered, on the village green, in noblemen's halls, in squares and market places. It is said that King Alfred the Great (849-899) was entertained by a wild beast show, and that William the Conqueror brought troupes of contortionists, rope-dancers and acrobats from France to England. At the same time, throughout Europe, the aristocracy, the wealthy, even bishops and popes were keeping exotic animals in private menageries, the forerunners of today's public zoos. The captive animals served much the same purpose as they did for the fallen emperors — prestige, power, the vanity of being the first to exhibit a particularly unusual exotic beast, such as Henry III in 1251 displaying a polar bear and elephant, the first of their kind to be seen in London. Many simply died in their own filth, of starvation, disease or suicide. Some of the European aristocracy even tried on occasion to revive Roman-style "hunts" with the animals trapped in their enclosures. One of the favourite pastimes of Charles IX of France, for example, was to stage combats with his menagerie animals. It is recorded that on the night that followed such a contest, 14 October 1572, he dreamt that his wild beasts had turned upon him. Evidently believing the nightmare to be prophetic, the following morning he strode purposefully to his menagerie and killed every single animal that it contained. In the thirteenth and fourteenth centuries, mystery plays, originally devised by the Church to teach its illiterate flock the Biblical scriptures, were staged in the old Roman amphitheatres, epic and grandiose performances often as spectacular as the emperors themselves had witnessed. "Christ rose through a trap door," wrote Murray. "Yawning jaws opened to spout fire and sulphurous smoke from hell... Saved souls ascended to heaven on a platform, while the damned fell into a pit. There were machines to make angels fly, to bring animals on stage, and to create the illusion of thunder, lightning, and wind."

Travelling animal show in the Middle Ages. "Bärenführer" by Gottfried Mind.

A wood-cut from 1820 depicting the shooting of an elephant in Geneva.

"Inneres einer Tierbude" (1835), Johann Geyer; Museum für bildende Künste, Leipzig.

But it was the fairgrounds of Europe which breathed life into the circus. Ever since the 7th century, these gatherings of merchants had enjoyed the strong backing of the Church and they rapidly began to play a fundamental role in developing international trade. The early circus folk quickly seized upon a golden opportunity to perform to what was virtually a captive audience. Just as migrant farm labourers followed the harvest from the Mediterranean to the Alps, so the show people trekked across the continent from fair to fair, thus eventually earning the circus its international character. Attesting to their popularity, when in the late medieval period merchants began to desert the fairs as more standardised means of long-distance trade had evolved, the fairgrounds did not die out but rapidly became characterised almost exclusively by entertainment. With snake charmers, rope dancers, animal trainers, magicians and jugglers, these exotic and colourful events were slowly but surely coming to resemble the circus as we know it today. Once again, explorers began to return from distant lands with animal curiosities which were set on display in the fairs, and reviving yet another practice of ancient Rome, almost every fair began to boast side-shows of human freaks. St Bartholomew's in England offered a typical assortment of "monsters" as they were known: a man with one head and two bodies, a hermaphrodite, a "child with a Bear growing on his back alive", a woman with three breasts... Their owners were even prepared to grant private audiences "at any gentleman's house, if desired". These freaks of nature were regarded as subhuman, on a par with animals and thus treated and exploited as such. A handbill circulated in London in 1784 united the freak and exotic animal in a masterful display of promotion that was to become a hallmark of the modern circus. Depicted as "the Link between the rational and brute Creation", the "most astonishing creature, called the Oriental Satyr or Real Wild-Man of the Woods" was actually an orang-utan.

It was not until the 18th century that the long evolution of the circus brought about the beginnings of the familiar ring show, which, like its early Roman ancestor, was basically a display of equestrian skills. Indeed, right up to the present day, trick riding is often staged with showmen dressed in charioteers' costume, with plumed helmet, tunic and breastplate. Furthermore, in American shows like the mammoth Barnum & Bailey Circus, the traditional grand finale was often billed as the *Great Roman Hippodrome Races*, which according to their own advertising blurb actually incorporated the "ancient arts of chariot racing and Roman standing riding". Similarly, the exotic and often garish circus parade, which used to be an essential feature of the American circus, held more than a passing resemblance to its ancient Roman counterpart, with a procession which featured "Roman" charioteers driving gilt chariots presenting strange and unknown animals in barred caravans to the gawping masses.

*"Press agents turned the power of the press to the purposes of
the circus."*
— Encyclopedia Britannica

Commonly acclaimed as the "father of the modern circus" is the
Englishman Philip Astley (1742-1814), son of a cabinetmaker from
Newcastle-under-Lyme, and a former sergeant-major in the 5th regiment
of Dragoons with a genius for trick riding. He is credited with being the
first to practise daring equestrian and acrobatic skills within an open ring
enclosure, though in the beginning this served no other purpose than to
advertise his newly-founded riding school in London, called the
Amphitheatre Riding House. These impromptu displays proved so
immensely popular that after years of nagging uncertainty Astley became
convinced that he had stumbled upon his true vocation. That conviction
was borne out by the ecstatic public response to his show's premiere, and
soon bareback riding and acrobatics was to be augmented by tightrope
walkers, tumblers and a troupe of dancing dogs. According to most circus
historians this was the time and place which saw the basic elements of the
modern circus brought together for the first time. Significantly, the display of exotic wild animals was still missing. Indeed, all of these shows
were confined almost exclusively to the equestrian arts and human skills
in acrobatics and juggling. Exotic animals were still unheard of in the circus and it was not until 1828, fourteen years after Astley's death, that the
first elephant was seen in the circus arena.

But it was one of Astley's horsemen, Charles Hughes, who in 1782 first
coined the term "circus" to describe this new and spectacular form of
entertainment, borrowing the word from the Latin. Opening his own riding school nearby on Blackfriars Road after witnessing Astley's astounding success, Hughes dubbed the show "The Royal Circus". Competition
between the two adversaries, and among the litany of upstarts who wished
to mimic their success, gave birth to another circus tradition — rivalry
and feud — destined to be conducted with a vengeance in the most flamboyant period of circus history and still much in evidence today. Astley,
it is said, rode around town proclaiming Hughes a fraud and impostor
while Hughes retorted by posting bills which called into question his
erstwhile boss's riding skills. In the same way, promotion and advertising, with all the trappings of exaggeration and hyperbole, became essential to the circus's survival, especially when it severed its roots and began
roaming from town to town. Advance publicity teams, travelling to the
next venue, would plaster the streets with posters, handbills and printed
heralds. Over the years, circus press officers also became adept at influenc-
ing and even manipulating the media, a phenomenon still in evidence to
this very day. As the circus was growing up as an institution, it was also
quite normal to produce so-called "rat sheets" which would be liberally

distributed to disparage the quality of a competing circus if it should be in the vicinity. Often, fights would also break out, sparking a ruthless vendetta between rival showmen in which animals were poisoned and circus caravans and tents burnt to the ground. Again, even this has not entirely disappeared from the contemporary circus world.

The decline of the fairs, the danger of the roads and poor modes of transport which discouraged people from travel — all of these factors combined to create a favourable climate for the evolution of the travelling circus. With the exotic, the garish, the phenomenal, the romantic, the circus brought welcome relief to the monotonous and uneventful lives of the sleepy towns and isolated communities they passed through, and perhaps simply because of this, their instant popularity was assured, even preordained. Piece by piece over the following years, separate skills and disciplines would be added to the circus concept, which despite its future potential was still restricted to equestrian acts. First of all there were the rope dancers, acrobats and jugglers who were already searching for alternatives to the declining fortunes of the fairground and discovered that the circus, with its round arena, was ideal for them to display their dexterity to an audience which could for the first time clearly discern that their skills were not faked. Following this, in 1815, there was the introduction of the menagerie, and in 1820, the premier "jungle act" of taming wild beasts. Shortly afterwards, Americans Aaron Turner and Seth B. Howes introduced the first "big top"; such canvas tents eventually become so large and ubiquitous that they were dubbed "canvas colosseums". The year 1859 saw the invention of the flying trapeze by the French acrobat Jules Leotard, and this major contribution to circus culture was followed by the inimitable clown, the champion of parody and mime, who provided welcome comic relief from the preceding suspense of acrobatics and lion taming. Fast on the clown's heels came the live orchestra, now as much a tradition of the circus than any other single act, and in 1871 the exotic side-show of freaks.

Philip Astley and a few of his contemporaries had set all this in motion. When in 1772 the English stunt rider travelled to France to perform his "daring feats of horsemanship" before the king and the French court, he discovered a similar enthusiasm for the fledgling circus concept, particularly from disenchanted showmen who were willing to forsake the fairgrounds. Though he was to play an instrumental role in founding the French circus, with visits to Belgrade, Brussels and Vienna, he was also destined to bring the circus to the whole of Europe, and, by chain of influence, to America and the world. Indeed, during his lifetime Astley was to open no less than 19 permanent circuses at home and abroad. A decade after his first visit to Paris, at the invitation of Marie Antoinette, Astley launched his own amphitheatre. When hostilities erupted between Britain and France after the French Revolution, he leased it to Antonio Franconi (1738-1836), a hot-tempered nobleman turned trick rider who claimed to be in enforced exile following a fatal duel in his native Venice. Landing up penniless in Lyon, so the story goes, he was offered a job in lion taming, but was quickly mauled. With the little money he had earned, he bought himself a cage of canaries, somehow induced them to stand on their heads, pull miniature carriages and fire toy cannons, and promptly went on tour with them through France and Spain. Evidently impressed by the gory spectacle of the Spanish matadors tormenting their victims in the bull ring, he set about promoting bull-fighting in France. Eventually Franconi was to be hailed as the father of the contemporary French circus. Astley's arch-rival Charles Hughes, on the other hand, is credited with introducing the circus to Russia, where, said unkind tongues, he not only held private circus performances for the royal court in the palace in St Petersburg, but also enjoyed the personal favours of Catherine the Great. In any event, the Russian circus was soon destined to become one of the country's most popular forms of entertainment, apparently boasting more than a hundred itinerant and stationary shows. Even to this very day, approximately 22 million people every year watch acrobats, horse riders, animal trainers, and clowns being taught at the state circus school.

The first circus to be seen in the New World was in 1792 when John Bill Ricketts, a celebrated English equestrian who had once been a pupil of Charles Hughes, presented a show in Philadelphia and New York City. It is recorded that George Washington, an ardent horse-riding enthusiast, not only attended Ricketts' show but even rode frequently in the countryside with the father of the American circus. Notwithstanding friends in high places, Ricketts eventually fell foul of the kind of disaster which was to ruin many a circus entrepreneur. In 1799 his amphitheatre in New York burned to the ground, an accident attributed to a drunken stage-hand dropping a candle, though it has also been speculated that special effects aimed at creating "a sea of flame" in the arena went disastrously out of control. Nor was that the end of his streak of bad luck. Leaving America virtually penniless, the ship taking him back to his native England foundered, and all on board were lost.

By the turn of the century, the circus had found its way to every corner of Europe and had also become firmly established in America. Yet despite its success with the crowds, the circus was a tough and often pitiless life, with showmen constantly battling against poverty, injury and death. It was an existence governed by the "survival of the fittest", and despite its showy and sometimes genuine camaraderie, it was marked by ruthlessness. Fire was a haunting and enduring threat which was to ruin many a circus czar and kill many a panic-stricken animal. The early buildings used to house the shows could well be described as death traps, traditionally made of wood, the arena illuminated with hundreds of candles, the show cannons emitting flames and sparks and the ground littered with sawdust. Between them, Astley and Ricketts alone were to lose five of their circuses to fire, major disasters which not only killed their animals and destroyed their equipment but almost wiped them out financially. Small wonder then that they and their competitors became calculating, hard-bitten men, with little sympathy even for their fellow human beings let alone their animals. In America, home of the brave and land of the pioneering spirit, the adversity that the circus faced was perhaps even harsher. Having to combat religious prejudice, the elements, shortage of money, floods, droughts, fires, and other "acts of God", circus life here required an even greater degree of shrewdness and fortitude, not to mention a propensity for gambling and ruthless opportunism.

It was not until the early part of the nineteenth century that the travelling circus was born, the idea of holding shows under canvas and playing to America's predominantly rural population inspired by a group of New England circus pioneers. Although these crude, impoverished affairs were dubbed "mud shows" because the show grounds were so often trampled into swamps during rainy weather, people flocked to them because they provided desperately needed relief from their parochial, monotonous lives. Indeed, the circus was destined to become the principal form of entertainment for most Americans for many years to come. Three of the trail-blazing New England group, Lewis B. Titus, Caleb Sutton Angevine and John J. June, were the first to import wild animals expressly for display in the travelling menageries. Prior to that, they were in the habit of buying the luckless creatures from sea captains who had picked them up on their voyages to the most exotic reaches of the globe. At first, during the slack and cold winter months, they were forced to put their animals in country barns and cellars, but this was unsatisfactory in many ways, not least because profits dwindled drastically. They then struck upon the idea of having their headquarters on New York's Bowery where they could not only keep the animals but also exhibit them. As soon as winter loosened its grip, the animals would be leased out to other entrepreneurs — usually the highest bidder. It was thus that the idea of a touring menagerie corporation was born. By January 1835, the animal-dealing trio had persuaded more than 125 menagerie exhibitors to set their seal on forming "one joint stock company for the purpose of exhibiting wild animals belonging to them in company or co-partnership for profit". The resulting organisation, boasting combined assets in the form of animals and equipment of over $300,000, was named, with typical grandiosity, the Zoological Institute. To avoid antagonising America's religious fundamentalists, notes Murray, "the Zoological Institute was advertised as scientific and educational, but even that did not protect its beasts, for two elephants were killed, and other animals were either shot or poisoned by fanatics." Despite such attacks, the Zoological Institute paid huge dividends and, in shades of ancient Rome, catching expeditions were dispatched across the globe in search of exotic beasts. When the first giraffe to be seen in the USA was imported in 1835, it was billed as "The Stupendous Giraffe or Camelopard"; its life was brief, like many of the other animals imported to satisfy human curiosity and their owners' greed. Because the hunger for ever more exotic animals could never be satisfied, a lively trade developed in fake animals — such as sharks and whales made of leather, as well as mermaids and sea monsters. The slick ruthlessness exhibited by such men as Titus, Angevine and June gave them and their Zoological Institute the whip hand when it came to control over the burgeoning menagerie industry. Exerting tremendous power, their reign over the kingdom of animal import, lease and sale lasted for sixty years. "Sitting behind their desks hundreds of miles from actual operations," wrote Murray, "they could route shows into town ahead of their rivals, cut prices, spread slanderous tales about competitors, hire ruffians to intimidate them, cut down trees and burn bridges to delay rival companies, and otherwise exert an influence that was effective though largely covert."

The introduction of performing wild animals to the circus arena was also an American innovation, inspired by one Isaac A. Van Amburgh (1801-65) of New York who is credited with being "the first to enter a cage of jungle beasts in a public exhibition", some time between 1820 and 1833. Legend has it that at the impressionable age of nineteen, he was reading the Scriptures and came across Daniel in the Lion's Den, promptly deciding that his true vocation was that of lion tamer. His dream came true at the Zoological Institute's winter quarters in New York when he walked nonchalantly into a cage of snarling, ferocious beasts and began lashing them into obedience to the thunderous applause of spectators. His unique style was so appealing to the public that it would be mimicked by countless other animal tamers. Dressed in jungle fatigues, wielding a whip and firing blanks from his pistol, he would stride into the cage, deliberately baiting and taunting the animals to bring out as much ferocity and jungle savagery as he could, whereupon he would proceed to bully them into submission. His *pièce de résistance* was forcing the lions to approach and lick his boots as the ultimate sign of his conquest and the animals' abject subservience. Turned into an instant hero, the young, intrepid animal tamer soon found that he could even dictate terms to the likes of Titus and Angevine. By the time he was 23, he boasted his own travelling menagerie, and in 1838 even performed six times before an enthralled Queen Victoria. Van Amburgh's publicity agent Hyatt Frost declared that, prior to one of these royal command performances, the lions had been starved for thirty-six hours, and that when Van Amburgh was putting them through their paces they were so hungry that he had to lash them furiously with his whip "into the most abject and crouching submission". Soon he was to be honoured both in Europe and America as the "greatest lion tamer in the world". With fame, came riches. By the mid 1840s he owned the largest travelling show in England and was leasing animals to many other menageries and zoos around the world. Perhaps it was these great landmarks of circus history at the Zoological Institute which later inspired the shrewdest animal tamers to claim that their routines possessed inherent educational and conservation benefits for the public. In any event, Van Amburgh is also credited with being the first man to put his head in a lion's mouth which, while not being very educational, is certainly spectacular. By this time, European animal trainers had been following the fairground circuit for centuries, but the Frenchman Henri Martin (1793-1882) has the distinction of being "the first great trainer to appear in the circus". Both he and Van Amburgh also appeared in theatrical productions, such as *The Lions of Mysore*, and, closer to home, *The Brute Tamer of Pompeii*. But while it would never fall again into such depravity and horror as its Roman namesake, tens of thousands of exotic wild animals were destined to suffer and die for human entertainment in the circus, victims of human ignorance, cruelty, supremacy.

It is generally accepted that a conspicuous distinction exists between European and American styles of exotic animal dressage, commonly known as "jungle acts" — though the distinction becomes blurred with time, nationality and the preferences of the individual trainer. In the archetypal American style, it is said, "the trainer, with his gun blazing and whip cracking, is pitted against roaring animals, apparently on the attack, with the final outcome seemingly in doubt. By an apparent hair's breadth margin, the disciplined routine imposed by the trainer triumphs over jungle fury." Following in the footsteps of Van Amburgh, the unchallenged maestro of this style was the American Clyde Beatty (1903-65), who is said to have "subjugated as many as 40 black-maned African lions and Royal Bengal tigers at one time." Indeed, a 1934 poster presented Beatty as "The Jungle King In A Single-Handed Battle With 40 of The Most Ferocious Brutes That Breathe". By comparison, the European style might seem rather sedate, if not a trifle bland, as the trainer attempts to "prove his mastery and skill by presenting his jungle charges in the role of obedient, even playful pets. The wild character of the animals, however, is revealed just often enough to remind the spectator that what he sees is indeed the result of masterful training."

The pioneer and leading exponent of the so-called "soft dressage" technique of animal taming was Carl Hagenbeck, later honoured as the "father of the modern zoo". The son of a Hamburg fishmonger, the boy acquired the first taste of his future vocation when some fishermen brought ashore six seals that had accidentally been trapped in their nets. They were put into wooden tubs and young Carl exhibited them at a penny per head. Concluding that the ubiquitous dressage techniques of the day could only inspire an animal's deep-seated hatred for its trainer, and that they were not only cruel but also uneconomic in the long run, Hagenbeck set about trying to train animals with "kindness", substituting praise and rewards for successfully accomplished tricks instead of beatings and other punishment for failures. The reality may not be quite so glowing as the legend however, since the reward — mostly food — can soon become a punishment when deliberately withheld from a misbehaving or noncompliant animal. By the time he was forty, Hagenbeck was sending tamed animals all over the world, as well as exhibiting them at home. He gained further fame, this time in the zoological world, by modifying the very physical structure of the permanent menagerie, up until then characterised by cramped, barred cages. Through the judicious use of landscaping, he established the forerunner of today's zoological park, providing animals with large open-air enclosures which went some way towards simulating each species' natural environment — at least from the point of view of the public.

In 1887 Hagenbeck bought his imagination to bear on the way in which the wild animal spectacle was presented in the circus. Dissatisfied by the customary method of having the animals perform inside their beast wagons which were drawn into the ring, he invented the large "cage arena" that is still seen today, though often in collapsible form. This provided more space for the trainer and his animals' repertoire, and allowed the now staple equipment of the wild animal act to be utilised for the first time, such as pedestals, ladders and seesaws. But despite this reputed new departure of innovative and humanitarian thinking, circus animals were still confined to tiny and squalid beast wagons, and thousands of creatures continued to suffer and die in the wild at the hands of those animal catchers who made a living stocking up the "civilised" world's zoos and menageries — amongst them Carl Hagenbeck and his heirs who became Europe's foremost animal dealers. Indeed, from 1866 to 1886, at the height of his animal-catching and selling career, Carl Hagenbeck imported 1,000 lions, 400 tigers, at least 700 leopards, 1,000 bears, 800 hyenas, 300 elephants, 17 Indian, Javan and Sumatran rhinos, 9 African rhinos, at least 100,000 birds and tens of thousands of monkeys. It often took months of arduous travel before the captured animals arrived at their final destination. As Bill Jordan and Stefan Ormrod report in their book *The Last Great Wild Beast Show*: "If you add to the fearful experience of capture, the horrific sensation of being confined to a crate or cage for months on end, bumped and jarred over rough terrain, tossed and pitched across unseen oceans, to arrive in a strange, cold and completely alien environment, only then is it possible to comprehend the suffering and anxiety caused, and the resulting mortality rate. Stress is still one of the major killers when wild animals are captured; in Hagenbeck's day its effects must have been terrible." Moreover, even the much-vaunted notion that Carl Hagenbeck instituted a revolutionary change in dressage technique from the brutal to the tender and merciful is as exaggerated and illusory as the circus show itself. Cruelties remained endemic, as they still do today, with trainers continuing to subdue their animals by means of the whip and chair, the noise of the gun, starvation, or simply violent kicks. "Even into the late nineteenth century," concedes Murray, "no matter how the training was accomplished, the exhibition of great jungle cats was still very often a matter of scaring them into a state of hysteria by firing guns, beating gongs, cracking whips, and prodding them with red-hot irons as the Romans had done. The beasts then roared and raged enough to satisfy the onlookers. Audiences were so bloodthirsty that accidents were sometimes even faked, though there were a shocking number of occasions (as there still are, and probably always will be) when the trainer actually was torn to bits."

The Menagerie

Hailing from Somers, New York, one Hachaliah Bailey has the dubious distinction of founding America's first travelling menagerie. That was in around 1815, when he toured New England with his solitary elephant called "Old Bet" which he had supposedly purchased for $1,000 from a sea captain who had bought her at a London auction for $20. The pair travelled by night, probably in order to guard against the prying eyes of those who would not pay to see what they could just as easily see for free. In the daytime he exhibited her in barns and tavern yards. But in 1828 Old Bet fell victim of the righteous and puritanical wrath of certain New Englanders who believed that the elephant display was as shamefully irreligious as the theatre, saloon and dance-hall. Taking the law into their own hands, just before dawn they waylaid the party that was leading Old Bet to the next town; half a dozen shots rang out and the great beast fell bellowing to the ground, dead. Yet Bailey & Co.'s success with the crowds soon resulted in imitations, business investment and an amplifying of the concept by the likes of Titus, Angevine and Van Amburgh. In England, there was Wombwell's Royal Menagerie founded in 1807 by Captain George Wombwell who amassed an impressive collection of animals mostly from visiting foreign ships. It is interesting to note that a contemporary of his, the bookseller William Hone, lambasted the menagerie proprietor for his avarice and cruelty, citing an incident in the city of Warwick when the publicity-hungry Wombwell had two of his lions, Nero and Wallace, baited by dogs. After encountering him at St Bartholomew's Fair in 1825, Hone wrote that Wombwell "exhibited himself, to my judgement of him, with an understanding and feelings perverted by avarice. He is undersized in mind as well as form, a weezen, sharp-faced man, with skin reddened by more than natural spirits, and he speaks in a voice and language that accord with his feelings and propensities." In brightly coloured wagons displaying jungle scenes, Wombwell's Royal Menagerie travelled throughout the British Isles with wildcats, wolves, monkeys, giraffes, elephants and camels, and eventually gained such fame that on five occasions it gave royal command performances, three times before Queen Victoria herself. For the public, the animal freaks of the menagerie were not appreciably different from the human freaks of the side-show or mental asylum. Indeed, this was an age when the insane were also on public display, with a Sunday visit to Bedlam being one of London's greatest attractions where visitors were charged a penny each at the turnstile. As authors Bob Mullan and Garry Marvin point out in their book *Zoo Culture*: "In the asylums the often cold and damp cage-like rooms had nothing more than straw and a pallet for the 'patients' to sleep on, and the more dangerous were often chained. Madmen were not treated as full human beings, because they were thought to be related to the animal world in all its strangeness. It is highly significant that what is normal behaviour in animals — their unrestrained wildness — is equated with human madness, that is abnormal behaviour." And just as the visitors to Bedlam goaded and provoked the inmates, so too did the visitors to the menagerie in order to incite a lion to roar, a bear to growl or a monkey to scream.

Yet only gradually did the menagerie and the modern circus form their supposedly traditional alliance. Indeed, it was not until 1851 that the two elements appeared together for the first time, when George F. Bailey, a nephew of Hachaliah's, bought six cages of animals from the conglomerate Zoological Institute, and added them, together with several elephants, to his ring show. From then on, the menagerie was destined to become a major feature of the American circus, usually exhibited in a separate tent through which the public passed on their way to the big top. The collections were often extensive, and included wild cats, giraffes, elephants, chimpanzees, gorillas, rhinos and polar bears. But what is especially ironic is that the founding of the circus menagerie — which contemporary circus entrepreneurs so resolutely insist is an innate and inviolable part of their golden tradition and heritage — was little more than an inflated circus illusion, perhaps the greatest conjuring trick to beguile the public ever seen under the big top. Indeed, that "golden tradition" actually came into being entirely artificially, through the same deliberate falsehood that we hear today, namely the circus's spurious claim that the menagerie and the performing animal play a vital educational role. As we have already seen, by this time the circus, as well as some of the small travelling menageries, were experiencing strong opposition from religious fundamentalists who viewed the conjuring tricks and illusions of the circus as works of the Devil. Declared an editorial in the *Weekly Recorder* of Chillicothe, Ohio on 2 August 1815: "The principal object pursued by the conductors of the circus is to enrich themselves at the expense of others... Believing that these men are prosecuting an unlawful calling — one that cannot be defended on Scriptural grounds, or on principles of sound reason and good policy, we presume the good sense of the citizens in general would lead them to treat their exhibitions with that unqualified neglect and contempt which they so justly deserve." The citizens of Sunbury, Pennsylvania, even went so far as to charge six members of a circus company with witchcraft, following a performance on 19 April 1829. The charge sheet accusing them declared that they possessed the "power of witchcraft, conjuration, enchantment and sorcery and being moreover persons of evil and depraved dispositions, and as magical characters having private conferences with the spirit of darkness, did... expose to the view of diverse and many people of this Commonwealth various feats, acts, deeds, exhibitions, and performances of magic and witchcraft."

Although the case was dismissed and those arrested freed, the incident brought home to the circus proprietors of the time just how formidable the opposition had become. It was thus that they ingeniously contrived to bring the menagerie into the circus — after all, the reasoning went, although the magical quality of the circus unavoidably seemed to suggest witchcraft and devilry, animals had been collected by pious humans since the time of Noah. Indeed, although the churches had declared circuses "immoral", ambitious entrepreneurs like Titus and Angevine at the Zoological Institute were convinced that by introducing exotic animals, the whole caboodle could be passed off as "educational". To sweeten the pill, great spectacles were held which depicted some historical or biblical scene, such as Solomon and the Queen of Sheba. With typical ingenuity, another way to overcome puritanical resistance was to give attractions biblical names. P.T. Barnum, tongue in cheek, dubbed his hippopotamus, "The Behemoth of Holy Writ Spoken Of by the Book of Job". The zebu was converted into a "holy cow", and the vile animal cages referred to as "dens" to evoke Daniel and the den of lions. Robinson and Lake's circus in 1883 even went so far as to dub their big top the "Superb Firmament Pavilion", while another travelling menagerie went by the name of "Animals of the Scriptures". Like the murals which adorn the menagerie today showing animals roaming free and wild in an untouched environment, the sides of the gilded animal cages depicted colourful biblical scenes, such as Noah's Ark, Jonah and the whale, and the lion and the lamb lying down together. As they intended, these new features gradually overcame public hostility and the menagerie thus became a permanent if artificial fixture of the modern circus. There can be little doubt that the relentless competitiveness between circus rivals led to great resourcefulness and ingenuity, but apart from being put through ever more bizarre, perverse and cruel routines, the concept of the performing circus animal has never been able to keep pace with the genuine imagination and innovative ideas that other circus performers brought to their respective arts and disciplines.

A slight variation on the circus theme in the USA was the Wild West Show, the first of which was founded by William F. "Buffalo Bill" Cody in 1883. They featured reconstructions of historical events such as Custer's Last Stand, the Indian attack on the stage-coach and the inevitable last minute rescue by the US Cavalry, as well as sharpshooting — starring the legendary Annie Oakley — bronco busting, roping and other ranch-hand skills. So fallen had the Indian nations become by this time that even Indian ceremonials were held to entertain the public, the crowds lured by the imposing presence of Sitting Bull. Although not kept in quite such deprivation as the circus's exotic animals or P. T. Barnum's freaks of nature, the Indians were nevertheless displayed as curiosities. For the proud Indian, like the proud tiger, it had now come to this, paraded from town to town, no longer a threat but a "quaint heritage" of the white man. And indeed, this kind of exploitation glaringly revealed the white psychology and the faith of its Bible-toting priests: to civilise the red Indian according to God's wishes. The savage, the wild animal: the two were virtually indistinguishable, even to the Christian religion, which had concluded that both were soulless — perhaps because both were close to Mother Earth.

Back in Britain, one "Lord" George Sanger was becoming the country's pre-eminent circus chieftain. In the rags-to-riches tradition that proves so endearing to circus culture, from a poverty-stricken boyhood Sanger emerged to became a multi-millionaire. One of ten brothers and sisters, he was born in 1827 to a peep-show impresario. As a child he worked at the pitiful little circus as a barker but when his father died in a cholera epidemic, George Sanger moved on to a freak show at Richardson's Theatre where, beside the usual fat men, two-headed woman and living skeleton there was also "Madame Stevens, the Pig-Faced Lady". This was actually a brown bear whose face had been shaved and the rest of its body hidden in a dress, shawl, bonnet and gloves. The wretched animal was strapped into a chair and seated close to a table from under which it would receive prods to make it produce the supposedly life-like grunts of a pig-faced lady. After experiencing many years of hardship and poverty, Sanger started his own circus and then hit "lady luck". During its heydays in the 1850s — with amphitheatres in Plymouth, Exeter, Bristol, Bath, Birmingham, Manchester, Liverpool, Glasgow, Dundee and Aberdeen — his company was to consist of 1100 persons, 180 horses, 18 lions and countless other animals, making it the biggest collection of menagerie animals in the UK. By 1930, it was the respected Bertram Mills circus which led the field in Britain, followed by John Sanger and Sons. Four other large companies were to join the fray by the 1950s: Chipperfield's,

Billy Smart's, Sir Robert Fossett's and Robert Brothers, all sporting such huge menageries that wild animal acts were also dispatched to perform on the Continent.

The German circus world during the 19th century was characterised by the extravaganzas of the Busch and Krone dynasties. Busch's "Siberia" show featured 120 polar bears, all sliding down a specially constructed metal slope into an arena filled with water; in "Sevilla", the circus baron even presented bull fighting in the circus ring. The Krone dynasty was born in the 1870s when Fritz Krone founded a small impoverished menagerie which roamed from fair to fair. By the 1930s, thanks largely to the shrewdness and imagination of Fritz's son Carl, Krone had become a flourishing circus with an unrivalled collection of exotic animals. Some twenty years later it was known as the greatest travelling circus in Europe, with a menagerie containing 70 elephants.

> *"Under the pressure of growing competition the owners of elephants had to spur on the animals that were no longer marvels in themselves to ever more marvellous feats... In 1846 an elephant in England was taught to walk the tight-rope, in 1853 the first specimen stood on its head, not long after that an elephant could be seen riding a bicycle and doing a single-armed handstand. The impossible had thus been made possible — by man, not by elephant. The heaviest and most imperturbable of animals, the ambling mountain from the mists of the past, had been forced into a feather-light, labile equilibrium. It was not the elephant, it was nature itself that here seemed to be standing on its head."*
> — Dr Stephan Oettermann

Elephants, it has been said, are the very hallmark of the circus, the awesome size of the animal making its submission to *homo sapiens* a curious and compelling paradox. The first recorded presentation of elephants performing together in one ring occurred in 1874 in Howes' Great London Circus and Sanger's Royal British Menagerie. In the USA, the largest herd ever employed by a single circus was the 50 elephants of the Ringling Brothers and Barnum & Bailey Circus in 1955. Though countless other species have performed in the circus ring, few are more associated with circus "tradition" than the elephant. In America, explains Murray, the elephant was "a stupefying novelty" the appearance of which eventually became woven into the very fabric of the circus tradition, so much so that "no American feels he has seen a real circus unless he has found in it at least a couple of elephants."

Elephants walking on enormous glittering balls, elephants dressed up as Charlie Chaplin, playing musical instruments or sitting neatly at the dinner table, elephants standing on one leg, forming pyramids, carrying tigers on their backs. Perhaps the fascination in all of this is the paradox of a great, and at first sight clumsy beast, performing with such delicate balance and control. Yet almost without exception the stunts that the animals are induced to perform in the circus arena turn them into grotesque caricatures of their true selves. To this very day, elephants are still trained to walk the tightrope — a trick first seen at Rome's Circus Maximus. "To walk a rope is no harder for an elephant than for a man," asserted Marian Murray. "The difficulty lies in making the elephant get up onto the rope in the first place." As we shall see in the following chapter, one method employed by the Swiss National Circus, Knie, was to beat the young elephant's legs repeatedly until they bled.

But elephants, especially the great tuskers, are unpredictable and notoriously difficult to control; many a trainer has been trampled, crushed to death, or impaled on tusks, either by accident as an animal panics, or deliberately as the creature exacts revenge for some earlier abuse or mistreatment. Van Amburgh's great tusker, Hannibal, brought to the USA in 1824, killed at least seven persons, and according to the animal tamer's publicity man, Hyatt Frost, the elephant possessed "an almost unparalleled reputation for viciousness". On one occasion, says Frost, men had to stab the elephant repeatedly with pitchforks in order to subdue it during one of its frequent rampages. On another occasion, it took several men three days to subdue the tusker Romeo when the elephant flew into a rage after they had tried to chain it. "When an elephant grew too dangerous," writes Murray, "or had killed too many persons even for a sensation-avid public, the owner had several choices. He could shoot the offender; he could give him to a zoo; or he could sell him to another circus where he would appear under another name. The last was one of the commonest procedures — and of course the most dangerous."

Impresarios soon learned that elephant babies were the paramount attractions with which to draw the crowds. In 1955, Ringling Brothers and Barnum & Bailey imported 27 elephant calves of varying sizes to take their place alongside 27 adult "aunties". As usual, it was brilliant publicity, and few of the public can have questioned the origin of those babies and what had happened to their mothers. According to a 1952 census, all except 6 of the 264 elephants in the USA were female, making sheer nonsense out of circus claims that the animals would be bred in captivity.

The civilizing of nature: the Ringling Brothers' elephant brass band seen in a poster from the beginning of the century.

Elephant "Sandry" as Charlie Chaplin in 1953, appearing with Rolf Knie, Circus Knie. (Circus Knie)

Freaks of Nature

But it was Phineas Taylor Barnum, later destined to become a household name, who introduced one of the most lucrative variations of the menagerie — the circus side-show. The freaks of nature displayed here appealed to people's prejudice, their unquenchable curiosity for the outlandish and the unknown, and the paradoxical human attraction and repulsion toward the diseased and deformed. For more than a hundred years, the side-show was to remain an indispensable appendage of American circus culture. The first of its kind systematically organised was contained in "P.T. Barnum's Great Travelling Museum, Menagerie, Caravan and Hippodrome", and the countless imitations which followed in its wake habitually featured the same classic attractions, including the giant, the fat lady, the midget, the three-legged boy, the armless wonder and the thin man. For the freaks who never gained fame and fortune like General Tom Thumb, the 25-inch midget who brought Barnum riches beyond his wildest dreams, life was often a misery, more akin to slavery than employment.

In yet another circus rags-to-riches story, Barnum was born into a poor family in Connecticut in 1810. He was not a practical man by any means, yet exploited to the full his own dramatic personality, his genius in interpreting human psychology to meet his own ends, and his talent for hatching the most sensational and bizarre schemes. In her book *Circus!* Marian-Murray notes that he was known to many as a "trickster, a perpetual liar and unscrupulous cheat who perpetrated a series of clever deceptions on a public he looked upon as fools." Yet his basic philosophy — "the bigger the better" — was all-American, and he is believed to be the author of the now traditional American motto, "There's a sucker born each minute." Barnum was also undisputed trail-blazer in the hyperbole and superlative of circus language. "By the end of Barnum's life," notes Murray, "such adjectives as mammoth, monstrous, gigantic, colossal, elephantine, amplitudinous, stupendous, marvellous, magnificent, glorious and superb were to have lost virtually all meaning."

Barnum stumbled upon his true vocation when he heard about a crippled and helpless black woman, called Joice Heth, being displayed in a freak show in Philadelphia. She was reputed to be 161 years old and to have been George Washington's nurse. Upon seeing the old crone for himself, Barnum promptly bought her for $1000 and took her to New York to exhibit, where she earned him $1500 a week. When the old woman died within a year following a strenuous tour, an autopsy revealed that she was no more than 80. Although branded as a hoaxer and fraud, thick-skinned Barnum merely shrugged off such attacks, declaring that they served his purpose by "keeping my name before the public." Thereafter he was to acquire a taste for notoriety.

In 1841 Barnum invested everything he owned in a gamble which, during his thirty-year reign, was to bring him undreamt-of wealth, buying Scudder's American Museum on Broadway and renaming it Barnum's American Museum. By the end of the following year it had become the city's most popular place of entertainment. Huge garish panels on the outside of the building depicting strange exotic animals attracted customers in hoards. Baby shows, dog shows, poultry shows and flower shows, unknown species from distant impenetrable jungles, tamed red Indians who whooped their way obediently through war dances — these became the standard fare of the Museum. In 1864 Barnum even bribed an interpreter to let him display a group of imposing Indian chiefs who had expressly gone to Washington to conduct negotiations with President Lincoln over land rights and the white man's continuing injustice.

It was the Museum's policy to offer curiosities from all over the world, ranging from flying fish and mud iguanas to grizzly bears and the "first and only" hippopotamus in America, from human freaks such as the Bearded Lady, Siamese twins and Albino family, to "educated" dogs and seals. In yet another blatant fraud, Barnum even displayed a "Fejee Mermaid" — a shrivelled monster a metre long ingeniously constructed from a fish's body tacked to the head of a monkey. Displaying his unrivalled expertise in promotion, Barnum first set about wearing down the scepticism of New Yorkers as to the existence of mermaids. In part, this was achieved by having one of his business associates pose before the press as an expert from the Lyceum of Natural History in London. By the time the mermaid arrived in New York, Barnum had succeeded in creating such avid curiosity among the public that his Museum was mobbed by the crowds, his revenue from ticket sales more than doubling. Increasingly desperate for other curiosities, Barnum himself travelled up the St Lawrence to obtain two white whales, sent them 700 miles back to New York by train, and put them in a tank of fresh water. Needless to say, they died within a few days. He then built a 7-metre square tank, piped sea water into it and brought in another pair of white whales, but they promptly died as well. Not one to surrender to adversity, Barnum acquired yet another two replacements which this time lived long enough to be displayed to the public; his marine collection was later augmented with sharks and porpoises.

The Museum burned to the ground in 1865 and the only animals saved were the "educated" seal, one bear, and a few birds and monkeys. But the indomitable Barnum began again, establishing the New American Museum which he stocked with animals from all over the world. This too was gutted by fire in 1868 with the same devastating loss of animal life. Although the ageing Barnum at last decided to retire, he was soon to become the father of "The Greatest Show on Earth", and America's pre-eminent circus dynasty.

In 1871 "P.T. Barnum's Travelling Exhibition and World's Fair on

Wheels" took to the road — equipped with the largest number of caravans ever seen in a circus, and a tent that held 10,000 people. The sideshow's star attraction was four "Fiji Cannibals" who, Barnum solemnly declared to his gullible public, had been educated and converted by missionaries. But the inimitable showman soon found himself entangled in a bitter feud with another circus chieftain of the time, Adam Forepaugh. At one point, the two rivals fell into vying with each other to be the first to procure the "Sacred White Elephant of the Orient". Forking out $75,000 for one of the rare mottled pink, albino-like animals in Burma, Barnum gleefully concluded that he had out-tricked Forepaugh only to discover that through some treachery his elephant arrived painted red and blue. A cunning Forepaugh used the incident to publicise his adversary's empty promises to the public and promptly presented to them a real, brilliant white elephant — one that had been given a liberal coat of whitewash.

> *"On 15 September 1885 came the event for which the age of progress had long been secretly waiting: the confrontation of nature and technology. Jumbo, the elephant of flesh and blood, met the elephant of the technical world, the steam locomotive, head on. The elephant paid with its life, but for once it also won a moral victory: the locomotive was derailed! But this victory was the final downfall of the elephant. The remains of the specimen concerned can be seen in the Museum of Natural History in New York, while the remains of its species now vegetate in the world's zoos. They have lost their dignity forever. They are now only the sad trophies of progress."*
> — Dr Stephan Oettermann

In 1882 Barnum and his new and relatively unassuming partner James Anthony Bailey set in motion a plan to buy "the world's largest elephant" from London Zoo. Jumbo, as the 10 ft, 10 ins tall, eight-ton beast was known, was to become so famous that he would eventually bequeathe his name to the English language as a simile for greatness. Despite protests over the transaction — which the matchless showman Barnum actively encouraged — the sale went through, with Jumbo netting London Zoo $10,000. But when Jumbo set his eyes upon the huge iron-bound cage that was to transport him to America, he began to trumpet in distress and lay down on the ground and refused to budge. A distraught agent then cabled Barnum for urgent instructions, and the impresario replied: "Let him lie there a week if he wants to. It is the best advertisement in the world." Less than three years later, the "greatest elephant the civilised world had ever seen" perished during a derailment of circus railway wagons in Ontario, Canada. As Jumbo appeared from his wagon, he was struck by an oncoming train. In a typical display of consummate bad taste, and to minimise his losses from the highly popular elephant, Barnum promptly bought Jumbo's "widow", Alice, from London Zoo and exhibited her beside the skeleton and stuffed hide of Jumbo.

Frequent travel over long distances in cramped and filthy conditions made the circus animals' life a misery — as it still does today. In 1876, the then independent James Anthony Bailey, after playing to audiences in San Francisco and grossing as much as $6000 a day, chartered a steamer and took his menagerie across the Pacific to Australia, Tasmania and the Dutch East Indies. But as Murray records, after leaving Tasmania, the circus ran into a violent storm: "In the first moments of excitement, the rope around the bears' cage broke, and the cage with the lions slid down onto them. All the boxes overturned, and several washed overboard, occupants and all. Above the screams and roars of pain and terror from the animals, the shouts of the men, and the wild shrieking of the storm, a terrific splash was heard as the rhinoceros went into the sea. Cage after cage followed. Nearly half the menagerie was lost, and the giraffe lay dead with a broken neck. When the ship reached Sydney, so the story goes, the giraffe was skinned and stuffed, and a mechanism inserted. In a darkened cage, the head on the neck nodded gently, and no one was permitted to go near enough to discover the truth."

By the end of the 19th century there were over 100 circuses criss-crossing America, spawning a sub-culture which gave rise to many a circus dynasty, the greatest family trees becoming a veritable puzzle of boughs and branches as circus families intermarried. Father would teach son and mother would instruct daughter in the vital skills necessary to achieve perfection in the discipline the child seemed most suited for. With a life on the road, an upbringing within a proud and insular culture, and education or schooling a rarity, there were few opportunities for a child to choose a profession outside the circus world. Upon reaching a certain age, having honed his talents, the child would perhaps take to the arena, join a rival circus, be married off into a different circus family, or simply start a poor ramshackle travelling show of his own. Competition and the search for pastures new prompted many circus families to leave their native countries, emigrating to Asia, South America, South Africa, and Australia. But while in Europe circus families tended to split up, in the USA there was a mania for mergers — though agreements were sealed and then broken with bewildering regularity. This trend culminated in 1907 when Ringling Bros. bought out Barnum & Bailey, creating the world's largest circus corporation. The two circuses combined in 1919, and according to *Encyclopedia Britannica*, "the last competing syndicate, the American Circus Corporation, which comprised five circuses, was bought in 1929 to remove the last serious challenge to Ringling supremacy."

Soon destined to become star of the Ringling conglomerate's menagerie was Gargantua, depicted as the largest and most ferocious gorilla the world had ever seen — an advertising ploy that revealed the crass cynicism of America's pre-eminent circus chieftains. The gorilla, which made its public debut in 1938, had actually been captured in Africa as a weak and vulnerable baby. Following an acid attack by a disgruntled sailor during its transport to America, the disfigured Gargantua was to harbour a bitter grudge against every human being he ever encountered, including his own trainer who rarely dared to approach the animal. Yet the ugly, deformed face of the beast and its unbridled fury were guaranteed money-spinners.

Resembling the culture of ancient Rome more than they would care to admit, *Circus Americana* was also characterised by its obsession for the grandiose. The big top of the Ringling Bros. and Barnum & Bailey Circus covered the equivalent of a hectare, was supported by centre poles 20 metres high and sheltered 12,000 people. Unlike the European circus which has traditionally focussed the audience's attention on just one ring, at Ringling Bros, Barnum & Bailey crowds could watch as many as seven rings and stages at one time, the show's rough-and-tumble character stressing the rapid and dynamic pace, and the quantity of the performers and exhibits. By 1941, their famous "Greatest Show on Earth" was transported around the country on four trains with a total of 107 twenty-one metre long carriages and freight wagons. Sometimes the show, with its glittering pageantry, displayed such overwhelming grandiosity that it simply back-fired. Writing in the *American Encyclopedia*, F. Darius Benham and Arthur Perrow report that some pre-show parades, designed to give a tantalising preview of what would later be on full show under canvas, "were so huge that when the Barnum and Bailey Greatest Show on Earth visited Germany, the watchers of the parade, after it had passed, returned to their homes thinking that was the whole show."

But the American hunger for the grandiose soon led to financial woes, and eventually the demise of the big top in the USA. In 1956, in what marked the end of an era, increased freight charges forced "The Greatest Show on Earth" to give up its itinerant way of life and appear only in exhibition halls and other metropolitan buildings. According to a statement by the owners, the circus had become the victim of television, bad weather, traffic congestion, labour troubles and mounting costs.

The Dolphin Circus

Following P.T. Barnum's ill-fated display of white whales in his New York Museum in 1860, it was not until 1913 that cetaceans were again seen in captivity, this time when C. H. Townsend, curator of the New York Aquarium, stumbled upon the idea of exhibiting dolphins as an unbeatable novelty to attract the crowds. Thus on 12 November 1913, five bottlenose dolphins — the first ever to be brought into commercial captivity — were caught in North Carolina and transported on a three-day journey to New York. In June 1914 Townsend wrote that there had never been a more successful display in the Aquarium's 12-year history. The last of the dolphins, succumbing to pneumonia, died in 1915 after 21 months in captivity. It was another quarter of a century before a captive dolphin would be trained and put through its paces to entertain a human audience. The year 1938 saw the inauguration of Marine Studios in Florida and the arrival of the facility's first bottlenose dolphins. According to anecdotal accounts or stories that have gradually turned to fable with age, the very beginnings of dolphin dressage were conceived here more or less accidentally. During feeding time at Marine Studios, it is said, dolphins gradually fell into the habit of jumping up to catch the fish that were thrown to them, and this miniature spectacle always amused the public, the keepers and curator. Then a year later in 1939, Cecil M. Walker, responsible for maintenance of the water purification pumps on the night shift, observed one evening how a dolphin pushed a pelican feather across the surface of the water towards him. "Just for the hell of it" he took the proffered feather and threw it back into the water, whereupon, to his great surprise, the dolphin brought it back again. The game continued with Walker experimenting with a ball, an inner tube of a bicycle, small stones and other objects. As the game took shape with other dolphins joining in the act, it began to resemble the repertoire seen today in every dolphinarium in the world. At least, that's how the story goes, a tale which has its fair share of Hollywood ingredients, even for the humans involved: from the lowly position of night foreman, Walker was quickly promoted to the position of general director at Marine Studios.

Soon, spellbound tourists and day-trippers beating a path to see the only, the original, the amazing, performing dolphins were joined by world renowned scientists, and it is interesting, even amusing, to see how rapidly the notions and "discoveries" of science fall into obsolescence, blinkered as they are by the pride of human intellect, divorced from a timeless spiritual respect for the sanctity of life. Internationally respected zoologist Heini Hediger, for example, could scarcely contain his enthusiasm for Marine Studios' sensational new animal act. Describing his visit in a 1954 paper entitled "Sketches about Animal Psychology in the Zoo and Circus", Hediger enthuses: "The most important in this town situated directly on the sea are two aquaria of distinctly American proportions — hence the biggest in the world — so that those enormous pools are rightly no longer called aquaria but oceanaria." In fact, one of those "enormous" pools, home to no fewer than 11 dolphins, measured a mere 22.5 metres in diameter and 3.6 metres deep — grossly inadequate even by today's standards.

Similarly, a Hediger paper entitled "Dressage Experiments With Dolphins", published in 1952, begins by recalling Pliny's fable of a boy who had gained the love of a dolphin by feeding it regularly with bread, and who was carried across the sea every day to school on the animal's back. Hediger notes that scientists have always viewed such stories as lacking any foothold in reality and that they are best left to poets and writers of fairy tales. But 2,000 years later, he goes on to say, there is at least a dolphin in Florida which obeys the commands of its trainer and even allows itself to be harnessed to a surf-board. Thus, he concludes, for humans to be carried over the water with the help of a dolphin is today quite feasible. Hediger goes on to record how sea-lion trainer Adolf Frohn was appointed to teach the dolphins their dressage stunts in the "generous facilities" provided by Marine Studios — a pool about 8 metres in diameter and 1.5 metres deep. It was in this special dressage pool, notes Hediger, that Frohn trained the especially gifted *Tursiops truncatus* called "Flippy". Reading between the lines of the scientific treatise, one can perceive a subjective struggle between scientific intellect and what could best be described as the human conscience. "But 'Flippy' wasn't a fish," Hediger solemnly declared, "and one nearly had to suppress the question as to whether it was an animal at all, when it was looking at you sideways with a twinkling eye from less than half a metre away." Indeed, if it were not for the intellect's constant calling to heel by scientific rationality, Hediger continued, he might have been tempted to look at the dolphin instead as "an enchanted creature". The same conflict between thought and feeling, the same uncanny, mystical experience of kinship, has haunted many a dolphin trainer, scientist and visiting child. Sadly for humanity, sadly for the dolphin and sadly for the world, the more delicate sense of feeling or intuition is so often regarded as a threat to the intellect that it is either overruled, suppressed or trampled. "Flippy", Hediger notes, was fed a strictly weighed portion of 6 kg of fish, an amount "determined by the relatively small possibility of movement." Because the pool was so shallow, Hediger blandly recorded, the dolphin was exposed to the summer sun without adequate protection, the resulting sunburn manifesting itself "in a strong reddening mainly of the light parts of the grey, smooth, plastic-like skin". The scientist could find nothing morally repugnant in the showbiz style of the exhibition. Here at Marine Studios, Hediger commented, it was not a question of "scientific dressage but of show dressage, but the fact that even this circus-like dressage can, in principle, be of scientific value cannot be denied."

The Unlearnt Lessons of Clever Hans

In attempting to pin-point the circus's true identity, the *Encyclopedia Britannica* declares that "Dramatising real life may be appropriate in the movies or television, but the circus must remain a fantasy, forever unreal and divorced from life's routine." This prescription, unfortunately, also includes the myth that animals are happy and well-treated in the menagerie and dolphinarium, content under a rigorous training regime. Hagenbeck's so-called "soft dressage" provided a convenient alibi for the numerous trainers who had neither the patience nor the wits to adopt his methods. Even to this very day, cruelty and deprivation is common in the training of animals, whether in circuses, films and television, or in science. Surprisingly for an institution which prides itself on being at the forefront of scientific and technological advancement, primates owned by the USA's *National Aeronautics and Space Administration* (NASA) have regularly been trained for space flight by the use of electric shocks and beatings with sand-filled hose pipes. Such treatment prompted American astrophysicist Carl Sagan to declare: "If chimpanzees have consciousness, if they are capable of abstractions, do they not have what until now has been described as 'human rights'? How smart does a chimpanzee have to be before killing him constitutes murder?"

But it was probably an episode at the turn of the century that became a landmark in modern attitudes towards animal intelligence. It was then in Germany that a horse called Clever Hans was baffling both scientists and public audiences alike with his intellectual abilities, which included mathematics, an aptitude for identifying musical intervals and a working knowledge of the German language. If someone were to ask him the square root of 16, Hans would dutifully reply with four taps of his hoof. So sceptical were scientists that an investigating panel was formed, composed of two zoologists, a psychologist, a horse trainer and a circus manager. Yet even they could find no flaw in the horse's talents. Indeed, Clever Hans seemed to be on the verge of embarrassing the entire scientific community until one young psychologist set out to discover how Hans would perform if asked questions by someone who didn't know the correct answers. It was then that the horse's score plummeted to almost zero. Thus it transpired that Clever Hans had not mastered mathematics, music or German after all, but had in effect learned to read people's minds by observing subtle changes in their posture, breathing and facial expressions. A triumphant scientific community promptly declared poor Hans a fraud, and portrayed the entire affair as final, unequivocal proof that animals can only react, not think. But ironically, perhaps the same could be said of the scientists themselves: merely labelling it the "Clever Hans Syndrome", they displayed not the slightest interest in understanding the horse's uncanny, extra-sensory abilities. It was as though science was betraying its own superstitious fear of the unknown and indulging in one of the most comforting tenets of Descartes' brand of scientific enquiry — "that which cannot be proved conclusively does not exist." This is often lauded as objectivity and yet even today, when it comes to animal intelligence, it seems as though reality has to conform to existing scientific theories rather than the other way around. But at least Hans the horse had showed up the absurdities of gauging the intelligence of animals by strictly human criteria.

Unfortunately, few researchers were prepared to learn this profound lesson from Hans. In 1947, for instance, a young American psychologist adopted a four-week old chimpanzee which, for six years up until its premature death, was brought up like a human child, and subjected to an intensive language-training programme. During those years the animal learnt to utter only four barely coherent words — Papa, Mama, Cup and Up — which finally led scientists to conclude that non-human primates simply do not possess the vocal apparatus necessary for human speech. Similar research is continuing today using hand gestures and abstract symbols instead of speech and so far the results have proved quite remarkable, with some chimps learning 150-sign vocabularies. Falling back into their old anthropocentric habits, however, the scientists are now being tormented by another momentous question: are the animals only capable of memorising unordered strings of signs or are they able to grasp grammatical rules? It is thus that to pass an intelligence test in a behavioural laboratory, animals are still required to master singularly human skills. Out in its own domain, however, the animal is often more than a match for the human being in terms of observation, cunning, conscious deliberation and other survival skills.

The mysterious theft of abundant quantities of bananas was baffling an harassed plantation manager in Sri Lanka. Suspicion initially fell on some anonymous gang of local thieves, but only after mounting several armed, all-night vigils did he finally discover the true culprits. Hardly believing his own eyes, he watched as a troop of working elephants from a nearby forest padded stealthily into the banana groves for their midnight feast. So as not to disturb the slumbers of the plantation workers and guards, every night before setting off on their raid the ingenious creatures had stuffed mud into the great bells slung around their necks.

The power to reason, the ability to differentiate, to analyse and associate, to perceive continuity and arrive at the concept of cause and effect — these qualities have all been cited as definitions of intelligence. But if intelligence means different things to different people, just consider what it might mean to the animal kingdom as a whole with its mind-blowing diversity. Out in their own environment, animals must use their cunning and intelligence to survive. And as if each species inhabits a separate reality, intelligence is unique in form to each and then varies widely again with the individual. The skills they demonstrate are similarly unique, with certain animals displaying everything from abstract thought to complex communication abilities. For at least a thousand years, humans have believed that they are the only beings on the planet capable of conscious thought. This conviction did not change even when society accepted the fact that human beings were physically descended from, and related to, other species. Yet the implication of contemporary research into animal intelligence is that our minds too are also part of an evolutionary continuum, with conscious thought not a special aptitude that divides us from the animal world, but something that joins us intimately with it.

> *Reuter, 17 November 1988. — A school of dolphins nudged and guided two sailors, shipwrecked in rough seas off the coast of Indonesia, through the night to the safety of a small island. The men were able to raise the alarm and rescue teams plucked another nine of the ship's crew from the sea, a spokesman for the ship's owners, the Indonesian state oil company Pertamina, said yesterday.*

As we have already seen with the "talking" chimpanzees and those swotting up their teacher's grammatical rules, the same ubiquitous anthropocentrism that afflicts the human race is even glaringly apparent in this branch of science. It is perhaps especially ironic that in such behavioural experiments, the researchers study the animal with that special brand of stilted impassiveness so peculiar to modern science. It is typified by the many hard-line behaviourists who, rather than stooping so low as to admit that animals care about their young, describe a monkey's, or wildcat's attentiveness and grooming as "instinctive licking behaviour". The reductionist approach so inherent in establishment science is also much in evidence, not least of all because even research into comparative psychology is invariably conducted not in the animal's natural habitat, but in the most artificial of conditions in the laboratory. Yet evidently having been unable to see the wood for the trees for years, increasing numbers of scientists are now coming to the momentous conclusion that valid tests of animal intelligence can only be conducted in a species' unique natural environment. Indeed, as field biologists have been discovering for years, outside the artificial conditions imposed upon them in behavioural laboratories, animals may display their cognitive powers in the wild with far more complexity than the ones the scientists are so eager and insistent upon teaching them in captivity.

Dolphins have become favourite subjects for the behavioural laboratory in recent years. Internationally acclaimed cetacean expert Professor Giorgio Pilleri of the Brain Anatomy Institute at the University of Berne, Switzerland, has long denounced the anthropocentric nature of such research. "Keeping dolphins in artificial conditions can do little else than produce artificial scientific results," he reasons. "We are dealing with animals of the highest levels of development, intelligence and sensitivity," but these qualities he adds, "are only evident in the dolphin's own unique aquatic environment where that intelligence has evolved to meet specific needs. It is nonsense to attempt to teach the dolphin algebra or human language, in just the same way that it is absurd to try to test animal intelligence in general by human criteria." Furthermore, Pilleri believes that the pressures of captivity often cause a "profound psychological disturbance" in the animals. Ironically, one of the first symptoms of this condition is a "loss of communication" and Pilleri insists that he has "proved that dolphins actually become less intelligent in captivity."

Out in the open sea, a dolphin school, composed of anything from a dozen to over a thousand animals is kept together by means of acoustic communication. While high-frequency sonar clicks are used for orientation and hunting, lower level sound serves as language. "In the wild, dolphins are highly gregarious creatures with pronounced individuality," says Pilleri. "On numerous occasions, wounded dolphins have been observed being supported by their companions, brought to the surface of the water to breathe, and nursed until they become well again. Females, acting as midwives, assist each other in giving birth. They help the exhausted mother by raising the newborn calf to the surface to enable it to breathe. Even before the onset of labour, the other females surround the mother. This also points clearly to a capacity for differentiated communication."

In some dolphin species the sonar emissions can reach frequencies of 200,000 Hz, Pilleri continues. "The *Platanista* or blind river dolphin is capable of detecting balls 2 mm in diameter at a distance of several metres as well as distinguishing between materials — whether an object is made of wood or stone for instance. And in addition to identifying the species of fish, it can tell whether it is alive or dead." From all the available evidence, Pilleri concludes, "the ultimate status of man's brain in the ranking of mammals is today beginning to be in doubt."

A curious episode which took place on the Black Sea several years ago may also shed light on dolphin thought. A small Russian fishing boat was suddenly surrounded by several dolphins who began to push the vessel towards a buoy. There, the bemused fishermen discovered a young dolphin trapped in the buoy's anchor line. The men proceeded to free the dolphin baby and when they succeeded, the dolphin school let out whistles of joy and thanks. They then escorted the fishing boat all the way back to port. Other incidents also attest not only to the intelligence of dolphins, but also their ability to grasp the abstract concept of cause and effect.

Danish ethologist Holger Poulsen related an episode in which two dolphins were playing with an eel. When the eel eluded them by swimming into a hole, one of the dolphins seized a small fish with a poison sting, took it carefully in its mouth, and pushed it into the eel's hiding place. The eel immediately fled the hole and thus the game continued.

The legendary compassion of the dolphin, of course, also extends to the human race, with numerous stories from every corner of the Earth recounting how the animals have protected swimmers in shark-infested waters, or saved drowning seafarers. But to a science still steeped in speciesism, there is always a "rational" explanation, as evidenced by the views of unabashed dolphinarium fan Prof. Paul Schauenberger, a researcher at the Museum of Geneva. Though "there are countless examples" of dolphins coming to the rescue of human beings, Schauenberger reasons, "we shouldn't believe that the dolphin is saving people intentionally. It is rather that all dolphins, from the smallest to the biggest, show an innate tendency to carry on their foreheads every object drifting on the surface. It is a game, an instinct." Schauenberger seems reluctant to explain why the dolphins habitually carry their human objects to the nearest shore rather than out to sea.

> "There is no creature among all the Beasts of the world which hath so great and ample demonstration of the power and wisedome of almighty God as the elephant."
> — Edward Topsell; *The Historie of Foure-Footed Beastes*, London 1658

Elephants Never Forget

Research at Kenya's Amboseli nature reserve has discovered that elephants, like dolphins, can also communicate with each other over several kilometres using calls inaudible to the human ear. "Such communication could explain coordinated movements by separated elephants and herds which have puzzled observers," says Peter Jackson of the International Union for Conservation of Nature. "The elephant's use of tools also implies a well-developed intelligence," reports Dr Fred Kurt, a lecturer in ecology and a specialist on elephants both in captivity and the wild. The tip of an elephant's trunk, says Kurt, "is a kind of olfactory hand and it is used for shaping and manipulating tools, such as tiny pieces of wood for grooming the skin, or logs that it can throw with considerable skill at its adversaries." Their intelligence is also reflected in their nimbleness of movement. An elephant, says Kurt, despite its massive bulk, "would be quite capable of cautious movement in a china shop, and not be at any means as clumsy as the popular phrase implies." Memory is cited as yet another test of intelligence, and according to Kurt, the memories of elephants, for so long regarded as legendary, "can measure up to those of humans." As evidence for this, he points out that the elephants of Knie's Swiss National Circus "know the way unaided from the railway station to the circus ground in at least sixty towns — and wild herds are just as good at finding the way to their feeding grounds." American ecologist Cynthia Moss has spent 13 years studying an elephant family in Kenya. She concludes that the animals not only possess virtues of loyalty and kindness but can readily grasp the concept of mortality. Using the tips of their trunks, she reports, they rarely fail to examine the skeletons of fallen companions. On one occasion, Moss observed how a grown elephant gently fondled the sun-bleached skull of her long-dead mother, as if in recognition.

But even intelligence research in an animal's natural environment can sometimes have an amusing way of showing up a scientist's own intellectual limitations. When chimpanzees embark on a termite hunt, for instance, they will look for a suitable branch, carefully strip off the leaves and, with great concentration and dexterity, probe down into the openings of the termite hill. Much to their embarrassment, researchers who tried to mimic the practice discovered that they were as clumsy and ineffective as the adult chimps' children who had not yet fully learnt their skills.

> "It is not in great animals alone that we see unapproachable
> wisdom; no less wonders are seen in the smallest."
> — St Basil, *Hexaemeron*, Homily IX

But what of smaller creatures? For many years, science has attempted to categorise the comparative intelligence of animals with the concept of "cephalisation" — measuring the ratio of brain to body weight. Thus, allowing for complexity of the brain, dolphins, gorillas, chimpanzees and orang-utans share the same level of cephalisation as human beings. But by this criterion, the complex behaviour of smaller animals with low degrees of cephalisation can only be explained as being dictated almost entirely by instinct — a legacy of Descartes' "clockwork" mechanisms. It may be, however, that the entire basis of such scientific theory is at fault. Donald Griffin, emeritus professor at Rockefeller University and author of a 1984 book entitled *Animal Thinking*, dismisses the automatic-instinct theory. He argues that few animals' brains could even store the huge volumes of behavioural instructions they would need to survive in constantly changing environments. Making conscious decisions, he declares, is far more economical than carrying around automatic responses to all the many contingencies of daily life. Indeed, he adds, "animals with relatively small brains may have greater need for simple conscious thinking than those endowed with a kilogram of grey matter."

This might explain the sophisticated abilities of some migratory birds which are believed to navigate by stars and by measuring subtle changes in the Earth's magnetic field and polarised light. In one recent experiment in the USA, for instance, a number of shearwaters were tagged and then released several thousand miles outside their customary migration route. Although their subsequent journey involved flying over alien terrain with no familiar landmarks, the birds arrived at their usual nesting sites only a few days late. Other small animals also show convincing signs of conscious intelligence: the intricate dance language of honey bees discovered by Karl von Frisch in which a bee scout will explain to its compatriots at the hive in what direction and at what distance food can be found; a species of desert ant in southern India which has developed its own water management system by piling feathers around the entrances to its underground colonies, trapping morning dew; the woodcock, wagtail and robin who are known to nurse their wounded companions, expertly plastering fractures with mud.

Without doubt, the very concept of animal wisdom raises profound implications for human society; for, if animals can think and reason and are conscious of varied emotions, what possible justification could there be for their mistreatment in industrial farms, their exploitation in animal shows and zoos, their abuse in laboratories? What would be the fate of the current brand of establishment science, with its neutered morals, always ready to serve the highest bidder? Yet for expedience's sake, to preserve a self-serving utilitarian view of creation, perhaps human society would prefer to stick to the belief in the non-thinking clockwork animal, and let the worn-out ghost of Descartes continue to haunt.

"Learned men of the forests in their imitation of the human comedy." The chimpanzees Romeo and Juliet, a menagerie poster from the turn of the century.

A 1988 poster of the "Cirque National Italien" alias "Circo Medrano", depicting their "largest and most ferocious gorilla in the world." (Matthias Schnellmann.)

II. ENDANGERED SPECIES — IN ABUNDANCE

"Over the years the dealer has obtained a reputation somewhat akin to the slave-trader; and it is a reputation many rightly deserve, for like the slavers they travel widely, enjoying the not inconsiderable profits of their venture, whilst their cargoes of horror lie concealed below decks, hidden from sight so as to disturb few consciences."
— Bill Jordan and Stefan Ormrod

If, as Schiller said, "World history is the world's court of judgement," how then should we regard the circus menagerie today, so plainly a product of a bizarre and brutal ancestry? From its earliest beginnings in the circuses and amphitheatres of ancient Rome, the blood games of species supremacy drove many animals systematically towards extinction. When its malevolent ghost reappeared centuries later, the circus soon came to play a pivotal role in the vast international trade in endangered species. Today, even by those favourite catchwords of the zoo and circus fraternity, "education" and "conservation", it must be difficult to explain to any wide-eyed child just why there are now more tigers inhabiting barred menageries in Europe than the Asian wilderness.

Without doubt, history has seen anthropocentrism grow into such a rampant and insidious force, so deeply ingrained in human attitudes and reflected so destructively in human deeds that it is difficult not to ascribe its cause to some kind of perverse subconscious death wish. As I have already described in *The Monk Seal Conspiracy*, anthropocentrism's long and bleak tradition has taken a devastating toll upon the Earth. Its effects could be compared to a state of chronic war or to some debilitating malignant disease, inexorably draining the resistance of the body and the fortitude of the spirit. Environmental scientist David Sarokin has written: "Like any ailing patient, a sick planet displays symptoms. Dead dolphins wash up inexplicably on the beaches; tropical coral reefs and temperate forests are dying around the world; gaps in the ozone layer appear like open sores in the upper atmosphere. Rain, snow and fog are often hundreds of times more acidic than normal. Fish populations have unprecedented numbers of tumours. The planet is even running a fever: The summer of 1988 may one day be looked back upon as the first clear warning that the greenhouse effect had fundamentally changed the heat balance of our planet." This vivid analogy of Earth as a living being also forms the basis of Dr James Lovelock's *Gaia hypothesis*, and although bolstered now by detailed ecological evidence, in substance it is a belated rediscovery of a world view that once nourished the cradle of civilisation more than 2,000 years ago in ancient Greece. As one of the forefathers of contemporary ecology, Plato described Gaia, the Mother Earth, as "a living creature... endowed with soul and reason". Today, we can say that this ancient God, this creature upon which we dwell, is on the verge of mortal illness, final proof perhaps that we, like the emperors of old who were so intent upon their own apotheosis, have, by means of the most brutal subjugation, won our much-cherished supremacy over the Earth even if it threatens to end in our own demise.

Despite all the petty conflicts between nations, races, religions and philosophies, outside every single home, in every single village, town or city, in any country or culture in the world, there is the devastating irony of this uniting force: a species graveyard which stretches before the eyes, a graveyard that by·the turn of the century may well contain a million headstones. Within a decade, the pall-bearers passing before our homes will be delivering to their graves at least one extinct species every hour. The fact that few people actually mourn the passing of these souls is a glaring testament to that deathly and virulent anthropocentrism which afflicts the human race. Indeed, even within the environmental movement, there are those who only seem to be saddened by these extinctions because their "usefulness to man" has been irretrievably lost — either as a food or medicine source, as components of a gene pool, or most hypocritically of all perhaps, as part of "man's natural heritage". Though they assert that this utilitarian philosophy will appeal to human nature's inevitable selfishness, it must, almost by definition, ultimately prove self-defeating, if only because the Earth will never be saved by deception, even Plato's well-intentioned "magnificent myth" or "noble lie". Such conservationists seem to have forgotten that at the very heart of our battered relationship with the planet — and often with our fellow human beings too — lies the festering wound of utilitarianism. As former UN High Commissioner for Refugees, Prince Sadruddin Aga Khan, has said, "The gulf that separates speciesism from racism is a narrow one indeed."

But while they face genocide in the wild, there are endangered species in abundance in the menagerie. Even a casual stroll around the circus can reveal this bizarre logic of an all-conquering species, the exhibits in barred beast wagons that seem to bear an uncanny resemblance to those freaks of nature which were so lucrative in circus sideshows during the last century — curious relics of the wild which *homo sapiens* is, according to God's wishes, civilising into oblivion.

Blind Justice

The chimpanzee, gorilla and orang-utan, the elephant and rhinoceros, the leopard and tiger — all of these species, so common to the circus menagerie, are listed in the *Red Data Book*, once rather cynically described as the ecologist's version of the *Tibetan Book of the Dead*. Published by IUCN, the International Union for Conservation of Nature and Natural Resources, it lists every kind of animal and plant according to its perceived ability to survive the onslaughts of the "Alpha" species, as either rare, threatened, or endangered. People may be forgiven for assuming that these animals are under strict protection; laws have the habit, even though they are only made of good intentions, paper, compromise and loopholes, of deluding the public into believing that a particular conservation problem has been irrevocably solved. Unfortunately, this too is little more than brittle illusion, as testified by the enduring billion dollar slave-trade in the most endangered of Earth's inhabitants.

The first international efforts to stem the traffic in wildlife took place in Washington, D.C. in 1973, when 80 nations met to draft the Convention on the International Trade in Endangered Species (CITES). Prior to this there were few restrictions imposed upon this secretive industry, based, like any other, on encouraging mass consumption as a part of the inviolable law of supply and demand. More than any other factor, it was the hideous realities of animal dealing which finally awakened the public and brought pressure to bear on governments to clamp down on the barbarity of the trade — at least its more obvious, offensive barbarity. The industry which supplies the world's zoos, menageries and pet shops was exposed in graphic detail in the press: suffocated tigers packed in crates scarcely bigger than themselves, their faces still frozen into a grotesque mask of terror and agony; monkeys that had died of panic and overcrowding, spilling out of crates onto the concrete floor of the freight terminal; eagles with their eyelids crudely sewn together with stitches of string; a sun bear which had strangled itself on its own chain during the endless journey from Malaya. Though CITES has made substantial progress in curbing such outrageous abuses, few would pretend that the Bergen-Belsen of the animal kingdom has been eradicated; it has in fact merely been sanitised by regulation.

Under the Convention, which came into force in 1975, species are listed under Appendix I, II or III according to their estimated survival status. Except for "scientific considerations" (a loophole which sees thousands of exotic animals end up in laboratories and zoos every year), trade is banned in Appendix I species, those considered seriously threatened with extinction. Animals in this list include the chimpanzee, gorilla and orang-utan, cheetah, clouded leopard, Asiatic lion, tiger, snow leopard, Indian elephant and rhinoceros. For Appendix II species, potentially threatened by trade, commerce is permitted provided that the transaction is officially authorised by the country of origin. Included in this list is the bottlenose dolphin, that ever-smiling clown of world oceanaria and, until very recently, the African elephant which faces extinction by the turn of the century. It is ironic perhaps that in practice traffic in Appendix II species is so liberal that many *taxa* now contained in this annex will probably have to be promoted aloft in years to come. Some 90 per cent of all monkeys required for research, for example, are still being trapped in the wild. The International Primate Protection League estimates that one million primates are taken in this way every year, 200,000 reaching their destination while the other 800,000 die during capture or transportation. Appendix III enables individual governments to list certain regional or endemic species which, while not considered endangered by the world at large, are deemed worthy of protection in their country of origin.

> *"One of the principal weaknesses of the Convention on International Trade in Endangered Species is that the 'Mr Bigs' of the animal trade can sit in places like Nairobi or Nuremberg concocting sordid deals for which they will never be punished."*
> — International Primate Protection League

It has been said that in any law ever conceived there must exist a loophole, and this is certainly true of CITES which, in recent years, has begun to look distinctly tattered. Even the CITES secretariat itself, based in Lausanne, admits that "there are loopholes which can be exploited by unscrupulous traders," adding that countries which resist becoming signatories to the Convention — such as Mexico, Cuba, the United Arab Emirates, Taiwan, Hong Kong, Singapore and Burma — remain centres or conduits for international trafficking. Furthermore, despite some cursory monitoring by Interpol, the regulations are severely weakened by organised corruption, particularly in Third World countries where most of the species originate. While it is true that stricter enforcement of CITES has curbed the activities of some traders, it has also had the added effect of driving the more resilient, professional smugglers into the sleazy underground world of organised crime, with the Mafia controlling large chunks of a thriving black market. Even embassies and consulates, with the privilege of diplomatic immunity, have been implicated in smuggling live endangered species. The animal trafficker, like his counterpart in the illegal drugs trade, stands to make stupendous profits. Indeed, according to former animal dealer Jean-Yves Domalain, many animal traders also traffic in drugs. The contraband is concealed in crates holding venomous snakes, snapping crocodiles or other similarly daunting beasts which understandably tend to deter rigorous inspections by customs officers. Sometimes, drugs may even be hidden inside the bodies of living animals.

In terms of profits — currently estimated in the region of $5 billion a year, including $1.5 billion worth of illegal deals — the international trade in endangered species is also said to rival global drug trafficking, and one could make similar parallels as regards its propagation of misery and its power to corrupt. These however, are "only animals", and although drug addicts are not generally regarded as very much more superior by those who rule and regulate, when it comes to law enforcement the analogy stops dead. While a veritable army of professionals is arrayed against drug growers, refiners, smugglers and dealers, by comparison there is little more than a rag-bag Dad's Army sent out to intercept poachers, local and international animal dealers. Then there is the discrepancy in the penalties and sanctions of the law. If apprehended, members of an international heroin syndicate will face long prison sentences and confiscation of assets; an international dealer in endangered species on the other hand will be given little more than a slap on the wrist — a minuscule fine entirely out of proportion to his profits. This is just one of the reasons why CITES is being described as the animal dealer's charter. But there are others which are far more serious. Greenpeace, for example, has laid the blame squarely on CITES for the continuing market in endangered species, stating that a "momentum has gradually developed to change the purpose of CITES to one which promotes the trade in wildlife."

The reasons for such charges are highly complex, but by way of an introduction, they can best be illustrated by the CITES secretariat's attitude towards two most pertinent issues, the poaching of lowland gorillas, and the illegal trade in ivory. All gorillas are strictly protected as Appendix I species under CITES, and normally the juvenile individuals so much in demand in the menagerie can only be caught by first killing their mothers and protecting adults. But in 1984, IUCN, which also acts as scientific adviser to CITES and is a sister organisation of the World Wide Fund for Nature (WWF), inexplicably paid for seven lowland gorillas to be exported from Cameroon to Holland, their final destination being Burgers' Zoo, a commercial safari park in Arnhem. The juvenile animals had been captured by French expatriates Robert Roy and his wife, veteran animal dealers specialising in trafficking gorillas and chimpanzees. Though the International Primate Protection League (IPPL) and leading primatologists were actively campaigning to have the gorillas stay in their natural habitat by creating a survival and rehabilitation centre for orphaned individuals, their efforts were to no avail; behind the scenes, the transaction was being hustled through CITES' legal bottlenecks with scarcely more than a rumour of consultation, even though IPPL is actually a member of IUCN. When a furious Dr Shirley

McGreal, chair of IPPL, discovered the surreptitious operation, she stated: "We couldn't believe that a conservation group would sink so low. They are even paying the dealers so-called 'expenses' for catching and exporting the gorillas" — an amount reputed to be in the region of $32,000. McGreal went on to say that in the closing stages of the deal, pressure was exerted on the president of Cameroon by high officials of the Dutch government and only then, with his apparently reluctant seal of approval, was the export permitted. The undermining of CITES for such demonstrably spurious reasons was underlined by the fact that the CITES authority in the USA had previously denied import permits for the seven gorillas, partly on the grounds that the dealers in question had already decimated wild gorilla populations in certain areas of Cameroon. Indeed, although the director of Burgers' Zoo heaped praise upon the dealers, even going so far as to describe them as "conservationists", IPPL provided evidence that the Roys and their suppliers had, over several decades, slaughtered hundreds of free-living gorillas during their capture of profitable gorilla babies for the world's menageries. "It appears strange," declared IPPL, "that the CITES secretariat does not seem to have files on known or suspected animal dealers, especially dealers as well-known and long-established as the Roys. Even though IPPL existed before CITES did, we have never been invited to contribute data to CITES files." But both IUCN and CITES remained distinctly unmoved by such revelations, IUCN declaring that the gorillas "indirectly serve the conservation of nature if they breed and one can give the offspring to other zoos." McGreal concluded that "it will be very hard for IUCN to intervene with any moral authority now to seek an end of trade from the Cameroon or anywhere else in Africa." With the price on the head of a baby gorilla having reached $125,000, IPPL emphasised that none could be considered safe from poachers. Although justified by CITES and IUCN as a "one-shot deal", gorillas continued to be exported from Cameroon, including three destined for Taipei Zoo in 1987 in a transaction orchestrated by the notorious German dealer Walter Sensen, with export papers which the Cameroon government later declared to be forgeries. Two of the young animals, already having seen their mothers and families shot before their very eyes, died of panic and suffocation during transport. But like most live animal cargoes, this one too was insured, to the tune of $445,000. Thus, even if an animal, confined to a metal or wooden crate, does perish during a long and arduous journey, most dealers still stand to make a lucrative "insurance killing".

The annual trade in ivory continues to kill 89,000 elephants every year, according to IUCN. Those deaths translate into some 825 tons of raw ivory, with a market value of $50 million. Most of this is sold in Asia where it is converted into worked ivory worth about $500 million. Despite the much-vaunted rigours of CITES, the ongoing trade is inexorably driving the African elephant towards extinction. There are now thought to be only 700,000 elephants left on the entire continent compared to 1.5 million ten years ago, and many ecologists predict that by the year 2000, the species may well have disappeared forever.

Proclaiming 1988 the "Year of the Elephant" in the USA, the African Wildlife Federation (AWF) launched a consumer boycott of ivory products aimed at stemming the death toll. At that time, the USA and Japan were supporting almost two-thirds of the world demand for ivory, representing the deaths of 60,000 elephants a year, while EEC countries, up until June 1989, were annually importing ivory amounting to 12,000 elephants. According to Cynthia Moss, a senior researcher at the AWF, "at least 80 per cent of ivory on the market today is from poached elephants — even if it comes with all the correct papers certifying it as legal." The trade, she added, is systematically circumventing the provisions of CITES. While strenuously denying the charge that CITES is becoming an institution which promotes rather than regulates the trade in endangered species, Jacques Berney, deputy director-general of the CITES secretariat in Lausanne, described the ivory consumer boycott as "unworkable", adding that "CITES is actively campaigning against it." The basis for this extraordinary stand was the claim that much of the ivory on the international market is in the form of antique worked pieces. Yet even Berney himself conceded that such ivory "could be from poached animals" because it is "impractical to make a distinction between old and new worked ivory at border controls." Hoping to stem illegal traffic in ivory, for many years CITES put its faith in the so-called "quota system" which allowed individual African governments to decide annually how many elephants could be "legally culled" in their own countries. This was despite the fact that it is virtually impossible to ascertain the difference between "legal" and "illegal" ivory and the fact — well known to CITES — that several governments in the region are also intimately involved in black market trafficking. CITES' reasoning however, was based upon the notion of "sustainable utilisation" of the elephant, revealing once again just how successful avarice can be when masquerading as objective, hardheaded pragmatism. "Any import ban will backfire on conservation because it will halt legal elephant hunting under the quota system," insisted Berney. "Countries would have no incentive to protect their elephant populations." Though the notion of protecting animals by shooting them may seem somewhat peculiar, Berney justified the CITES policy as being grounded upon the IUCN and WWF policy of "sustainable development", adding that "probably the best chance for the survival of wildlife is to give it an economic value as a renewable resource." Yet even discounting the offensive notion of viewing the elephant as no more than a human asset, it was patently obvious that the "utilisation" of the species was not, by any means, "sustainable". Declared elephant specialist

Dr Fred Kurt: "These dealers fully expect the African elephant to become extinct and that is precisely why they're stock-piling as much ivory as they can lay their hands on. I've been told by people involved in the trade that in the future ivory will be worth more than its weight in gold. Now you can imagine why there is this free-for-all over ivory. These dealers are actually *speculating* on the elephant's extinction." Despite such warnings, however, even WWF International campaigned against the boycott — until an unexpected wave of public sympathy for the elephant suddenly overturned its ill-fated and increasingly embarrassing policy. It is reported that in 1988, shortly before his retirement, EEC environment commissioner Stanley Clinton Davies was preparing a report to submit to the Council of Ministers which would espouse the cause of the ivory boycott. It was then that WWF International stepped in, eventually persuading him to scrap it. Yet with opposition to the quota system mounting steadily even within Africa, CITES, WWF International and other diehards were soon shown to be fighting a losing battle. Indeed, under massive pressure, the EEC finally imposed a ban on ivory imports in June 1989, and a blanket — though still provisional — import ban was achieved a few months later when the parties to CITES, meeting in Geneva, voted to promote the African elephant into Appendix I. Unless it is undermined by certain African nations applying for exemptions, this move will also have the added effect of closing down the trade in African elephant calves destined for the circus — these animals usually being the offspring of those killed under the quota system.

Ruthlessly efficient, the animal-trafficking industry is actually producing greater annual wealth than the gross national product of some Third World countries where much of the trade in endangered species originates. And it is here where we stumble across one of the inherent and most intractable of all problems confronting CITES. That is the insidious seesaw of supply and demand for endangered species, involving the chronic poverty of the Third World on one hand, and the over-consumption of the rich, industrialised world on the other. In 1979, according to IUCN — four years after CITES came into force — the demand for luxury goods in the developed world led to the deaths of 2 million crocodiles, 500,000 wild cats and 70,000 elephants. Bowing as usual to the sacredness of the free market, those who originally drafted CITES took little or no account of the fact that free enterprise would inevitably continue to be the dynamic driving force of the industry — those haute couture boutiques in New York, Paris, London and Rome for instance, where the closer to extinction an animal is, the more exclusive, luxurious and coveted is its skin. The same principle governs the entire market, from authentic turtle soup to genuine turtle-shell spectacle frames, from real crocodile handbags and shoes to ivory carvings. Even for a wild animal destined to be incarcerated for life, free enterprise is the guiding principle, whether that be for the zoo, the circus, the private menagerie or the laboratory. It is a vicious and cut-throat business, and although it may be pragmatic to say, as apologists for the trade so often do, that "responsible animal traders take measures to prevent any contravention of CITES," this may well be regarded as being just one more testament to this golden age of illusion. With profit as the sole motivating force, it would be more accurate to say that illegal trafficking is even implicitly encouraged by a convention that does not prohibit but only regulates the trade in endangered species.

For a network of international dealers, dealing syndicates and national brokers, the incentive for the trade is greed grown rampant with cold-blooded cynicism; for the locals they exploit as poachers and animal catchers, however, the incentive is often no more than grinding poverty and ignorance — at least in the beginning. If poachers are now materialising who have undergone rigorous military training and who are equipped with kalashnikov assault rifles, machine-guns and hand grenades, then that is the result of growing sophistication on the part of an industry that believes that having been given an inch, it can take a mile. Indeed, if the trend continues as it has, then — just like those 12-year-old cocaine barons in the United States equipped with an electronic armoury already daunting even for the police to challenge — within a decade we should not be surprised to see poachers furnished with mortars, armoured cars, even tanks. Indeed, that day may have already arrived. Only recently, poachers within Kenya's Mount Elgon national park killed several elephants with an antitank gun. Even more disturbing, in 1988 South African military forces were implicated in a huge ivory racket reputed to have caused the decimation of Angola's elephant population. Over 100,000 elephants are said to have been massacred by the Unita rebels of Jonas Savimbi in Angola, in order to finance the war there. Condemning South Africa as "one of the largest wildlife outlaws in the world", Craig van Note, vice-president of Monitor, a consortium of US environmental and animal welfare groups, reported that most of the elephant tusks were being carried out on South African air transports or trucks — all with the complicity of South African officials at the highest levels. Savimbi, in an interview with *Paris Match*, recently admitted that he has financed much of the war with ivory, diamonds and teak.

There is a reason for this escalation of the animal trade beyond the capitalist canon that all money must grow. In this case, endemic poverty, chronic injustice and abuse of power has provided fertile soil for a politicisation of the trade, by now resembling an insurgency in several countries. To some extent, poaching may also be a result of "leadership by example" — the idea that the "man in the street" should look up with pride towards his leaders and thus inspired, adjust his lifestyle accordingly. But when the president, his army chiefs and security forces are all on the make, sooner or later the entire bureaucracy becomes riddled with corruption, and all that remains of respect for the law is cynicism. The fact that heads of state have regularly been implicated in organised poaching is hardly likely to inspire reverence for the protection of endangered species. In 1984, for example, no less than five African presidents were accused of fostering the killing of elephants. Adding to the confusion, former big-game hunters now appear on the scene as the heads of international conservation organisations, preaching the creed of "sustainable utilisation of endangered species". The subsequent culling of "excess" animals — excess in this context usually meaning that they have outgrown the reservations allotted to them, not that they have suddenly become un-endangered — can do little else than encourage poaching. Furthermore, as Jacques Berney himself admits, despite the efforts of CITES, "there will always be poaching — anti-poaching units are just too expensive and no one is prepared to pay for them."

On the other hand, some people are prepared to pay handsomely to shoot elephants, hippos and wildcats — as much as $1500 a day for African hunting safaris. Indeed, in this new concept in tourism and recreation, business is booming. Take the example of *Jet Tours*, an enterprise run in association with Air France. In its hunting and fishing catalogue 1988/89 the company offers the adventure of a life-time for the would-be big game hunter, together with detailed advice on how to mount trophies. The European bison can be hunted in Poland, while Bulgaria offers the European brown bear, the much-despised wolf, and the European wild cat. For something a little more exotic, the brown bear and the lynx can also be shot in Mongolia. At the top end of the price list, the crocodile, lion, leopard, hippopotamus and even elephant can be hunted in a variety of countries including Cameroon, the Central African Republic, Ethiopia, Rwanda, Zambia and Zimbabwe. A discreetly presented box on the last page of the brochure has the heading "Washington Convention" where it is stated: "For certain animals like the brown bear, wolf, Turkestan deer, Hartmann's zebra and Roanne's antelope, that are listed on Appendix II of the Convention, it is necessary to obtain a certificate of origin to ease the import of the trophy into France. We provide advice on this matter." In case it is difficult to tell from the small print the difference between the legal and illegal shooting of an elephant in Africa, just imagine what it's like for the down-trodden and hungry where laws have always stolen, never given. In such a climate seething with contradictions, poaching and smuggling rapidly become endemic in one form or another. Not that Third World countries alone are liable to graft and corruption. In what it derisively calls the "revolving door phenomenon", the International Primate Protection League states that "ex-government officials find work as consultants because they know their way around the departments where they used to work and how to get information, and even, occasionally, which officials are subject to bribes. At least one former senior official of the US Fish and Wildlife Service 'revolved' out of the Service's door to become a lobbyist for animal dealers, big game hunters, ivory traders and furriers. Mr Richard Parsons was formerly director of the Federal Wildlife Permit Office, which is supposed to regulate the importation of endangered wildlife to the United States. In 1983, Parsons quit this position and turned up at the meeting of CITES as a representative of an animal dealers' lobby. At subsequent meetings, Mr Parsons has represented the trigger-happy big game hunters of the Safari Club International (who had applied in 1981 to import to the US 'trophies' of gorillas, orang-utans, and over 50 other endangered species) and a US fur industry lobby."

But what of loopholes affecting the trade in live animals for display, loopholes which allow animal dealers like Walter Sensen of *Zoo Agentur* in West Germany, for example, to trade in lowland gorillas, or offer rare Commerson dolphins for sale with full CITES documentation? Or circuses throughout the world to obtain Appendix I elephants from Asia?

"Animal supplies to the circus are all subject to the Washington Convention," insists Dr Thomas Althaus, an ethologist at Switzerland's Federal Veterinary Office. "It is impossible now to import endangered species from the wild for primarily commercial purposes. It's not possible to import leopards, jaguars, tigers or snow leopards or Asian elephants. Most are captive bred or the others are pre-convention animals — old elephants for example that were imported in the 1950s." Yet by hook or by crook, some circuses are still managing to acquire Appendix I Asian elephants by exploiting CITES loopholes. Switzerland's prestigious Circus Knie for example recently imported two new baby elephants from Burma which is not a member of CITES. Explains Dr Fred Kurt, who was once a close associate of Circus Knie: "In the 1970s, Lufthansa, on its inaugural jumbo jet cargo flight from Delhi to Frankfurt, carried a dozen baby elephants and they went to Walter Sensen, the German animal dealer. Now I always thought that with the Washington Convention things would change but it didn't stop circuses like Knie getting new Asian elephants, even though it is officially not permitted. But Althaus — who gives out the permits — is a very close friend of Louis Knie and whether he sees these matters very objectively, I'm not so sure. To me it seems very strange indeed that Burma allowed the export of these two baby elephants when at the same time the country — worried about the decline of its elephant population — has requested international assistance for their elephant captive breeding project." Vigorously opposed to such trade, Kurt believes that the elephants should stay in their natural habitat. "In certain elephant camps in Asia," he explains, "there are often too many baby elephants. Because there may be no work for them, the people who run these camps then try to sell them but in my view it would be better to keep these elephants in Asian national parks to use them for traditional forestry work where there are no roads, and with local people. And there they can always play an ecological role." Instead, the two Burmese baby elephants are now destined for a life in chains. Reported Zoo Check's co-founder, Bill Travers, who visited Circus Knie in Zürich in April 1989: "The worst sight was the heaving and shuddering of the two baby Asian elephants. This they did continually when they were not tugging at their chains which fixed them to the centre of their wooden platform. One elephant, standing next to them, was acting as an auntie, and reached out frequently with her trunk to touch and comfort them."

Even CITES itself reluctantly admits that much of the illicit trade in live animals for display is carried out with the help of people assigned to protect them, though it rarely, if ever, names names. In some countries in Africa, Asia and Latin America, dealers can purchase signed but blank health certificates, and — with appropriate baksheesh — official export documents. Over the years, this has led to a strengthening of documentary requirements, though they can still be by-passed through several exploitable clauses. One is that a "Pre-Convention" Appendix I animal is officially regarded as being Appendix II and CITES concedes that the Pre-Convention clause "can be used to cover continued illegal trade." Similarly, an animal of a strictly endangered species testified as being captive-bred is also summarily demoted to Appendix II. Basically, all that is needed to prove this is an "official" paper from the country of origin — even if that country is not a member of CITES.

A slight variation on the "captive-bred" ruse is to declare that a wild-caught animal has been in human hands too long for it to be returned to its natural habitat. In 1988, for example, German trafficker Walter Sensen wrote the following letter to a menagerie client eager to obtain an Appendix I gorilla:

> "We could supply you from Equatorial Guinea (West Africa), at short notice, a 0,1 gorilla. Depending on age and weight the price will be between DM 80,000 - DM 120,000...
>
> We are certainly the only firm which can still export from West Africa gorillas and chimpanzees because we have an exclusive contract with the government of this country for five years. If you are interested in this gorilla, I could send you by fax a sample of an export permit.
>
> In this export permit is written, amongst other things, the following text: *'The gorilla in question is a specimen which has been in human care and can't be returned to the wild.'*
>
> This text is important when one applies for the import

permit. — Zoo-Sensen GmbH, Import-Export Wholesalers."

For the travelling circus crossing international borders there may be another exploitable loophole when it is intent upon buying or replacing an animal. This revolves around the "transit" or "temporary export" permit afforded to circuses under CITES. Before leaving their country of origin, circuses are obliged to make an inventory of the animals they will be carrying with them in their wagons. Though in principle customs officials should check against the list the animals being exported, in practice such a thorough inspection is seldom made, allowing the circus to add animals unnoticed to their menagerie. Pier Lorenzo Florio, director of the Italian branch of TRAFFIC, a WWF-affiliated organisation which monitors the trade in endangered species, advocates stricter CITES control of circuses. "Only God knows where they get their animals from," he declares, "but they are undoubtedly dealing in animals, and contravening the terms of the agreement. It cannot be explained for instance why so many circuses in Italy have infant chimpanzees, which are photographed for a fee being held and cuddled by members of the audience." Florio, who is also a member of the Italian CITES management authority, surmises that Italian circuses buy the chimps while on tour in Spain, and then import them illegally into Italy, failing to declare the new additions to their menagerie on inventory forms. Itinerant beach photographers who ply their trade along the holiday coasts of Spain and the Canary Islands are thought to be at the forefront of this continuing black-market trade. Wild-caught in Africa, the chimps are crated up, six to eight to each wooden box, and put on a tramp steamer bound for Spain. Transported with no food or maternal care, it has been estimated that for every chimp that arrives in Spain, 10 have died. As 180 individuals are thought to be in use at any one time by the beach photographers, this is calculated to represent the deaths, from capture and transport, of 1,620 others. To render them docile, the chimps, who are often worked for 16 hours a day, are shot full of sedatives and some have their teeth broken off so they can't bite the customers. They are routinely killed or sold off after two or three years when they become unmanageable. Though a party to CITES, Spain has yet to seriously crack down on the trade, and the country also remains a major centre for trafficking in gorillas. "In late 1987," IPPL reports, "two gorillas were exported from Spain to Japan. A CITES export permit was issued by Spanish wildlife authorities claiming that the gorillas were 'captive-born.' An investigation conducted by IPPL (Spain) revealed that the gorillas were probably 'captive-born in the jungle'! The animals were supposedly bred at the Ringland Circus in Aldea, Spain. Spanish conservationists visiting the circus found the place 'fenced like a fortress' with 'at least six guard dogs roaming around to discourage unwanted intruders'. They also learned that, in a recent police raid on the facility, inspectors found five young chimpanzees, one large adult chimpanzee, one bonobo (Pigmy chimpanzee), five leopards and a Pigmy hippo. The chimpanzees were found by accident: as the inspectors were leaving, a large circus trailer drew up. The inspectors ordered it opened up, and found the chimpanzees inside. From the documents, it appeared that the animals had arrived that very morning by a boat entering the port of Valencia from an unknown location (presumably somewhere in Africa, most probably Equatorial Guinea, a former Spanish colony, from which four gorillas were exported in late 1987). Equatorial Guinea is also the suspected supplier of 'beach chimpanzees' to Spain." Black-market trafficking to supply the needs of the circus and menagerie has also included other endangered species. In 1988, a forlorn and ailing Asian elephant was discovered in a crate in Rotterdam. Her skin had turned to parchment during her month-long journey from Vietnam and she was reputed to be "in a pitiful state". Similarly, even the critically-endangered Mediterranean monk seal has been made to pose in the circus arena. In 1985, it is reported, the last seals of Tunisia's Galite archipelago became extinct when two of the animals were captured for an Italian travelling circus, the remaining individual succumbing to the harpoon of a snorkelling Italian tourist.

On top of all this, CITES regards conservation as something entirely different from animal welfare. A government which provides export documents to an animal dealer has no obligation or right to enquire into the standard of facilities which that animal will be subjected to upon arrival, and this may be one reason why there is a lively re-export trade in animals to establishments in the Third World where conditions can be so primitive that a life of suffering or a premature death is virtually inevitable. "It is only for Appendix I species that it is clearly mentioned that the importer must be suitably equipped to house and care for it," says Jacques Berney, adding that this is the sole responsibility of the importing country. "For Appendix II species, there are no provisions, since animal welfare and husbandry concerns are expected to be covered by national legislation." All too often, however, such legislation may be either inadequate or non-existent. It was thus that in 1988, the Swiss authorities permitted the export of two dolphins to Egypt, where they ended up languishing in a hotel swimming pool for a year, and another dolphin belonging to the same dealer became the sole occupant of a minuscule open-air pool in a safari park in Austria, even though solitary confinement of this kind is well-known to be cruel to such gregarious animals. According to Berney, there are no provisions within the agreement which might prevent a person who is incapable of ensuring an animal's welfare from owning a dolphin or any other similarly-classified species.

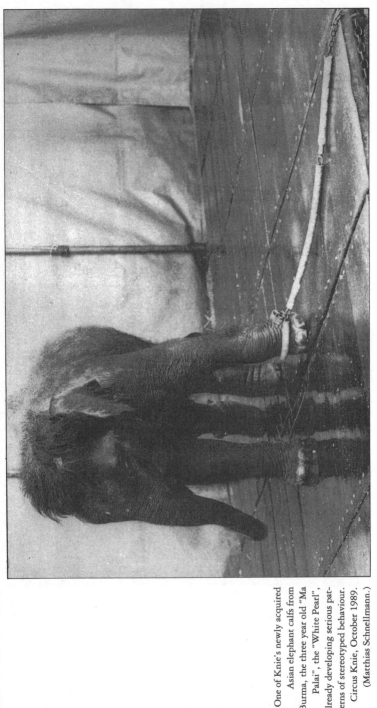

One of Knie's newly acquired
Asian elephant calfs from
Burma, the three year old "Ma
Palai", the "White Pearl",
already developing serious pat-
terns of stereotyped behaviour.
Circus Knie, October 1989.
(Matthias Schnellmann.)

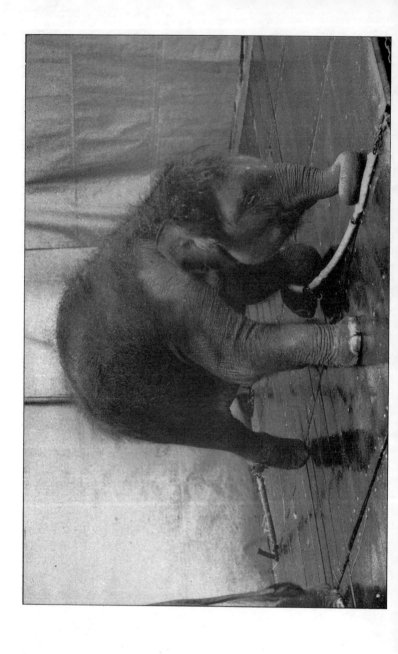

The Potemkin facade of the circus menagerie, depicting animals roaming free in a pristine wilderness. Circus Krone. (Holger Vogt.)

Education and Conservation

As we have already seen, the modern circus was almost strangled at birth by those who condemned it as the work of the devil. It was only by portraying the menagerie as educational and marrying it off to the circus that the "Zoological Institute" and similarly dubious enterprises were able to pacify the pious wrath of the American puritans. Although this amounted to the most blatant and systematic of all circus deceptions, it was also the most triumphant and enduring. Indeed, it is ironic that precisely the same justification is being used today, this time to deflect the criticism of those who are opposed to the display of exotic species under the big top.

Because of a burgeoning public concern for nature conservation in recent years, the more astute and affluent circuses — like their counterparts in the oceanarium trade — recognise that they must alter their image if they are to stay in business. The lesson may be as illusory as the brightly coloured facades to the menagerie which depict animals roaming free in a pristine natural habitat, but the circus would still have us believe that there is no anomaly in confining animals which are on the verge of extinction to cramped beast wagons or training them to perform feeble-minded tricks in the arena. With the perfidious clout of today's public relations experts and image consultants, such degrading spectacles are now portrayed not only as "education", but even "conservation", the circus menagerie becoming a modern Noah's Ark, striving to rescue animals from impending doom. The more sober facts — that the Noah's Ark may be a rat and disease-infested prison whose inmates can literally be driven insane by their captivity, that some rare animals are bred to such abundant excess that they must either be put down or sold off as "models" for scientific research, are studiously exorcised from the illusion. Says David Hancocks, director of the Arizona-Sonora Desert Museum: "The people who operated the travelling menageries, wild beast shows and circuses soon learned that aggressive promotion and media hype can be an effective substitute for a poor show. Building on the image of 'nature red in tooth and claw,' tigers were billed as man-eating monsters, elephants as gargantuan deformities, gorillas as devilish freaks. The entire picture of wildlife was distorted beyond recognition." Those myths, says Hancocks, still prevail. "Each and every day wild animals are being subjected to deprived environments. The fact that this occurs merely so that people can see tigers riding on horses under pink spotlights, or laugh at chimpanzees dressed as senile tramps, or watch an elephant in a yellow tutu stand on its hind legs, or see a bear on a motorcycle — the fact that these imbecilic and useless actions are considered to be a justification for such exploitation adds an especially tasteless irony." It may also reflect, by way of the circus's much-coveted traditions, the extent to which rabid anthropocentrism afflicts the human race, the spoilt child amongst species, and explain how this utilitarian view of creation is bequeathed to future generations. Circus, menagerie, zoo and dolphinarium managers routinely insist that the public has the *right* to see captive exotic species, almost as though it were a God-given prerogative. Recently, however, the cause of pure entertainment in the animal show has given way under pressure to the manifestly dubious claim of education of the young.

As the charity Animal Aid points out: "It is often stated in defence of circuses that they are of educational benefit to children, who might otherwise never see these animals. But what exactly do we teach our children about animals through a visit to the circus? All a child can see is the size, shape and colour of the animals. Their behaviour patterns, social interaction, intelligence, hunting instinct, maternal instinct, sibling behaviour, food gathering patterns and all the facets of animal behaviour that makes a species so unique and interesting, are not apparent in circus animals." Nor, one might add, are they apparent in the dream-machine promotional techniques of the circus, the typically garish Italian-style circus posters, for example, depicting ferocious gorillas in the mould of King Kong and snarling polar bears which seem to be on the verge of pawing a sultry and scantily dressed model. Yet the circus, with the survival of the performing animal at stake, clings ever more tenaciously to the subterfuge of education.

British circus czar Gerry Cottle, forever asserting that his animals are only "performing natural extensions of their normal existence in the wild," seemed to have received divine benediction for that point of view when Canon John Morris, apparently at Cottle's behest, bestowed his blessing upon the animals at a Christmas 1988 service held under the big top at Battersea. "I discovered to my horror that they needed it," writes journalist Tessa Dahl who attended the spectacle. Yet surely no irony was intended when the prayer for the animals was read out, echoing through the arena:

> *Creatures of the home and woodland,*
> *Jungle and sea,*
> *We would ask for God's protection*
> *Wher'er you be.*
> *When men in their greed oppress you*
> *We will ask the Lord to bless you*
> *And a loving hand caress you,*
> *Making you free.*

"As the little band played its rousing music, animals were carted on and off in cages or boxes," Tessa Dahl reported. "Lions were forced through a steel tunnel, assistants banging sticks against the bars to hurry them along. They looked mangy, with pathetic soulful eyes. Otto Vohringer cracked his whip and they jumped through hoops. We watched three Himalayan black bears being led out of tiny cages by a girl in Cossack dress. The bears had thick leather muzzles and chains around their necks. The baby bear was clawing at his muzzle, desperately trying to pull it off. The 'natural extension' of their existence was then demonstrated as the bears drove out of the ring in a car." Next on the programme was Jan and her Nile Crocodiles. They were "dragged out of a coffin-like casket for Jan to dance around while the ringmaster told of the dangers. The largest crocodile endured Jan's head in his mouth once his sleepy jaws had been prised open and Jan's body pressed seductively against his. The act complete, he was carted out in his box, with his tail hanging out of the back." Though the adults in her party were "devastated", writes Dahl, the children were "enthralled", and it was this that disturbed her most of all. Surely it is "wrong to bring children up with the notion that animals are there to be used and dominated by humans," she concluded. "They are creatures with their own dignity, they should not be parodied and forced into this ignoble pursuit. How can we start expecting our youth to have a different attitude towards the natural world when this is their holiday entertainment?" The elephants, she continued, "paraded in and climbed resignedly onto each other's backs, limbs straining, eyes watering. 'I'm sure they're crying,' said my neighbour. I think he was right. They suffered indignity and so did we watching them."

Understandably, sometimes the rose-tinted veil wears perilously thin, even for children. In April 1988, the *Daily Mail* published a letter from a 16-year-old girl who had just returned from a school holiday in Russia and a visit to the Moscow State Circus: "Several people walked out crying," she wrote, "after seeing them whip the horses around the face to make them walk on their hind legs and hitting them to make them fall over. The bears had be dragged in, as they obviously didn't want to perform and they looked so sad walking on their hind legs." While such incidents undoubtedly serve to dispel the illusion of the circus as an educational institution, ironically, even a seriously conducted organised tour through the circus menagerie might achieve the same effect.

In a beast wagon at Switzerland's Circus Olympia, for example, in a filth-spattered cage measuring just three metres by two, there are two adult chimpanzees, their bodies tense, rocking deliriously to and fro, their faces often buried in the straw. At other times, they seem to stare into nothingness with grotesque, contorted faces, or frantically smear their own excrement across the walls of the wagon. There is no label attached to the bars which confirms their identity or origin, least of all the fact that the chimpanzee is actually the closest living relative of *homo sapiens*, sharing 99.8 per cent of human genes, even its blood compatible with ours. So-called "Pre-Convention" Appendix I animals, there is nothing to protect them except an inadequate and desultorily applied animal welfare law. Their brothers and sisters in the wild are decreasing rapidly, the result of human encroachment, poaching by animal dealers and trophy hunters, a long history of exploitation in biomedical research, and an enduring demand by zoo and circus menageries which gives life to a quietly thriving black market. During capture, almost invariably the infant or juvenile chimpanzee will first of all see its mother and any other defending adult shot down before its eyes, the killing/capture ratio reported to be between 5:1 and 9:1. Yet few casual visitors to this menagerie would even begin to suspect that the chimpanzee is actually a native of the dense forests and open woodlands of west and central equatorial Africa. Much of their life — sometimes spanning 50 years — is spent in the trees, where they sleep and obtain the fruits that constitute the bulk of their diet. A sleeping nest is built each night and a resting platform may be built during the day. The great exuberance and versatility which makes the chimpanzee so popular with animal trainers and the public is, if anything, even more apparent in the wild, with individuals fashioning improvised tools and displaying a profound ingenuity in solving the problems that confront them. Although classified as a single species, *Pan troglodytes*, there is as much variation among chimpanzees as among races of humans. As the infant chimp grows, it begins to explore the world, riding on its mother's back as she travels. The young chimpanzee will remain under adult — primarily maternal — supervision for years, during which time it acquires the knowledge that will allow it to become fully integrated into a complex social system. Deprived of all this in captivity, aberrant behaviour becomes virtually inevitable, including an inability to foster offspring or care for them.

The psychotic chimps of Circus Olympia, Switzerland. (Matthias Schnellmann.)

Formerly the star of the dear departed Chimp's Tea Party, a favourite for children on a day's outing to the zoo, chimpanzees at the circus are still dressed in human clothing. Infants, clad appealingly in toddler's blue or pink, are carried around the audience before the show commences to sit in laps, cling to necks, posing for a cute and memorable photograph for an additional fee. This is not nursery school however, but work, and the chimpanzee child is given sound raps over the knuckles or pinched hard if he misbehaves. Juvenile individuals later undergo rigorous training to perfect "their own" circus act — riding small motorbikes or monocycles, acting as clowns, rickshaw drivers and performing diverse tumbling and gymnastic feats. Cruelty is all too often just a fact of life. Because they are only manageable as performing circus animals when young, the chimps soon outlive their usefulness. Though often castrated, males become vicious and unpredictable as they grow older and females, because of the swelling of their genital organs when on heat, are regarded as ugly. For this reason adult individuals are confined for the remainder of their lives to the menagerie cage as display animals, or are sold off to a zoo or vivisection laboratory.

Inhabiting yet another bare cage in a circus beast wagon, this time in the Italian *Circo Italiano* alias *Medrano*, there are a male and female lowland gorilla, a species that was once the big game hunter's dream. Once again, the inherent discrepancy between the wild gorilla and its counterpart in the circus cage is all too apparent. Rising at sunrise, wild gorillas, often in permanent and gregarious social groups of between five and twenty individuals, spend their days leisurely feeding, resting and sleeping. Rarely remaining more than one day in a single place, they'll travel up to five kilometres between dawn and dusk, uttering soft grunts as they move along to help them keep in touch with one another in the dense undergrowth. Towards nightfall, each gorilla builds itself a nest, either on the ground or in a tree, infants snuggling up to their mothers to sleep. The first intrepid jungle explorers portrayed the gorilla as a ferocious and unpredictable beast who attacked humans without the slightest provocation. Although the gorilla is the largest of the anthropoid apes, adult males with their striking grey or silver backs attaining a height of about 2 meters, the creature is actually shy and peaceful, a vegetarian who subsists on a variety of bark, leaves, roots and fruits. Yet the myth of the fearsome gorilla still persists to this very day in the "educational" world of the circus. Medrano, for example, portrays its male gorilla as "the largest in the world", its posters depicting a ferocious King Kong, a swooning abducted woman clasped in one of its giant hands. According to Pier Lorenzo Florio of TRAFFIC, "Medrano pretends that its current female gorilla was born in the circus and that its mother died during delivery, but this is probably just fantasy. It is far more likely that the gorillas came in as contraband in 1980, just as Italy joined CITES."

Even gorillas can still be found in circus-menageries. (William Johnson.)

In the same wagon, behind a flimsy partition, there is a single orang-utan, or "person of the forest of Malay", a creature which first appeared in an English menagerie in 1784, advertised as an "Oriental Satyr". Condemned to life imprisonment in a typically bare circus cage, its living conditions in captivity have not appreciably changed since then, despite the fact that study of the species in its natural environment has revealed much more about its needs and its way of life. A long-armed arboreal ape, covered with flowing red hair, the orang-utan lives in the forests of north Sumatra and Borneo. Unlike other species of monkey or ape, they are solitary animals, with up to four individuals inhabiting each square kilometre of forest canopy. They spend their days feeding, roaming from tree to tree, rarely, if ever, touching the ground. At night, like chimps and gorillas, they construct sleeping nests by breaking branches and weaving them together.

"The elegant trainer Billy Wilson Smart and his charming wife Ingrid present their three splendid Indian elephants, Bully, Quato and Ongeli who can both crawl and form astonishing pyramids." So declared the press kit of the 14th *Festival International du Cirque* in Monte Carlo in January 1989. This annual five-day gathering is regarded as the most prestigious event in the circus world, with clowns, acrobats, jugglers, trapeze artists and animal tamers competing for much-coveted golden awards, presented at a glittering ceremony presided over by avid circus fans Prince Rainier and his daughter, Princess Stephanie. Perhaps the event can best be summed up by a comment, expressed with an American twang, that I overheard at the Festival during the intermission: "You couldn't wish for anything more at Monte Carlo. Oh, it really is the best time of the year! You have glamour, royalty, sex, even exotic animals!"

> *"That great bulk, which looks so phlegmatic, is in fact a mass of nerves and emotion. The animal gives obvious proof that he experiences affection, love, fear, jealousy, resentment, tenderness, stubbornness and rage. The sudden noise of a firecracker has thrown many an elephant into temporary insanity. Using that incredibly adaptable trunk, with equal ease the beast can pick up a pin or kill a man. An elephant sleeps very little, usually just an hour or two at a time, and sometimes, like a naughty child, uses the hours when mankind is sleeping to perpetrate deliberate mischief."*
> — Marian Murray

More than any other single animal, it is undoubtedly the great grey elephant with its small curious eyes, its fan-like ears and its giant pad-like feet, which is most traditionally associated with the circus world. Today as traditionally, when not performing in the ring circus elephants are kept almost permanently fettered, chained to the ground by one foreleg and one hind leg so that social interaction between the animals invariably becomes crippled. Walking through the elephant tent of the menagerie, under the passive and attentive gaze of these sagacious creatures, it is unnerving to think that as infants, many of the wild-caught African elephants have seen their mothers, sisters, fathers and brothers shot dead in front of them. Despite their bulk, elephants are agile and even nimble on their feet, able to move virtually without a sound, walking on the tips of their toes. The trunk, besides being used to give themselves frequent dust and water baths, is also a keen olfactory organ, capable of detecting unerringly even supposedly odourless poisons. Gregarious animals with complex social rules and recognisable customs, herds of between 25 to 30 elephants will roam through the jungle or bush feeding from a wide selection of grasses, fruit and nuts. Other females in the herd, called *aunties* by the Burmese, assist a mother before and during the birth of the young. The animals also possess pronounced personalities and such complex emotions that once in captivity, deprived of the intricate social customs of the herd, they become prone to neurosis and can be driven insane. Writes Ivan T. Sanderson, author of *The Dynasty of Abu*: "They have been known to cry from sheer frustration; to commit 'mercy killing' on an incurably ill member of their herd; to help — by lifting and supporting — a wounded or ill member of the herd; to rescue captured members of the herd; and to rescue humans from other elephants or from natural or man-made disasters."

Elephant training session with Billy and Ingrid Wilson Smart at the Monte Carlo Circus Festival. (William Johnson.)

Still billed as an electrifying attraction in the majority of circuses is the wild cat, from the most exotic species such as the Bengal and Siberian tiger and the Himalayan snow leopard, to the puma, jaguar and of course that dethroned king of the jungle, the lion. Once again, the bare menagerie cage characterises their existence when not performing or training in the arena. Though they are often seen crammed together in the beast wagon, apart from the lion most cats are essentially solitary animals in the wild. While in the circus cage they must make do with no more than one or two square metres, in their natural habitat the individual tiger, depending on availability of prey, inhabits a range of anywhere between 60 and 500 square kilometres. Of the eight races of tiger — living in diverse habitats from temperate oak forests to dry thorn scrub, from humid rain forests and mangrove swamps to the snowy Manchurian spruce forests — six are threatened with extinction. Only about 12 Javan tigers remain, no more than 110 Siberian tigers still survive in the Soviet Far East, and the Chinese tiger is already thought to be extinct. Even in India, commonly regarded as the traditional home of the tiger, only some 4000 remain alive.

Similarly, the powerful spotted cat known as the leopard or panther inhabits semi-deserts, rain forests and mountains up to the snow line, the individual animal often wandering far and wide in search of prey. Unlike other big cats, leopards are also proficient climbers, and in the wild they can often be seen while at rest draped rather precariously high along the branch of a tree.

The ritual justification of the circus for keeping lions in the menagerie cage is that even in the wild the animals spend some 20 hours a day at rest, either sleeping, dozing, or sitting. While it is true that lions typically lead a leisurely life when prey is plentiful, they must still hunt to survive and this, on average, entails walking eight kilometres a day for up to three hours, the pride's territory extending between 40 and 400 square kilometres. Their favourite habitat, savanna sparsely covered with thorn scrub and acacia trees, may also be regarded as being somewhat more stimulating than the naked menagerie cage with its aluminium floor covered with sawdust. Unlike the solitary habits of the other great wild cats, lions are gregarious, forming prides of up to 35 individuals that have a complex social organisation, with lionesses raising the young and hunting cooperatively. Venerated in the Middle East in ancient times as an animal god because of its loud roar, strength, and majestic beauty, the lion is now extinct over a large part of its former range, which stretched through Iran to India and over much of Africa. Only about 175 Asian lions still survive in the wild, they are already extinct in North Africa, and are only found in larger numbers south of the Sahara.

Victims of poaching and a habitat constantly shrinking through human overpopulation and encroachment, other great and exotic beasts are also to be found in the circus ring and menagerie, including the rhinoceros, the polar bear, the Himalayan brown bear and even the world's most famous endangered species, the giant panda. Though animal acts are alien to Chinese circus culture, pandas have been seen in some shows. On one occasion, for example, the Shanghai circus featured a trumpet-blowing panda reclining in a gilded cart being towed around the arena by an Alsatian dog. Then in November 1988, a circus tour of Australia by the giant panda Wei Wei, organised by the New Zealand impresario Christopher Cambridge, was abruptly cancelled when the government imposed an import ban. Wei Wei's repertoire includes motorbike riding, blowing a trumpet and eating with a knife and fork.

The black rhino population has declined from 65,000 in 1970 to 13,500 today, while the Sumatran, Javan and great Indian rhinos together probably number fewer than 2000. Similarly, there are thought to be less than 3000 Southern white rhinos still to be found in their natural habitat in Africa and according to IUCN, the Northern white rhino — with only 15 still surviving in a national park in Zaire — is the most endangered animal in the world. Grazing animals, rhinos inhabit open plains, sparse thorn scrub, savannas, thickets and dry forests, as well as mountain forests and moorlands at high altitudes. In the circus, however, they must content themselves with a beast wagon in which they are scarcely able turn around in, and if they're lucky, a small improvised enclosure set up on the grounds of each venue. Paraded under the spotlights under the big top, in circuses like Knie rhinos have even been featured galloping around the arena with tigers on their backs, the animals portrayed as being "no longer enemies, but partners". Rather more mundanely, "the magnificent African rhinoceros" of the Italian *Stefano Nones Orfei* "can even hold out his foot as if to shake hands." Even the amphibious hippopotamus, which in the wild is often found in groups of six to 15 animals, spending the day wallowing lazily in muddy water, can be found in the circus menagerie, often — as in the case of the Italian *Datrix Togni* circus — without so much as a tub of water to bathe in.

Perhaps because the crocodile is not quite as endearing as the typical "Noah's Ark" animal, their welfare in the circus is afforded even less consideration. For most of their lives they are quite literally stored in minuscule covered tanks or boxes, often with their mouths taped up. Yet to the sensation-hungry circus manager, they provide the audience with the thrill of the untamed ferocious jungle beast, the most "spectacular" trick being for the trainer to place his head between the animal's toothy jaws. In a promotional blurb for the Monte Carlo Circus Festival, for example, Karah Khawak of Poland was portrayed as "the only person apart from his brother to learn the fantastic secret of how to hypnotise these enormous saurians only a few centimetres away from the spectators." The audience's safety, however — including that of Prince Rainier and his entourage

Panda bear appearing in the "Shanghai Acrobatic Troupe." (Courtesy Bayerischer Rundfunk.)

Performing Rhino with Stefano Orfei-Nones (Circo Moira Orfei), Monte Carlo International Circus Festival, 1989. (William Johnson.)

who suddenly found themselves face to face with daunting reptilian fangs — was ensured by the discreet use of wire-like bands to clamp the animals' mouths tightly shut.

Also on the programme at Monte Carlo were the "farmyard animals" of Evgeni Schmarlowski of the USSR, a supposedly comical repertoire that featured a donkey, fox, raven and monkey, and numerous mink, chickens and ducks. "His brand-new finale," announced the press office, "will not fail to intrigue all the ladies in the audience who dream of owning a mink coat." After Schmarlowski's trained monkey dutifully terrified a certain dour lady in the audience — obviously the Russian's assistant —by jumping into her lap, she was invited into the ring, and, behind a dressing-screen, was invited to don a mink coat as recompense. Just as she was admiring her new attire, Schmarlowski fired a shot from a pistol, at which point the coat disintegrated into scores of live mink running frantically across the arena. Such treatment might explain why so many replacement animals were to be found under canvas in Schmarlowski's corner of the menagerie tent, housed in minuscule green metal boxes to enable him to travel the world with his show. The fox was confined to a wire mesh cage with a bare wire floor, less than half a metre square.

Although somewhat slow and clumsy at first sight, all except the very heaviest of bears climb trees and are agile in moving over rocks and ice, leaving a human-like footprint on soft ground. Most are also innate wanderers, subsisting on a varied diet which includes fish, insects, fruits and honey. They tend to live alone except during courtship, and hibernate during winter. If cornered or attacked, they can become one of the most dangerous of all animals, as many a circus trainer has discovered to great cost. In India, it is not uncommon to come across dancing bears in the streets. The World Society for the Protection of Animals reports that the immature animals are caught in the Himalayas; their teeth and claws are extracted, a hole is drilled through the upper palate and a rope inserted by which the bear is led and restrained. Training the bear to jig or dance is accomplished by the use of hot coals, a similar technique employed by other travelling showmen, including the Gypsies of western Europe. Writes Rodney Manser, a former public relations man for the Gerry Cottle Circus: "The major part of the training consisted of getting the bears to rear up at the sound of a tambourine and to stay up while it continued to be played. This was achieved by pulling the bear up onto its hind legs and then letting its forepaws down onto scalding metal trays. At the instant the forepaws touched the metal the tambourine would sound. The bear's automatic reflex obviously being to rear away from the source of pain, it would rear up on its hind legs. This process was repeated until the bear firmly associated the sound of the tambourine with searing pain to its forepaws should they be placed down — so whenever it heard the tambourine it would rear up and stay up until the music stopped."

Polar bears, once numerous around the north pole, migrate over vast distances, sometimes even swimming many miles. No more than 12,000 still survive, their numbers having declined drastically since the 1920s due to human exploitation. When hunting, they are known to rub snow on their black noses so as to make their dazzling white camouflage complete. Normally two or three cubs are born in a litter, hairless, blind and scarcely bigger than guinea pigs. The mother bear encourages her young to use ice slopes as toboggan runs to help them gain strength. The cubs slide down on their bellies, legs spreadeagled, with mother catching them at the bottom in her paws. Once in captivity, most polar bears are simply driven insane. Zoo Check reports that twelve out of 20 polar bears in Britain show signs of mental illness. At Bristol, embarrassed zoo officials have even been obliged to hide the polar bear Misha — who spent a decade in a Chipperfield circus beast wagon — because the animal had become too deranged even for the public gaze. Ursula Boettcher of East Germany remains the leading exponent of polar bear dressage in Europe, the Circus Fans Association describing her act as "awe-inspiringly impressive", with a "sensational new trick" that features one of the animals "standing over Miss Boettcher who is lying on the ground — head to head". Hardly educational perhaps, and at first glance, not even particularly sensational, yet with the unpredictable bear, there is scarcely any warning of an impending attack. But it is the brown bear of Europe and Asia that is the most common occupant of menageries on this side of the Atlantic, and in the arena they can often still be seen riding motorbikes, roller-skating, playing football and even ice-hockey.

In what was portrayed as "The Peace of the Jungle", the Clubb Chipperfield organisation, vying for a golden award, presented a combined exotic animal routine at the International Circus Festival of Monte Carlo in January 1989. According to Prince Rainier's press office, the act, masterminded "with infinite patience" by impresario Jim Clubb and trainers Luis and Marcia Palacios, featured tigers, lionesses, leopards, bears, as well as a solitary wolf and striped hyena. In the ring, they would form "splendid pyramids and a marvellous tableau in which the numerous wild beasts stand up majestically on their stools." In actual fact, the two Himalayan brown bears were never once taken out of their beast wagon during the prestigious five-day gathering at the jet-set capital of Europe. The reason, according to one of Clubb's animal handlers, was because the bears "are too unpredictable. We're after the golden award and they can mess up the whole show." Similarly, the only exercise that the distraught and cowering wolf and hyena experienced during their five-day sojourn on the gold and concrete coast was to be prodded into the arena to pose under the multicoloured spotlights, clearly intimidated by the presence of their "jungle friends". Small wonder then, that the wolf and hyena — both roaming pack animals in the wild — and the two bears, all displayed

Confined to a wire mesh cage with a bare wire floor, less than 0.5m square, this fox is the property of the Russian performer Ewgeni Schmarlowski, appearing at Monte Carlo's International Circus Festival, January 1989. (Matthias Schnellmann.)

typical stereotypic behaviour in their wagon, pacing up and down, and biting and sucking the bars of the cage. Though the distinction between the working and non-working menagerie animal is constantly emphasised by those who wish to justify their continuing use in the circus, the bare, cramped cage remains the habitat even for the performing animal for at least 20 hours of every day. In the case of Clubb Chipperfield's animals at Monte Carlo, this meant a cage size of four square metres per species for the wolf, the two bears and a pair of tigers, five square metres for three leopards, and six square metres for two lionesses and another pair of tigers.

It is perhaps all the more ironic then that Jim Clubb is chairman of the Association of Circus Proprietors of Great Britain (ACP) and its animals sub-committee, which introduced a revised code of conduct early in 1988, ostensibly aimed at improving the welfare and living conditions of captive circus animals. Says ACP secretary Malcolm Clay: "This association is recognised by central and local government as being responsible for the conduct of the circus business in this country. It imposes on its members very strict standards of animal welfare, including veterinary inspections, exercise areas etc. Because of this, certain of the large circuses refuse to join and are content to trade at the very minimal levels required by law." Despite such self-regulatory and self-policing measures, typically conducted with great fanfare, it is all the more curious that in an interview with an American television crew in Monte Carlo, Clubb heaped praise upon one of the most notorious of British circuses where his mixed exotic animal act had previously appeared to great acclaim. At the Blackpool Tower Circus, owned by First Leisure Corporation, animals are consigned for the five months of every season to a dimly-lit cellar, deprived of fresh air, sunlight and physical exercise. A 1987 report by two independent veterinarians, Bill Jordan, formerly a consultant to several international zoos, and Dr M. Woodford, an elephant specialist, concluded that no animal should be kept in underground accommodation. They stated: "In spite of the recent expenditure of £15,000 on 'improvements' to the animal accommodation we do not consider that the premises are suitable for the humane maintenance of captive, large, wild animals. They are, in fact, barely adequate for domestic animals which can be exercised outside." They found two twelve-year-old elephants housed in an area measuring twelve metres by four, the animals taken out for exercise only twice a week. Because "they are never allowed into the exercising area," the vets concluded, "partly because they refuse to go past the lions to get into this area, and partly because it is barely big enough for them to enter and turn around, the accommodation provided for elephants is inadequate." The show's eight lions were accommodated in a row of cubicles, and although provided with an "exercise cage", Jordan and Woodford noted that it was "hemmed in by tall buildings and it is doubtful if the sun ever penetrates that far." They concluded that "the mauling of the trainer which took place on the 18th July, after our visit, supports the contention that there are too many lions performing in too small an area."

Jordan and Woodford reserved some of their harshest criticism for the deplorable living conditions of the Pygmy hippopotamus: "This animal is kept alone in a small L-shaped enclosure measuring six metres by four in which there is a water tank just large enough for it to clamber into. To get into the tank it has to climb up four or five steps and then drop into the water. This is a tropical species which normally lives in small groups and so it must suffer from being kept underground, alone, in artificial light for five months. The staff admitted that this animal is kept as a gimmick as it does not perform in the ring... We question the morality in exhibiting an IUCN Red Book vulnerable species for entertainment purposes..."

Lancashire County Council, following a subsequent inspection, unanimously condemned the animals' living quarters, though because Blackpool Tower is privately owned, their hands were tied. Unexpectedly, it was then that the chairman of First Leisure Corporation, Lord Delfont — admitting that he was bowing to public pressure — announced that there would be no more animals in the Tower Circus when the current contract with impresario Peter Jay expires in 1990. Lady Delfont also played a leading role in opposition to the Tower's circus animals. "She said 'close the damn zoo or I will divorce you' — what choice was I left with?" asked the besieged lord. A hastily formed association, the Blackpool Tower Support Group, its ranks and influence swelled by members of the ACP and the Circus Fans Association, then promptly set about undermining the decision, launching a petition drive in a bid to have it overturned. Publicity material states that "as a member of the Association of Circus Proprietors, the Tower circus is subject to regular inspections by internationally famous TV zoo vets David Taylor and Andrew Greenwood. The animals are cared for and housed subject to their rigorous guidelines." Indeed, the Blackpool Tower Support Group quoted Taylor — whose veterinary escapades formed the basis for the popular BBC television series *One by One* — in support of their petition and publicity drive: "In my experience, animals in the circus are very healthy, certainly as healthy as animals in zoos and safari parks. Circus animals have no occupational diseases. They have more personal care and attention from their keepers and trainers... The animals in the circuses operated by members of the Association of Circus Proprietors are certainly kept healthy, using the most up-to-date veterinary equipment... based on my knowledge of animal behaviour in the wild and captivity and on medical evidence, I would say they are are pretty content with their lot." Incredibly, the Circus Fans' petition went on to claim that the Blackpool Tower elephants "have their own living area and pen where they can roam freely," and that the "only basis for proper animal training is patience and respect and a rapport between animals and their trainer. They enjoy working with people — it is of therapeutic value as it provides them with something interesting to do and prevents them getting bored." David Taylor, however, evidently seething that his name had been dragged into the controversy, declared: "I have never inspected the Blackpool Tower Circus premises." He went on to complain in the press that "I haven't been to the Blackpool Tower Circus for 18 years. They have taken my remarks, which referred to circuses in general, and quoted them completely out of context. They are distorting and falsifying the facts... There are some animals which should never be kept in circuses." What is beyond dispute, however, is that Andrew Greenwood — who shares the famous veterinary consultancy with Taylor in West Yorkshire — is the official vet for Blackpool Tower Circus. Also beyond dispute is the fact that Greenwood has expressed his satisfaction with animal-keeping standards at the Circus, stating in one instance that the wild cat cages are "large and airy, even though they have no access to direct sunlight."

In view of David Taylor's more general comments in applauding the standards of animal welfare in the circus, it is perhaps all the more interesting to note that in his book *Zoo Vet*, he remarks: "Although many circus animals are trained without cruelty, there are still a few terrible black spots. You will find them in the smaller, tatty circuses and menageries if you can penetrate the closed, suspicious, obstructive world behind the scenes. It is a world skilled in repelling outsiders and deceiving humane society inspectors and, most important, able to move on if trouble is brewing. At first hand I have seen bears encouraged to move from travelling box to circus ring by flaming newspapers being thrust underneath them, and I have heard the regular, sickening thuds as a chained African elephant was beaten systematically with bamboo rods by two keepers to break it by literally torturing it until it collapsed. The most repellent feature of the process was the calm clinical way in which the keepers administered the beating. It was a job, just like grooming, which called for a repetitive movement for long periods of time: no anger, no emotion, just a boring job of beating. Of course, when the police arrived the men were indeed grooming the elephant. Bamboo rods applied with all a man's might across the rib-cage of an elephant leave no marks." Taylor continues: "At another circus I watched an act purporting to be a chimpanzees' tea party where the animals were not just as good as gold, they were almost automatons. The audience marvelled at the obedience of the little apes and smiled as the trainer fondled their hairy heads. It was all in the fondling. The man showed me his thumb-nail, which had been allowed to grow long and then filed to a vicious point. It was strong and horny, and he used it with cruel skill to gouge and twist the sensitive flaps of the chimpanzees' ears. It was really a display of brutal sleight-of-hand carried on in full view of the public. I was to find that this method of controlling chimps by their delicate ears was commonplace in the world of chimpanzee training; even mature specimens were subdued by the agony of a quickly applied hold."

Though many creatures to be found in circus beast wagons are currently listed as under threat or in danger of extinction, they are known to the zoo and circus fraternity as the "Noah's Ark" species not because the menagerie truly believes its own spiel about playing a vital role in conservation, but because it is these varieties of animals which are believed to be the crowd-pullers, those depicted in the colourful and comfortingly naive pictures in children's story books or those incarnated into Disney-like characters, anthropomorphised, endowed with human personalities, human desires and human vices. That may seem a marginal improvement on anthropocentrism, but the catch is that in the circus business, one has never cancelled out the other. Indeed, whether by accident or design, the anthropomorphised Noah's Ark animal is merely the projected illusion for public consumption; behind that warm image there is the hard reality of a circus manager trying to turn a profit, and an animal tamer who is under the stress of an ever-looming deadline to have his new and ever more spectacular act ready for public presentation. Such creatures may be portrayed by the circus dream machine as coming straight off Noah's Ark, but the fact is that for the sake of expedience, an animal, however endangered, is not only systematically deprived of its freedom and its innate dignity, but also the wild environment that gave it birth and shaped its very character and spirit.

Jim Clubb is part-owner and managing director of Clubb Chipperfield, an ambitious enterprise that specialises in training exotic animals not only for the circus arena, but also for television and film advertising, the famous Esso tiger being a prime example. A former wild animal trainer himself, Clubb gained a prestigious company name when he married Sally Chipperfield and for several years he toured with the Sally Chipperfield Circus. But with image-consciousness becoming ever more imperative in recent years, Clubb distances himself from the often scandal-afflicted Chipperfield dynasty, reputed to be one of the largest exotic animal-dealing concerns in the world. "My wife is a Chipperfield but we are completely different from the other Chipperfield Circus. I originally worked for Chipperfield's but I have run my own business for the last 10 years. But we are completely different — it's very important you say that. There are three Chipperfields you see. There's my company, there's Chipperfield Enterprises which is the circus belonging to my wife's father, and then there is his brother Jimmy Chipperfield who has all the big safari parks. But I would say that we are probably one of the leading animal suppliers in the world now of trained circus acts." Echoing the almost identical sentiments of his contemporaries in the circus world, Clubb insists on the ecological credibility of his animal shows: "Let's put it this way, we are not taking animals from the wild. That is quite ridiculous. When everyone was saying that the tiger is in danger of extinction, we were breeding tigers at a rate of 50 a year. But the danger of putting captive-bred animals into the wild is that they can't hunt properly and they become potential man-eaters. The problem is that the animal is dying out in the wild but it's not dying out in captivity. Nevertheless we believe that we educate people into how beautiful and intelligent these animals are — that's our conservation message." It is a message that Clubb also promotes vigourously in the circus press. Apart from publicising "James Clubb's pigs with baboon jockeys", recent advertisements have also touted the Clubb Chipperfield organisation as "Breeders of Endangered Species of carnivores — tigers, leopards, jaguars, rare black jaguars, and, even rarer, striped hyenas." They are "the only striped hyenas in any circus in the world!" the advertisement continues breathlessly, adding that the enterprise owns and trains 250 animals of 50 different species. Similarly, Clubb's star attraction, Doutschka, is billed as "the only snow leopard in any circus in the world!"

Chris Krenger, public relations manager for one of the most respected circuses in Europe, Circus Knie of Switzerland, claims that "there is no doubt that the circus plays an important role in ecological education," because the performing and menagerie animal "provides people with the impetus to donate money to endangered species when seeing these animals face to face." David Hancocks, on the other hand, believes that animals in captivity have had a profoundly detrimental effect upon people's understanding and appreciation of wildlife. "In truth it must be recognised that many commonly held attitudes towards wild animals have grown from public contact with captive wildlife," he declares. "The use of the word 'monkey' in the English language is an illuminating example. The English had no natural contact with monkeys, and learned of them only from the aberrant behaviours of psychotic specimens in deprived environments; today the word monkey is used as a verb to illustrate grotesque actions, or as a noun synonymous with a mischievous child. Our concepts of many other wild animals are also distortions fostered by the conditions of menageries in circuses... To compound and extend these attitudes by exhibiting animals as 'freaks' in a circus is a serious threat and insult against wildlife conservation. It is impossible to excite the interest of the public in conserving bears and elephants when they are presented as mere curiosities under multi-coloured floodlights against the background of a show band... The fact that circuses are doing a disservice to the cause of wildlife conservation, and are actually helping to add confusion and delay to progress in this area by their methods of exhibition, is therefore a matter of urgent importance and is a particularly insidious danger."

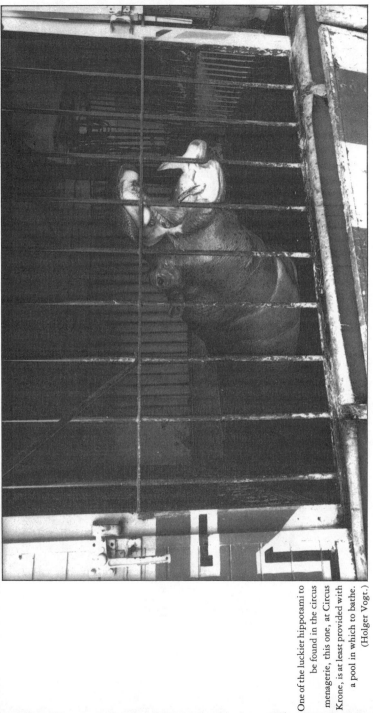

One of the luckier hippopotami to be found in the circus menagerie, this one, at Circus Krone, is at least provided with a pool in which to bathe. (Holger Vogt.)

The habitat of Circus Krone's giraffe. (Holger Vogt.)

Natural Behaviour

Though afforded an increasingly high profile as part of an aggressive and ingenious sales pitch to put critics on the defensive, one should not underestimate the support that the concept of the educational circus animal has found among active circus fans, government inspectors and some influential zoologists and ethologists. At centre stage of this new public relations strategy is the claim that the exotic animal performing in the arena displays only the most natural behaviour, fully in tune with its own innate instincts. To proponents of this view, even the most bizarre forms of animal dressage can now be justified as "mere extensions" of an animal's natural behaviour, almost as though the trainer, far from exerting a coercive influence, actually played a completely passive and incidental role. Examples of such dressage are legion, and if they appear to drag not only the animal but also science into the theatre of the absurd, then that must be a testament to the circus's unrivalled proficiency at spinning a potent and compelling illusion. Accordingly, even the archetypal "boxing kangaroo" — which only a few seasons ago also appeared at Peter Jay's CPA-approved Blackpool Tower — is portrayed as being true to its own natural instincts. More extreme styles of dressage, too preposterous even for the most ardent circus fan to justify in terms of "natural behaviour", are rarely condemned but greeted with a telling and uncomfortable silence: the ice-skating polar bears starring in a circus in the Ukraine, for example, the muzzled animals also riding a sledge, performing acrobatics, and dancing the waltz; or the "great musical and comical spectacular" of Spain's Toronto Travelling Circus, which features chimpanzees dressed as matadors, the terrified animals entertaining the holiday crowds by desperately trying to escape the charging bull in the arena.

Yet even the more mundane wild animal acts seem to stretch the idea of "natural behaviour" far beyond the bounds of credibility. The undisputed star of one of Clubb-Chipperfield's wild cat shows, for example, is a single snow leopard, one of Earth's most endangered species, with less than 500 surviving in the wild. But second generation captive-bred in Winnipeg Zoo, this exquisite animal, like many others, will never return to its natural habitat. Indeed, what some ethologists have denounced as a "degrading spectacle" is vigourously defended by Jim Clubb in the belief that a display of the snow leopard's "natural behaviour" in the circus arena not only provides the public with entertainment but also "ecological education". "We only train the animals to do natural things, not unnatural things," Clubb asserts. "I mean they naturally jump, they can naturally sit, or when they walk the double ropes in the air they would walk along the branch of a tree in exactly the same manner. So everything we teach them to do is only an extension of what they would naturally do in the wild. We are simply exploiting their natural abilities." But in the final analysis, as Clubb himself admits, it is the bottom line that counts:

"We're in this business because we love it, but the only way we can keep these animals is to make money from them through public exhibition."

Similarly, Emil Smith, trainer and presenter of the Clubb-Chipperfield show, denies that his act is either degrading to the wild cats, or that his showmanship exhibits an archaic human supremacy over the animal kingdom. "Jumping, climbing, walking a pole — these are just slight variations of what the animal naturally does in the wild," comes the pat reply, as though he's been asked the question for the millionth time. In 1987, the act, which also features jaguars and African leopards, was put on tour throughout Europe, with Clubb having negotiated lucrative seasonal engagements in what are regarded as some of the best continental circuses, including Krone in Germany and Knie in Switzerland. To the sound of the Knie brass band playing the "Pink Panther" and "Jesus Christ Superstar", the climax of the act features the cats jumping onto glittering discotheque balls, and balancing themselves in a begging position as the silver globes revolve under the spotlights. In all honesty, could this be described as "natural behaviour"? Says ethologist, government inspector and circus fan Dr Thomas Althaus: "This has to be put into perspective. For the animal, it doesn't care if it stands on a rock or a mirror. It jumps on that thing, it sits upright and it jumps down. That's its behaviour and there's absolutely nothing unnatural about it. The effect that is being added by use of the mirrors is just show. It's a way of presenting the beauty of the animal and the people are thrilled. They may be less attractive on a rock."

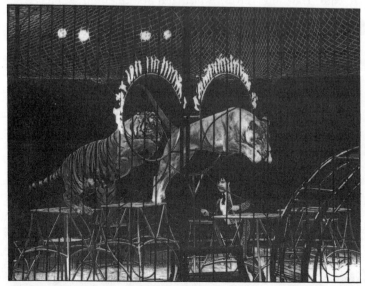

"The Peace of the Jungle" — Club Chipperfield's wildcat show at the International Circus Festival in Monte Carlo. (Matthias Schnellmann.)

Ice-skating polar bears starring in a circus in the Ukraine. (Associated Press.)

Captive Breeding

Yet for the pro-circus lobby there is another argument in favour of having critically endangered species confined to the menagerie beast wagon: conservation through captive breeding. For Dr Thomas Althaus, an ardent supporter of this view, the picture is clear-cut: "People have always had animals in their care — I don't like the word 'captivity.' If you are against keeping wild animals in the zoo or circus then you are also saying that if a species is highly endangered, you are prepared to let it die out. Those are the consequences — which I'm not prepared to accept." Despite this rediscovered credibility of the travelling menagerie, once again the inherent illusion of the circus is ever present, masking a much bleaker reality.

As we have already seen, the international trade in animals has been subject to the provisions of the Washington Convention since 1975, forbidding the importation of strictly endangered species for purely commercial purposes. It is thus that most of today's circus animals are either captive bred, or were caught in the wild before the Convention came into force. And yet due to difficulties in captive breeding, some circus animals such as chimpanzees and elephants are in chronically short supply — perhaps presaging their eventual disappearance from menageries. Circus Knie's elephant population for instance is far from being self-sustaining, even though it claims to play a valuable role in the conservation of the species and enjoys an international reputation in the circus world for its captive breeding efforts. Indeed, although the first Asian elephant to be bred in a zoo was more than a century ago, since then, in all of Europe and America, only about 120 have been born. Even today, says Fred Kurt, "It's still very rare for an elephant to be born in captivity, and in the second generation, there's not even half as many born. From what I've discovered this is because the wild male baby elephant has to learn about copulation and reproduction, something that's not easy when the animal is constantly fettered in a row in a circus tent." The spectre of disease also haunts the young elephant in circus captivity. The third captive-born elephant at Knie, Lohimi, lived for just three years, succumbing to disease in 1988. According to Fredy Knie Snr, Lohimi died of herpes and he states that "now all the elephants in Switzerland are infected with herpes." Fred Kurt believes that it was the stress of training and performing in the ring which made Lohimi's herpes infection break out, and that the young elephant was just too weak to combat it.

At the same time, lions, tigers and leopards have been bred to such abundant excess that there are now more of these animals to be found in European menageries than in their country of origin — where some subspecies are on the brink of extinction. Apart from very few species, however — such as the Arabian Oryx which does not have to relearn survival skills, or animals such as orang-utans or chimpanzees which must first be put through exhaustive and failure-prone rehabilitation programmes —

most zoo and circus species are virtually impossible to reintroduce into the wild. Are circuses then merely pretending to play a vital role in conservation? Not so, says Thomas Althaus: as endangered animals in the wild become the victims of poaching and habitat destruction, the zoo and circus may provide the species with a final refuge, thereby preventing their extinction.

Asserting that "breeding in zoos has become an essential part of conservation," science writer and broadcaster Colin Tudge, writing in *New Scientist*, concedes that "unless such breeding is carried out on a large scale, through cooperation between zoos, and between well-chosen animals, it would be bound to fail. The results would be inbred and probably infertile parodies of wild creatures that, at best, were only fit for life in captivity. The task of matchmaking is becoming so large and the orchestration so intricate that only computers can cope. No one doubts that the ideal way to conserve animals is to do everything possible to save their habitats; the loss of wilderness, rather than the direct assault of the hunter, now endangers an estimated 25 per cent of all species." Unfortunately, even the world's most renowned and prestigious zoos can only point to a few limited successes in reestablishing such animals in the wild. No more than 20 species currently benefit from coordinated breeding programmes and even the staunchest proponents of captive breeding admit that it could only save a minute fraction of the Earth's endangered species. Given the results of the first comprehensive survey of zoos in the EEC, such dismal results may not seem altogether surprising. In the more than 1000 registered zoos, holding an estimated one million animals, inspectors found "depressing" standards of welfare, education and conservation. Animals used to wide open spaces were discovered kept in pits where they could only see walls and sky; a gorilla in Rome zoo was confined behind glass to a barred enclosure with virtually no light; polar bears in Naples were forced to endure the summer heat with temperatures soaring to over 40 degrees C; and at Marwell zoo in Hampshire, animal facilities were so badly designed that when two black rhinos died, their cages literally had to be cut into pieces to remove them. Small wonder then that the notion of captive breeding for conservation in the even less sophisticated environment of the circus beast wagon resembles a theatre of the absurd. Even so, apologists for captive breeding have some remarkable plans for the future of wildlife, as outlined by Colin Tudge, apparently without irony: "As human populations decrease from the 26th century onwards," he writes, "it will be possible for animals to live in the wild again. So the task of conservation breeders is not to keep animals for ever, but to tide them over for 500 to 1000 years in a state in which they are able to return to the wild — albeit a 'wild' that is very different from the wilderness of today." This grand vision is expected to be accomplished utilising "huge genetic banks of animals as frozen sperm, eggs and embryos," reminiscent of the 1970s cryogenics fad in the USA which saw deceased humans frozen in liquid helium with the vain hope that in generations to come they would be thawed out and given new life by the future miracles of science. The fundamental flaw in the equation is the inconvenient fact that once thawed out, the endangered species that had been kept on ice for a thousand years would have no one to teach them their survival skills. Indeed, in all of these grandiose, high-tech solutions that cannot seem to tolerate the idea of the unquantifiable and elusive elements of creation's life-force, one can still perceive the stalking ghost of Descartes and his belief in the clockwork animal.

> "Denied access to their natural habitat these animals become marginalised from their wild nature and begin to lose access to the mentalities and behaviours which would have been appropriate there. Such animals have a status akin to that of refugees. They are in enforced exile, but a false one at that because realistically there is no 'home' to return to."
> — Bob Mullan and Garry Marvin

Even for more prosaic methods of "conservation" through captive breeding, the dilemma remains virtually the same, but with some familiar and ugly twists. Bill Jordan and Stefan Ormrod, for example, in their book *The Last Great Wild Beast Show*, point out that if 48 gorillas are captured in the wild, only 30 will survive initial trapping and handling, only 12 of these will survive their journey to the zoo and only half a dozen will live to maturity. Before even considering "conservation", those six individuals would have to produce 48 progeny simply to ensure no depletion of stock — an impossible feat since the animals are slow breeders. As there are now some 400 gorillas in captivity around the world, this represents an astounding death rate and hardly an endearing or efficient form of conservation. The chronic condition that seems to afflict the human race — fragmentation, perhaps even some virulent but as yet unrecognised form of schizophrenia — is all too evident, particularly the irrational notion of conserving wildlife as something extraneous to their natural habitat and its intricate ecology. Indeed, perhaps the most difficult species to reintroduce to the wild is *homo sapiens*.

To pro-circus scientists like Thomas Althaus, the stud book is the circus's testament to its role in conservation, despite the slow but inevitable degradation of a species' genetic identity in captivity. "You have stud books for endangered species like the Siberian tiger or the snow leopard to enable the circus people to keep the genetic changes as low as possible," he insists. But strangely enough, for all this faith in preserving the "genetic material" of the wild, reintroduction is a four-letter word to most circuses, usually met with scorn and derision. A reflex reaction that betrays such extreme defensiveness is perhaps predictable since successful rehabilitation of circus animals into the wild would become one more reason for the menageries to be closed down altogether. The catchword that all seem to have learnt is "Man-Eater!" though it is difficult to see how, even after twenty years of captivity in a beast wagon, an elephant, rhinoceros, chimpanzee or orang-utan would begin preying upon human beings. Obviously, by focussing attention only on the profound difficulties which have surrounded attempts to reintroduce wild cats, raising the spectre of mauled children, the circuses hope to destroy any notion of reintroduction — even though it is ostensibly central to their justification for "keeping species on ice". Dr Thomas Althaus: "These wild cats in the circus are now all captive bred and it's impossible for example to reintroduce captive-bred tigers into the wild. This has been tried several times but has always failed. The only thing that might work is the reintroduction of captive-bred snow leopards. This is because their habitat is a very vast area without human population — so the risk that they begin eating livestock or killing people is less acute. But it is also a big risk for the animals themselves since it's difficult to ensure that they'll get their food — there's a chance they may survive and a chance they may die." Under the present regime, it is a risk that the animals will never have to take since no circus that I have heard of is engaged in any reintroduction programme.

According to Dr Fred Kurt, although not fully wild, working elephants from Asia which now provide a small reservoir of supplies for circuses, could theoretically be used to repopulate the wild — if room could somehow be made for them. "During colonial times, the British used elephants for their teak forestry in Asia," he recounts. "They shipped elephants from Burma to the Andaman islands and these elephants escaped, and their offspring still survive — at least 30 or 40 wild elephants or former working elephants. But working elephants in the forests of Asia are, ecologically speaking, not tame — although hobbled they are quite able to find their own food, you don't have to teach them what can be eaten and how to find water. But an elephant who has lived 20 or 30 years in chains in a circus just wouldn't know what to do — it would be almost impossible to reintroduce them to the wild."

For other species, perhaps the gravest and most intractable obstacle to reintroduction is a consummate lack of will and effort. Such programmes remain chronically short of funds, and attract little or no interest from the self-professed conservationists of the zoo and circus world. Indeed, while the global zoo budget is estimated to be about £1 billion, the national parks of black Africa are afforded an annual budget of £60 million. Similarly, for all the talk of conserving species in captivity with the vague, dim and distant aim of eventual reintroduction, even the zoological community plays virtually no role whatsoever in attempting to protect the disappearing natural habitat of these animals, thereby making the cryogenic process even more irrelevant. Furthermore, with indiscriminate cross-breeding in both zoos and circuses, there is the very real danger that reintroduction could pollute genetically pure strains in the wild with animals of uncertain parenthood. In the final analysis, only reserves and national parks which hold together an intact ecology will have any hope of saving a species from extinction, something that has already been proved time and time again. The Indian tiger population, for example, fell from an estimated 40,000 at the turn of the century, to about 2,500 in 1969 and 1,827 in 1972. It was only when Indira Gandhi, with the collaboration of the WWF, stepped in to conserve the species, selecting nine areas to become special reserves as part of the successful *Project Tiger*, that the the wild tiger population once again began to increase. Indeed, for both the zoo and circus, it seems that it is easier just to play at conservation, and studiously keep the stud book as an alibi. Fuelled by the fatalism of seeing vast areas of natural habitat destroyed, such complacency may give rise to an even more daunting prospect. Says Althaus: "Well, you never know. The few remaining rhinos that we have in the wild may end up in Africa behind a fence with military guards in helicopters and jeeps around those fences with machine-guns. That's the future, unfortunately, that many wild animals face. Of course many species are not quite so spectacular and nobody really takes any notice until they've already disappeared. But for the spectacular animals — the risk is that the few remaining animals that there are will be left in zoos and circuses."

Sadly, it can hardly be denied that these captive animals now inhabit a strange limbo of existence where they are neither wild nor domesticated. Deprived of their natural habitat and behaviour, as unique species they face almost certain biological and psychological disintegration. Although circuses proudly insist that stud books are kept in order to ensure the genetic purity of these animals, in the final analysis, these may be of no more significance than the breeding records of pedigree poodles. Indeed, says Dr Fred Kurt, after several generations in captivity, where genetic change is almost unavoidable, these species become merely deformed shadows of their former selves. Facing eternity behind bars, eventually the menagerie animal may bear more than a passing resemblance to the white tigers displayed by the likes of the American animal tamer John Campolongo of the Hawthorn Circus Corporation, based in Richmond, Illinois, which currently owns 40 of the animals. Cruel mockeries of creation, perhaps more than any other single example, the white tiger acts as a devastating indictment of the menagerie's avowed role in conservation and its respect for the sanctity of wildlife. Though many circus owners and animal trainers feel a kind of repugnance for these pitifully bizarre freaks of nature, as "super-exotics", they have nevertheless proved to be an irresistible money-spinner. Grotesquely over-bred, they are known as "star-gazers" because their bluish eyes, sadly disconcerting, are slightly crossed and raised towards the heavens. Explains Fred Kurt: "All of these white tigers originally came from Delhi zoo, bred from a single male that was caught in the wild in the 1960s. He was obviously discovered at a lucky moment because normally, a genetic mutation of this kind couldn't possibly survive for long. On top of anything else, a white tiger, without any camouflage, how could he hunt? He would be completely lost. At Delhi zoo he was bred with a normal tiger and then was re-bred again with his own daughter to keep the purity of the strain. The result was total inbreeding and today these animals all suffer from liver and kidney deficiencies and other physiological problems."

Triangle of Trade

As certain species are bred to excess, individual animals, unwanted and often uncared for, face an ominous future. In recent years, to cope with this overbreeding, a triangle of animal trade has developed between circuses, zoos and research laboratories, often with specialised animal dealers acting as well-paid intermediaries. Says Fred Kurt: "Circus Knie had a tiger some years ago which had been trained to ride on the backs of horses and rhinos. But after a time this is passé, you can't show this act every year in any circus. Then of course the circus management looks for another place for this tiger and they become increasingly desperate to be rid of it, but the fact is that there are just so many of these animals in captivity that sooner or later they always end up with a rather dubious animal dealer."

In 1983, press reports revealed that for several years, a 150-strong colony of rhesus monkeys at Woburn Animal Kingdom, a safari park in Bedfordshire, had been utilised as a reservoir for terminal laboratory experiments. Woburn's animals — including lions, elephants, and giraffes — were under the care of director John Chipperfield, yet another member of the great British circus clan. The rhesus monkeys, on loan from the notorious Shamrock Farms in Sussex which specialises in the purchase and sale of animals for the laboratory, were periodically rounded up to be sold off as "models" for drug and chemical testing. Similarly, when chimpanzee trainer Mickey Antalek, a performer of 15 years' standing at Ringling Bros, Barnum and Bailey Circus, died suddenly of a heart attack in August 1984, his four chimps were hurriedly shipped to the White Sands Research Center in Alamagordo, New Mexico. As IPPL pointed out, White Sands, whose facility holds over 500 monkeys and 70 chimpanzees, earns most of its profits from the giant Hoechst Pharmaceutical Company of West Germany and advertises the availability of its chimpanzees for the testing of insecticides, cosmetics and new drugs. Efforts by IPPL to have the chimps released were met with disdain, the immensely rich Ringlings stating that they were under no moral or legal obligation to ensure the animals' future welfare.

At the same time, however, the caring image was of paramount importance, as evidenced by the statement in *Circus Reports*, a trade publication, that the chimps had gone to a wildlife sanctuary. "Ringlings washed its hands of the animals," announced IPPL, "despite the fact that they had been 'star attractions' for years, since the chimps were able to do such complex tasks as riding motorbikes." But then perhaps Ringlings' obligation did not even start at their own circus. According to the testimony of one vet, the chimps were "in very bad shape" when they were transferred to White Sands, and "had many scars and some burns, possibly from motorbike training." Determined to have the chimps released from the research facility, IPPL issued an Emergency Alert to its members and supporters. Demonstrations subsequently took place outside the arena where Ringlings were performing and thousands of letters poured into the circus's headquarters in Washington. Foreseeing pickets, boycotts and unfavourable publicity, by February 1985 Ringlings had finally succumbed to media pressure, and wishing to preserve image, that most valuable of all commodities in the circus world, had the chimps transferred, at IPPL's behest, to the Wild Animal Retirement Village in Waldo, Florida. Interestingly, the case also shed light on the training methods that the chimps had endured at Ringlings, probably the most famous and prestigious circus in the world. According to Nick Connell, a former trainer at Ringlings, the chimps had been subjected to systematic cruelty by Mickey Antalek — adding that he had also witnessed similar abuse in the training of bears and lions. He wrote: "I first saw him training these four chimps in winter quarters. They were on a long multi-seated bicycle on which three of the large chimps rode as passengers while the large chimp Louis steered and pedalled. The vehicle was difficult for even a human to ride in these conditions, and Louis had a hard time of it, spilling the ensemble repeatedly. And, repeatedly, he was struck with a sturdy club. The thumps could be heard outside the arena, and the screams went further than that. My blood boiled. I am ashamed to say I did nothing!"

The chronic problem of surplus animals in the menagerie also sheds light on the absurdity of the circus's new rallying cry of "Captivity for Conservation". Explains Fred Kurt: "Every subspecies of tiger is on the endangered list, but in the circus, the vast majority of these animals are never on a stud book. They are bred in such large numbers that eventually they either have to be killed or sold. But who on Earth wants to buy a tiger? Tigers are sold at between 50 and 300 Swiss francs (£20-£120) because there are just too many of them in captivity. And so sooner or later these animals always end up with a dubious animal dealer or at a primitive menagerie." Indeed, some surplus species, he adds, may also end up as fashion wear, or even on the dinner table, in much the same way as some of the famous bears of Berne, still held in a medieval pit in the centre of the city, are served up as *haute cuisine* in city restaurants. The bear and tiger cubs may look cuddly when born, but they soon outgrow their usefulness as a crowd-puller. It is then, says Kurt, that the animals either end up on the dinner table in restaurants that specialise in exotic meats or as fashion wear in stylish department stores like the *Kaufhaus des Westens* in Berlin where customers with a weakness for curiosities can buy tigers' tails or bears' paws. Again, the law is blind to such dealings.

In the USA, unwanted circus or zoo animals may find themselves as cut-price bargains in such outdoor sales as the "Annual Southeast Exotic Animal Auction", held in Atlanta, Georgia. Among animals offered for sale in 1984 were squirrel, owl, and macaque monkeys, llamas, antelope, bears, wolves, cougars, giraffes and ostriches, Bengal tigers and mountain lions, all to be sold to the highest bidder regardless of the customer's experience in keeping wild animals or the standard of their facilities. Shoppers at the fair included speciality restaurants, pet shops, and also recreational "game farms". Also known as "shooting ranches", it is here that the unwanted circus or zoo animal must surely suffer the ultimate humiliation. Catering for those jaded and image-conscious city slickers afflicted with a craving to play the fearless white hunter, lions, tigers, leopards and other wild beasts can be "wasted", for a price, with automatic weapons, and their heads mounted to adorn some New York penthouse or Miami condominium. The irony of it all is that having lost their wildness in the beast wagon or the zoo cage, these animals even have to be "spooked" with shouts or gunfire otherwise they just lie there passively and wait to be shot.

Often, these surplus circus animals may simply languish behind bars until the day they die. In May 1988, for example, a male chimpanzee was discovered in a roadside menagerie at La Place, locally known as Snake Farm, 50 miles north of New Orleans. The animal, a former circus performer billed as "Gorilla" and "Jungle Killer", had endured solitary confinement for 20 years, in a cage measuring 2.4 x 2.4 x 1.6m with a bare concrete floor and with nothing but a swing for exercise. Extricating the chimpanzee and the other primates from their cages proved a daunting task. Reported IPPL: "None of the primates had been let out in approximately two decades and the rusted doors had to be hammered and pried open with a crowbar and winch."

One might well ask why measures are not taken to prevent overbreeding in the beast wagon. The answer, unfortunately, is that overbreeding, particularly of lions, tigers and leopards, is actively encouraged because those cute and fluffy cubs remain one of the star attractions of the circus menagerie. Furthermore, there are other problems which show the situation in its true squalid light. Castration will make the male lion, the king of the jungle, lose his mane — and a bald lion is probably going too far even for the freak-hungry menagerie.

Clubb Chipperfield trainer
Emil Smith with snowleopard
(William Johnson.)

Bred to excess, many animals in
the circus face a cruel and
uncertain future. Often, overbreeding is actually encouraged
in the beast wagon — particularly of lions, tigers and
leopards — because those cute
and fluffy cubs remain one of
the star attractions of the circus
menagerie. Here, Emil Smith
shows off a leopard cub.
(William Johnson.)

"In the circus an animal has a much better life than even in a zoo. He has a complete routine, he has a life to look forward to."
— Jim Clubb

The Beast Wagon

Trucked around Australia during the blistering hot summer of 1987 was a troupe of Siberian brown bears, owned by one of the 70 units of the Moscow State Circus. Their star turn in the ring saw them walk a tightrope suspended six metres above the ground at an angle of 45 degrees. The once proud animals, ranging in age from two to ten years, were dressed in sailor suits and from the neck of one of the youngest bears swung a out-sized baby's dummy. Following this colourful spectacle, the animals were returned to their "living quarters" — cages just one metre square. Few members of any circus audience will care to realise that performing animals such as these spend much of their entire lives cooped up in containers or crates in which they are scarcely able to turn. In the Australian heat wave, the Russian bears were understandably reluctant to return to their containers, but by all accounts their protests were met only with contempt and harsh treatment by their handlers. Only demonstrations by animal welfare groups in Sydney and Melbourne eventually forced the circus to rehouse the bears in larger cages. Said Wayne Stevens, a spokesman for the promoters, Michael Edgley International: "Public opinion seems to be changing and I dare say we have to be adaptable enough to change with it when it is required." Even that grudging change however was only temporary: the Russians have traditionally used such minuscule cages ever since the days of Peter the Great. In August 1988, the Toronto Humane Society gave another unit of the Moscow State Circus 48 hours to find bigger cages for its 12 performing bears or face criminal charges. The bears, declared the society, were being "psychologically tortured" by their confinement. Revealing once again the hidden sordidness of the rose-tinted illusion, the 15-city tour through the USA and Canada, with 200 scheduled performances, was sponsored by "Snuggle", a fabric conditioner produced by Lever Brothers Corporation, their endearing marketing symbol being a cuddly teddy bear. These animals "do the tricks out of love and not out of fright," asserted the bears' trainer. Yet it is reported that in Las Vegas two members of the audience accidently witnessed an incident backstage in which one disobedient animal was struck with what appeared to be a steel rod. Nevertheless, the Russian bear-tamers did find some friends amongst American zoologists. While admitting that he had witnessed stereotyped pacing and cage-gnawing behaviour in the bears, the curator of animals at San Diego zoo insisted that "it provides a form of regular exercise."

Even in the most prestigious of circuses, it is normal practice for wild animals to be confined for life to cramped and bare beast wagons. The ritual defence for this is that "they know of nothing else" and that an animal experiencing fear or deprivation in their confinement would howl, scratch and gnaw at the bars. But would even a human prisoner continue to howl after realising that there is no use in doing so? Certainly, before learning the hopelessness of its situation, many a captured animal scratches and cries in a frenzy of desperation. Only with time and a realisation of futility, is this distress gradually translated into stereotyped behaviour, the defiant and noisy chain-rattling of elephants, for example, bears biting and sucking at the bars of their wagons, mad-eyed monkeys indulging in compulsive masturbation and self-mutilation. But, insist the circuses, the performing menagerie animals receive regular exercise, and therefore their welfare is even superior to that of zoo animals which may have far larger enclosures. Such "exercise", however, may only amount to a stressful appearance in the arena, either for training or during show time under the glare of the lights and the cacophony of the audience's applause, cheers and whistles. In the case of a wild cat, the animal will be prodded with a stick or metal bar out of its cage into the tunnel which connects the beast wagons to the arena, face its trainer brandishing a whip, perform several tricks, and then be prodded once again down the tunnel back to its cage. To pro-circus ethologists this is called "occupational therapy", which amounts to quite a stunning admission in itself since in my dictionary the definition is *"the therapeutic use of crafts, hobbies, etc., esp. in the rehabilitation of emotionally disturbed patients."* Says a former officer of the British Veterinary Association, James Allcock: "I am not in favour of the traditional 'wild' animals living in travelling circuses. The big cats — lions and tigers — cannot possibly have an acceptable life in the unfurnished cages (large wood and steel boxes would be a better name) that they have to live in... They may be in the ring for a couple of hours a day, but the remaining 22 are spent looking at solid walls, bars or passing people."

Predictably, drugs are used extensively to blunt the psychological terror of these freak-show animals. Only recently has "occupational therapy" become a more expedient and respectable course of action, though all too often even this is no more than a sugar-coated pill for the public. "Elephants, apes and bears — they're the greatest problems for the circus," says Fred Kurt. "I would say that they should never be allowed to travel with them any more. Often in the menagerie you can't even see the apes — they're hiding in the back of the wagon or under the straw. It's the same for the bears in the Russian and East European circuses — they're hidden away in boxes — boxes that are so small that the bears can't even turn around. Most are kept permanently under drugs."

The RSPCA finds similar cause for complaint in the way elephants are held in captivity in the circus: "Elephants are shackled nearly all the time, and although the chains are often enclosed in rubber pipe or sacking, some elephants have been permanently scarred by lifelong leg-chains."

In most countries, the law makes no distinction between a performing and non-performing animal, the travelling menagerie being exempt from any legislation which might govern standards in zoos, such as providing accommodation specifically attuned to the unique needs of individual species. Indeed, for every single animal in the menagerie, even the most rudimentary conditions which characterise their life in the wild are missing: climbing possibilities for arboreal apes, for instance, or bathing facilities for polar bears and hippos. The only "justification" for this exemption is monetary, quite simply because even the most elite travelling circus cannot hope to provide the space required for animals under zoo legislation. Noting that a wagon measuring 6 x 2.4 x 1.8 metres is considered adequate for seven polar bears, and that it is deemed acceptable for 14 lions to be housed in a vehicle with a volume of 6 x 2.7 x 1.5 metres, the RSPCA concludes that circus cages "are designed only for transportation. They must, by definition and design, always be inadequate... Frequently old, dilapidated and rusting, these wagons offer no outlet for the animals' instincts to explore, to 'play' or do anything other than exist." Indeed, few animal living quarters can be as bare as a circus beast wagon, save for those in a laboratory or a factory farm. Even hiding possibilities — to allow the animal to retreat from the inquisitive eyes and teasing of the crowds — are generally non-existent, quite simply because the public won't pay to see a hiding animal.

A rare insight into just how the frustrated and neurotic menagerie animal regards the public on the other side of the bars is given by zoologist and anthropologist Dr Desmond Morris, former director of London Zoo: "Apes and certain monkeys have sometimes been known to develop the habit of throwing their faeces at visitors. The colony of adult chimpanzees living on an island at Chester Zoological Gardens frequently tears up clods of earth and hurls them with remarkable accuracy at onlookers on the other side of the water-ditch. The dolphins at Marineland in the United States were observed to pick up pebbles from the floor of their large tank and flip them out of the water at certain visitors." He adds that "Apes, monkeys, cats, corvids and parrots may sometimes develop an enticement device. The visitor is attracted and then attacked. In most cases this involves an intense and extremely friendly invitation to groom. The mammal presses or rubs itself against the wire or bars, the bird cocks its head and ruffles its feathers. Then, as soon as the visitor has started to scratch, stroke or rub the soliciting animal, it swings round in a flash and scratches, bites or stabs at its victim."

A non-performing Black Bear of Circo Medrano, displaying typical stereotyped behaviour in the form of compulsive bar-biting. (Matthias Schnellmann.)

Bear at Circus Krone, Germany. (Holger Vogt)

"A mistake often made by humans is to apply human psychology to animals. Because humans — and a minority at that! — appreciate a beautiful sunset, they assume animals must prefer beautiful surroundings too, whereas the truth of the matter is that animals are thoroughly satisfied provided their basic wants — food, shelter, general comfort etc. are catered for and, in some species, toys or apparatus provided (for example, a large rubber ball for a rhinoceros, swings for apes etc.)... Protected from the hazards of disease, famine, predators etc. that make life in the wild a precarious business, the animals in leading zoos and circuses today lead a virtually utopian existence."
— Rodney N. Manser

Plagued by rising costs and falling attendance, many travelling shows are run on a shoestring, and thus the animals often suffer from inadequate care and veterinary attention. According to the Washington-based group *People for the Ethical Treatment of Animals*, circuses "may visit 150 towns in the spring, summer and fall months, and a clean water supply is not readily available in every location. As a result, drinking water is limited, and cleaning the animals and their cages may take low priority, causing real hardship for animals like elephants, who are accustomed to frequent bathing." Not even when the circus has come to the end of its touring season will the animals be allowed more spacious accommodation. During the slack winter months, most animals will still be kept in their beast wagons or travelling crates. Few circuses have the funds or the desire to invest in comfortable winter quarters since off-season housing is only used for a few months a year. Because of quarantine regulations, other animals will simply continue touring abroad, as far afield as Asia, South Africa and Australia. Jim Clubb: "When we send an act onto a European tour we usually keep it there for a minimum of five years because when we come back to England we have to go through quarantine — that would mean that we would have to stay on one premises for six months without working." Adds Chris Krenger: "When an animal act leaves Knie at the end of the season they'll go to another circus to tour Germany, Italy and Holland for example. They're always in these wagons, that's for sure, but they're all born in the circus in these wagons. They don't know anything else."

Asked whether it can be justified to have animals confined to their cages for life, Dr Thomas Althaus replied: "Well what else should the circuses do with their animals? Kill them? You can't let them out: to an animal that's the most frightening, terrible experience. He fights to get back into his environment where he feels secure. If they open their cages the animals are more than happy to get back in again." But is this not a psychological phenomenon similar to that suffered by human beings who have spent years in prison or other institutions? "Well these are not people. Animals are animals and people are people. A person can realise that there is an outside world and can have a wish to go from Berne to Zürich, for example. An animal cannot." So both morally and legally one must accept different standards between animals and people? "Absolutely. An animal is an animal, constructed in a completely different manner. For these leopards or tigers, the cage is a home where they feel at ease. They go through their tunnel to the circus ring and even there on their pedestal, they may fall asleep or doze off or begin to lick themselves. An animal that is not at ease wouldn't do that. If the animal was stressed it would begin to shiver, try to run away, urinate, defecate, vocalise, scratch." But such statements may simply reflect the contradictions that inevitably infest the pro-menagerie argument, especially that perennial warning to avoid anthropomorphism — while almost in the same breath the practice of placing plastic sunglasses on a dolphin or infant's clothes on a chimpanzee is defended as just enhancing "show value". Perhaps it was significant then that although regarding "animals as animals", when I outlined to Dr Althaus the psychologically depressed state of two chimpanzees inhabiting a beast wagon at the dilapidated Swiss Circus Olympia (the animals burying their heads in the straw or gazing dementedly through the bars, hugging themselves and aimlessly rocking from side to side), Althaus stated, apparently too deep in thought to realise his error: "Yes, that may be a very bad sign — like an autistic child."

Stereotyped Behaviour

Both for menagerie and dressage animals, the pressures of captivity, coupled with the almost inevitable destruction of some species' complex social structures, can often lead to severe neurosis and stereotyped behaviour, leading some circuses, says Kurt, to keep many of their animals under "psycho-pharmaca" or other "headache pills". Such treatment becomes necessary when the stress of confinement provokes fighting between animals, aggression towards the trainer or even self-mutilation. Despite appearances to the contrary, many wild animals are only superficially "tamed" by their captivity. Their instinctive behaviour patterns and social needs remain largely intact within their genetic make-up, and it is the continual frustration of these natural impulses which drives the captive wild animal relentlessly into neurosis. As the RSPCA points out, prolonged social isolation in primates can lead to autistic-like behaviour, stereotyped rocking and thumb-sucking, the animals often withdrawing into the corner of their cage, hugging themselves or relapsing into fits of severe self-directed aggression, such as banging their own heads continually against the bars, walls or floor. Young monkeys reared away from their mothers display typical deprivation symptoms, aggression, apathy, lack of exploratory behaviour and general listlessness, and as adults, they are often unable to foster young. Females that do manage to give birth under such wretched conditions have been known to neglect their offspring, even attack them or over-groom them.

Says Dr Desmond Morris: "Parent animals sometimes become too parental if they have nothing to divert their attention. There is then the danger that they may spend too long cleaning or licking the offspring and damage them in some way. They may insist on carrying them in their mouths for long periods of time, or they may eat parts or all of them." Self-mutilation, he adds, may start in an entirely different fashion. "Usually the animal concerned is isolated and is so underoccupied that it over-cleans itself. A simple example is the 'running sore'. An animal experiences a very minor superficial injury — a scratch or a small cut. It starts to lick or rub it and soon it develops into a larger and larger area. In the wild, the normal amount of licking that the animal would have time for would help to clense the wound and it would heal normally. In captivity, on the other hand, the animal may go on worrying the place until it becomes really serious. A large percentage of all captive monkeys are without the extremities of their tails for this reason." Morris goes on to note that "young apes taken from their mothers at the clinging stage may develop a clinging response to their bedding, grasping a bundle of straw or hay tightly to their bodies. It is significant that such individuals, even when sexually mature, may resort to this distorted infantile pattern when they experience insecurity." As the RSPCA points out, it is highly significant that "'deprivation symptoms' such as rocking, pulling out hair, chewing fingernails, obsessive scratching and playing with their genitals have been observed in parentless children living in institutions." Chimpanzees, says Morris, are particularly susceptible to such deprivation. He graphically describes their inventiveness in the ultimately futile effort to cope with the deadly monotony of their lives in captivity: "And how ingenious they are! Over there is a young chimpanzee with nothing to play with except his own body. He invents new kinds of locomotion — rolling, spinning, dropping on his head from the roof. He stuffs straw into his ears, smears his faeces over the cage wall and traces patterns in the mess, pulls faces, claps and waggles his hands. But with no companions and no complexity in his environment to manipulate and investigate, he will, despite his brave attempts at inventiveness, grow up to become a dulled, stupid clown instead of one of the most brainy and fascinating creatures on the face of the earth." There is, he concludes, "something biologically immoral about keeping animals in enclosures where their behaviour pattern, which has taken millions of years to evolve, can find no expression... until this knowledge is applied all we can hope for is to see animal lunatic asylums." Often, not even a larger enclosure can heal the psychological wounds caused by years of confinement in a circus beast wagon. In one instance, a circus polar bear sold to a zoo continued to pace out precisely the same circuit that conformed to the measurements of its beast wagon.

Once in captivity, stereotyped behaviour in an elephant often manifests itself as a compulsive weaving movement. Fred Kurt: "This is always a sign of an animal which is not well kept. The movement starts when the animal walks or stretches to the point where the chain ends and then back again. They feel the natural impulse to move — to eat perhaps, or because it is too cold or too hot or they want to go out, or they're frightened and they want to run away from something, or they're nervous before the show — but because they're restrained by the chains, this impulse is translated into the weaving pattern. It may also occur because very often, the elephants have such little room in their circus tent that not all of them can die down at the same time. And so when an elephant wants to lie down but it can't, then this very neurotic weaving behaviour begins again." Imagine the psychological injury continually inflicted upon these creatures, he adds, by being almost permanently chained up in a row: "An elephant realises that there are eight different individuals in the tent but it will only know two of them, the one to the left and the one to the right. Like this, their entire social behaviour is bound to become crippled, and this is what is always forgotten. Normally the people in the circus have little or no idea how these animals would live out in the wild, free, nor can they be bothered to know. They have only ever seen them in circuses and if for instance you try to persuade a circus to keep elephants without chains — as I have done many times with Knie — they simply don't understand it. For the circus owner or animal trainer, elephants have always been kept in chains." Indeed, in his book *Elefanten und Artisten*, published in 1987, Rolf Knie declares that "without chains the elephants would tear the tent apart, tear the canvas to pieces and eat it."

"It was thirty years ago that as a university student I first spent several months at Circus Knie because animal behaviour interested me very much," explains Kurt. "Through Knie I also spent time at other circuses, such as Bertram Mills in England. At this time I saw the animals through the eyes of the circus trainer: elephants had to be kept like this and nobody criticised it. And then when I began my behavioural study on elephants I started to observe this stereotyped behaviour, which was evident even in newly-caught baby elephants. Now even today, thirty years on, these problems still exist." But what are the precise causes? To begin with, says Kurt, much of this neurotic, compulsive behaviour is induced by the destruction of the species' complex social structure: "Often baby elephants are taken away too early from their mothers. Even Zürich zoo's head elephant keeper told me that he believes every elephant has already gone mad before it arrives. In the wild, you see, the young may suckle for up to two years. The presence of the mother is of tremendous importance

— she protects the baby and teaches it a great deal, from stripping the bark of a tree to eating grass. The young one will be about four years old when the mother gives birth again — then it acts as an assistant to the mother to help raise the younger brother or sister, and learns how to give them food, how to play with them, how to protect them when they sleep. These animals are taken away to the circus in one of the most important phases of their life."

Even something as seemingly elementary as how the animals are fed in captivity can have a profound impact upon their psychology and well-being. "In the wild, the larger an elephant becomes," Kurt told me, "the more time it spends on feeding, including the preparation of food — some plants they eat only the bark, for instance, others, only the leaves. But in the circus, the food is delivered highly prepared. Maybe once in a while they get some branches but even these are quickly removed because everything has to look so tidy. So instead of spending 16 hours a day feeding, they spend two hours — and because this leftover time is not replaced with anything else they can do little else than become mad. If they could only walk, or play... as highly social animals they could also spend more time in social interaction, but in the circus they're in chains so they can't even meet each other, perhaps only their two neighbours in the row. Of course, none of these things kills the elephant — and that's why it just doesn't matter."

According to Kurt, another cruelty routinely imposed upon the circus elephant is to deprive it of its ritual bathing and mud baths. The very least circuses should do, he declares, is to take their elephants out into the nearest wood or forest, the nearest stream or lake. "If you don't do it for the elephants," he implores them, "then at least do it for yourselves because that creates a hell of a lot of goodwill amongst the public." Yet there are additional reasons that make bathing for elephants imperative, reasons that the circuses just don't understand, he adds. "The elephant skin has a velvet kind of quality which even bleeds if a horsefly stings it. With its funny hairs, the elephant feels what it doesn't see. The skin is also very important for thermo-regulation. It is highly sensitive, so it needs a lot of care, not only a bath. They use leaves, sand or earth to cool the body and retain the moisture of the skin. But now when you see these circus elephants they always have to stand there clean, naked, whereas you never see a clean, naked wild elephant, they're always covered with water, mud, leaves, sand, earth or something to protect the skin. I believe this may add to the unhappiness these elephants must feel in the circus."

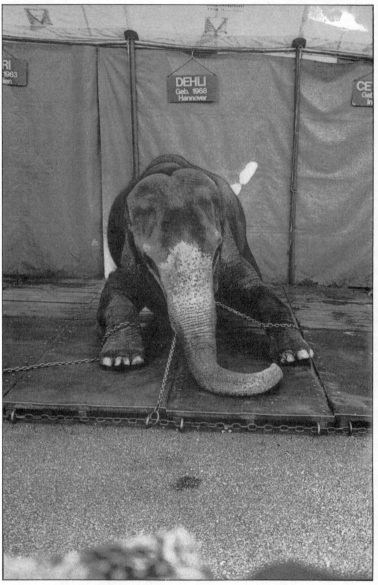

Life in chains. (Matthias Schnellmann.)

The Prisoner's Chains

On a sweltering summer's day in Berne, Circus Knie's elephants, as is customary, were standing side by side in their tent, their feet locked into thick chains. The air under the sun-drenched canvas was humid and musty as the elephant keeper moved slowly along the line, hosing and scrubbing down the animals. The last elephant in the row, however, was lying on its side, and despite gentle coaxing, shouts and then more violent prodding, could not be persuaded to lift itself up. As the keeper began to lose his patience, the other elephants in the tent became increasingly restless. It is perhaps one of the first rules of the circus that the animal trainer or keeper cannot afford to back down before a disobedient creature; he must at all times in the relationship maintain the clearly defined status quo and his own dominant position as the "alpha" or master. As the keeper began to brandish his elephant-goad at the stubborn animal — a short stick with a metal hook on one end — tweaking the thick yet sensitive skin, each and every one of the other elephants in the line began stamping their feet and rattling their chains. So rhythmic and tumultuous was the sound that it seemed startlingly reminiscent of a spontaneous protest by the inmates of a human prison.

Thomas Althaus was reluctant to comment on the elephants' chain-rattling, ducking behind clinical ethology rather than admit that even his favourite circus possesses prisoners of conscience, their wildness somehow regarded as a crime against civilisation: "That's very difficult for me to interpret because I have not seen it first hand," he declared. In all his years as a circus fan, all that he had observed with "scientific objectivity" was the chain-rattling which greeted the keeper bringing food. "So this might be compared to begging behaviour, like a child that wants attention," he told me. "Of course this might also be the reason that the inmates of a prison make a noise — to get their food quickly or whatever they want in prison."

I then asked Fred Kurt what could have provoked such a reaction. "When elephants suddenly rattle their chains like that it could mean that they foresee that one of them is to be beaten," he replied. "Some of these elephant keepers are not as clever as the elephants — macho individuals with loud voices and big muscles — and sooner or later they get trampled on or even killed. Of course Knie, because of its reputation, is not very proud to have information published about the accidents they've had with elephants. But Knie had an accident in Berlin in 1979 when a little elephant stood on top of two of those idiots and broke their bones. Even so, this is not exceptional, this happens every year in the circus because the animals are physically and mentally tortured." In taming the innate wildness of the animal and breaking its spirit, such abuse may be virtually inevitable. For an unruly elephant, for example, there is the punishment of "spanning" — where all four feet are fettered by chains, and then its front legs pulled forward and its hind legs backwards. An elephant that finally loses its long-tried patience and turns against its trainer is almost invariably shot. Says Kurt: "The elephant calves are normally mentally broken before they reach Europe. I mean what must it be like for an elephant baby to put it in a box, in an aeroplane or for weeks on a ship? In the beginning when they are still little they're spoilt, but afterwards..." The same phenomenon may be equally true of elephants born in the circus, adds Kurt, citing the case of Knie's second captive-born elephant, Madura, which was shot after killing its Moroccan keeper in Austria in June 1984. Speculating on the cause of the attack, Kurt says: "It could easily have been because she was spoilt when she was small. And then of course as she grew bigger she had to be handled a little more roughly — with hooks and so on — and then she became aggressive. When you are spoilt as a child and from one day to another you suddenly realise everybody who spoilt you has now started to knock you down and beat you, then it comes as a big shock. And then of course you react. And there are some keepers in the circus who like to show their authority so that every morning they beat the elephants — there are these traditions in the circus."

Chris Krenger, however, denies that Knie's training and dressage is in any way cruel or degrading to the animals: "They like it, it's good for them, and they live much longer than in the wild. Elephants in the wild, for example, hardly ever reach the age of 20 because they suffer from hunger and disease, they die because there is not enough water, they have accidents and there is no vet who can treat them. But in the circus, elephants easily reach 60 years old." So for Krenger it seems, the elephant's own preference must be obvious: a life of 60 years in chains against only 20 years in the wild. How strange that we humans must even impose upon the wild animal our own atavistic prejudices against nature, and convince ourselves that even for the elephant, human civilisation must be infinitely more preferable. Similar sentiments to those voiced by Krenger are also echoed by Emil Smith, describing the benefits enjoyed by his captive bred wild cats: "No freedom, no suffer. A blind man born blind won't suffer half as much as a man who has a car accident and becomes blind all of a sudden. So they enjoy it here, you can see they're happy animals with an interest in life."

The Endless Journey

Confined to its beast wagon, the exotic circus animal must somehow learn to cope with the ordeal of being carted around from country to country by ship, plane, train and truck. In 1986, for example, it was disclosed that three Chipperfield elephants had been chained in a dark crate in the hold of a ship for three months, while on a problem-plagued 40,000 km journey around the world. Eighty-two-year old patriarch of the circus family,

Dickie Chipperfield, insisting that "we love our elephants," blamed the incident on a "paperwork mix-up"; RSPCA wildlife officer Stefan Ormrod, on the other hand, declared that circus animals forced to endure such conditions were "better off dead". The elephants, Camilla, Leila and Mina, were being shipped by Chipperfield to the Far East for a set of performances in Hong Kong and Taiwan, and it was here that they were refused entry by port authorities. According to the RSPCA, while Chipperfield's vainly tried to have their paperwork ironed out, the elephants were stored on a barge in the steamy harbour of Kao-Hsuing, still manacled in their metal container measuring just 12 x 2.4 x 2.7 metres. Here, in the stifling humidity, with temperatures soaring to over 30 degrees C, the three luckless elephants were destined to spend two months. The animals were then moved to Hong Kong where they were also refused entry, finally obliging Chipperfield's to return to the UK to sort out the tangle of red tape. Upon arrival at Southampton, an inspector from the port health authority found the container to be so badly damaged by the frenzied kicking of the elephants that it was not even roadworthy. Also returning, in a container with seven compartments, were a black bear, four polar bears, two tiger cubs and four lion cubs, one of which was found to be paralysed and was declared physically unfit to have made the 24-day voyage from Hong Kong.

But billed to appear at a circus at Hong Kong's Ocean Park — together with a boxing kangaroo, eighteen lions, performing pigs dressed as racehorses and a troupe of monkeys in jockey costumes — even then the ordeal of Chipperfield's three elephants had not yet come to an end. With fresh entry permits and a new container, they set off once again on their arduous journey back to Hong Kong, completing what was described by the press as a "25,000 mile Voyage of Hell".

Revealing just how the law countenances such abuse, only the most flimsy legal action could be levelled against Chipperfield's for the three-month nightmare that their elephants had to endure — " overcrowding" is an offence under the Transportation of Animals Act of 1973. Indeed, the most serious charges that could be brought against the circus related to the allegedly illegal import of animals into the UK and to the distress caused by the long journey to the paralysed lion cub. At the end of the five-day hearing in January 1989, Chipperfield's were fined just £1000 by city magistrates in Southampton for transporting the sickly animal in an overcrowded and unfit container. The six-month-old cub, the court heard, had died in quarantine three weeks after the traumatic journey, and had been discovered in the container suffering from a swollen foreleg, enlarged hocks, curvature of the hind legs and partial paralysis. Eleven charges of illegally importing polar bears, brown bears, two tigers and four lion cubs were not proven. Denying all 13 charges relating to the voyage, Dickie Chipperfield declared: "I would not have shipped the animals if I did not think that the container allowed space enough." But a court trying the shippers, P & O, disagreed. Magistrates in Southampton fined P & O and its captain P. J. Clark a total of £1000 for failing to ensure that the animals would not be caused injury or unnecessary suffering.

Predictably, such insignificant penalties do little or nothing to improve standards of animal welfare, even with previous offenders. Due to another wrangle over import papers and unpaid bills, seventeen Chipperfield lions and tigers were left practically deserted in two rusty and dilapidated trailers at the end of the circus's New Zealand tour in 1988. The tour was cut short after poor ticket sales forced some shows to be cancelled. Problems then arose as the circus was preparing to leave for Indonesia. The necessary import permits for the eight tigers and nine lions had not been received, and further delays ensued when the circus was accused of still owing money for previous transportation costs. Consequently, these animals were for some three months confined to their beast wagons — part of the time on a car park — unable to be exercised due to quarantine regulations. According to a Ministry of Agriculture and Fisheries vet, the animals were crammed together in pitch darkness, lying in their own filth. One tigress, who had died after giving birth to twin cubs, had been partially eaten by the others.

Reward and Punishment

Citing the views of Dr Heini Hediger, the renowned zoologist who is commonly credited with being the "father of the scientific zoo", the RSPCA asserts that fear plays a central role in animal training and dressage: "Virtually all animals have distinctive flight motivations which may be measured by a quantitive value — the flight distance. If a potential enemy comes within the flight distance of an animal, it will attempt to flee. If confined and unable to retreat, the animal will cower, show 'fear' and issue a low intensity threat. If the intruder continues to approach, a critical distance is reached, at which the insecure, apparently cowering animal will attack. Thus the lion trainer's 'skill' is largely based on the ability to assess this critical distance." For those who know how to read animal behaviour, the RSPCA continues, this fear is apparent in almost every wild animal act. "Ear and tail movements, facial expressions, body postures and vocalisation provide a fairly accurate indication of the animal's experience. In the circus ring, the big cats frequently display these signals very clearly. They will often respond to the trainer's commands by slinking across the ring, belly close to the ground, ears flattened, sometimes snarling loudly. A clear indication of fear. Aggression is often the first response to fear, and a lion or tiger may be seen to paw threateningly at an outstretched whip. An audience may well misinterpret these aggressive approaches, and marvel all the more at the trainer's daring."

A tiger of the Swiss wildcat tamer Erich Leuzinger. (Matthias Schnellmann.)

Walking the tightrope; 'natural behaviour' of the tiger as seen in Circo Medrano. (Matthias Schnellmann.)

For the performing circus animal, food may also become the incentive for it to accomplish the desired dressage tricks of its trainer. A wild cat being trained to stand on its hind legs, for example, will generally be more cooperative if it is hungry and then coaxed into obeying its master with occasional pieces of meat. While such methods are often condemned as cruel and coercive, others maintain that food deprivation and reward keeps the animals active and healthy. Thomas Althaus: "If these animals were to be fed and watered all the time, they would not run around and do things. You see this in zoos or safari parks — where they have more space and food. They just stuff themselves and go to sleep again. So I think it's good to give them a little bit of exercise."

Though ever careful to distance himself from the other scandal-afflicted enterprises run by the Chipperfield clan, Jim Clubb insists that cruelty to animals is now a thing of the past. "It may have been common in the last century, but not any more. To get the best out of an animal you have to treat it with respect and today the vast majority of animal trainers realise that." The same view is echoed by Malcolm Clay, a Lancashire solicitor who is secretary of the Association of Circus Proprietors: "Circus animals are very expensive, much-loved creatures. Nobody in a well-run circus would dream of treating them with cruelty or neglect." But Fred Kurt is adamant that cruelty is still a way of life in many travelling animal shows. "Knie is very proud that its animal training is made during public visiting times to the menagerie," he points out, "but tell me why the training of young elephants is not to be seen by the public?" Yet the training of elephants calves in the circus ring has been witnessed by some independent observers, including the celebrated Swiss artist Hans Falk, who spent about twelve months travelling with Circus Knie between 1977 and 1979. With soulful compassion, Falk speaks of the animals which inspired him to draw and paint as he toured the country with Knie in his own circus caravan. "It was so very beautiful to see the power of the elephant — this great power and yet this quietness, this gentleness," he remembers. Recalling one of the first training sessions of the young African elephant Malayka, Falk says: "They were training her to do a kind of balancing act, walking over a wooden plank only about 50 centimetres off the ground. But the elephant refused to do it — she was afraid. After a while, the trainer and even Louis Knie lost their tempers and began to use a stick with a metal hook on the end, pushing and pulling her. They wanted to get the act ready in the shortest possible time but the elephant was just unable to do it. Then in this certain moment it became a little hell in the circus ring. The trainer beat the elephant on the legs until there was blood."

According to Fred Kurt, such brutality can be common in the training of wild animals in the circus. While hastening to affirm that he regards Knie as one of the finest circuses in Europe, he also adds, somewhat mor-

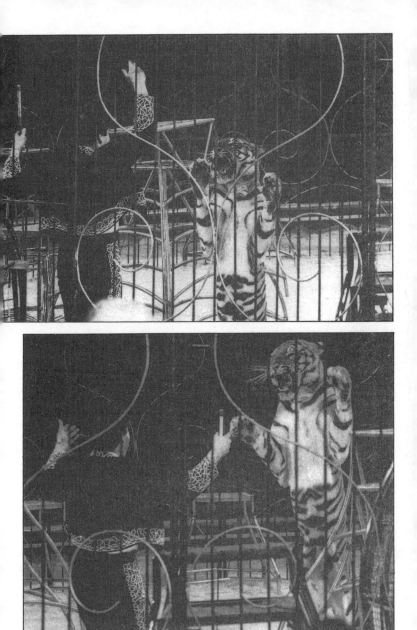

"The Peace of the Jungle" — Club Chipperfield's wildcat show at the International Circus Festival in Monte Carlo. (Matthias Schnellmann.)

dantly, that "the best of the worst doesn't have to be a good one." Today, he says, there are many circus trainers who equip themselves with sharpened sticks, screwdrivers or walking sticks with nails concealed in the crook and tip to control or prod the desired response from a stubborn animal. Unnoticed by the public, he adds, there are also circuses where electric shocks are used — a method that was even employed by Knie in the past: "The presenter of the act may have artificial flowers in his hand for instance, and these flowers are connected with two wires to a battery, hidden somewhere in his costume. In much the same way as pigs are driven into the slaughter house, this method may be used to make old elephants stand up on their hind legs when they are just too weak to do so. Even Knie recently sold elephants because their backs had become weak through overwork." Kurt asserts that elephants are physically unsuited for such strenuous dressage techniques. "A young elephant can be made to do these tricks," he says, "but as it grows older and heavier, you reach the point where their muscles can't take the strain of lifting the whole body weight any more. And even to train these little ones is a problem. There is a long-standing joke in the circus: 'You know how an elephant learns to stand on one leg? You just have to beat the other ones.'"

Recently, an article in the Italian magazine *Nuova Elettronica* revealed that the editorial staff's technical service had been approached to produce a "micro-electroshock" device to train circus animals, powered by a 9-volt battery. Declared the magazine: "We knew that among our readers there were students learning to become electronic engineers, company directors, radio hams and many others operating in different fields: doctors, office workers, photographers, musicians etc., but we could never have imagined that there would also be 'animal tamers'. And we would never have known, if one day the lion tamer of a circus which had just arrived in Bologna, had not come to us with several free tickets for the show in exchange for a 'project' which in his opinion only we could put into being.

What could an animal tamer want from us?

Simply a circuit to help to tame animals. We learnt that in order to make an animal perform a certain action, for instance lift the front legs, dance, lie down etc., the means used are rather rough and at times cruel. Every time an animal tamer utters a 'key word' some electrical discharges are transmitted to the stand on which the animal is standing and, whether the animal likes it or not, it has to lift its legs. After several attempts, the animal associates that painful feeling with certain words, with the snapping of the whip or with other actions and therefore it will have the same reaction even if there is no electric shock. Though we were not completely unaware of this, we felt emotionally involved when we came into direct contact with this, especially when we heard that this technique is not the most painful used by less scrupulous animal tamers."

Elephants performing hind leg stands in the arena. Such dressage techniques are depicted by the circuses as "natural behaviour" but according to elephant specialist Dr. Fred Kurt, the animals are physically unsuited to perform such strenuous tricks. (William Johnson.)

The white tigers of John Campolongo, Hawthorn Circus Corporation, USA. (William Johnson.)

Ironically, as international conservation treaties cut off the supply of Asian elephants, such cruelties may become more common, claims Kurt. Because of the ensuing scramble to obtain the few that are obtainable from plantations, some circuses are now having to resort to the African elephant which is weaker and less heavily built than its Asian cousin — and therefore even less adept at performing arduous dressage tricks such as forming pyramids and standing on their heads. Because of this, says Kurt, "there will be beatings of elephants even in the very best of circuses".

While some of the internationally renowned circuses may have suspended overt systematic cruelty such as delivering electric shocks to animals during training sessions, many circuses, under constant economic pressure to produce unique and ever more spectacular acts to the public, find themselves with no alternative but to use the stick or riding crop. "In many Italian circuses for instance," says Kurt, "even a casual visitor would be able to see the wounds of the elephants. Because one way to stop elephants or to make them run is to push a sharp stick between the nails. There the skin is usually not well maintained because the elephants can't bathe enough and can't rub and groom themselves, and there you can see the wounds. And of course, they are very sensitive there. Just imagine, always being given pain in the bed of your nails — it hurts tremendously." Dr Rolf Keller considers this kind of abuse virtually inevitable in the circus: "They use these pointed sticks even with sharp, knife-like edges — and I've heard that it's used regularly between the toes. I would say if you have to train elephants in a circus and have to be around elephants, you need some kind of pointed stick. They brought the method over from India — where it's used everywhere. But it's difficult to say whether it's a bad thing or not because that depends on how the stick is used. In Basle zoo we used sticks, not very sharp, but we never used them at the foot — never."

Despite the much-vaunted "soft dressage" techniques championed by Carl Hagenbeck which are themselves rooted in coercive mental control, even Fredy Knie Snr, patriarch of the Knie dynasty, states that "50 per cent of the dressage of horses today is criminal." Declares Nancy Burnet of the California-based Coalition to Protect Animals in Entertainment: "Animals in entertainment are treated second only to those used in research laboratories. The animals that endure the most abuse at the hands of the entertainment industry are probably elephants and primates. Elephants are hit with axe handles or beaten with sledgehammers — primates are beaten with axe handles or rubber hoses filled with sand or pebbles." She adds that it is not unusual for animals in the entertainment industry to be dyed, drugged, burned, beaten regularly and have their food withheld. An orang-utan, for example, was fatally beaten with an axe-handle while under training for the Hollywood movie *Every Which*

Way But Loose, starring Clint Eastwood. Similar cruelty was reported in 1988 by actor Howard Mann in the filming of a television commercial on behalf of a company producing suntan lotion. Mann was to act the role of Tarzan, while a performing chimpanzee called "Mister Kokomo" was chosen to play Cheetah. After spending all day outside gathering coconuts for dinner, Tarzan was to return home sun-burned and hence in dire need of lotion. The chimpanzee would then pick up the can and spray him on the back, as Tarzan declared, "Good Cheetah, make my day!" Mann reports that the chimpanzee was somewhat less than adept in acting out its pre-assigned role, spraying him first in the face and then on the chest. After three hours and 40 takes, the lotion was at last being directed at the right place on the Tarzan hulk, but in the process, the all-important brand-name was hidden from the camera. Having lost the last shreds of his temper, the unidentified trainer, screaming at the chimpanzee, dragged the animal out of sight behind some bushes. Mann then heard what he calls "a loud crashing whack and a series of heart-rending moans". Seeing the expressions of disgust on the faces of those present on the film lot when he returned with the anguished chimp, the trainer announced, according to Mann's recollection: "You gotta remember! These are animals. You can't be too nice to them. They don't understand that. You have to show who's boss, see?" The subdued chimp, Mann reported, finally got the scene right.

Occasionally, overt animal abuse may even be evident in the circus arena before a packed house, as I myself witnessed during a matinee performance of the *Circo Italiano* in Marseilles, in November 1988. From the very beginning of their performance, the circus's troupe of tigers seemed unusually nervous and disconcerted, displaying indifference to the commands of the *dompteur* who himself rapidly began to lose his composure seeing his well-rehearsed act disintegrate before the public. The final embarrassment came when one pedestal-sitting tiger decided to repay his tormentors in the audience by spraying them with a jet of urine, leaving some unfortunate mothers and children in the front row to frantically wipe their faces. Finally, consumed with rage, the trainer hurled a metal bar at one tiger, and overturned a pedestal on another.

III. JUSTICE UNDONE

"The time will come when public opinion will no longer tolerate amusements based on the mistreatment and killing of animals. The time will come, but when?"
— Albert Schweitzer

"No one here can play the missionary," declares Dr Thomas Althaus, in his official capacity as head of the Endangered Species Section at Switzerland's Federal Veterinary Office. Sadly, it is these few words which seem to sum up the attitude prevailing in similar government departments throughout Europe, departments which are vested with the profound responsibility of ensuring the welfare of circus animals. The basic creed of such bureaucrats, apparently, is: "Don't rock the boat, don't upset the status quo, but at the same time, beware of offending public sensibilities, bruised by recurrent disclosures of animal abuse in circuses." Small wonder then that such government officials often seem to use the letter of the law as an alibi for inaction, while studiously ignoring its ailing spirit.

It may of course be logical to assume, as so many government inspectors do in order to conceal their own complacency, that the welfare of these animals is assured simply because they are the "bread and butter" of the circus. Yet as elephant specialist Dr Fred Kurt points out, "while none of the circuses have an interest in killing their animals because there is a lot of time and money invested in them, this doesn't mean that systematic cruelty doesn't take place." Another problem, this time also confronting the most diligent of officials, is that legislation has conspicuously failed to keep abreast with society's changing attitudes towards conservation and its contemporary understanding of the needs, behaviour, sensitivity and social customs of wild species. The wilful or wanton infliction of pain, suffering, or death upon an animal or its neglect may be illegal in many countries throughout the world, but because cruelty of this kind is notoriously difficult to prove, such laws are seldom enforced. "To obtain a conviction under the Protection of Animals Act 1911," the RSPCA explains, "there is a need to prove substantial unnecessary suffering. But the law has not kept pace with changing attitudes. The practices involving the treatment of circus animals to which the Society has the strongest objections are, at the moment, perfectly legal."

While the use of animals in entertainment has already been banned or severely restricted in several countries, including Denmark, Sweden and Finland, in others, such as Italy, Spain and Portugal, laws relating to the welfare of circus animals are virtually non-existent. In Britain, there has been no change in the law for over 60 years, and there is little prospect of more stringent legislation in the foreseeable future. While the Labour Party manifesto in the last two years has included a pledge to phase out exotic animals in the circus, the Tories believe that existing legislation is perfectly adequate to ensure their well-being. Curiously, the government appears to put its faith in the Performing Animals (Regulations) Act of 1925, an archaic piece of legislation which requires circus exhibitors and animal tamers to be registered by County Councils, and which originally seems to have been designed with bureaucratic red tape rather than animal welfare in mind. Though the Act empowers council officials or police officers to enter circus premises at all "reasonable times" in order to inspect animal facilities, RSPCA inspectors do not have a similar statutory right of entry. And although circuses are subject to inspection by council veterinarians, there are few in the UK who possess the necessary knowledge and experience of wild exotic animals to be able to adequately interpret their nutritional needs, behaviour patterns and symptoms of stress. Though constrained by the inevitable limitations of the Act, growing public concern for the plight of circus animals has prompted other forms of action to be taken by local government. So far, as many as 120 local authorities in the UK have resolved not to lease sites under their control to circuses which contain animal acts.

Circuses in Britain are specifically excluded from the Zoo Licensing Act of 1981, even though the Act actually lays down only minimum standards of care and welfare for animals in captivity. This exemption appears to be based solely on economic considerations since there is not one travelling menagerie in the entire country that could ever hope to comply with its provisions. One requirement of the Zoo Licensing Act, for example, is that acceptable accommodation should be provided "in accordance with the needs of the species... to aid and encourage normal behaviour patterns." As those officials who formulated the Act must have realised, providing such accommodation in circus beast wagons that are designed to travel the roads would be an impossible feat. Indeed, should they ever be obliged to comply with zoo licensing regulations, the travelling menageries would be confronted by the Hobson's choice of either being forced out of business or continuing to keep the circus tradition alive without the help of captive wild animals. Though the time may well have come for precisely that ultimatum to be delivered, such a move is unlikely for a variety of reasons. To begin with, both circus and government departments alike defend the menagerie's cramped beast wagons on the grounds that the animals incarcerated within them receive regular exercise in the arena and subsequently require less space than zoo animals.

We have already seen the fallaciousness of this argument. Secondly, lobbying pressure on behalf of the European circuses is surprisingly potent. Wealthy and influential circus dynasties such as Chipperfield,

A tiger in its add-on 'enclosure' in Circus Krone. (Holger Vogt.)

Knie and Krone, the *Circus Proprietors Association*, the *Circus Fans Association* of England and America, the *Société du Club du Cirque* in France, the *Gesellschaft der Circusfreunde* in Germany and Austria, and the *Ente Nazionale Circi* in Italy, all continue to actively promote the myth of the performing animal as an inviolable centuries-old circus tradition. By judiciously raising the spectre of unemployment, economic hardship, and the needless aggravation of tens of thousands of ardent circus supporters, they have systematically fostered government reluctance to take measures to protect the rights of circus animals. And finally, governments seem habitually disinclined to solve any conservation or animal welfare problem by outright action that might cause economic upheaval.

If forced to act under such circumstances they prefer gradual "reform" rather than outright prohibition. All too often, the end result is a law that does little else but legitimise the crime — larger cages, for example, instead of no cages at all. In this respect, government inaction in Britain has been encouraged rather ingeniously by the self-policing efforts of the Circus Proprietors Association. Representing the ten largest circuses in the UK, the CPA claims that its "continually self-improving code of animal welfare" constitutes the highest possible standards for caging, stabling and transport. Its guidelines, revised in 1988 with the help of exotic animal vets David Taylor and Andrew Greenwood, call for larger exercise cages to be erected on site alongside the animals' sleeping quarters. Says Malcolm Clay, secretary of the CPA: "We are interested in raising standards, in even more regulation, not less. Proper exercise facilities for example: ideally elephants should have an exercise area possibly surrounded by low-voltage electric fencing as much to deter and protect inquisitive dogs as to keep the circus animals in." Yet the cages, even though slightly bigger, are still bare and the scope for "self-improvement" seems to be as limited as the dimensions of the beast wagon itself. Indeed, for as long as circuses are permitted to cart animals around the world for show, wild cats and bears will continue to be kept in cages small enough for transport, and elephants will still spend much of their lives chained to the ground. Moreover, although the guidelines prohibit menageries of non-performing animals, they can do nothing to alter fundamentally an environment characterised by the most squalid deprivation, not least of all the wild animal's continually frustrated natural instincts to play, roam and explore.

So inevitable is this deprivation, that pressure is mounting constantly for the central government to take firm legislative action to curb animal abuse in the circus. Speaking recently at a seminar organised by the Animal Welfare Foundation of the influential British Veterinary Association, the well-known radio and television broadcaster Johnny Morris declared: "Circuses should be banned from keeping certain animals because of the cruelty involved in their training and the conditions in which they are kept. There is little doubt that cruelty is involved in training circus animals, but the most disturbing aspect is clearly the way they are kept when not performing."

A similar inadequacy in the law exists in the United States. According to Alex Pacheco of People for the Ethical Treatment of Animals: "The Animal Welfare Act merely requires that the animals have enough space to stand up and turn around when confined, yet even these minimum regulations often are not enforced." This view is shared by Nancy Burnet of the Coalition to Protect Animals in Entertainment, a consortium of over 50 US animal welfare groups: "The laws are really meagre. Trainers seem to have carte blanche when it comes to animals. Beatings are actually considered acceptable training methods." Indeed, the law seems quite incapable of preventing even the most crass abuse of animals for the sake of dollars and sensation. In 1984, for example, Ringling Brothers' Greatest Show on Earth presented four goats with surgically implanted horns in the middle of their skulls. The Circus's publicity machine touted them as "living Unicorns".

For the past 50 years, declares Burnet, it has been the American Humane Association that has been solely entrusted with the responsibility of watching over animals in the entertainment industry. "The American Humane Association has failed miserably," she asserts. "No complaint of animal abuse has been filed in 20 years from the American Humane Association. The Coalition is seeking their removal as the purported protectors of animals in entertainment. American Humane cannot solve the problem of animal abuse in entertainment because, unfortunately, they are part of the problem. American Humane is more interested in protecting the producers and trainers than the animals." Indeed, according to the International Primate Protection League, at the three-day annual meeting of American Humane in 1984, one of the star attractions was a performing orang-utan dressed up in human clothing.

"In order to stop the rampant abuse of animals in the entertainment industry, standards and guidelines need to be set up which trainers must adhere to," Burnet insists. "Personally, I'm a total abolitionist. I'd rather not see any animal exploited by being used in the entertainment industry or under any circumstances. Unfortunately, our society is not ready for that right now." For the time being, the Coalition focuses its efforts on trying to convince the public to boycott any circus, film, or advertised product which involves animal abuse. "People who love and respect animals the most are often unknowingly financing this cruelty," explains Burnet, "and in this way, our ultimate goal is to take the profit out of animal abuse in the entertainment industry." Also seeking fundamental amendments to the Animal Welfare Act, the Coalition advocates statutory right of access to animal training sessions by independent inspectors, and wants trainers found guilty of abuse to be prohibited from working with animals.

In countries such as Italy, Spain, Portugal and Greece, animal welfare laws are still, to all intents and purposes, non-existent. Says Pier Lorenzo Florio, director of the Italian branch of TRAFFIC: "There are over 300 circuses in Italy, and only about eight or ten of these are considered 'first rate' like *Medrano* and *Togni*. Most of the others are much more primitive affairs, wandering from town to town with a couple of aged lions, gorillas or chimpanzees. Because they are poverty-stricken, their animals are bound to suffer continual deprivation, but we have no laws that can prevent it. As it is at the moment, a tiger could literally be kept in a box, or a dolphin in a bath tub. Although one minister submitted a bill to Parliament five or six years ago to outlaw exotic animals in circuses, because of the impending elections it was left sleeping and has never been revived." Florio goes on to note that Italy is also lacking any law to prevent private individuals from owning dangerous exotic animals as pets. "Keeping exotic pets such as wildcats is becoming very fashionable, especially around Palermo and Varese," he warns, adding that in Lombardy alone, "there are at least 50 lions and 20 tigers" in private households. "All told," he says, "there are perhaps 3000 wild animals kept as pets in Italy and in fact there's less paperwork in owning a tiger than an ordinary dog. There is even no law to prevent a private individual from taking a lion or tiger on a leash and walking it down the street." In 1988, he reports, a three-year-old girl was critically injured after being mauled by a leopard in a busy city street, and just two weeks later, in northern Italy, a sixty-year-old woman and a boy of eighteen were killed after being attacked by two rampaging lions.

With circuses habitually changing their animal shows and roaming around the country, it cannot be denied that the authorities throughout Europe and America face serious obstacles in enforcing even the most cursory of regulations pertaining to veterinary hygiene and public health and safety. In the Federal Republic of Germany, for example, local government vets are responsible for implementing such measures, but besides being ill-versed in the biology and behaviour of exotic animals, they are seldom even notified of a circus's arrival until the beast wagons have moved on to another district. Furthermore, it is reported that there are so many districts with local vets that even the federal authorities are not always aware of their existence. Says Achim Bollmann, circus specialist at the Hanover branch of the *Tierschutzbund*: "There are almost 100 small travelling circuses in Germany and because most of them are unable to sustain a living, many must resort either to begging in the streets with their animals or to petty crime. Only very rarely will their income from summer shows be enough to tide them over winter. Many of these people are illiterate and it's wrong that their burden of poverty should fall on the backs of the children and the animals. The efforts of our government offices are so poor that these circuses can often work without any form of control at all, even though they should be checked and given a permit by the veterinary authorities. Even when a case is brought against a circus for some kind of animal abuse, it is very difficult for a vet to justify his position before a court as there are no standards defined by the law."

Without doubt, Finland boasts the most progressive performing animals legislation in the world. Issued on 12 September 1986, a decision by the Ministry of Agriculture and Forestry stipulated that "monkeys, elephants, predatory animals, pinnipeds, rhinoceroses, hippopotami, wild ruminants, marsupials, raptorial birds, struthious birds, crocodilians and ungulates must not be used in circuses or other similar performances." Indeed, the only animals that may appear under the big top in Finland are dogs, domestic cats, sea-lions, ponies, tame horses and donkeys. Though Sweden's Animal Protection Ordinance, promulgated in June 1988, includes similar restrictions, under pressure from the circus lobby elephants have been exempted from the ruling. Travelling menageries, however, are explicitly forbidden under this ordinance. The Norwegian government has enacted similar measures. According to the Ministry of Agriculture's Veterinary Services Department, under "Section 15 of the Animal Welfare Act of 20 December 1974 there is a general ban on exhibiting animals in public. The Ministry of Agriculture may allow exemptions, but is very restrictive with regard to which species to use in circuses. It is not permitted to exhibit monkeys, other carnivores than domestic dogs and house cats, rhinoceroses, hippopotami, deers, kangaroos, birds of prey and other seals than sea-lions. We suppose that, from the welfare point of view, it is very difficult to keep exotic reptiles and amphibians in a circus, moving them from place to place, and permission is not given to exhibit such animals either."

The wide discrepancy in animal welfare legislation in Europe has prompted the *Eurogroup for Animal Welfare*, a coalition of organisations representing each of the 12 member states of the EEC, to seek the introduction of uniform minimum standards throughout the Community. One of their avowed priorities is to press for tighter legislative control of "animals in exhibition situations", a wide category covering not only zoos, dolphinaria and safari parks, but also circuses, films, television and advertising.

According to Eurogroup, the EEC bureaucracy already has every intention of introducing standardised regulations governing animal welfare, from farm animals to laboratory animals. Somewhere on the periphery, as a lost cul de sac of concern, will be those creatures who inhabit the travelling menageries. Because only "minimum standards" will be introduced, however, the law will almost certainly do little to alleviate the deprivation suffered by the circus animal. Indeed, if past performance is anything to go by, such standards will probably do little more than legitimise the industry, for while it is true that many of the smaller squalid circuses and menageries will at long last go to the wall, the more affluent and image-gifted impresarios will be able to bask in their new-found approval by officialdom.

When the powers that be in Brussels finally get around to drafting Community-wide regulations governing exotic animals in the circus, reviewers will almost certainly look to Switzerland which already has in place Europe's most comprehensive legislation based on "pragmatism" and "compromise", the *Schweizerische Tierschutzgesetz*, introduced in 1981. It is all the more important, then, to look at this law in detail, to discover its intentions, its merits, its flaws, and loopholes.

At the Mercy of the Law

Varying in size and sophistication, there are 14 circuses in Switzerland, seven of which keep animals. They range from top-of-the-line establishments such as Knie and Nock, to more down-at-heel enterprises like Olympia, Royal and Stey. But whatever imperfections or merits there are to individual circuses, there is little public scrutiny of what goes on behind their colourful facades. Despite the undeniable difficulties in keeping track of roaming menageries, my investigations have revealed glaring and inexplicable inadequacies — not least of all on the part of authorities which seem either unable or unwilling to apply even the letter of the law, let alone its spirit. Some of these deficiencies have been excused on the grounds that the law is still in its infancy, though critics assert that no amount of refining will be able to make much impact on its severe flaws and plug its gaping loopholes.

Asked whether the new law and its application can be considered satisfactory, ethologist Dr Rolf Keller replied: "No, certainly not. As is typical in Switzerland it's a compromise, and in this case a bad one. On one hand it shouldn't really be allowed to keep any animal in a circus — especially the ones which do not perform and are confined permanently to the menagerie cage. But on the other hand, there's the justification for display animals — that they receive adequate exercise through dressage and show performance." And indeed, like any Swiss compromise, this one too hinges not on any altruistic ideal, but on economic interests.

Under the terms of the Animal Protection Law — which also defines minimum cage dimensions — there is a clear distinction made between menagerie animals that are kept strictly for display, and those which are classified as "performing." Non-working animals in a travelling menagerie must thus be provided with the same sized cages that are applicable to any permanently sited zoo. In this respect, the law incorporates a two-stage period of adjustment to allow both circuses and zoos time to conform to its provisions. By the end of 1986, the law obliged them to have achieved 50 per cent of these space requirements, and by

1991 they must be in full compliance. For performing animals, however, the law is considerably less benevolent — ostensibly because their training routines and appearances in the arena help them to lead a healthier, more active life. This means, for example, that a pair of lions kept in a menagerie only for display would, by 1991, be entitled to a cage size of 24 square metres, plus an extra outside enclosure of 40 square metres. If they are performing, however, they must be content with a mere 5 square metres of living quarters and a 4 square metre exercise cage, though these are no more than "flexible guidelines". Only at the circus's winter quarters would the lions' cage size have to conform to zoo requirements of the law whether the animals are then "working" or not.

Paragraphs Made of Rubber

When it comes to defining a working or performing animal, however, the law is vague, providing a convenient loophole for circuses to exploit. Like a Chinese riddle, one might ask, "When is a non-performing animal a performing animal?" The answer apparently is when the circus management decides it to be so. A prime example of this loophole is the Knie rhinoceros, a friendly and docile creature originally wild-caught in Kenya, which, to all intents and purposes, was not performing during the 1987, 1988 and 1989 seasons. Did this mean that the small wagon and enclosure in which it was kept was illegal? Fred Kurt: "This is really a rubber paragraph. What does 'working' mean? The rhino may well be regarded as working if it's taken into the arena in the morning and then walked around for a little 'training'." Kurt goes on to say that he recently complained to the Federal Veterinary Office about the living conditions of the snakes and crocodiles appearing in Knie's 1989 programme. "These animals are kept in small boxes, and to me this was an obvious contravention of the minimum size ordinances. But Thomas Althaus replied that these animals were 'working' — revealing just what a rubber paragraph it is. Can you imagine — a *working* python?!" Apart from these reluctant show-business animals, adds Kurt, "there are also the animals starring in cabarets and nightclubs — and how they have to live! Really, I wouldn't like to know. Because most probably they're kept in boxes somewhere in a hotel room and in the evening taken out for ten minutes or so, and this all falls under the paragraph 'working animals'."

Dr Rolf Keller sheds further light on the apparent anomaly of the Knie rhinoceros, whose rights under the law have been drastically curtailed: "The rhino was performing — once. That was when it was in the arena with the tigers several years ago now." He then adds with a mordant laugh: "But it's difficult to say for how long it'll be regarded as a performing animal." Dr Thomas Althaus, for his part, insists on the rhino's legality: "It's not in the show but it's going into the arena and running about. Under the law, training — perhaps for the next year's programme

— naturally counts as performing."

While admitting that the Federal Veterinary Office would "like to put more pressure" on Switzerland's smaller and often less responsible circuses, Althaus defends Knie's compliance with the law as exemplary. He points to the circus' swift decision to sell its two pre-convention lowland gorillas which, up until 1986, had been the stars of its non-performing menagerie. "Even though Knie would have had until 1991 to adjust its gorilla wagons," he declares, "it just discarded the whole thing." Knie's decision however may have been dictated more through hard realities than pure altruism. As Chris Krenger, the press officer of Knie, readily admits, the new law meant that Knie "would have had to construct such a big enclosure that it would have been impossible to construct and to travel with." Furthermore, by 1991 Knie could well have faced difficulties in finding customers for its aging gorillas — one of which was captured in the wild as a baby. It was thus that the circus apparently jumped at the chance to sell them. "They are now in a very nice safari park at Woburn, near London, owned by the Chipperfield's," says Krenger — neglecting to mention that the various enterprises run by this famous circus family have been rocked by a series of animal welfare scandals over the years, including the terminal vivisection experiments on Woburn's tribe of rhesus monkeys.

But what other tangible effects has the law had upon the circuses of Switzerland? Knie, also known as the "Swiss National Circus", enjoys an impeccable reputation and exudes a professionalism and confidence which enables it to take criticism in its stride and to deflect it with ease, often utilising its financial might and its high-level political and media connections. It has dealt with the law's ramifications in the same way. Chris Krenger: "Knie is now in full compliance with the law. There is not another circus in Switzerland which does more for its animals." Krenger, however, remains doubtful that the law will have much impact on the smaller circuses. "In theory, once the new law comes fully into force, it should no longer be possible to abuse animals in the circus, but I'm sure that some circuses should not be allowed to keep animals at all because some of them just don't treat their animals correctly. But when they are inspected, they are often given the benefit of the doubt." It was significant perhaps, that Dominik Gasser, owner of Circus Olympia, declared: "We have always had a good standard of keeping animals and big cages, because we act according to the animals and not the law." Circus Stey: "The law has added a great burden, mainly of a financial kind. We need more animal keepers, more wagons, and it also means more work for us all." Ruth Buser, Circus Nock: "Our animal wagons had to be converted and now one thinks more carefully about what species are still acceptable to travel with. The public — though not because of the law — has generally become more sensitive towards animal protection. And yet despite the public concern which was reflected in the December 1978 vote in favour of the Animal Protection Law, circus animals are still regarded as private property, making it virtually impossible for independent observers to check on the fate of individual animals. In effect this means that for the public at least, records of animal purchases, sales, deaths and injuries are non-existent, and that a circus is even legally entitled to kill an animal which has lost its usefulness and which it is unable to sell. Moreover, the law provides no protection for excess or unwanted animals that may well end up in the most unscrupulous menageries abroad, so medieval in character that animals are regularly beaten and starved and live in nightmarish conditions.

Further complications are found in the practical application of the law whose responsibility rests exclusively with cantonal veterinary offices, often already overworked with agricultural animals. Fred Kurt: "In theory the law is quite strict on the sizes of cages for circus and zoo animals, but it doesn't say anything about the *quality* of these cages. Furthermore, the cantonal vets take no notice of the psychological defects of the animals — they have no experience, and no one cares if the animals are mad. Indeed, mad animals are often the best attraction. Bears and monkeys with stereotyped behaviour are considered as clowns, something absolutely funny."

In what is a common phenomenon throughout Europe, even the circus vet, says Kurt, has little or no understanding of such stereotyped behaviour. "These vets are not animal psychologists. Because many of them have never even seen a tiger or an elephant in the wild, these behavioural problems they just can't comprehend. It is the same for the animal trainer. For instance, ask Louis Knie, 'why are your tigers always walking on aluminium where they can hardly make a step without slipping?' And he'll reply, 'don't worry, tigers have always lived like this,' and for him they *have*."

Cantonal vets are also responsible for ensuring that accommodation provided for the menagerie animal conforms — at least superficially — to the unique behavioural needs of individual species. "But what can a cantonal vet possibly know of what a camel, a tiger or an elephant needs?" asks Kurt. "Even if he would like to find out, he would have no time to do so. He has to control everything from imported meat to milk and slaughter houses — and so a circus for him is something he goes to in the evening with his wife." Hans Huggel, professor of animal biology at Geneva University, and president of the *Ligue des Droits des Animaux*, agrees with that assertion. "The law is supposed to guarantee the welfare of these animals, something that it conspicuously fails to do. In our opinion, these animals are stressed by their confinement and psychologically deformed. Such sordid displays should be forbidden."

But of course, any law can only be as effective as its enforcing officers, and here, the Animal Protection Law leaves much to be desired. The looming 1991 deadline requiring full compliance with the law does not only seem to be a cause for complacency among the more down at heel circuses, but also, apparently, at the Federal Veterinary Office as well. "I always think it important to make the distinction between good and bad circuses," Dr Thomas Althaus told me. When I asked him to name just one "bad" circus, he told me that he was unable to do so because he had only visited two of them — Knie and Nock. It should be remembered that this was already 1987, nine years after the initiative was accepted by the public, six years after it had become law. At this time, Althaus, by his own admission, was attempting to locate the winter-quarters of Circus Olympia. Evidently several protests had been received regarding the standards in which the circus' two chimpanzees were being held, a 15-year old male, and a female aged 13. "We have already heard about these chimpanzees and are taking the necessary measures," Althaus told me. Although this could not include confiscation, he explained, "the cantonal authorities could refuse them a permit." But as we shall see later, it actually took the Federal Veterinary Office no less than three months to locate the circus' winter quarters, and even longer to intervene — not on behalf of the chimpanzees unfortunately, but merely to rectify "a technical breach of the law".

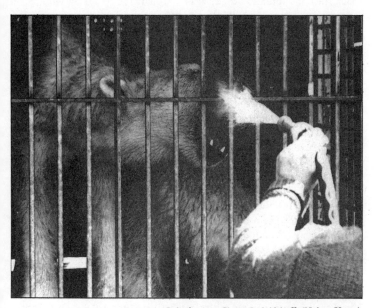

Polar bears at Circus Carl Althoff. (Holger Vogt.)

Spotlight on the Law

Endowed with official credibility, such attitudes may explain why the Animal Protection Law is today more likely to give the circus manager the benefit of the doubt rather than the animals themselves. This is perhaps nowhere more evident than at more primitive animal shows which teeter on the brink of illegality and exploit every loophole that the law has to offer, including its inefficiency. It is thus that, with apparent impunity, a tiger at Erich Leuzinger's wild cat show is confined to a box-like metal cage where it scarcely has sufficient room to stand up or the lions of Jerry Wegmann's *Raubtierschau*, an off-shoot of the Plättli-Zoo in Frauenfeld, so cramped that they literally sprawl over each other as they try to move. Sometimes, even to the casual visitor, the distress suffered by such animals is all too evident. At Circus Olympia for example, two chimpanzees were discovered inhabiting a hovel-like wagon spattered with filth, and displaying the manic behaviour of animals that have been driven to the verge of insanity. Indeed, the sordid conditions in which these chimps were kept, and the chronic confusion surrounding the circus' very legality, seems to spotlight a law that is not only tattered with loopholes, but that is both incoherent and dilettanteish in its application. The law stipulates that they must be provided with "climbing possibilities": an old car tyre hung on a chain from the roof of the cage. Allegedly performing animals, the law stipulates a cage size of 10 square metres for the chimps; at least one occasion in 1987 they were found to be inhabiting a cage of 6 square metres. The law also stipulates that when in their winter quarters, their cage must conform to zoo specifications, a total area of 20 square metres; at Olympia's winter quarters however, the animals simply remained in their beast wagon. Wearing thick chains, which Olympia's owner, Dominik Gasser, described as being no more bothersome to them than "necklaces", the chimps lay face-down in the soiled straw as though trying to hide or escape from their misery; they sat huddled together in one corner of the wagon, rocking aimlessly to and fro, their eyes either blank and expressionless or rolling grotesquely. One of them, its neck and hands bearing mysterious wounds, gnawed repeatedly at the metal bars.

For circuses to obtain a valid permit — which must be renewed annually before the commencement of the touring season — they must first be checked at their winter quarters by a cantonal vet to ensure that their animal facilities conform to the law. In Olympia's case there seemed to be only one snag; although registered in Derendingen in the canton of Solothurn, its winter quarters were nowhere to be found.

While the circus was on tour during 1987, the cantonal veterinary office of Geneva discovered that the chimpanzees were not performing and were therefore being held in illegally small cages. "We told them that the cage size must comply with the law," says cantonal vet Dr Bernhard Walker, who has the reputation of insisting on the strictest control of circus menageries. "If chimpanzees are working in the circus arena," Walker told me, "the conditions of the law are less strict. But because these animals were only kept in their cage, we demanded that the size conform to the law. My philosophy is that animals from nature do not exist to be put in the circus. The Swiss law allows it, but if the law's conditions are not observed then I am not satisfied." Because Olympia originated from another canton, however, there was little Walker could do except report the incident to the federal authorities. "Mr Althaus knows about this," Dr Walker insisted, "so why doesn't he collaborate with the veterinary service where Olympia has its winter quarters? He has to do it."

Back in Berne however, Dr Althaus, who by this time had managed to locate Olympia's winter quarters in Bassecourt in the canton of Jura, declared that he had "no idea" whether Olympia's chimpanzees were working or not and was therefore unable to judge their legality. Asked why the circus had left Derendingen, Althaus replied: "I think they have never been there. This was just a contact address." It was in fact the local post office. And yet even several months later, the cantonal veterinary office of Solothurn still believed that Olympia was in Derendingen. By their own admission, they had provided their non-existent circus with permits "for at least two years", certifying the legality of its animal facilities by post. Upon hearing this news, a somewhat subdued Althaus confirmed that Solothurn had acted illegally. Even this, however, did not mark an end to the saga. According to the cantonal veterinary office of Jura, which described the whole problem as "a mess", the circus had been stationed at the village of Bassecourt for no longer than six months, and had received its last permit from the canton of Basel Land. This information had apparently been passed on to them by Dominik Gasser who claims that, prior to moving to Jura, Olympia had its winter quarters in the Basel district of Schweizerhalle "for over ten years". Dr Jean-Pierre Siegfried, cantonal vet of Basel Land declared however, that the last time he had inspected Olympia was "three years ago". In effect, this means that although based in Basel Land, Olympia was obtaining its convenient inspection-free permits from Solothurn. Althaus, however, doubted that this amounted to a deliberate evasion of the law, and seemed to infer that the Federal Veterinary Office was reluctant to help the chimpanzees: "We know of some chimpanzees which have been killed here in Switzerland because their owners did not have the necessary room or money. It's easy for some people to say that a circus has to make bigger cages or that circus animals have to disappear — they pass a sentence of death on these animals. That's the consequence. If you say for instance that Circus Olympia has to get rid of these chimpanzees, they'll kill them. They have no possibility of selling them to someone else."

And so here once again, image took precedence over substance, with the Federal Veterinary Office resorting only to token measures in order to rectify a "technical violation" of the animal welfare regulations. Althaus' superior at the Federal Veterinary Office, Dr Peter Dollinger, together with the cantonal vet, visited Olympia on 9 March 1988 to inspect the circus and issue a valid permit to allow it to operate. But although the circus was refused permission to take the chimpanzees on tour, zoo conditions — which would have required an enclosure of 20 square metres — were not imposed. This second breach of the law was justified on the grounds that Dominik Gasser was in the process of building a menagerie and lunar park at his winter quarters, which, when complete, would provide the chimps with accommodation in full compliance with the law. Yet the ritual show-style mendacity and exaggeration that characterises the Gasser family apparently escaped the attention of the two vets, since at this time Olympia had not even been granted planning permission for its menagerie and amusement park. At the same time, responding to the threat of a scandal over the chimps' plight in the press, both the federal and cantonal authorities imposed an arbitrary information black-out. When I returned to Bassecourt, I discovered why. Although Althaus had assured me that the chimpanzees "would have to be given bigger cages," I found the animals confined to a smaller space than ever before, a section of a beast wagon measuring no more than 5 square metres.

Conflict of Interest?

Such methods of administering and applying the law do not surprise Prof. Hans Huggel, who accuses Dr Thomas Althaus of "gross conflict of interest". Althaus, he says, "is really the worst man for this job. He is actively portraying to the public that wild animals are happy in their captivity and tries to prove that the circus is an important tool in educating young people about nature. He is even paid by Knie in spite of his position at the Federal Veterinary Office where he is responsible for the protection of circus animals. We consider this to be entirely unethical." Althaus, however, rejects such criticisms: "It doesn't bother me at all because I consider people that are working against the keeping of zoo and circus animals to be people that do not know what they are talking about. This Prof. Huggel for instance is a so-called biology professor, but if you look closer you see that these people are dealing with cells and enzymes and biochemical experiments — they have no idea of the lives of animals as a whole. To me, experts of whole animals are people who are working with whole animals — people in the zoos for instance or circus trainers." Defending his relationship with Knie — which includes weekend lectures on animal training under the big top — Althaus says: "When I work with Knie on a Saturday I get only 200 Sfr. as paid expenses — including travel."

IV. THE INTERNATIONAL DOLPHIN DEALERS

"One of the most typical — not to say reprehensible — examples of man's continued ignorance as regards the keeping of animals in captivity is the latest trend towards keeping cetacea in oceanaria or dolphinaria to train them, an activity which became fashionable in the 1940s. In essence this is no different from the old attempts to satisfy man's curiosity by means of performing animals in miserable travelling circuses or showmen with their pitiful dancing bear acts."
— Professor Giorgio Pilleri

A strong and often mystical bond of friendship has existed between human and dolphin since the dawn of civilisation. In ancient Greece, the killing of a dolphin was regarded as a sacrilege against the gods to be punished with death. The human-dolphin empathy upon which this edict was based was rooted partly in spiritual intuition and an appreciation of the creature's profound intelligence and compassion. But it also reflected an uncanny recognition of biological kinship. Not only had Aristotle correctly classified them as mammals, but it was widely believed that these "marine cousins" of humanity had once lived upon dry land, together with the earliest ancestors of man and woman. "Diviner than the dolphin is nothing yet created," the poet Oppian wrote in *Halietica*, 1800 years ago. "They exchanged the land for the sea and put on the form of fishes." In a similarly glowing tribute, the philosopher Plutarch declared that dolphins are the only creatures who seek friendship for purely altruistic reasons, without any thought of personal gain. Greek civilisation's luminous legends, frescoes and mosaics often depicted the animals rescuing shipwrecked sailors, or portrayed children riding on the backs of wild dolphins. But perhaps the greatest human homage to the dolphin is the legend surrounding the Delphic Oracle. Here, where the forces of the universe converged at the centre or navel of the Mother Earth, the benevolent dolphin god Apollo Delphinos became the interpreter between his father, Zeus, and a wayward humanity.

But while the ancient Greeks venerated the dolphin, the Romans simply butchered the animals and ate them. These extremes of relationship are much in evidence to this very day. Stories of dolphins befriending humans and playing with children, or saving bathers by fighting off shark attacks are still heard frequently, but they are usually eclipsed by distinctly macabre reports of dolphins being slaughtered by angry fishermen. A scapegoat for our own species' greed in fishing the oceans to exhaustion, in many parts of the world they are despised as "gangsters" or "thieves" because they damage nets and dare to eat fish that "belong" to human beings. For many years the governments of France, Greece and Japan even paid a bounty for the head of every dead dolphin that was brought in, simply because the animal was regarded as being in unfair competition with the fishing industry. Elsewhere, dolphins suffocate as they become trapped or entangled in fishing nets, or are maimed and mutilated by heavy machinery as the nets are winched on board. In the eastern tropical Pacific tuna fishing industry, which has claimed the lives of almost seven million dolphins since 1959, at least 125,000 individuals continue to be slaughtered every year with no justification apart from an all too respectable ambition to maximise profits.

Perhaps it would be logical to surmise from all of this that the ancient friendship between our respective species is no longer reciprocal. But that conclusion would be hotly disputed by the world's dolphinaria, who like to pretend that their dolphins have been rescued from a terrible fate in the wild. And indeed, judging by the numbers of dolphins in circuses, zoos and amusement parks around the world today, one might well assume that humanity's fascination for the intelligence, compassion and playful humour of these creatures has not diminished. But can this really be the same sincere and time-honoured friendship between distant cousins? Or is it the kitsch and cuddly illusion of Disneyland, a commercial dream-machine through which the dolphins are processed to feed an industry's dementedly-ringing cash register and an insatiable human craving for distraction and entertainment; stripped of their natural identity, deprived of their own culture and environment, and subjected to a purgatory sometimes no less brutal than their slaughter in the wild?

The Secret Trade

The Swiss-owned International Dolphin Show (IDS), a "postbox company" registered in Liechtenstein, is just one of many enterprises involved in the multi-million dollar industry of dolphin capture, sale and lease. The workings of this industry are shrouded in secrecy, partly because the exploitation of dolphins in circuses and amusement parks depends upon the public's belief that the animals are happy in their captivity. Despite a wealth of evidence to the contrary, this is an illusion carefully nurtured by the industry's public relations experts. Of the thirty-two species of dolphin scattered throughout the world's oceans, it is the Atlantic bottlenose, *Tursiops truncatus*, which is able to survive captivity the longest. But it must certainly be an added bonus to the owners that the bottlenose has that distinctive upward-curving mouth, giving an often deceptive impression to the public that the animal is smiling. The pain and misery, and the depressingly recurrent deaths of dolphins in captivity, are systematically shielded from the public eye in order to preserve the vast profits spawned by that illusion.

The commercial competition in the international dolphin industry is intense, with the United States leading the world by providing 9000 full-time jobs and an annual budget estimated to be in the region of a third of a billion dollars. According to the American Association of Zoological Parks and Aquaria (AAZPA) there were 1135 marine mammals in captivity in the USA in 1975, and of these, 359 were cetacea. This relatively small number supposedly "provided educational displays" for over 130 million visitors or 114,537 visitors per animal per year. By 1983, that number had risen to 1341 sea mammals representing 27 different species.

Between 1938 and 1980, the USA took a minimum of 1500 live dolphins from the sea, and in the last ten years, Japan alone has captured 500 dolphins for various amusement parks. Altogether, it is speculated that at least 2700 bottlenose dolphins have been taken worldwide, though according to the International Whaling Commission, 4500 small toothed whales are known to have been kept in captivity. These include 300 Pacific striped dolphins, 250 short-finned pilot whales, 150 spotted dolphins, 120 killer whales, 100 white whales, spinner dolphins, common dolphins, and finless porpoises, over 80 harbour porpoises, and limited numbers of at least another 20 species. But these statistics are grossly deceptive; they do not take into consideration the official apathy which reigned during the 1960s and 1970s when record-keeping was either inept or non-existent, nor do they even speculate on numerous illegal dolphin catching operations. More importantly, they do not take into account the slaughter which so often accompanies the dolphin catch. This "wastage" — as traders euphemistically refer to dolphins fatally maimed during capture — can sometimes exceed 50 per cent, including pregnant mothers and nursing calves. It is here, in the brutal capture of dolphins in the wild, that the industry's tacit conspiracy to beguile the public is most evident. The International Dolphin Show, for example, owned by the Swiss entrepreneur Bruno Lienhardt, has been specialising in the capture of dolphins for 18 years, mainly in Mexico, Guatemala and Taiwan. As we shall discover later, Lienhardt's catches off Taiwan's Penghu Islands in 1980 resulted in the deaths of sixty dolphins, without so much as a murmur from the authorities or the dolphinarium-owners' lobbying organisation, the European Association of Aquatic Mammals. Similar catching operations are conducted regularly by enterprises in numerous countries, from Japan to Mexico, from Iceland to Thailand, the Philippines and Indonesia. It is merely the law of supply and demand, for as dolphins inevitably die off in their cramped pools, it is just as inevitable that they will have to be replaced.

Those dolphins that survive capture then have to undergo the terrifying ordeal of transportation which often claims more lives. The animals are usually transported in an aluminium or wooden crate, on an irrigated stretcher suspended with belts to give some protection to their vital organs which become all the more vunerable once the animal is taken out of its natural weightless environment. This stretcher, when bound up with tape, can also become a "strait-jacket" for dolphins which are liable to panic, while valium, a sedative, is often used in an attempt to calm the animals. Those that manage to survive transportation are then consigned to their new habitat, perhaps a zoo, dolphinarium, circus or travelling show. According to statistics provided by the UN's Food and Agricultural Organisation (FAO), dolphins in the wild can live up to 30 years, but their average life expectancy in captivity is a mere 5.3 years. Though longevity may have improved in some institutions over the years, conditions vary a great deal, with travelling shows offering such primitive facilities that the dolphins may live no longer than a season or two — but long enough for the owners to make a substantial profit on their investment.

"The Inherent Contradiction"

It was a 1983 report by cetacean specialist Professor Giorgio Pilleri, director of the Brain Anatomy Institute of the University of Berne, Switzerland, which embroiled the world's dolphin industry in an international controversy. In Volume XV of his *Investigations on Cetacea*, Pilleri concluded: "Whatever efforts are deployed, the keeping of cetaceans in captivity will always pose problems because of the inherent contradiction on which it is based: the keeping in cramped conditions of creatures which are accustomed to vast open spaces." But Pilleri shies away from the unexpected attention which the publication of the report has brought him. A mild-mannered man in his sixties, Pilleri seems more like the archetypal absent-minded professor than someone intent upon stigmatising a lucrative international business. His twenty-year study of dolphin behaviour and intelligence — both in captivity and the wild — earned him worldwide respect in the scientific community, but he was soon to renounce both the vivisectionist methods which researchers often use to probe the mysteries of the dolphin mind, and the conditions in which the animals are held in captivity. "It is true that I kept dolphins here at the Institute," Professor Pilleri told me. "I feel ashamed at having done so. I feel ashamed for my lost dolphins. They were a rare river-living species from Pakistan, known as *Platanista* dolphins, unique in that they are almost blind and live in a totally turbid medium. They were nothing more than an alibi for scientific research since keeping dolphins in artificial conditions can do little else than produce artificial scientific results. Four of my dolphins died — three from skin disease caused by chlorine in the water and from consuming fish polluted with mercury and parasites, and one which died after breaking its beak." But although he feels anguish for the dolphins he lost, Pilleri is also adamant that his efforts eventually brought lasting protection for the river dolphins in Pakistan when a national park was established with the help of the World Wildlife Fund.

"Dolphins are usually netted by local fishermen," explains Pilleri, "who tend either to be poverty-stricken and in desperate need of some extra income or else they regard the dolphins as pests and are keen enough to be rid of them." However much care is taken, and whatever the precautions, he continues, deaths are almost inevitable. "I remember that in Assam when the fishermen tried to capture the *Platanista* river dolphins, on one occasion, all six died in the net, including three pregnant females. But for the industry this is by no means exceptional. After capture comes the ordeal of transportation, with the stress involved causing all manner of illnesses to break out because stress has the effect of suppressing the immune system. Noise — especially high frequency — is very distressing to the animals. Many are likely to become sick or die during transport, particularly if the distances covered are great."

Dr Petra Deimer, a delegate on behalf of Germany to the International Whaling Commission, and an officially-appointed cetacean expert for the Scientific Authority of CITES, came to the same conclusion when investigating the capture of rare black and white Commerson or *Jacobita* dolphins found only in the waters of Patagonia. Between 1978 and 1983, she relates, 24 *Cephalorhynchus commersoni* were supposedly caught in Argentinian waters for dolphinaria abroad. Eleven of those were intended for Duisburg Zoo — though its director, Wolfgang Gewalt, claims the figure was only eight — and four destined for a dolphinarium in Japan. The fate of the nine missing dolphins was to become yet another enigma in the industry's long history of contempt for accountability, and Deimer speculates that they might well have died during capture. "Of the eleven — or eight — dolphins destined for Germany, only two males survived," she told me. "The four animals — one male and three females – intended for Japan never reached their destination. They were confiscated during a stopover in New York because of illegal importation into the USA — they had no permits. One female was already dead on arrival. The other three were brought to the Mystic Marinelife Aquarium in Mystic, Connecticut, where a second female died after four and a half hours. The male died after eight days. The autopsy revealed pneumonia, gastroenteritis, gastric ulcers and pancreatic fibrosis. The fourth animal — a female — suffered a chronic curvature of the spine; she died in July 1981 because of 'multiple complications'." Prior to her death, the crippled animal was only able to swim with its flippers, and Deimer cites evidence to suggest that this was a result of the dolphin being injured in its shipping crate. She also notes that the male Commerson which had managed to survive for just eight days at Mystic, displayed typical captivity neurosis from the moment it was put in the pool: "Within minutes the male began to dash about erratically, hitting the walls of the tank, until it was treated with Diazepam," a sedative.

Dolphin circuses, like their counterparts under the big top, like to portray their animals as well-adjusted beings displaying nothing but the most natural of behaviour. But in reality, little could be more *unnatural* than a captive dolphin, if only because from the moment of capture, every single individual must be kept afloat by injections of synthetic vitamins, broad spectrum antibiotics, fungicides and hormones. Without them, they would live no longer than a few days, succumbing to infections and malignant parasites as stress ravages their natural immunity. Indeed, once captured and confined, most dolphins will never again escape their nightmare world of stress, insecurity and neurosis except through the merciful release of death. Apart from the devastating trauma of capture, there is the inherent stress of confinement itself, which reduces highly-evolved dolphin society into a primitive pecking order, with the stronger and more aggressive animals not only fighting each other for supremacy but also hounding the weaker ones into submission, illness or death. Besides the tyranny of their own companions, there is also the tyranny of the show-master, the stress of performing to the crowds five times a day, and rigourous training methods of food deprivation and reward which can only incite further stress and jealousy among the captives. Indeed, recent studies in the United States suggest that an inordinate number of captive dolphins are succumbing to typical stress-related illnesses such as heart attacks and gastric ulcers. It can hardly be sheer coincidence that virtually identical disorders affect millions of human beings forced to endure tedious and repetitive menial work.

Yet it is not only aggression that manifests itself with this extreme and artificially incited social hierarchy. According to some cetacean scientists, including Giorgio Pilleri, aggression may just be one symptom among many in a fundamental desocialisation of the animals, a mortifying indictment of dolphinarium culture since the Jekyll and Hyde character-change which can so often afflict the captive dolphin must, to some degree, reflect the human influence which provoked that metamorphosis. While in the wild the dolphins hunt co-operatively in schools, herding the fish and sharing, in captivity they have been observed to display acute selfishness, even sadism. In an oceanarium in Florida, for example, it was observed how several bottlenose dolphins persistently chased away one of their ailing companions to prevent it feeding, even going so far as to pull the fish out of the dolphin's mouth. This antisocial behaviour continued even after the "thieves" had gorged themselves to excess. Such constant intimidation inevitably causes debilitating stress since the victim simply has nowhere to hide. Physical aggression has also been witnessed regularly *between* species held in close confinement, including instances of bottlenose dolphins attacking Risso's dolphins, spotted dolphins, common dolphins, pilot whales and pigmy sperm whales. Similarly, a false killer whale was reported to have set about and killed a young pilot whale, while at another establishment an Amazon river dolphin killed a smaller Amazon *Sotalia*. Sometimes, the much touted "natural behaviour" of unnaturally mixed species can be even more macabre. In one American oceanarium, a demented female dolphin was observed pushing her stillborn baby around the pool, perhaps out of some pitifully futile effort to breathe life into it. This compulsive grieving continued until a male pilot whale took the little corpse away from her, held it between its teeth for half an hour and then swallowed it.

Another much-neglected source of tension and anxiety which haunts the captive dolphin is incessant noise pollution, something to which the animals are particularly susceptible. From the constant racket of filtration pumps to the rhythmic booming of rock music, vibration and echoes are conducted so efficiently through the steel or concrete pool structures that dolphins may suffer almost permanent distress. By pretending that the problem isn't there, most dolphinaria hope that it will just go away. Petra Deimer reports that the respected Dr Klaus Hagenbeck of Hamburg Zoo, following consultation with the world's pre-eminent dolphin vet David Taylor, came to the conclusion that "there are noises in the sea as well." But perhaps not the constant, inescapable drone that can evidently turn some animals insane. The reasons for this extreme sensitivity become more apparent when one realises that the dolphins live more by sound than any other faculty. Scientific experiments over the years have revealed that the dolphins' ability to "see" underwater utilising high-frequency sound is so advanced that it is at least ten times more effective than any sonar system yet devised by the US military. Some researchers also believe that the dolphins' use of sound might enable them to look into the minds of their companions, to detect emotions and even thoughts. Dolphin communication, writes Carl Sagan in *The Dragons of Eden*, may involve "a re-creation of the sonar reflection characteristics of the objects being described. In this view a dolphin does not 'say' a single word for shark, but rather transmits a set of clicks corresponding to the audio reflection spectrum it would obtain on irradiating a shark with sound waves in the dolphin's sonar mode. The basic form of dolphin/dolphin communication in this view would be a sort of aural onomatopoeia, a drawing of audio frequency pictures — in this case caricatures of a shark. We could well imagine the extension of such a language from concrete to abstract ideas..." As we shall discover later, this sophisticated natural sonar system is one reason why both the American and Russian navies have invested heavily in dolphin research, though the animals have proved their worth to military minds not only in the improvement of radar and sonar — they have also been trained as "living torpedoes".

Other hazards that the captive animal must face include ingesting toxic paint applied to the pool liner, as well as an astounding variety of foreign objects apparently tossed frequently into the pool by visitors, from camera cases to gloves. At the shallow "Petting Pool" of Florida's Sea World, visitors both young and old are actually encouraged to feed dolphins with fish purchased at a nearby kiosk. Being confined to the pool, and unable to escape the attentions of the clamorous human visitors, the dolphins soon become consumed by boredom and relapse into expedient begging behaviour. Yet in the stomachs of the animals, not only fish is found, but also coins, hats and tennis balls, the kind of objects that regularly prove fatal to dolphins in oceanaria all over the world.

Counting the Dead

Often, not even drugs can keep a dolphin afloat for long, a fact attested to by the rudimentary mortality statistics that somehow manage to escape the industry's systematic policy of camouflage and secrecy. Notwithstanding this subterfuge, Professor Pilleri's controversial report, *Cetaceans in Captivity*, provided a rare insight into the death rates that plague the world's dolphinaria. Of the 21 dolphins transported to Europe in 1977, he revealed, 18 died within a year, while the 17 dolphins that were imported during 1979 had all perished by Christmas. The report concluded that the bottlenose dolphin has a 50 per cent mortality rate after 24 months of captivity, while the more sensitive common dolphin is cursed with an almost 99 per cent death rate over the same period of time. In Switzerland from 1975 to 1982, the report divulged, 19 dolphins and one orca whale were imported, of which six died and six were re-exported, including the orca which was sold off to an amusement park in Argentina. This gives a death rate of 30 per cent, but does not include those which may have died after being re-exported, nor those killed during capture. Similarly, in the space of one year (1976), infection caused the deaths of 24 dolphins in European and South African dolphinaria. Statistics from the USA were similar and also showed a 40 per cent death rate at capture. In New Zealand, Napier Marineland admitted that their death tally in 12 years of operation (1956-1968) stood at 68 animals, not including those killed or maimed during capture. The mortality rates affecting killer whales were similarly gruesome. Between 1962 and 1973, 50 orcas were caught for oceanaria in the USA and Canada, not including 12 that died in capture. After two years in captivity, the death rate amounted to 25 per cent in immature whales and 87 per cent in adults.

Though the industry has consistently refuted Pilleri's statistics, similar figures from other sources are just as bleak. According to the Russian cetologist Awenir G. Tomilin, out of 118 dolphins of nine species being kept at the oceanarium of Enoshima, Japan, between 1957 and 1965, 118 died, including 18 which had swallowed foreign objects. Similarly, as Dr

Susan-Jane Owen revealed in her 1984 report for Greenpeace, between 1972-1982 Japan captured 647 dolphins for 27 aquaria, of which only 293 still survived. In Indonesia (1975-1983) the mortality rate stood at 39 per cent and in Hong Kong (1974-1982) 96 per cent for the subspecies *Tursiops gilli*. At Hong Kong's Ocean Park, a total of 110 animals were captured between 1974-1982, of which 12 were released, 8 transferred and only 9 remained alive.

Appalling as these figures are, Professor Pilleri does not smother his own passionate feelings for dolphins with abstract statistics. "In the wild, dolphins are highly gregarious creatures and live in schools having a well-developed social structure — something which is entirely destroyed when they are brought into captivity," he told me. "They will assist a wounded companion by holding it up to the surface of the water and nurse it until it becomes well again. Certain members of the school will even act as mid-wives to assist the delivery of a calf. Can you imagine the utter heartless-ness of destroying such communities, the individual dolphins and their family members being killed and maimed during capture and transporta-tion? This is something that the business never cares to consider. They've created out of the dolphin a Walt Disney character, a perpetually smiling, happy and funny dolphin called Flipper. But 'Flipper' is not a dolphin, any more than 'Mickey Mouse' is a mouse."

The same cultural annihilation may be no different for the orca whale netted for display, nor for the dazed and dismembered families which are left behind in the sea in the wake of the capture expedition. Orcas live in "pods" which range in size from three to several dozen family members of varying ages. They swim at speeds approaching 55km per hour, are often regarded as being even more intelligent than the bottlenose dolphin, and are believed to be the only non-human mammals whose vocalisations have constantly changing regional "dialects". Also known as the killer whale because of its fearsome reputation as a ruthless hunter of seals, dolphins, porpoises and other whale species, it is nevertheless as gentle towards humans as its cousin, the bottlenose. Once in captivity the animal even becomes docile enough to peaceably share a pool with those species that were once its prey. But conversely, only in captivity, pushed beyond the limits of endurance, have they come close to killing humans. In the wild, male orcas might expect to live 50 years and females even 100. They are unlikely to live for more than ten years in captivity. Indeed, up until 1984, the average life-span of those orcas which had died in Britain was just two years and nine months.

> *"Some people contend that it is morally wrong to remove animals from the wild and hold them in captivity, either because they believe that some animals have evolved suffi-ciently to acquire rights equivalent to those recognised for*

> *human beings, or because they believe animals are severely*
> *harmed by life in captivity. These beliefs are not currently*
> *supported by sufficient scientific evidence. Consequently,*
> *they do not provide a factual basis for an overriding moral*
> *objection to displaying animals in captivity."*
— American Association of Zoological Parks and Aquaria

A Labyrinth of Mirrors

In the unlikely guise of a West Sussex fireman, former whale and dolphin trainer Doug Cartlidge has in recent years become the UK dolphin industry's most formidable and outspoken critic. His career began 20 years ago at Scarborough Marineland and Flamingo Park Zoo in Yorkshire. He went on to become head trainer at Windsor Safari Park in 1971 and Curator of Sea World Australia in 1974. It was at Windsor that his already gnawing doubts over the treatment of captive cetaceans at last came to a head and in 1976 he led a strike in protest against conditions. But it was a harrowing experience during a dolphin catch for Sea World Australia off the Great Barrier Reef that eventually prompted Cartlidge to quit the business for good.

"We caught three dolphins in our net and were bringing them in slowly," he recounts. "The first old one was too big for a show dolphin. The next one was scarred where sharks had had a go at it and was too big anyway, so they both went over the side. The next one was a beautiful six-footer and as clean as a whistle. 'We'll have this one,' we decided, and we started to pack up. Then I saw the two dolphins we had put over the net just sitting about 30ft away, looking at us. I don't know what it was but I just felt guilty. And then suddenly it hit me. I realised what we had was their two-year-old baby. All the way back to the main boat they followed us. I was near to tears. It was the way they were looking at me. They weren't sitting up in the water, they were just lying on their sides and watching with one eye out of the water." More than any other single factor, says Cartlidge, it was this experience which caused him to turn against the industry, and take his case to the public. "It is no crusade," he insists. "I can only publicise what is wrong in the industry until the public sees it's wrong. When that happens, at least two childless dolphins out in the Pacific Ocean will finally have made their point."

Ardent proponents of the industry like Professor Paul Schauenberger, a researcher at the Museum of Geneva, scorn such criticism as being anthropomorphic and emotionally-biased. "There are about 600 dolphins living in captivity today, which is only a negligible number" compared to wild populations, he maintains. Furthermore, he asserts, most dolphins originate from shallow coastal waters in the Gulf of Mexico where the depth of the sea rarely exceeds four or five metres, making the animals "naturally suited for adjustment to life in the aquarium." Conveniently,

One of the first priorities in taming the newly caught and delivered dolphin is to condition its attention away from the underwater environment to the 'open-air' environment of the stage, the trainer, the props and the audience. To expedite this subtle form of brain-washing, the animal — much to its initial reluctance and instinctive fear — is actively encouraged to wriggle out of the water and onto the stage. (Matthias Schnellmann.)

nothing is said of the spatial needs of the dolphin in other dimensions, nor of the comparative quality of the two environments. The reader may also notice that it is the dolphin that must adjust to the aquarium and not the other way round. This kind of thinking is typical of the industry and the particular brand of science which supports it. In the anthropocentric scheme of things, the individual is habitually subjugated to the species and because of this, animal rights are, by implication, either severely curtailed or non-existent. It might be more logical to assume that the wild population cannot be assured unless its individual members are also afforded some measure of protection. It is not so much a matter of numbers but of human attitudes towards creation in general. A consumerist, utilitarian outlook, even if restricted with quotas, can hardly be conducive to cultivating human respect for the Earth, let alone encouraging people to see themselves as an integral part of creation rather than an extraneous and dominant force over it.

What makes the dolphin show a unique attraction is precisely the very thing that reduces the industry to the role of slave-trader, for behind the frozen clown-like smile, the optical illusion of flippering happiness, there is the grotesque tragedy of a highly-perceptive and intelligent being incarcerated to provide humans with entertainment and profit. But how do the dolphin dealers themselves rate the intelligence of their animal possessions? On one hand, as part of the whole publicity charade, they capitalise on the mystical aura of these animals, such as Windsor Safari Park declaring in their advertising blurb: "You're bound to start wondering, 'Am I watching them? Or are they watching me?'" Such promotion implicitly conveys the impression that the dolphins are not only content in their captivity but are virtually there by choice. Another view is given by Mike Riddell, the hard-headed military-style director of Antibes Marineland who seems to regard the dolphin just as he would any other animal utilised by *homo sapiens*, declaring himself "fed-up to the back teeth with people who'd like to portray dolphins as super-intelligent extra-terrestrials visiting Earth from some enlightened civilisation." Others, less cynical, like Fredy Knie Snr, compare the dolphin's intelligence to that of a dog or ape.

But dolphins are not pets. They must work for a living, and if they refuse then in many cases they'll just go hungry. Indeed, it is an essential part of the Pavlovian conditioning regime that the dolphin must be kept sufficiently hungry in order to perform tricks at the command of the trainer. During show time, small morsels of food, judiciously controlled by the trainer, become the incentive and reinforcing stimulus for the animal to successfully accomplish each stunt. Any careful observer attending such a show will sometimes notice that a dolphin or sea-lion may not receive a reward after completing a certain trick. This, almost without exception, is because the stunt was not performed to the trainer's satisfaction — perhaps the jump not high enough, the response to a command too dilatory, or the exuberance of the animal just too impudent. As I learned from young dolphin trainer Rocky Colombo at Italy's Ocean World Aquarium, one of the first priorities in taming the newly caught and delivered dolphin is to condition its attention away from the under-water environment to the "open-air" environment of the stage, the trainer, the props and the audience. To expedite this subtle form of brain-washing, the animal — much to its initial reluctance and instinctive fear — is actively encouraged to wriggle out of the water and onto the stage. Hunger and the tempting reward of a fish dangling just out of reach helps the dolphin to weigh up the decision on whether to trust human orders or animal instinct. No doubt the unparalleled deprivation of its new under-water home also motivates the dolphin to take a greater interest in the "terrestrial world".

Conversely, perhaps this is why oceanaria consistently refuse to design pools which have some resemblance to the dolphin's multi-faceted under-sea environment. Although it is technically feasible, the dolphin would then have little inducement to escape its chronic boredom and sing "Happy Birthday" to the crowds. Deliberate punishment is also an integral part of the training regime, claims Doug Cartlidge: "The tricks are not performed because they enjoy doing them. First you find out how much they'll eat and still work. After that you condition the dolphin to associate certain hand signals with certain tricks that will result in the dolphin getting fish. You then find out if they are loners or prefer company because one of the punishments if they are not working properly is to lock them away on their own. You put them in a pen and ignore them. It's like psychological torture."

Yet the trainer also realises that being under constant stress, these are not exactly the peaceable, loving creatures that were once kidnapped from the sea. The animals show their anger by snapping their jaws, or speeding towards a swimming trainer as if to ram him, only veering away at the last moment. With a memory as long as the legendary elephant's, the dolphin will also bide its time before wreaking its vengeance for any blow or blatant injustice that it has suffered at the hands of the trainer. Conny Gasser's dolphin Flipper (No. 1) for example, having received a cuff from his nervous and overworked trainer while on tour in the Far East, waited several weeks until the ideal opportunity presented itself to take revenge. The moment came during a show in Indonesia as the trainer leaned precariously out over the pool for the spectacular climax where the dolphin would leap out of the water to gently snatch a fish dangling from his lips. Defying the training manual, Flipper burst out of the water, and, ignoring the fish, slammed the trainer in the head, rendering him unconscious.

Perhaps even more than the human prisoner, every single aspect of the dolphin's life is controlled by its keepers, from the administering of food

Killer whale show at Antibes Marineland, France. (Matthias Schnellmann.)

to the actual chemical composition of the environment in which the animal swims. Known as "synthetic sea-water", it is composed of H_2O, chlorine, salt and hydrochloric acid and, as many dolphins have discovered to their great cost, it is held at a vital and precarious balance. Says Pilleri: "Salt is expensive, particularly the large amounts needed to get the osmotic pressure identical to the natural habitat. What is usually achieved is little more than brackish water." Doug Cartlidge goes further: "If the zoo visitor were to see a chimp with its skin peeling off, a tiger with its eyes screwed tightly shut, an elephant with its whole body irritated by a chemical imbalance in its environment, how long would it be before something was done? Captive marine mammals endure all this as well as many more discomforts due to water problems. Unfortunately few visitors understand these problems."

But perhaps the deadliest of all for the dolphin is boredom. As "occupational therapy", dressage undoubtedly helps to relieve the stultifying monotony of their 24 hours a day locked in a concrete prison, but to pretend that the dolphins actually enjoy training and performing is rather like saying that the human prisoner enjoys the twice-daily half hour spent in the exercise yard. Three, four, five times a day the captive animals, in whatever dolphinarium one cares to look, are required to perform the same stale and frivolous routine. Says Switzerland's pre-eminent dolphin showman Conny Gasser: "One show a day would be too little — dolphins have to be moved. In the sea they would swim for kilometres when accompanying the ships on their journey."

"Dolphins in captivity have been *stolen* from the wild," Professor Pilleri insists. "It is nothing short of torture to take these animals — who are accustomed to the infinite beauty of the open seas, covering vast distances at speeds sometimes reaching 60km an hour — and then imprison them in tiny concrete or metal pools." The tedious uniformity of the captive dolphin's environment, he adds, is a universal trait of all dolphinaria, from the most sophisticated establishments in the USA, to the most menial travelling show. "In the sea the environment is multi-dimensional," explains Pilleri, "with interesting plants, animals and scenery. In the pool, there is literally nothing." It takes only a little insight, he suggests, to recognise that a dolphin held under such conditions must become psychologically deformed. Indeed, Pilleri believes that captivity, coupled with the destruction of the dolphin's sophisticated social structure, causes "profound psychological disturbance, and neurotic behaviour almost identical to that of humans when held in solitary confinement". These symptoms, he adds, "exacerbated by the utterly degrading tricks they are forced to perform in captivity," include loss of communication, despair and suicidal behaviour, and an unnatural aggression probably induced by feelings of intense claustrophobia. "Such disorders," Pilleri believes, "are not only apparent in the form of neurotic, compulsive acts

Land of make-believe:
Jon Kershaw with dolphin and
sea-lion before the backdrop of
a fairy tale village at Antibes
Marineland.
(William Johnson.)

symptomatic of stereotyped prison behaviour, but also in more subtle ways such as the refusal to reproduce."

Twenty years ago, the marine explorer and film-maker Jacques-Yves Cousteau came to roughly the same conclusion after seeing his own captive dolphins commit suicide. The animals, confined for study, quite simply hit their heads against the hard edge of the pool until they died. This prompted an anguished Cousteau to recommend that the animals be left in their natural environment: "The dolphin's life in a pool leads to a confusion of the entire sensory apparatus, which in turn causes in such a sensitive creature a derangement of mental balance and behaviour. Moreover an inner spiritual crisis is produced by the destruction of the social structure." Suicide, which has no relation to mass strandings of dolphins and whales, has never been witnessed in the wild, except as some individuals appear to panic and take their own lives during capture. Once in confinement, the animals may also attempt to starve themselves to death, so that force-feeding becomes necessary.

According to one of Pilleri's most controversial findings, once in captivity, cetaceans gradually begin to suffer from severe mutism, a phenomenon which manifests itself in the cessation of high-frequency echo-sounding for the purposes of orientation, and of two-way communication. As with other wild species held in captivity, he claims, dolphin brains have been found to shrink by up to 42 per cent, with the regions responsible for communication most affected. Upon reflection, such degeneration seems inevitable. To begin with, the dolphins have no need to use sound for hunting purposes since dead fish are provided as a minimum wage. Indeed, as the Russian cetacean scientist Awenir Tomilin reported in 1974, hunting reflexes and prey-catching reactions sometimes become so suppressed in captivity that the animals will make no attempt to hunt living prey in their pool even when hungry. Secondly, the tedious and all too familiar uniformity of the environment not only renders the use of echo-location meaningless, but it has also been suggested that high-frequency sound waves bouncing off a circular steel or concrete wall can cause distressing disorientation to the animals. Says whale specialist Dr Petra Deimer: "If, in their innate way, the animals were to make use of their 'acoustic eye' in a normal dolphinarium pool, they would feel at the very least like a man in a labyrinth of mirrors."

Perhaps it is even less surprising that communication suffers between neurotic animals in a crippled social structure, mindlessly performing the same routine day in and day out. Daring to look at it from the dolphin's point of view for once, perhaps there is basically nothing much to say about a featureless concrete prison. The Dutch communications scientist Dr Cees Kamminga, of the Technical University of Delft, confirmed Pilleri's findings during a comprehensive study of captive toothed whales' expressions of sound. At Duisburg Zoo in Germany, for instance, Kamminga used a hydrophone to tape the "verbalisations" of white whales or belugas which, because of their unique songs, are also known as the "canaries of the polar seas". But despite many hours of determined effort by the director of the Duisburg Zoo, Dr Wolfgang Gewalt, and one of his trainers, the animals remained silent, prompting the Dutch scientist to confirm what dolphin owners so vociferously deny: "In captive toothed whales I observed a constant decline in the quantity and intensity of their sound utterings."

In 1983, at the IWC *Whales Alive!* conference held in Boston, cetacean scientists recommended that dolphinaria should, "in due course", be replaced with coastal marine reserves, an idea long favoured by Professor Pilleri. Though perhaps fenced-off from the surrounding ocean, the dolphins would nevertheless be free to come and go as they please, indeed, to *choose* whether or not they would like contact with human beings. The only "performance" for the public would be the experience of observing the dolphins' natural and spontaneous interaction with each other. Devoid of pretence and artificiality, such marine parks could serve the legitimate needs of both education and science. Unfortunately, this more enlightened solution seems a very long way off, and being a realist who prefers some measure of improvement now rather than ten years hence, Cartlidge is prepared to be slightly more lenient in his demands. "If they must keep dolphins I would like to see similar set-ups to the Living World exhibit in Florida," he says. "There, the dolphins are surrounded by underwater flora and fauna, can eat whenever they want because the pool teems with fish, and revolutionary filtration techniques mean the water is crystal clear and free from any dangerous build-up of added chemicals. There is also no degrading show, though people go in to watch the dolphins play."

> "Even the standards themselves have been formulated with human ignorance as their foundation."
> — Professor Giorgio Pilleri

International Law
With the advent of the US Marine Mammal Act in 1973, Flipper Inc., having enjoyed years of lucrative trading entirely unhindered by any legal restrictions, was to face a formidable crisis. American citizens were prohibited from catching dolphins anywhere in the world without US government permission; the capture of dolphins in US waters would be subject to review by the Marine Mammal Commission of the National Marine Fisheries Service (NMFS); computerised records, updated annually, would be kept of all illnesses, deaths, births, and transactions; and even foreign facilities wishing to import American cetaceans would first have to comply with minimum standards governing pool size and veterinary

care. Although these standards were at best rudimentary — a pool with a surface area of 89.2 square metres and a depth of 1.83m is considered adequate for six *Tursiops truncatus* — the tightening legal noose led to the demise of many of the world's most notorious "dolphin cowboys" by the late 1970s. More tenacious enterprises however banked on a systematic exploitation of loopholes and bureaucratic confusion in international law, particularly CITES. Some found shelter in the lax and bribery-prone bureaucracies of the Third World, others in business arrangements with Russian and East European dolphinaria. Still others have managed to carve out a comfortable niche in Western Europe, no longer the operators of primitive travelling shows, but the proud managers of marine zoos-cum-circuses, sparkling dolphinaria enjoying a facade of respectability while their cupboards, so to speak, are crammed with dolphin skeletons. Even some of the most infamous dolphin dealers of the 1970s are still able to find shelter in complacent bureaucracies which have turned a Nelsonian eye to the abuse and exploitation of dolphins.

Although intended to curb the most conspicuous abuses of the trade, stricter enforcement of the law has also encouraged illegal trafficking in dolphins. Since 1973, when the Marine Mammal Act came into force, the US authorities have broken up a number of smuggling rings conspiring to catch hundreds of dolphins in the Caribbean and sell them all over the world for several million dollars. The controversy which shook Montreal's municipal dolphinarium in 1980 served to spotlight other inadequacies in the law. When workers went on strike, preventing anyone from entering the dolphinarium for 21 days, all four dolphins starved to death. The resulting public outcry prompted stricter regulations governing dolphins caught in US waters, and by 1984 even dolphin trainers in European establishments applying for new US animals were obliged to sign affidavits promising they would never strike.

Dealers have also been implicated in insurance fraud, attempting to recoup investments which died with a dolphin's fragile health. There are vast profits at stake. A show-trained dolphin might be worth up to $80,000, and an orca whale half a million. Although several large brokerages now refuse to insure dolphins and whales, policies in the USA are apparently easier to arrange, including cover for Europe. Says Doug Cartlidge: "It seems certain that some owners have been swindling the insurance companies. When one dolphin dies for instance, they collect the insurance from the company which has no way of knowing whether or not the dolphin that died was actually the one that was insured." An insurance analyst at Lloyds in Zurich admitted that "this could be a method of defrauding insurance companies", particularly since "a health certificate could be supplied by any qualified veterinary surgeon, and not necessarily an independent one."

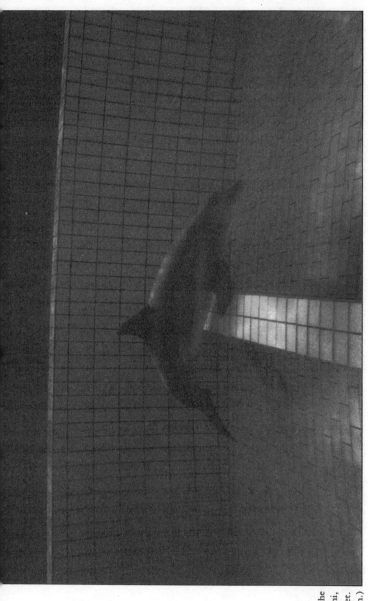

An underwater view of the dolphinarium in Rimini, reminiscent of a public toilet. (Matthias Schnellmann.)

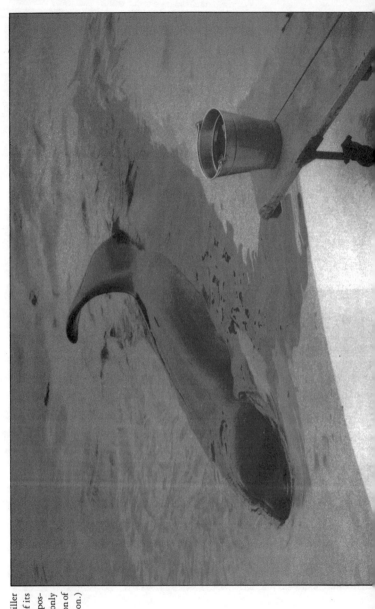

The limp back fin of a killer whale is a symptom of its restricted swimming possibilities, since the fin can only be kept rigid by a circulation of blood. (William Johnson.)

Like the itinerant menagerie's elephants or chimpanzees, under CITES, dolphins too can officially be regarded as circus animals, their owners provided with temporary import/export permits to facilitate frequent travel and display. Partly because of this, the bureaucratic confusion surrounding the export — import — re-export cycle of dolphins has frequently been used as a smoke-screen to conceal mortalities. There is a great reluctance, even on the part of the authorities, to reveal the exact statistics on the numbers of dolphins dying in captivity often they don't care enough to know themselves and revert to formal protocol to conceal their own professional inadequacies. Furthermore, it is the testimony of numerous former dolphin trainers that to avoid adverse publicity, dolphins that die are often replaced by newly-acquired ones which bear the same names. Hence the "Flipper" or "Lady" which the public may see performing tricks in a dolphinarium may in reality be "Flipper No. 2" or "Lady No. 3". In practice, the regulations seem to serve the interests of the dolphin-owners rather than the dolphins themselves. This is because dolphins are generally regarded as "private property" — and in fact almost as inanimate commodity items. Attempts to trace the fate of individual dolphins are routinely frustrated by the refusal of the authorities to release import-export documents and autopsy reports without permission of the owners. Legislation has also not succeeded in halting the cynical re-sale of dolphins to amusement parks outside of Europe and the USA, sometimes to Third World establishments whose facilities are so primitive that the export certificate actually represents little more than a death warrant.

In theory at least, domestic animal welfare laws should prevent the abuse of dolphins in captivity, yet in most countries that boils down to archaic anti-cruelty regulations which are either virtually impossible to enforce, or simply have no relevance. In Germany, for example, where there are no minimum requirements as regards pool size, state veterinary officers are responsible for ensuring the welfare of the animals. But as journalist Udo Tschimmel points out, these government vets are experts on cattle and poultry, not marine mammals. Trainers, he reports, joke that the vets don't even know where to take a blood sample from the dolphin and therefore prefer to leave the diagnosis to specialists like David Taylor and Andrew Greenwood, who count among their clients most of the dolphinaria in Europe. While this can hardly be an objective way of applying the law, at least Taylor and Greenwood possess expert knowledge of the fungus infections, parasites of the lungs, stomach ulcers and other common ailments that afflict dolphins in captivity.

Under Britain's Zoo Licensing Act 1981, dolphinaria must have permits to operate that are provided by local councils. The Act stipulates that a license may be refused if animals are not being properly cared for, but as we shall see in the following chapter, its dilatory application has done little to improve the welfare of Britain's captive dolphins.

Perhaps it is inevitable that such legislation — steeped as it is in species arrogance — should institutionalise the idea of the dolphin as an exploitable resource. Laws of this kind, dealing with controversial and emotive issues, are typically children of an unhappy marriage, or at least a marriage of convenience. It is thus that at the government altar, the groom — economic interests — and the bride — establishment science — will be joined in wedlock, the bride bringing with her a priceless dowry of credibility, despite her dubious morals, her overindulgent obsession for her man, *homo sapiens*, and her incessant charade of objectivity. Taking the analogy a little further, it might also be said that on the sidelines stand the nagging and unwanted mothers-in-law, the animal welfare organisations, rarely appeased and barely tolerated. Only later begins the embarrassing and awkward nuptial spectacle with Science practising the strangest contortions to satisfy the voracious fantasies of Economy.

The (Educational) Freak Show

The law, so conveniently blind to the dolphin's sophisticated social structure, reduces individuals to mere digits and statistics, their former lives, their experiences, dreams and relationships, obliterated. It is ironic perhaps that the same systematic stripping of identity has been a characteristic of almost every human prison, army or death camp. As human consciousness — and its conscience — slowly begins to awaken to such injustices, then the law, so often the skivvy of economic expedience, is merely reformed, given a face-lift or some minor cosmetic attention. As it is with every endangered species destined for the circus, this phenomenon, revealing as it does the uniqueness of human hypocrisy, is nowhere more evident than the legal requirement that shows should endeavour to be "educational". Dolphins wearing oversized spectacles, dolphins having their teeth cleaned with a toilet brush, dolphins singing a squeaky rendition of "Happy Birthday" — this, the most ubiquitous style of dolphin dressage — probably reveals more about the ailing human spirit and its self-imposed divorce from Mother Nature, than anything about the true nature of cetaceans. But is this surprising when the very parameters of the law and its terms of reference are morally bankrupt? By endowing the dolphin business with implied legitimacy, those who are responsible for drafting the law and its cosmetic amendments are — however inadvertently — actually encouraging the abuse to continue. Like the legalised exploitation of circus animals in general, the inherent flaws of such legislation betray a kind of institutionalised sophistry. Apart from the discomfort of added expense — a larger pool, more comprehensive veterinary care, "educational aids" — the international dolphin trade, can, for the time being at least, look forward to a reasonably secure and happy future. Like those who draft the law, they can continue to bank on illusion, so much in demand in today's world.

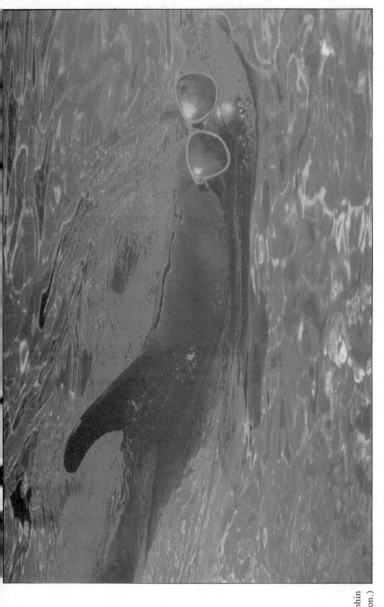

The 'educational' dolphin show. (William Johnson.)

Water skiing on dolphins.
(William Johnson.)

It was on 1 January 1984 that a new EEC directive — known as Council Regulation 3626/82 — came into force which had the effect of strengthening the Washington Convention. Those dolphins and whales that had once languished in Appendix II of CITES were promoted aloft to inhabit Annex C1, the EEC equivalent of CITES Appendix I. This meant that import licenses for both bottlenose dolphins and killer whales would now only be granted for the purposes of scientific research, education or captive breeding. Although a major stride towards the eventual abolition of marine circuses, it was not long before the industry had exposed enough loopholes for their replacement show animals to leap through. Asked in 1985 how the new EEC ordinance was affecting dolphinaria in member states, Dr Willem Wijnstekers, EEC officer responsible for monitoring Europe's wildlife trade, declared that "there is evidence that dolphinariums are rapidly putting together education packages just to be able to stay in business".

Trained to waltz, play "flipperball", wear giant sunglasses and straw hats, have their teeth brushed, and tow a child around the pool in a rubber dinghy — with only slight variations, the tricks are the same the world over, despite the much-touted "inherent educational value" of the show. Instead of a child, at Holiday Park in Hassloch, Germany, the dolphins used to tug a baby chimpanzee around the pool in a rubber boat, clad in life-jacket. In warmer climes — at Adriatic Sea World in Riccione, Italy, for example, or Pleasurama's Marineland of Mallorca — the show may also feature a bikini-clad woman "water-skiing" on a pair of dolphins. Nor is there any great difference in show style between the richer establishments who prefer to portray themselves as "marine zoos", such as Mike Riddell's Antibes Marineland in the south of France, and those which make little effort to disguise the fact that they are no more than marine circuses, like Franco Carrini's Florida Dolphin Show at Gardaland in Italy.

At Marineland, head trainer Jon Kershaw's speciality is to be launched out of the water on the beaks of two dolphins "at 18 Mph". Carrini's trick is almost identical except that it involves only one dolphin. All shows follow the same pattern. First, as the audience file through the turnstile and find their seats, the rousing rock or pop music begins, with the dolphins becoming visibly nervous and excited, leaping out of the water and making fast underwater circuits around the pool. But the music is not really for the benefit of the public at all, but used as a form of Pavlovian conditioning which the hungry dolphin associates with food-reward, alerting the animal that the show is about to begin.

At Windsor Safari Park, the female orca, Winnie, is expected to "kiss" the trainer, blow a trumpet, and glide around the confines of the pool with an oversized pair of plastic sunglasses on her head. "Of course there's a commercial side to it," conceded Andrew Haworth-Booth, then managing director of Windsor, quoted in the *Observer* in 1984. "But if there wasn't no one would ever see a dolphin or a whale. Winnie's sunglasses are nothing more or less than a prop. I don't see anything wrong in getting dolphins and killer whales to perform tricks. It all adds to their appeal." If all this seems somewhat reminiscent of the pseudo-intellectual debate over the alleged educational value of chimpanzees riding motorbikes, bears driving cars and elephants walking the tightrope, then that just goes to show how much time, money and effort has been invested by the industry in the field of "public relations". While one might well marvel at the extraordinary ingenuity of human affectation and hypocrisy, the "educational" dolphin show has nevertheless obviously found its legitimacy, being recognised not only by some respected cetacean scientists but also by international statutes and national legislation.

As long ago as 1973, John Burton, later to become secretary of the Fauna and Flora Preservation Society, wrote in the British magazine *Animals*: "One of the major problems confronting the dolphinaria is that they are all run for profit, and in many cases this shows. Many of the performances are pure 'circus' and have absolutely no relationship to dolphins as wild animals. For instance, this Christmas sees the first dolphin 'pantomime'." Nothing much has changed since then, least of all the refrain that there should be more "education" in the dolphinaria, as though this could somehow justify the rabid exploitation of the animals. Wrote Burton: "Already, by making the public aware of the animals — by showing them how they behave and what they look like — the dolphinaria may be helping whale conservation. But a lot more could be done. In the commentary which accompanies the performances I would like to hear mentioned the 250,000 bottle-nosed dolphins which drown each year in the nets of tuna fishermen or how the blue whale is nearing extinction through over-hunting; or the methods used to kill larger whales. 'The public wouldn't like it' is the main reason given for not stating such facts... but people ought to be told nevertheless." Thirteen years after this was written, UK government consultant Dr Margaret Klinowska was parroting virtually the same sentiments, the final effect being that under new legislation in Britain, the slave trade in dolphins would not be outlawed but merely reformed and given a public relations face-lift. Systematically ridiculed and demeaned in the process would not only be the pool-bound dolphins and whales wearing hats and sunglasses, but ironically, also science, education and conservation, the three alibis of continued exploitation.

Kiss of Death

Without doubt, few of the children or other eager sightseers filing through the turnstile of the dolphinarium will actually be aware of the fact that they are paying to gawk at animals condemned to an early death.

But perhaps this notion is just too naive for those who believe in "the law of the jungle" — or at least what they interpret that law to be where money-making is concerned. Even leaving aside the endemic commercial vulgarity of such establishments, the discrepancies in the educational argument are just too blatant to dismiss. While dolphins in the wild eat live fish, in the dolphinarium they must either eat them dead or starve. In the wild, dolphins live in schools with several generations playing vital social roles; in the pool, reduced to a male and his harem, dolphin society becomes crippled and perverted. In the wild, the dolphin will play and jump with spontaneous exuberance and the sheer joy of being alive; in captivity that is replaced by dressage that is artificial and conditioned, part of an enforced clockwork routine.

The industry emphasises the alleged potential benefits of scientific research as part of the learning process while guarding facts about miscarriages, deaths, sicknesses, and accidents like state secrets. The dolphinaria routinely portray dressage as natural behaviour, though with the ritual hyperbole of the circus many a stunt is billed as some kind of record-breaking spectacular, as evidenced by the all too familiar show spiel "the-one-and-only" or "unique-in-the-entire-world". Even stranger, while criticism of the industry is greeted by the mechanical rejoinder that the public shouldn't humanise the dolphin or become overly sentimental, the typical show continues to be crammed with such educational and scientific natural behaviour as dancing the twist and "shaking flippers". Leaping onto the conservation bandwagon, the industry has even begun to suggest — like Wolfgang Gewalt in Germany — that dolphinaria are playing a vital role in species protection; and yet when that very same industry is at the brunt of criticism over the capture of wild dolphins, the clockwork catch phrase is that "these animals are not endangered".

Similar contradictions are legion. Indeed, perhaps that rotting, fishy smell so evident in the dolphinarium is not necessarily the unhygienic fish kitchen or even a dead dolphin on the well-worn autopsy slab, but just the industry's chronic and inexorable hypocrisy. But there is also cynicism, pure and simple. Every trainer and every dolphin owner is well aware that dolphins in captivity are highly prone to contagious diseases carried by humans. They also know very well that some of these fatal infections are passed on to the dolphin in such seemingly innocuous ways that no one would even think of objecting. And yet it will remain a never-ending mystery how many dolphins have died because they have contracted some childhood illness, or even 'flu or the common cold. Certainly, those at the receiving end of the "educational" lesson won't be told. Nor will the shy yet delighted child who is encouraged to come down onto the stage, and whose loving kiss for the dolphin turns into a kiss of death.

To expect an industry with so much to hide to provide the kind of lucid, objective, and all-encompassing lessons which most parents expect from education, borders on criminal naivety. It is one thing for such "educational programmes" to include facts and figures on cetacean biology, behaviour and even — as Burton proposed so long ago now — the threats that they experience in the wild, but do we really expect the dolphinaria to openly discuss the abuse, deaths and misery of cetaceans in captivity? To do so would be tantamount to committing harikari, and however entertaining that might be for those still clamouring for *bread and circuses*, we must assume that it is unlikely. In any event, judging by a professional survey conducted on behalf of the Zoological Society of London, which revealed that less than 1 per cent of respondents were visiting the zoo and dolphinarium for educational reasons, everyone except the lawmakers it seems is well aware of the fact that dolphinaria are exclusively places of entertainment. Therefore it might well be valid to say that discussing earnestly all the ins and outs of the "education issue" simply plays into the industry's hands as it implies a legitimacy where there is actually none at all.

> *"For — even when the purpose is scientific study — the animals are so physically and psychologically deformed in the process that any discoveries made are distorted and give a thoroughly inadequate picture of true behaviour in the wild."*
> — Professor Giorgio Pilleri

Science — its ethical standards often leaving much to be desired — has long focused a jaundiced and clinical eye on captive cetaceans. The vast majority of research programmes — generally bland, feeble offerings with a strong alibi function — are self-serving forays into animal husbandry which can sometimes marginally serve to improve the animal's welfare and therefore the industry's high-risk investment. More esoteric research, long on nomenclature but short on tangible results, is occasionally conducted in liaison with local universities, an arrangement which can afford the dolphinarium a good measure of respectability and even an acceptable pretext for further dolphin imports. Then there is that brand of research detested by the industry because over the years it has served to highlight the physical and psychological deprivation of the animals in captivity. The potential legislative impact of such compelling scientific revelations continues to be muffled, however, not only because economy habitually speaks louder than ethics but because the most influential cetacean scientists actually owe their entire careers to studying the deformed caricature of the dolphin in captivity. That brings us to the ghoulish experiments perpetrated against immobilised, helpless dolphins in research laboratories across the world — a dolphin with its brain exposed in a laboratory in Paris, for instance, a plastic bucket under the canvas-sling "operating table" to catch the blood; or dolphins embalmed alive by a process known as "vital profusion". Notoriously difficult to anaesthetise because they breathe consciously, many a captive dolphin has had electrodes hammered into its skull while fully aware, fully conscious.

Yet dolphin vivisection is not only confined to those anonymous steel and concrete urban buildings where many a scientist, with such desolate futility, strives to find the heart of nature. By the late 1970s in the USA, research appendages to the larger dolphinaria were also becoming common, since the establishment would prove eligible not only for greater prestige in the zoological world, but also for substantial tax relief. Trainers such as Scott Rutherford, then working at Hawaii Sea Life Park, voiced concern that dolphins were ending up "as dead meat" in those shed-like laboratories, electrode wires trailing from pus-filled cannulas driven into the animals' brains — an experiment pioneered by Dr John Lilly, later to become the darling of the New Age movement in the USA. Unfortunately, those bleak, medieval days are far from over, as Willem Wijnstekers of the EEC confirms: "There are a number of scientific projects using dolphins in member countries. Yes, these include vivisection experiments."

> "As long as the public is satisfied with a couple of bottle-nosed dolphins having their teeth brushed in a seaside swimming pool, there will be little incentive for zoos to develop the art of cetacean husbandry"
> — John L. Adams

Born Captive
As for the last of the law's three great alibis, the "art of cetacean husbandry" — the absence of which John L. Adams lamented way back in 1972 — it is scarcely nearer to realisation than ever before. Indeed, it has never been a feasible proposition for most oceanaria simply because of cost. As long ago as 1977, a report by specialists concluded that producing second generation captive dolphins would cost over $1 million with a starting colony of one male and twelve females. Even the majority of the wealthier oceanaria in the USA and Japan have paid little more than lip service to captive breeding, partly because of their overeagerness to exchange the circus image for the more respectable scientific and educational credibility of the marine zoo. With typically uninspired leadership, instead of creating viable breeding colonies of a single species, and optimising their facilities to go some way towards meeting the animals' social needs, they set about mimicking the long outmoded menagerie collections of the early 20th century, emphasising the size and range of the animal collection, and fleshing-out the cetacean exhibits with seals, sea-lions and penguins. Japan has experimented with Gill's bottlenose and Risso's dol-

phin, while South Africa has kept the Indian Ocean bottlenose and the Dusky dolphin. With pioneering spirit, the USA has displayed the Amazon river dolphin, the Commerson dolphin, the Pacific white-sided dolphin as well as beluga whales, pilot whales, and the common dolphin. While Pilleri cites a 90 per cent death rate of young at pregnancy, proponents of the industry claim that as standards have improved so have the survival figures for newborn dolphins. That may be true in the USA but elsewhere around the world, the statistics continue to be bleak. The first known captive birth — to a harbour porpoise "rescued" from a fishing net — took place in 1914 at Brighton Aquarium. The calf — conceived in the wild as so many captive births continue to be to this very day — died immediately. That inauspicious event was to herald a veritable epidemic of miscarriages, stillbirths and infant deaths in the world's dolphinaria, plagued both by the behavioural problems of the animals themselves, and the incompetence or inexperience of staff. Thus, according to the *International Zoo Yearbook*, from 1965 to 1986, 134 dolphins of various species were born in captivity around the world, of which 106 died.

Sometimes, the temptation to deceive the public with a "phantom" pregnancy is irresistible, a fact attested to by Dr Margaret Klinowska in her government-commissioned report, *A Review of Dolphinaria*: "....'pregnancy' sometimes covered other reasons for failure to perform," she notes sardonically, "for example: required elsewhere, incompatibility, illness or death." But Professor Paul Schauenberger remains unimpressed by such criticisms. Up to the present day, he claims, approximately 180 dolphins have been born in captivity, and survival rates have improved so dramatically that the foremost dolphinaria in the USA are gradually reaching self-sufficiency. That may be good news for the wild dolphin as a species, but again, it does little for the long-term welfare of the individual animal. Indeed, one of the inherent dangers of captive breeding success is that commercial dealing in the animals would no longer be subject to international conventions governing the trade in endangered species. These have at least shown some appreciable results in curtailing the more obvious abuses of the dolphin dealing industry.

With inexplicable logic, the captive-bred individual is deprived of what few rights were afforded to its wild-caught mother as soon as it is born. With second generation animals now growing up into adulthood — neither they nor their parents ever having known the sea or ocean — it seems as though these animals, if the industry has its way, will not only be stripped of their true identity, but eventually will have no more rights than a battery chicken or a pig on an industrial farm. Major advances in husbandry and breeding success, concludes Schauenberger — albeit with an embarrassing dearth of evidence — herald a promising future for the industry. In much the same way that the cat, dog, pig, sheep and goat were domesticated thousands of years ago, so today, the wild dolphin is being tamed and domesticated by *homo sapiens*. Declares the visionary professor: "There is no convincing and justifiable reason at all to stop experiments to tame new species... At some time in the future there will be farms in the sea where man will increasingly breed fish for his own consumption. Then the dolphins will play a major role. They will, if we wish it to be so, be the sheepdogs of the seas!"

Even discounting such lurid fantasies, appearances that the industry is in a state of decline at present may well be deceptive. It would probably be truer to say that after several years of being under intense siege, it is now quietly plotting its future course of action, confident that it has been able to contend with EEC Council Regulation 3626/82, with a mixture of bluff, feigned respectability, and political connections. No doubt the industry expects to be able to weather the storm of more rigorous animal welfare legislation in the same way. Some dolphinaria might go to the wall, but that is just one of the decrees of fate in a cut-throat business; the industry as a whole will survive, though not without ruthless strategy.

Part of that strategy has been aimed at dismantling Regulation 3626/82. Behind the scenes, the European dolphin industry remonstrated, lobbied, and cajoled every influential person they could think of to convince the authorities that the regulation was suffocating them, preventing "reputable" dolphinaria from mounting breeding and scientific research programmes, and discouraging even the less reputable ones from investing in new installations. Pressure to de-list the dolphins from Annex C1 to Annex C2 was first detected from the Netherlands — which was then also home to the dolphin industry's lobbying organisation, the EAAM — and Britain, home of EAAM president, David Taylor. It was thus that on 7 April 1987, Dr B. M. Lensink, vice-chair of the Netherlands CITES/EEC Scientific Authority, wrote to Claus Stuffmann of the European Commission, declaring that because fifteen species of cetacean — with the bottlenose dolphin and orca whale inexplicably heading his list — "cannot be considered as threatened with extinction," the Netherlands Scientific Authority proposed to relegate them to Annex C2. A similar confidential proposal, "adapted from a text by Dr Margaret Klinowska" was submitted in August 1988 by the UK CITES Scientific Authority. Later that year, the influential EEC-CITES Scientific Working Group decided to recommend to the Council of Ministers the relegation of the cetacean species along the lines proposed by Lensink. Given the current wave of public sympathy for the plight of captive dolphins, particularly in the UK, it is not surprising that such behind-the-scenes manoeuvring has been conducted with the utmost subterfuge. The move would again render the dolphins virtually unprotected from the brutality and ruthlessness of the trade. As Appendix II animals, not even the feeble legal requirement of "education" would stand in the way. Says Pier Lorenzo Florio, director of the Italian branch of TRAFFIC: "We have our hands full even now checking up on the legitimacy of the industry and its respect or otherwise for animal welfare. Should this measure go through, it will open the flood-gates, and we won't have any legal means to stop it."

V. THE GLOBAL INDUSTRY

The God Apollo saw the smallest whale, the dolphin,
As the embodiment of peaceful virtue, undisguised joy,
And as a guide to another world.
He sometimes exchanged his god-like status
To assume dolphin form;
And founded the oracle at Delphi,
Named in the dolphin's honour.
There, the god hoped,
Man might be guided by a sense of other-worldliness.
— Heathcote Williams, *Whale Nation*

THE AMERICAN DREAM

As the descendants of the *Mayflower* fanned out across the New World in their covered wagons, taming the land and its indigenous peoples with the Bible and the bullet, the circus-like merry-go-round of dream versus reality became firmly embedded in the American psyche. Confronted by an immense, unfamiliar and intimidating wilderness, many of these first pioneers and settlers, inwardly pining for comfort despite all their showy bravado, subsisted spiritually on tall stories and golden hopes of the future. It was thus that the strange and paradoxical American Dream was born, a soft sweet with a hard-boiled centre, a seductive illusion encasing a harsh reality, a pretence of moral altruism all too often veiling a ruthless competition for wealth and self-aggrandisement. It may be said that the same unquenchable passion for make-believe is evident almost anywhere, given the natural human impulse to escape the common afflictions of daily life, the dreary routine of the work-place, the spiritual deprivation of the modern city, the stress of the rat race, or just plain chronic unhappiness. But it was in the USA that the manufacture of make-believe first became a national institution, mass-produced to feed a hungry world, a unique synthesis of commerce and fantasy typified by the conveyor-belt offerings of the "Hollywood Dream-Machine" and the boundless wonders of Disneyland. Small wonder then that in this surfeit of lucrative unreality, the idea of happy dolphins in minuscule concrete pools was destined to thrive.

As we have already seen, the pioneer of the contemporary dolphinarium was circus chieftain P.T. Barnum who displayed white whales in his New York Museum of freaks in 1860. Like most of his other

The frozen smile. (Matthias Schnellmann.)

exhibits, Barnum's mermaid-whales were no more than disposable gimmicks and, confined to tiny metal tanks, their swift and sudden deaths
only added to their magic and mystique. Barnum's fitful attempts at
whale and porpoise husbandry were followed by Marine Studios of
Marineland in Florida, which, also under the pretext of public education,
began keeping small, toothed cetaceans in 1938. But what set the dolphin entertainment industry on its money-spinning course, providing it
with a sudden boom in consumer demand, was the 1962 B-movie *Flipper*, directed by James B. Clark, and starring Chuck Conners and a conscripted dolphin from the Miami Seaquarium. The film, an irrevocably
poor production only salvaged by some endearing acting by the dolphin,
was dedicated to "Adolf Frohn who trained the first dolphin 13 years ago"
at Marine Studios in Florida. Although make-believe in the archetypal
Hollywood style, the film, with pungent irony, inadvertently seems to
condemn the very idea of cetaceans in captivity. When 12-year old Sandy
Ricks finds a wounded dolphin stranded on the Florida coastline, his first
impulse is to tie it to his skiff, take it to his seaside home, nurse it back to
health, and then proceed to hold dolphin shows for the neighbourhood
kids. But the crux of the story is the *release* of Flipper — on the insistence
of Sandy's disciplined yet caring Paw, a homespun fisherman played by
ex-gun slinger Chuck Conners. Initially heart-broken, the boy soon re-
establishes his relationship with Flipper, but this time in the dolphin's
natural environment, the wild. There can be little doubt that this inconvenient discrepancy between fact and fantasy escaped the attention of the
film's audience, principally children in their most impressionable years.
Few must have realised that in several shots, wounds are even visible
under the dolphin's flippers, consistent with poor handling in transportation.

The movie proved so successful at the box office that a long-running
TV series followed, with yet more implausible adventures featuring the
free-swimming dolphin. Flipper, the Hollywood star, superceded Fury
the black stallion and Lassie the collie dog in the hearts and minds of children. All this kitsch of course did wonders for the nascent dolphin industry, as witnessed by the hundreds of newly caught animals to be christened "Flipper". The dolphin deaths were all too easy to conceal, recalls
Doug Cartlidge: "If one died another would be bought from somewhere
else, tipped into the pool and renamed Flipper." Rapidly becoming an
international craze, the "Flipper Show" concept was flogged for all it was
worth — Flipper t-shirts, Flipper water-wings, Flipper beach towels.
With new dolphin shows sprouting everywhere — and with no laws to
inhibit capture or keeping in the most primitive conditions — the only
problem was for supply to keep abreast with constant demand. As is so
often the case whenever megabucks are at stake, the alluring American
Dream shielded a more sordid American Reality: behind the exaggerated

smile of the dolphin painted onto the billboards of the travelling Flipper shows, the animals were actually being so ruthlessly exploited that they were dying *en masse*, their entire lives reduced to nothing more than feeding the shark jaws of the industry's cash registers.

Like any gold rush, this free-for-all also attracted a bizarre spectrum of humanity, from beach boys to professional wrestlers, trapeze artists to fishermen, investment brokers to New Age cultists. The trailblazing sub-culture was not without its criminal elements, including those with Mafia ties. It has even been alleged that one dolphin dealer stuffed his dead show animal with cocaine in a lucrative smuggling operation from South America to Europe — assuring customs officials that the animal was merely "sedated". Perhaps it is axiomatic of the dolphin trade that many companies at the time were fly-by-night, founded on an unexpected opportunity but expiring as soon as the cash and dolphin flow shrank to a trickle and then dried up. Says Rudolph Jäckle, a dolphin-catcher in South Africa during the boom years: "After the Marine Mammal Act came into force in 1972 it became more difficult — you couldn't buy dolphins any more, you know, like sausages. Before '72 you could go to the States and buy any dolphins you wanted to."

It was in the Florida Keys that most of the dolphin catchers set up shop to supply animals to circuses and amusement parks around the world — men like Jerry Mitchell who founded the Marine Productions International Corporation, and who provided most of Europe with dolphins during the heyday of the late 1960s. Or entrepreneurs like Harvey L. Hamilton — "dolphin catcher and trainer" with "eleven years experience", who even today continues to be owner and operator of Florida's Ocean Attractions Inc. Most dolphin-trading at the time, including imports and exports, was so frenetic in order to keep pace with demand that no accurate records were kept of dolphin deaths and replacements. Indeed, the industry was quick to realise that its very survival was dependent upon the public's unquestioning faith in the dolphins' happiness, well-being and longevity. It was for this reason alone that secrecy and deception became instrumental in preserving the lucrative lie. It was, after all, a conveyor-belt industry, mass production and mass consumption, with the dealers taking no notice of an animal's pregnancy, motherhood, illness, or nervous collapse. They were simply caught, stored for as short a time as possible, and then shipped.

In 1967 'for example, Jerry Mitchell even exported a mother dolphin and her suckling from Key Largo to a seasonal show in Wales. Attempts were made to forcibly extract milk from the mother for the baby, but this failed, and the calf died after just two days. Even eight years later — and despite those ritual claims of the industry of constant self-improvement — researcher W. A. Walker cited a 40 per cent death rate during capture operations in Florida. The implications of this become evident when one realises that by 1976 there were 286 bottlenose dolphins and 17 orcas in captivity in the USA alone, as well as 54 other species of whale. The history of orcas in captivity began in 1961 when an opportunistic Marineland in California caught an ailing fully grown female which had apparently strayed into Newport harbour. It survived for just two days, but it marked the beginnings of a new fad for captive killer whales. From November 1961 to March 1976, 303 orcas were caught alive in American waters, relates Prof. Paul Schauenberger. Of these, 237 were released again, 56 were taken into captivity, and ten died during capture and transportation.

Riding on the crest of the Flipper wave, it was the American dealer and showman James W. Tiebor who shipped the first dolphins from Florida to Europe for exhibit in 1966. The exotic displays were greeted with such public acclaim that Tiebor soon found himself carting the dolphins all over Europe to exhibitions, agricultural and trade fairs. The deaths, deprivation and cruelty that the dolphins suffered in such travelling shows amounted to little more than an inconvenience for an industry which regarded these animals not as individuals or even living beings, but simply as disposable commodity items with a limited shelf-life and "planned obsolescence". Though they routinely succumbed to disease, injury or suicide, replacements — often christened with the same names as their fallen predecessors — were freely and cheaply available from the USA, South America and South Africa. In the heyday of the 1960s, a carnival atmosphere suffused the dolphin industry, one of free-spending, driving ambition and luck, the American Dream come true. The result was intoxication, blindness, self-delusion, the inability to determine where the fantasy of the show began and where it stopped. Often, the suffering of the condemned was not even recognised, and perhaps that is the saddest thing of all.

With the advent of tougher laws regulating the capture sector of the dolphin industry, there followed a period of recession and also a much deeper crisis of confidence. Desperation among the dolphin cowboys, previously renowned for their swagger and conceit, sometimes resulted in drunken bar brawls and cases of illegal capture and smuggling. Despite such rushes of activity, for the small entrepreneur the boom years of almost unlimited profit, Florida sunshine and the pretentious depiction of their own ramshackle ventures as "corporations" were over for good.

As the more insecure of the rogue dolphin dealers discovered to their great cost when the law slammed down to decapitate their activities, a healthy bank balance and the right connections can do wonders for company prestige and personal self-confidence, not to mention business survival. As the saying goes, nothing succeeds quite like success. It was thus that the larger and more robust enterprises, boasting efficient managerial skills and secure capital, entered a period of consolidation, lapping up the equipment and occasionally the expertise of their fallen brethren. Like the most hardy and tenacious of weeds, they put down roots deep into mainstream society, their executives hobnobbing with the well-to-do, with fellow businessmen, bankers, and politicians. It is thus that even today one can still find the names of the industry's most notorious dolphin cowboys of the sixties — now in smart business suits, managers of dolphinaria and amusement parks with a brittle front of respectability, a Potemkin facade behind which there is the same old treadmill of exploitation, death and replacement. It must be said that tougher laws, coupled with a seemingly inexhaustible human weakness for euphemism and pretension, have inadvertently helped them on their way to respectability — with today's dolphin catches called "scientifically controlled" and "humane", and the animals' life-long captivity justified in the name of children's education and scientific research.

Today, comparatively few specialised dolphin catchers have managed to survive, feeding – with their compatriots in Japan, Central and South America – New Zealand and Australia, the global industry's constant hunger for dolphins. They include the International Animal Exchange based in Ferndale, Michigan, perhaps the world's largest company specialising in the trade in exotic species and which supplies dolphins to numerous establishments in the USA and Europe. In Key Largo, Florida, which is still a base for many dolphin catching operations, there is Dolphins Plus Inc., run by Lloyd A. Borguss. Another well-known dealer, Mobi Solangi, not only catches dolphins in the Gulf of Mexico, but also runs a string of travelling dolphin shows. Also based in the Keys is Dolphin Services International, led by Dr Jay C. Sweeney who styles himself as an "Aquatic Animal Veterinarian attending international clientele, and Collector of Marine Mammals since 1971". His fellow director, and also captain of the *Dolphin Doll*, one of the speedboats used to chase the dolphin schools to exhaustion, is Gene Hamilton, "a Commercial Fisherman since 1940, and respected Dolphin Collector since 1964". One of Hamilton's regular clients is the US Navy, and its $30 million per year marine mammal programme. The company's sales brochure assures potential clients of a full and professional service with "personal attention", including "Preparation of US Permits", and "Arrangements for all aspects of transport: transporters and stretchers, logistical details and swift routing from Miami International Airport". Only "Quality Dolphins" are offered for sale after capture by an "experienced, careful collecting crew". As if to reassure the customer, the brochure continues, point by point: "Healthy, alert dolphins; bright show quality"; "Will deliver to your size and sex specifications"; "Acclimation pens located in crystal clear natural ocean lagoon" in the Florida Keys; "Dolphins accustomed to hand feeding with top quality fish". And of course, just in case that dolphin you bought is not so healthy and alert after all, there is a "90 day replacement guarantee".

Despite cosmetic refinements, dolphin catching is as ugly as it ever was, though the expense has become astronomical. Most are still caught in coastal waters of the Gulf off Mexico and the Caribbean, but now, in this age of efficiency where time means money, a dolphin school will first be located using spotter aircraft. Then, equipped with nets, powerful motor launches move in, applying sustained pressure upon the dolphin school, chasing the animals to exhaustion. Slowly but surely the roar of the engines begins to disorientate the dolphins by disrupting sonar communication, so that the bewildered creatures finally end up swimming in ever-decreasing circles. Pulling up the nets, perhaps the first victims are found; those dolphins which became entangled and drowned, those that have injured themselves trying to escape, sometimes tearing off a flipper as they thrash around in panic. Then comes the strenuous effort of heaving the selected animals on board. A difficult and clumsy procedure at the best of times, many a dolphin has to be thrown back into the water, paralysed, after its spine has been injured. The boats then speed back to land, leaving the dolphin school with its own unseen, unrecognised bereavement, the sucklings which will die without their mothers to nurse them, the injured which are held aloft by their companions, perhaps for days until they take their last breath. The captured dolphins will suffer a similarly unenviable fate. Once they are transferred into acclimatisation pens, the animals, still in a state of shock but fortified with vitamins, antibiotics, and sedatives, will promptly begin to starve themselves to death. To prevent the lucrative investment dying on them, a gag is often employed to force-feed the captives and only gradually can they be encouraged to suppress their own instinctive revulsion for eating dead fish.

Although the specialised capture business is only a shadow of its former self, dolphins and whales are still very much in demand, so much so that the managers of oceanaria sometimes feel obliged to mount their own capture operations when the need arises, either to replenish their own supplies or to sell to others. They include people like Bob Wright and his Sealand in Victoria, British Columbia, who gained much notoriety for his captures of orca whales. Also in Canada is John Hickes, the half-Scottish, half-Eskimo businessman who trades in Beluga whales. The hunt takes place each summer as the white whales migrate to the warmer waters of Manitoba to give birth in the estuary of the Churchill river. Fast motor launches are used to chase and herd the whales, with Hickes' team of hunters beating the sides of their boats to disorientate the animals. Once a whale is driven into shallow water, then rather than using a net, a lasso is thrown over it. In rapid succession, one of the catchers, poised on the bow of the lauch, jumps onto the animal's back and, in much the same way as steers are ridden by bronco-busting cowboys in Texas, the frenzied animal is ridden until eventually subdued. The hunters then check to see whether their prey's sex, age and length complies to requirements; if it does, the whale is hauled ashore and consigned, pending sale and transport, to a rusting tank not much larger than a toddler's paddling pool. Other individuals, deemed unsuitable for sale, are simply abandoned. Describing the 1989 hunt, journalist Kevin Toolis reported: "Some don't survive to be rejected. They die, battered by the boats which have persistently rammed them." Toolis quoted Anne Doncaster, of the International Wildlife Coalition as saying: "The hunters laugh and scream. You would think they were having the time of their lives. There is this awful whoop of triumph when they find the right one. You would think they had conquered Everest instead of catching some poor animal. They say they are after adolescents, but it is more like stealing eight-year-old children."

Hickes however, was unrepentant over his "bronco-busting" activities. He declared: "We literally jump on the whale's back and hold on to it by a small piece of rope. In previous years we used nets and loop snares. These are dangerous and very stressful to the mammal. You can either drown it or cut it up badly. In "busting" there is a stress factor involved for the animal. Their white cell counts go real high. But it's hard to say what it's like. I'm not a whale. I can't tell you how it feels."

In San Diego, California, there is Sea World Incorporated, probably the most prestigious of the American oceanaria. In 1973, under the pretext of scientific research, Sea World captured ten orcas valued at $5 million . The resulting controversy ended with the amusement park having its capture permit revoked by a US court — but not for long. In 1976, Sea World again set about catching orcas, this time off Washington state, near Seattle. But in the resulting furore, the oceanarium was forced to release them. Undaunted, in 1983, Sea World proposed the capture of 100 Alaskan orcas for scientific study, including invasive research such as liver biopsies, extraction of teeth and stomach-pumping. At the same time — and almost incidentally — it would also take ten of the animals back to Sea World. Although permission was granted by the federal authorities, there was public outrage in Alaska — where it was widely suspected that the research was no more than a convenient smoke-screen for a commercial company to obtain ten orcas, free of charge. Alaska's governor declared that the state would not endorse the federal permit, and although this had no standing in law, even Sea World was loathe to inflame Alaskan hostility by going ahead with the plan. But even this did not put a stop to the oceanarium's cetacean catches. In early 1984, Sea World attempted to import twelve Commerson dolphins — listed as a threatened species by IUCN — from Patagonia and at least five of the animals promptly died.

Despite its ferocious-sounding name, no records exist of any killer whale ever making an unprovoked attack on a human being. And so what happened at Sea World in 1987 is especially significant. Indeed, despite the much-vaunted pseudo-scientific research into cetacean-human communication at US dolphinaria, none of the four orcas confined to the establishment had ever been heard to utter any reason for turning on their two trainers and nearly killing them. This time, no amount of institutionalised secrecy could contain the scandal, perhaps because much more than "animal rights" were at stake — never a very valuable commodity when measured against profit. According to journalist Robert Reinhold, writing in the *International Herald Tribune*, 21-year-old trainer Jonathon Smith, while in the pool on 4 March 1987, "was hit on the back by a male orca, grabbed in the jaws of another, dragged down and smashed against the bottom of the 12m deep pool. He suffered a lacerated liver, heavy internal bleeding and other injuries." Then on 21 November, another trainer, 26-year old John Sillick, was attacked. As he performed one of Sea World's star-turns, riding on the back of a six-ton orca, one of the other animals rammed him and he suffered a broken back, hip, pelvis, leg and ribs. As information leaks turned into a veritable flood, it was disclosed that there had been no less that 14 "recent accidents" involving the whale trainers at Sea World, yet to preserve image and profits no changes had been made to the show, in training methods or handling of the whales.

At that time, the corporate parent of Sea World was Harcourt Brace Jovanovich Inc., the publishing and insurance empire based in Orlando, Florida. The Sea World whales, reported Robert Reinhold, "are the superstars of three — soon to be four — marine theme parks that have become the most profitable arm of the company that is desperately cash-hungry because its debt grew to $2.7 billion last year fighting off a takeover by Robert Maxwell, the British publisher." Sea World draws approximately 4 million visitors a year, with adults forking out $19.95 as entrance fees for themselves and $14.95 for their children.

Predictably, the Harcourt management quickly resorted to "damage control" to protect its image and reassure the public as to the suitability of the whale spectacle for family entertainment, by firing its three top managers at Sea World. The publishing conglomerate dismissed charges that they were ultimately to blame because pressure for profits was causing the whales added strain, and the trainers to take risks and make mistakes. The behavioural abnormalities of the whales are said to have become apparent shortly after Harcourt, moving to drive competitors out of business, took over and closed down Hanna-Barbera's Marineland in Rancho Palos Verdes near Los Angeles. The establishment's killer whales, Orky and Corky, were shipped to San Diego to join Sea World's orcas. It was speculated that their arrival — especially that of Orky, an aggressive male — had sparked the social disorders, with the inexperienced trainers unable to interpret the drastic change of mood in the pool. Yet Harcourt dismissed such allegations and although faced with an increasingly bitter controversy it was a defiant William Jovanovich who took the stage to distance the publishing empire from the implied incompetence of Sea World's president, chief trainer and zoological director. "The fact-finding by our committee showed that there was negligence," the flamboyant Jovanovich declared. "There was not a supervisor in the park near the stadium, which there was supposed to be at all times. It showed that three of the trainers had such meagre training it was a wonder they could even perform the most elementary aspects of their positions." According to the *Los Angeles Times*, Jovanovich went on to criticise the training methods of chief trainer David Butcher, describing his philosophy of cultivating a personal relationship with the whales as seriously flawed, in contrast to more "traditional behaviourist methods of punishment and reward."

For Sea World, the episode cast a shadow over its year-long festivities to celebrate its 25th anniversary, especially since Harcourt were suddenly in no mood for spectacular and risky stunts. The orca show was abruptly given a new format, stripped of bare-back riding and young trainers trustfully placing their heads into the toothy jaws of the whales. The new president of Sea World, Robert K. Gault Jr., was quoted as saying: "We were doing some very spectacular things that enhanced the show value, but we overemphasised the importance of the entertainment." That was an admission indeed, coming from an establishment which normally prides itself on its "educational" value. But predictably, Harcourt's moratorium on the most spectacular elements of the show was limited to the time-span of the scandal being erased from the public memory. Six months later, the trainers were back in the tanks with the killer whales and it was "business as usual". But in September 1988, Orky died — just 18 months after being moved from Marineland. The whale had lost almost a third of its body weight, prompting charges that the animal had "starved to death." Orky was the fourteenth Sea World orca to die in captivity since 1965.

Unfortunately for the image of Sea World, the remaining orcas' behavioural problems continued to deteriorate, eventually culminating in a devastating blow to public relations. In August 1989, Sea World's orca whale Kandu died after colliding at high speed with her partner Corky during a children's show. Witnesses declared that blood from the blowhole of the mortally wounded whale spurted over 6m into the air. Her jaw broken, Kandu eventually bled to death while shocked parents and children apparently had to be escorted out of the stadium. One spectator was quoted as saying: "I saw one whale with a huge gash ripped in its side like it had been harpooned or something. It leaped out of the water with a huge groan. I knew it was her death rattle — and then there was blood, loads of it. It dirtied the whole pool and you couldn't see the water. It was just all blood. Women and children had to look away." Sea World spokesmen speculated that Corky had smashed into Kandu deliberately, out of jealousy over the attentions of the male orca Namu, who was pen-ned-up at the time. The incident prompted whale expert Erich Hoyt to declare that "There has never been a known case of a killer whale killing another killer whale in captivity or even in the wild."

And so once again, Sea World was obliged to use all the ingenuity it could muster for the sake of "damage control". Said a report in the *San Diego Union:* "Sea World officials... apparently instructed employees to downplay the violent nature of Monday's bloody encounter. 'It actually resulted because of a little bit of playing between the two whales,' one cashier said. 'They weren't fighting,' said another with a smile. 'They were altercating.'" The final official line was: "The outcome of this par-ticular case was tragic, yet the incident was representative of common behaviour that is unrelated to captivity, show presentations or the level of daily activity of the whales." Reacting to the charge that corporate profits have a greater value than animal welfare at Sea World, Jackie Hill, vice president of communications, declared: "Sea World is not ashamed of being a profit making company. We are part of the economic structure of a free nation, returning profits to our shareholders." She went on to describe the standards of animal care at Sea World as "exemplary" and its facilities as "state of the art". Not all Sea World trainers would agree, however. Quoted in *The Killing Tanks*, an article by US journalist Gary Hanauer, one former trainer who left Sea World after being injured in an accident in 1984, declared that they were "ordered to administer oral drugs to the animals without knowing what they were, to spray paint the stump of a whale's amputated dorsal fin to make it appear normal, and to shake a dead whale on a stretcher to make it look as though the animal was still moving." Reeling from its plague of animal welfare scandals, still desperate for cash after its takeover battle, and increasingly media-shy over the scandals at Sea World, Harcourt recently sold the establishment to the multimillion dollar brewery corporation Anheuser-Busch, based in St Louis, Missouri.

All the rage at the moment on the US dolphin scene are "swim prog-rammes" where the animals are more or less leased by the half-hour to Hawaii and Florida holidaymakers at a price of up to $65 per person. Dol-phin-catching vet Dr Jay Sweeney runs his exhibit at the $360 million Hyatt Regency hotel in Waikoloa, Hawaii, where, in a "high-tech", "state of the art" lagoon, six dolphins are involved in seven "encounters" a day with hotel guests. So lucrative is this new form of entertainment that according to one official of the National Marine Fisheries Service, "Every hotel in Hawaii wants to put a dolpin in the pool." The dangers posed to the dolphins by human infection — and to the swimmers themselves by dolphins that suddenly begin to face their claustrophobia with an uncharacteristic aggression — have so far been ignored, and although the authorities seem keen to regulate this booming side-show, they are proving so popular that an outright ban seems unlikely.

Indeed, the never-ending controversy in the dolphin industry and the perceived inadequacy of the law has also had the effect of putting the National Marine Fisheries Service on the defensive, the federal body which administers the Marine Mammal Protection Act. Declares Nancy Daves Hicks of the Animal Protection Institute of America (API): "In 1988, API undertook a complete review of captive marine mammal issues to determine whether or not the federal agencies charged with regulating marine mammal capture and care were doing an effective job." API discovered, according to Hicks, that "the permit process is so automatic and routine that only when a facility is outrageously unfit or there is threat of litigation will a permit application be rejected. Of 261 applications for display permits forwarded to the Marine Mammal Commission for review, only eight were denied."

SOUTH AMERICA

Mexico, Argentina, Venezuela, Guatemala and Cuba — these countries began to play a pivotal role in the dolphin industry when the US Marine Mammal Act came into force, compensating for the sudden shortfall in supplies. In Argentina until the early 1980s, there was Avelino H. Cobreros' *American Fauna* whose advertisements offered Commerson or *Jacobita* dolphins for $12,000. These animals had been "tamed in ponds" measuring just 3 x 6 x 1m prior to shipment, and Cobreros, in all seriousness, advised potential customers that the dolphins should be kept either in "sea or sweet-water" at a temperature of "8 to 19 degrees", although "other varieties are also acceptable". In Arica, Chile, there is Lothar Schwark, a Swiss expatriate who in the past has also specialised in the capture of Commerson dolphins. The Commerson, with its exquisite black and white markings, became a sudden fad in European amusement parks in the early eighties — until it was discovered that the animal's survival span in captivity rendered it uneconomic. Nevertheless, it is thought that Schwark was behind two 1984 efforts to import Commerson dolphins into Germany.

Based in Mexico until recently was another Swiss, Heinz Hugentobler, who in 1978 supplied four dolphins to Bruno Lienhardt's International Dolphin Show, and one to Heinz Pelzer's Safaripark in Gross-Gerau, Germany. In 1985 he was involved in the sale of a trained 4.5 ton orca whale from Toronto to Mexico City for the staggering sum of a quarter of a million dollars.

But it is in Fidel Castro's revolutionary Cuba that dolphin catching in South America has been given a new lease of life, under the auspices of the quasi state-run enterprise *Aguaria Nacional*. Complains trainer Rocky Colombo of Italy's Ocean World Aquarium, who lost two dolphins supplied by Aguaria Nacional within as many years: "They send over the dolphins healthy or sick — it doesn't matter to them."

UNITED KINGDOM

Apart from the capture of five white whales as scientific curiosities in the 1870s, and several so-called "rescues" of stranded cetaceans in the 1930s, it was not until 1962 that the dolphin display industry in the UK evinced its first spasms of birth. It was then that two female bottlenose dolphins, from "captive Italian stock" were transported by road and air to an out-door swimming pool in Plymouth. Brought in by Tony Soper on behalf of the BBC Television children's programme *Animal Magic*, they starred briefly in the production *Ride a Dolphin*, before dying on the eighth day of their confinement, apparently from malnutrition.

Since then, up to three hundred bottlenose dolphins and eight killer whales have been imported into the UK, according to figures gathered by Dr Margaret Klinowska of Cambridge University. No one really knows how many of those dolphins died during their enforced captivity, quite simply because accurate records of transactions and mortalities were as rare as public accountability. We do know that today, only 13 dolphins and one killer whale are left.

In 1984, zoologist Charlie Arden-Clarke of the Oxford-based Political Ecology Research Group declared that at least 100 dolphins had died in captivity in Britain since 1960. Instead of living up to 25 years in the wild, he concluded in a report commissioned by Greenpeace, dolphins were, on average, dying in captivity before their 12th birthday. Similarly, the natural life-span of killer whales, believed to be between 35 and 100 years, was being reduced in British aquaria to an average of just two years and nine months. Though his report was lambasted by the industry as an exercise in exaggeration, the BBC's *Watchdog* programme in May 1984 uncovered a death toll of 75 animals. During the course of his investigation, which was continually hampered by the industry's refusal to supply data, Arden-Clarke also discovered that from 1969 to 1983, a period of only 14 years, at least 57 dolphins and nine killer whales had been imported into Britain. Of these, only 17 dolphins and four killer whales remained alive. But of course, the trouble with any such report is that by the time it's written and printed, it's already out of date: the dolphins just keep on dying.

Repeated controversies of this kind finally prompted the British government to institute a temporary import ban on captive cetaceans and announce a Department of Environment review of UK dolphinaria in 1985. That review culminated in a 250 page report by consultants Dr Margaret Klinowska and Dr Susan Brown of Cambridge University's research group in mammalian ecology and reproduction. The study, which became known as "The Klinowska Report", cites 127 dolphin mortalities between 1965-1985. But this estimate may only represent the tip of the iceberg for several reasons. First of all, Klinowska's assessment is based largely not on verifiable documentation but on the memories of those who had or continue to have a vested interest in the dolphin trade — in other words those most prone to rosy-hued recollections of the industry's past. To illustrate just how convenient lapses of memory can alter government-approved statistics, take the case of dolphin imports to the now-defunct Animal Training School and Dolphinarium in South Elmsall near Wakefield. Klinowska, relying almost exclusively on the testimony of the dealers themselves, reported that eight dolphins had been imported to this facility between 1973 and 1974. However, documents discovered recently by the Animal Protection Institute of America "in an old box in a Florida government office" reveal that no less that 34 dolphins were actually shipped to the South Elmsall establishment in that two year period. Furthermore, Klinowska lists no fewer than 81 additional unnamed dolphins with question marks denoting an uncertain fate following their sale, or their owners' bankruptcy. Finally, no account is taken in the statistics of what Klinowska euphemistically calls "the subsequent careers" of those cetaceans destined for re-export. But even taking into account all of these anonymous "ambassadors" of the animal kingdom, our ad hoc statistics still do not include dolphins fatally maimed during capture and transport, dolphins simply forgotten by their owners, and dolphin babies conceived in the wild but delivered in captivity, stillborn, rejected or even deliberately drowned by their mothers.

In the golden heyday of the industry, there were at least 36 assorted dolphinaria or itinerant dolphin shows in the UK "The owners and operators of the reputable dolphinaria would welcome tighter controls," wrote conservationist John Burton in 1973, revealing not only the pathetic subservience of the conservation movement at that time, but also, ever-present, its outlandish naivety, since any repute was singularly in the eyes of the beholder. Indeed, judging by the rabid exploitation of their captive dolphins, even moral constraints were regarded by the industry as virtually non-existent, and later, it systematically exploited every loophole that the law had to offer. Burton went on to remark that "dolphinaria are incredibly easy to open," and that "the import controls are almost non-existent; it is more difficult to bring an owl or a squirrel into Britain than a dolphin!" In the absence of any legislative controls, conditions varied between wretched and woeful, from portable plastic pools measuring just 1.5m deep and 3.5m in diameter, to converted public baths, the forerunners of today's permanent dolphinaria. Although somewhat larger, these pools also acted as overwintering bases and storage facilities for animals awaiting sale, lease or transport to seasonal shows, and so it was not unusual for them to be literally crammed with dolphins. The dolphin trade may have been characterised, from its very inception, by illusion and deceit, but its *raison d'être* — profitability — was governed strictly by what would today be called "hard-headed realism". For most dealers at the time, it didn't matter if a dolphin died as long as it could be replaced without ruining performances or contracts. Compared with potential revenues, dolphins were dirt cheap. In 1976, one could be bought for as little as $450 from a dealer in the Keys. The causes of death were as similar as they were predictable: peritonitis or renal failure from dirty, infected water, chlorine poisoning, heart failure attributable to stress, attacks by other dolphins due to overcrowding, suicide by ramming the walls of the pool, and the compulsive swallowing of foreign objects — Bubbles, for instance, who died at Clacton after ingesting a child's plastic windmill or Sinbad who allegedly choked to death at Woburn after a visitor tossed a 2p coin into his blow-hole.

Although bottlenose dolphins are found in British coastal waters, Klinowska reports that there have never been any serious attempts to capture the animals. One of the main reasons for this appears to be the tangle and confusion over legislative protection of "British" cetaceans. First of all, there is the "Royal Fish Law" of 1324 which affords the Crown exclusive rights to all whales. Then there is the Whaling Industry Regulation Act of 1934 which prohibits the capture of any cetacean within 200 miles of the British coast. And finally, the killing, injuring or capture of bottlenose dolphins, common dolphins and harbour porpoises is expressly forbidden under the Wildlife and Countryside Act of 1981.

Predictably, an industry with a constant hunger for dolphins wanted nothing to do with permits and red tape, and so several British dealers were deeply committed to catching dolphins abroad where few restrictions existed. At the forefront of this lucrative sector of the industry was *Queen's International Dolphins* owned by Keith R. Franklin and Louis D. Holloway. Based in Kent, the company described itself as "suppliers, collectors and trainers of high quality dolphins, whales and sea-lions", and during its ten-year life-span organised dolphin catches in Panama, Mexico and Italy.

Franklin and Holloway's first dolphins, Turk and Britt, arrived from Florida in 1969, ready for the opening of their Cliftonville Dolphinarium at the Queen's Hotel in Margate. This was a converted indoor swimming pool, featuring an underwater panorama from the hotel bar. But Franklin and Holloway could not content themselves with the small-time in provincial Margate when the pickings elsewhere were so temptingly sweet and easy. Klinowska lists a maximum of 41 dolphins passing through their hands between 1969-1979, but in reality the figure is more than double that. With dolphins leased from Aquatic Mammals Enterprises — operated by dealer Joe Raber at the Battersea Fun Fair — Queen's Entertainment Centre, another Franklin-Holloway off-shoot, provided shows to northern industrial cities like Bradford and Liverpool where the dolphins were simply put in the municipal swimming baths. They also exploited the summer holiday trade, with outdoor shows in portable 9m diameter pools at the Pier in Southend-on-Sea and in Skegness in Lincolnshire. At this time, the dolphin duo were involved in almost every aspect of the industry, their dealings a tangled web which not only included leasing animals for their own use but also renting them out to the likes of Jimmy Chipperfield for the circus czar's West Midland Safari Park near Bewdley in Worcester. Dolphins were also put into storage awaiting sale or transfer to other shows: according to BBC's *Watchdog* programme in May 1984, at one time eleven dolphins were kept in the Margate pool which was only large enough for four. Franklin also sent out a travelling Flipper show to the Far East, but disaster struck in Indonesia when four people were crushed to death as the frenzied crowds converged on the makeshift arena.

For Queen's, circumventing or finding and exploiting loopholes in international law became a speciality. Says a now repentant Keith Franklin: "We had about 100 dolphins go through our company in ten years of operations. We also bought-up all of the 'Pre-Act' dolphins in the USA — those that had been caught prior to the introduction of the Marine Mammal Act, which virtually ended the trade in the USA. I went all over the States buying-up these dolphins, and we held and trained them in New York and then sold them in pairs all over the world. My last two dolphins — Bonnie and Clyde — I sold to Conny Gasser in Switzerland." In fact, Franklin had a number of dealings with the former circus trapeze artist. These included catching dolphins in Mexico and Italy to circumvent the constraints of the Marine Mammal Act which had resulted in a drastic shortfall in supplies. With many dealers desperate for dolphins and basic prices having rocketed from $900 in 1972 to $2300 in 1973 after the introduction of the Marine Mammal Act, dolphin catchers in other parts of the world, such as Central America, Hong Kong, Japan and Taiwan, stood to make a fortune. Even as late as 1977/78, Queen's was, by its own admission, involved in a "large scale six-month operation in Panama, catching dolphins," a project spearheaded by Keith Franklin, while Louis Holloway kept shop at home.

Since 1978, Franklin had also been the British representative of one of the world's most notorious dolphin dealers, Bruno Lienhardt, owner of the Liechtenstein-based International Dolphin Show. One of Franklin's first transactions on behalf of Lienhardt was the renting of two IDS dolphins to Don Robinson's Flamingo Park which were later sent off to entertain the tourists in Alicante, Spain. Here, at least two foreign-owned dolphinaria had sprouted to exploit the tourist season, the Safari Park at Vergel near Alicante, and the fairground Holiday Parque near Benidorm.

When it came to dolphin dealing in the UK, Don Robinson and his one-time associate Pentland Hick were undisputed lords of the manor. The eccentric and visionary Hick founded the zoological gardens in Kirby Misperton, North Yorkshire in 1959, with an ambitious ex-professional wrestler Don Robinson as one of his partners. Accompanied by Dr John Lilly, who was later to become a guru for the New Age movement and a pioneer in "human-cetacean communication", two dolphins, Flipper and her one-year-old female calf Cookie, were flown in from Florida to be Flamingo Park's new inmates. They arrived on 20 June 1963, making Hick's establishment the first to display bottlenose dolphins in the UK — and perhaps the whole of Europe. They lived for 24 months and six months respectively, and were quickly replaced by two others. In 1963, Pentland Hick, still with a visionary eye for future trends, formed Associated Pleasure Parks, a company dedicated to consummating his dream of fusing, with elements of Disney, the zoo and the fairground. The forerunner of today's theme-park, Hick's brain-child came into being with the opening of a second establishment, Cleethorpes Marineland and Zoo.

Associated Pleasure Parks also organised primitive travelling shows using surplus dolphins stored at Flamingo Park. In the winter of 1966, for example, dolphins were exhibited in the old tram sheds of Queens Hall in Leeds, in a circular plastic tank just 1.52m deep and 3.66m in diameter. Although their battered merchandise often could not with-stand the rigours of itinerant circus life, the money-spinning shows went on, with the dolphins of Associated Pleasure Parks pulling crowds in other northern industrial cities during winter, and exploiting the sum-mer tourist trade in resorts like Bournemouth and Weymouth.

Klinowska describes Hick as "very adventurous, not only in transport methods, but also in his search for new species to exhibit". *Ruthless* how-ever might have been a better word, as the temperamental and flam-boyant entrepreneur "sent his people far and wide" to collect the speci-mens which appealed to a sudden whim. They included white whales from Canada, pilot whales from the Shetland islands, and a pair of Adria-tic common dolphins from Riccione, Italy, which were so stressed by their journey that they survived only a few days. Some consignments travelled not by air but by ship, despite this entailing a longer and more stressful journey for the animals. In 1965, reports Klinowska, "four white whales were sent by sea from Quebec, travelling in tanks on the deck of the liner *Arcadia*. Two were lost overboard in a storm when the tank failed, one died and the other was injured. The survivor and the dead animal were landed. The survivor was taken to Cleethorpes, but died of its injuries about September 1965."

It is here, in recounting the bizarre, pioneering adventures of Pentland Hick, that we stumble across yet another contemporary personality in the international trade in dolphins and whales, David C. Taylor, intrepid roving vet for many of the world's oceanaria, a consultant to the Circus Proprietors Association, author, television celebrity, and president of the European Association of Aquatic Mammals. A Yorkshireman of acerbic wit, driving ambition, and a weakness for the limelight, it was in the early 1960s that Taylor, having abandoned the more sedate vocation of family practice, became a freelance vet treating the wild exotic beasts of the zoo, circus and dolphinarium. He began his new career as a consultant to Belle Vue Zoo in Manchester, and then joined Hick and Robinson, eventually landing the job of curator at Flamingo Park under the directorship of Reg Bloom. Also working here during the sixties was Mike Riddell, later to become director of Antibes Marineland on the Mediterranean coast of France after marrying the daughter of Roland de la Poype, the tobacco baron who founded the Antibes oceanarium.

Although one can always admire a man or woman of vision and ideas, it is unfortunate that Hick's all-consuming passion was inflicted upon the defenceless animals that were to compose his grand menagerie. David Taylor recounts that, at Hick's behest, he was even dispatched to Greenland to find a narwhal, probably because that beautiful and mysterious unicorn of the sea so appealed to his master. In his 1976 book *Zoo Vet*, Taylor also describes a mission to Pakistan to locate pygmy sperm whales, and although a new-born animal was traced to a pool in Karachi, this had apparently been killed by some prankster placing a firework in its anus. Klinowska wryly remarks that "ordinary sperm whales were considered to be too large, even by Mr Hick."

While Hick began to flounder in his imaginative schemes and gimmicks, the more down to earth Robinson became increasingly involved in business practicalities. The brusque Yorkshireman, who had worked himself up hook and claw from the grimy terraced streets of the industrial north to the exclusive housing estates of the new rich, was to become a formidable business adversary of others in the UK dolphin industry. As Pentland Hick succumbed to financial woes, Don Robinson was poised to take over. Within a few years, Don Robinson Holdings, based in Scarborough, would incorporate up to fifty companies including several enterprises which had dealings in the dolphin industry, firms like Scotia Investments — mainly concerned with bingo halls and package holidays — which bought out Flamingo and Associated Pleasure Parks in 1969, and Yorkshire's Trident Television. This gave the holding company control of several zoo-dolphinaria: Flamingo Park, Scarborough Marineland, Blair Drummond, Crick Castle in Wales, Dudley Zoo, Cleethorpes and later, in 1977, Morcambe Marineland. It was at this juncture that Robinson, aided and abetted by his right-hand man Tom Hanson, a former wrestling cohort, took over the reins, seizing almost any opportunity to expand operations into virtually every aspect of the dolphin industry, including capture, sale and lease.

In 1970, Robinson's Scotia Investments held a summer dolphin show for one or two seasons at Gwrych Castle near St Asaph in North Wales. The only "filtration" was a chronic leak in the minuscule free-standing portable pool, leaving the hapless dolphins stranded on several occasions. Such travelling shows proved so lucrative that other enterprises also took to roaming the countryside with collapsible pools and beast wagons containing dolphins on irrigated stretchers. Reminiscent of the fairground wanderers of the Middle Ages with their dancing bear acts, records from the late sixties and early seventies speak of dolphin shows in small tents or inflatable domes, playing at the Battersea Fun Fair, on the Golden Mile at Blackpool, at the Belle Vue amusement park in Manchester, and swimming pools in Bristol and Bradford. Dolphins from seasonal venues, such as Blair Drummond in Scotland, also went travelling far afield. Records speak of the animals appearing in shows in Malta, Gibraltar, Mauritius and South Africa.

"We started by buying two dolphins from Jerry Mitchell but one died on the way over," Don Robinson told me from his offices at the Royal Opera House in Scarborough. "Later on we caught our own dolphins in Florida because of the poor standard of dolphins being sent over from Mitchell. He was supplying the whole of Europe with dolphins and he'd only keep them a week before transport and if they didn't eat within two days he'd force-feed them." But with constantly expanding interests in the industry, Robinson soon found himself buying dolphins anywhere he could find them, including from Europe's foremost dolphin trader James W. Tiebor, based in Munich. Later, he obtained his dolphins through the International Animal Exchange in Michigan, but was reluctant to comment on his present business dealings. Indeed, when asked if he was still involved in the dolphin business, he replied: "Well that's hypothetical, why do you want to know that?" Upon further questioning he stated: "We are only involved in places abroad and I'm not prepared to say where." The company however does have some involvement with Marineland in Palma Nova, Mallorca, a member of the Pleasurama group of companies which gained considerable notoriety for its dolphin dealing in the 1970s when Robinson was a director of the company. This is a Flamingo Park-like establishment, part zoo, part circus and part fairground, featuring a sea-lion show and a parrot circus, the exotic birds trained to roller-skate and ride monocycles over a tightrope. Hitting on a new fad, at one time Marineland also starred "Polynesian Diving Girls". Imported from Japan, Marineland's glossy brochure announced, seeded oysters are "brought to our Pearl Lagoon, where you can watch our girls dive and collect them for your entertainment and delight."

"We have investments in various companies abroad, with merchant bankers and pension funds helping us," Robinson told me. "We have a capital worth of £18 million so we're not fly-by-night or anything like that." Allergic as many of his compatriots are to public criticisms of the dolphin industry, even today Robinson staunchly defends his animal welfare record. "A few years ago we had more dolphinaria in Britain than anyone," he declared. "We were at Dudley, Cleethorpes, Scarborough, Blair Drummond in Scotland, Crick Castle in Wales, and we lost less dolphins than anyone in the country." Yet Robinson was actually the "bête noire" of the animal welfare movement at that time, in part because his dolphins were housed in one of the country's smallest pools. According to the RSPCA, the facilities were just sufficient to keep the dolphins alive, but no more. Travel seemed to be the purgatory of Robinson's dolphins, the animals being shunted not only between Scarborough and Flamingo Park, but also, during the winter, to Malta, South Africa, and Robinson's Canadian dolphinarium in Hemingford, Quebec. Until 1974, Robinson's primary dolphin holding was at Flamingo, and he continued to pay homage to the legacy of Pentland Hick, maximising the menagerie collection to more than a thousand animals, and spotlighting the most exotic specimens, the polar bears, elephants, orang-utans, the "splendour of the big cats".

The park's brochure, its cover sporting drawings of a smiling elephant, chimpanzee, lion, crocodile, snake and dolphin, advised visitors: "Take a Zambesi riverboat on the Jungle Cruise. Your white hunter will guide you through untamed crocodile country, past Zulu villages and lifelike tableaux of Jungle scenes. There's even Tarzan, and a prehistoric monster." As always, the dolphins were not exempt from this spinning of money and make-believe. The brochure continues: "See the fabulous performing dolphins in Ocean World. You'll marvel at the antics of these fun-loving sea creatures from the moment they take their opening bow to the time they wave goodbye. Diving through hoops, pushing boats around the pool, tail-walking — it's all in a day's fun for the dolphins." Exuberant fun and systematically concealed suffering — that was and continues to be the fate of the captive dolphin. According to Klinowska's estimates, at Flamingo alone from 1972-78, eleven dolphins died, a mortality rate of 35 per cent. Conveniently absent from these statistics however are another 21 dolphins whose individual destinies have been forgotten but who are now almost certainly dead. Asked how many dolphins he had actually imported during his years in the business, Robinson told me: "About ten or twelve and we can account for all of them." That just goes to show how rose-tinted memories can be in the animal exploitation industry. In total, from 1968 when it opened to the public, to 1978 when

Scotia Investments sold-out to A. Gibb, at least 87 dolphins were processed through Flamingo, revealing the extent to which the company was
involved in animal dealing. Most, if not all of those dolphins are now
dead, some surviving only a few days, some a season, and others long
enough to be traded around the world to other up and coming "performers", men like Mike Riddell in Antibes, and Conny Gasser in Switzerland. Scarborough Marineland and Zoo was another of Robinson's important holdings, with as many as 36 animals passing through the establishment in its 17 years of operations between 1968-1985, at least five of
them called "Flipper". This was one of the last of Robinson's dolphin
holdings to be turned into an American-style theme-park, the unwanted
animals being packed off to Windsor Safari Park.

Robinson's animals can have fared little better at Cleethorpes Marineland and Zoo in Lincolnshire where the fibreglass pool was only 2.44m
deep. But according to Klinowska, not only dolphins were kept at
Cleethorpes, but also a white whale, a pilot whale and even Robinson's
second orca, called Calypso. It was here that celebrity vet David Taylor
attempted to artificially inseminate the doomed whale with sperm from
Cuddles, Robinson's killer whale at Flamingo Park. Evidently it was
thought that a baby whale would be a stupendous public-relations
windfall, but Taylor's efforts proved futile. In the end, Calypso died in
Antibes and Cuddles — who had already suffered from such serious intestinal ulcers and massive internal bleeding that the pool at Flamingo Park
had been turned blood-red — was transported to Dudley Zoo, on Castle
Hill, overlooking the smog and industrial desolation of the Black Country. According to Doug Cartlidge, who worked for Don Robinson during
the 1970s, and who later went on to be killer whale and dolphin trainer at
Windsor Safari Park, Dudley's appalling facilities undoubtedly contri-
buted to its premature death. "We were nursing Cuddles for 24 hours a
day for weeks at Flamingo Park. And when Robinson told me he was
moving him to Dudley Zoo I told him that if he did, I'd leave. And I did
leave. Cuddles was in a very bad condition, but I do know that he supposedly attacked Robinson in Dudley Zoo." There, the ailing creature
had been consigned to a pool "which was hardly big enough for him to
turn around in" — but enough to die in. The pear-shaped outdoor whale
pool was just over 15m long, 6m wide and 3.5m deep, while its inmate,
measuring over 6m from head to tail, was almost half of the size of its container. Taylor attended the last rites. He was seen clambering down into
the empty pool with a needle and a knife. Soon afterwards, Cuddles was
dead.

The blunt Yorkshireman, who "likes to call a spade a spade", was under
no illusions about his dolphin shows being "educational". "The kids enjoy
it," Robinson was quoted as saying in the *Observer* magazine in 1984,
when he still owned two dolphins at Scarborough. "It's a good day out.

It's more a pleasure thing than an educational show. But what's wrong with giving people pleasure?"

> *"The sole object of Pleasurama Ltd is to make a profit for its shareholders."*
> — Sir Harmar Nicholls, MP

Perhaps one of the most sordid examples of dolphin exploitation was the brain-child of Pleasurama, now one of Robinson's partners in Spain, but then led by Sir Harmar Nicholls, MP. Pleasurama's London Dolphinarium, at 65 Oxford Street, opened its doors to the public in 1971, as an up-market striptease revue featuring dancing "aquamaids" and several dolphins confined to a tank 3m deep, 14m long and 5m wide. In his book *Doctor in the Zoo*, David Taylor writes that the male dolphins had to be treated with anti-androgens to prevent them making passionate advances to the mermaid showgirls. Unlike the Moulin Rouge's similar revue, which spanned 14 years, the London Dolphinarium was never a great financial success for Pleasurama and it closed its doors in 1973. Always the optimist, Klinowska reports that "an experimental lecture and demonstration service for schools" also took place here, but presumably without the aquamaids.

Writing in the magazine *Animals*, journalist Nigel Sitwell declared that he was "shocked" by what he saw and heard at the dolphinarium's opening gala night, eagerly attended by striptease and circus voyeurs, fellow politicians of the chairman, investors and Pleasurama share-holders. "The nadir of my evening was when Sir Harmar Nicholls, MP, chairman of Pleasurama Ltd, announced that 'the sole object of Pleasurama Ltd is to make a profit for its shareholders.' This amazing remark was greeted with delighted cheers and applause. It does, of course, reflect a good conservative business principle — and in many business fields it is arguably quite acceptable. But not, I submit, when the business is keeping animals in captivity." Sitwell went on to deride the showbiz and glitz of the dolphinarium, its complete absence of any element of education, conservation, or scientific research, an observation as relevant then as it is today: "The standard of commentary at most of these shows is shockingly low, consisting almost entirely of pure corn. And I believe the surroundings are important too. In the case of the London Dolphinarium, one has to negotiate one's way past a battery of stalls selling an array of gimcrack souvenirs of the most spectacular vulgarity. The whole atmosphere smacks of blatant hucksterism — it is the land of the fast buck — and I think it is quite wrong to keep any animals, but dolphins in particular, in such undignified surroundings."

In March 1974, a similar nude review, the brain-child of soft porn impresario Paul Raymond, opened at London's Royalty Theatre, but closed after only six weeks due to adverse publicity. Klinowska writes that "the famous 'dolphin strip-tease' appears to have been accomplished by training the animals to press quick-release fasteners and the swimmers to position themselves appropriately; not by soaking the bikinis in fish meal or by hiding pieces of fish in the costumes." Klinowska, however, gives no sources for this claim, and there have been persistent rumours to the contrary, especially from the Moulin Rouge. In any event, it is now virtually beyond doubt that the dolphins in Paris had to be kept half-starved in order to make them perform. But this aspect of wild animal training — food deprivation and reward — is something that Klinowska consistently fails to address.

Other prominent personalities during the heyday of the dolphin entertainment industry include Terry Nutkins, currently general manager of Windsor Safari Park. Nutkins is a veteran dolphin owner and handler who had his fingers in innumerable business pies. Employed by Pleasurama as their assistant general manager, he was instrumental in founding the London Dolphinarium and its aquamaids revue in 1971. From 1970 to 1983 Nutkins was also general manager of four Trust House Forte dolphinaria which lost at least 12 dolphins during his tenure.

Reg Bloom is another seasoned practitioner in the arts of dolphin exploitation, with almost a quarter of a century of experience to draw upon. Formerly director of Don Robinson's Flamingo Park in Yorkshire, Bloom is now consultant to the same amusement park-cum-zoo, re-christened Flamingo Land by its new proprietor in 1978. He is also joint owner with his son, Peter Bloom, of Dolphin Services, an off-shoot of Bloom UK which supplies dolphins under contract to various establishments — including Flamingo Land where Peter Bloom is dolphinarium manager and head trainer. Having worked at Clacton and Windsor, Hong Kong, and two dolphinaria in Spain, Peter Bloom has accumulated over eleven years of experience in the industry, and was even commissioned to set up from scratch a dolphinarium in Manila, from designing the pool and having dolphins caught in Taiwan, to staff and animal training.

From 1971 to 1985, Reg Bloom operated the pretentious-sounding North Sea World Training Dolphins School at the pier in Clacton on Sea in Essex, which consisted of a former outdoor swimming pool. Although used for storing dolphins, Bloom's Dolphins School was also a training establishment, with many animals spending time there during transit from one venue to another. Bloom was also involved in the capture, purchase and transportation of dolphins for other owners, including Sir Harmar Nicholls' aquagirls revue in Oxford Street. In 1969, he went off to the Florida Keys to catch dolphins with Jerry Mitchell, and five animals which managed to survive capture and transport ended up at

Windsor Safari Park, then owned by the Billy Smart organisation. Later residents of Bloom's Clacton pool included three young killer whales, Nemo, Neptune, and another unnamed male, owned by the International Animal Exchange. They had been wild-caught from the same pod in October 1981 by Helgi Jonasson's animal-dealing company in Iceland, *Fauna*. Languishing in the seaside pool awaiting sale, their plight aroused the attention of Greenpeace which subsequently launched a campaign to "Free The Clacton Three". But within days — and only two months after they were fished out of the sea — the anonymous male died of traumatic shock following severe injury to its abdominal wall and kidneys, either caused by a transit accident, attempted suicide, or by the aggression of his brothers in the sloping 2.40m-3.20m deep former swimming pool. Neptune died 18 months afterwards of peritonitis, leaving Greenpeace with a campaign called "Free The Clacton One".

Without insurance, those deaths would have represented a stinging loss for the International Animal Exchange. But as it was, unable to find buyers for the animals, the mortalities may even have been financially expedient since the whales each cost £30,000 in insurance premiums and feed, consuming 220 kg of fish every day. Nemo languished for three years at Clacton, which meant that in terms of survival rates, he was already living on borrowed time. Greenpeace had raised £45,000 to buy the whale, with the intention of retraining him for life in the wild and eventually releasing him in his home waters to rejoin his family or pod. But neither Nemo's owners, the International Animal Exchange, nor Clacton Pier's manager Frank McGinty, were in the mood to haggle with Greenpeace, least of all in public. Release would have set a dangerous precedent, and some scientists, who should have known better, were quick to condemn the plan as a gimmick which would be both cruel and fatal — though it is ironic that they never termed the catching or imprisonment as such. McGinty stated that Nemo would cost at least £250,000, inflating the ailing whale's value to put it way beyond the means of the Greenpeace budget. A behind the scenes attempt by the International Animal Exchange to sell the whale to an aquarium in Mexico failed when the Department of Environment refused to issue an export permit on the grounds that Mexico was not a member of CITES. Finally the battle of nerves culminated not in Nemo's release back into the wild as Greenpeace had so fervently hoped, but in the creature's transfer on "humanitarian" grounds to Windsor Safari Park. Here, the whale, 7.5m in length and weighing over a ton, was to share a claustrophobic 26 x 14 x 3.5m pool with a female orca called Winnie, seven bottlenose dolphins, and, during show-time, a sea lion act and a high-diving performance.

Nemo's long solitary confinement at Clacton and the fate of his brothers had provoked considerable public controversy, and indeed, it was actually the plight of this single orca which eventually prompted the government to launch, in the autumn of 1985, an official enquiry into UK dolphinaria, to be spearheaded by Dr Margaret Klinowska. "For the whale whose plight started it all," wrote Kieran Mulvaney of the Whale and Dolphin Conservation Society, "the future of Britain's dolphinaria is no longer of any consequence. Shortly after Nemo had been moved to Windsor, I went to see him for the first time, and found him resting his head against a viewing window in the wall of his pool, vocalising to himself as he rocked gently from side to side. As I watched silently, a crowd of school children tried to attract his attention by jeering and banging on the glass just inches from his face. It was, at least, an indignity Nemo did not have to endure for too long. As 1986 drew to a close, he became seriously ill with cancer. By the time his trainers noticed any symptoms, it was too late to do anything. Within days, he was dead." "Cancer" was, at least, the official line, though no tissue samples were made available for independent analysis.

By 1986, only five dolphinaria had managed to survive an inevitable process of recession and consolidation, partly induced by public distaste for the ruthlessness with which the marine cousins of humanity have been exploited. Those establishments were Brighton Aquarium and Dolphinarium, Flamingo Land in North Yorkshire, Knowsley Safari Park on Merseyside near Liverpool, Morecambe Marineland in Lancashire, Whipsnade Park, and Windsor Safari Park Ltd.

Brighton Aquarium and Dolphinarium is owned by Aquarium Entertainments Ltd. Leased from Brighton Corporation, its main pool — 22m long, 9m wide and 3m deep — is normally shared by three or four dolphins. Although first opened in 1872 by Prince Arthur, it was not until 1968 that a display pool was constructed to house two bottlenose dolphins that had been captured in Miami. Brighton was also not averse to an occasional dabble in animal dealing. In 1977, in a joint venture with Don Robinson, six Mexican dolphins were ordered, their planned destination Scarborough Marineland. Five of the animals survived capture long enough to be put in wooden crates in the unheated hold of an aircraft bound for London. Chilled to the bone, the ailing creatures were then driven to Brighton for nursing, but four of them died. The one remaining dolphin recovered and was sent to Scarborough where it eventually became just another anonymous mortality statistic. Then, in 1979, in conjunction with the ubiquitous Reg Bloom, six animals were purchased from Ocean Park dolphinarium in Hong Kong. They were the survivors of a so-called "drive fishery" in Taiwan, where dolphins are slaughtered either for meat for human consumption, or because fishermen regard them as pests which deplete their fishing grounds. For about two months, Reg Bloom had the six dolphins put in temporary storage at a disused swimming pool in Worthing. From there, four animals went to clients in

Spain, and the remaining pair were taken to Brighton, one surviving another three or four months and the other dying a year later. Altogether, Klinowska speaks of 14 out of 17 dolphins dying here between 1968 and 1985, although she stresses that "Brighton have not kept systematic records of their animals and the veterinary records before 1983 have disappeared."

Pool size at Flamingo today is no different from 1968, when Reg Bloom's original 1966 design was expanded into a figure eight in order to accommodate the ill-fated killer whale, Cuddles. Its three current inmates must make do with a world 24m in length, 12m in diameter and between 2.74m and 4.27m in depth. However, as Doug Cartlidge wryly points out, during show time here, in line with the dolphin industry's new role in public education, it is announced "that these animals in the wild would never encounter water deeper than three metres".

Knowsley Safari Park in Prescot, near Liverpool, is owned by the Earl of Derby, and was opened to the public in 1971 following the lead of other stately homes which had to choose between bankruptcy and an invasion of day-trippers. The 18th Earl of Derby chose the latter, perhaps inspired by his distinguished ancestor, the 13th Earl, who had created his own menagerie of rare and exotic species at Knowsley early in the last century. Somewhat consoled by this, the Earl formed a partnership with circus baron Jimmy Chipperfield to operate the safari park. The Park's dolphinarium, operated under contract by Trust House Forte, was inaugurated in 1972. Perhaps for the sake of its reputation, the hotel chain prudently chose to revoke their contract in the beginning of 1983 because of what Klinowska terms "the difficulty and expense of obtaining replacement dolphins". In ten years of operating the establishment, Trust House Forte had lost at least seven dolphins at Knowsley alone and this could not be reconciled either from a profit or public relations point of view. It was then that the Earl and ringmaster Chipperfield called in Reg Bloom, who promptly obtained a permit to import two replacement dolphins from the USA. The first of these, purchased from Marineland, Palos Verdes, California, arrived in March 1983, became ill with phlebitis at Christmas and died the following February of liver failure. And so the show went on, this time with yet another two dolphins, called Sooty and Clyde, delivered by Terry Nutkins who had purchased them from Blair Drummond when Trust House Forte dissolved all of their dolphin interests. But ultimately, Knowsley was to become yet another victim of dying dolphins, financial constraints and public pressure, and by 1987 the dolphinarium had closed its doors for good.

Whipsnade Park and its Water Mammals Exhibit is owned by the Zoological Society of London (ZLS). It is a registered scientific and educational charity which is somewhat ironic since a succession of teachers have condemned every UK dolphinarium, including Whipsnade's, as being entirely devoid of educational value. Established in 1826, the ZLS has a proud and distinguished history, though how rose-coloured is open to question. A gentleman's club for much of its life, inspiration for its founding seems to have been sired by a passion for collecting as many unknown and exotic curiosities as could be found within the animal kingdom.

As early as 1860, attempts by the ZLS were made to keep harbour porpoises at Regent's Park, but from the fourteen that arrived, three died during capture, and the remainder soon perished in captivity, setting an unheeded and ominous precedent for the future. It was not until 1972 that the ZLS, having maximised its range of exotic species at Whipsnade Park since acquiring it in 1927, opened a "cetacean collection" to serve the callings of science and education. Concealed behind such pretensions were five frightened and travel-weary dolphins which had, with the usual degree of compassion, just been caught, bartered for, force-fed and dispatched by Marine Animal Productions Inc., operated by one Mobi Solangi, yet another Florida dolphin catcher. Notwithstanding a supposedly superior standard of animal husbandry at Whipsnade, one animal perished within the space of a week. Doug Cartlidge reports that "this animal had numerous infected ulcerated skin lesions caused by chafing in the slings during transport... No fat was found in any part of the carcass... Stress and trauma were also listed as causes of death. Therefore, it would appear that this animal starved to death and was transported even though it was ill." Two of the other imported dolphins died in 1974, the third in 1979, while the remaining dolphin had the luck or misfortune to live until 1984. A baby born in May 1984 lived less than a fortnight.

By 1985, only two dolphins composed Whipsnade's "Order Cetacea" despite an original avowed ambition to stock the pools with other species of dolphin and whale, and to establish a breeding colony. But behind such scientific affectations, it was in fact all the fun of the fair. Indeed, in his 1988 study, Doug Cartlidge reserves some of his harshest criticisms for this once eminent and prestigious institution. "The pool itself is wholly inadequate in terms of size for the purpose for which it was supposedly intended: as a pool for a proposed breeding colony for dolphins... it even fails the standards introduced in 1985 by the European Association of Aquatic Mammals, which is made up mainly of owners and operators of dolphinaria." Nor was Cartlidge impressed by Whipsnade's much-vaunted standards of animal husbandry. "The actions of the staff at this establishment towards their animals have appalled me," he wrote. Noting that a net had even been left in the pool with the dolphins, he commented: "Video film clearly shows that both animals were in the same area without any supervision. Even an inexperienced visitor commented on the inherent danger. Had either animal become caught in the net it would have drowned before any assistance could have been given. How 'qualified' staff could have carried out such an irresponsible act amazes me."

Cartlidge goes on to describe the plight of Samson, an animal who had become psychologically devastated by his confinement here. "For a number of years now the male, 'Samson', has been exhibiting severe mental and psychological problems. He goes into an almost psychotic trance, and on occasions he has been known to ram the underwater viewing windows. He fails to respond to any signal or stimulus for extended periods of time." Klinowska, in her report for the government, also cites Samson's erratic behaviour, though with explanations that appear unashamedly anthropocentric. "He began to 'attack' the underwater windows," she wrote, "building up to nine incidents in a month and damaging his beak and melon (the area above the beak). It was thought that he was attacking his reflection and many efforts were made to reduce reflections, by altering lighting, without much effect. Various 'toys' and extra play sessions with keepers were also provided, but to no avail. In the 1985 observation session we saw no 'attacks', but Samson did bump his head on the glass when inadvertently startled (by a dropped pencil) at 01.15 and produced a new (to us) very loud 'creaking' sound, which was repeated at increasing intervals and decreasing frequencies for almost 10 minutes." Noting that the behavioural problems first began when two of Samson's companions died in 1983, she went on to declare that Whipsnade's decision to bring in a replacement dolphin called Lady was a "reasonable solution to the problem". The scientific evidence for this diagnosis apparently, was that "in the six months since Lady arrived, glass attacks have only occurred three times".

Cutting its losses, Whipsnade Zoo closed its dolphinarium in June 1988, despite all the glowing plans for a large-scale breeding centre which had so impressed Klinowska during the government enquiry. Still battling with madness, Samson was moved out of sight and out of mind to Spain, while Lady was to end her days at the grimy and squalid Morecambe Marineland.

Evidently run on a shoe-string, the dilapidated *Morecambe Marineland* in Lancashire is owned by Ocean World (Marine) Ltd, a yacht building and fitting company which took over from Don Robinson's Trident Television in 1983. Once proudly claiming to be "Europe's first Oceanarium", it currently possesses a solitary male dolphin called Rocky. This individual is the only one left out of at least 13 others which either died or passed through on the way to some unknown and unenviable fate since Morecambe's opening in 1964. The establishment was never very lucky with dolphins: according to the BBC's *Watchdog* programme in 1984, seven out of eight dolphins died here within two years. Ironically,

Rocky has the deepest dolphin pool in the country — 5.5m — but all to himself. The animal had been held virtually in solitary confinement for four years, with only a brief respite when Sooty — who was destined to perish within two months — was acquired from Liverpool's Knowsley Safari Park. Lady, purchased from Whipsnade in June 1988 to enhance show value and give Rocky some company, died a year later after suffering a miscarriage. Although organisations such as Zoo Check had protested the proposed transfer, no reply from the government was received until after the deal and merchandise had been signed, sealed and delivered. "The wisdom of mixing Lady with Rocky must be questioned," wrote Cartlidge. "Although representation was made to the Department of the Environment pointing out reasons to refuse the move, they decided in their wisdom to sanction it. If Lady dies within a short time of arriving at Morecambe then the Department of the Environment must be considered, in part, responsible." Following a brief visit shortly after Lady's arrival at Morecambe, Cartlidge added the following comments: "She was not feeding, was very lethargic and all her skin was peeling badly. It was later discovered that there had been a problem with the chemical induction system, causing the severe burning. Her failure to feed would indicate possible, stress-related problems following transportation." The dolphin never recovered.

Windsor Safari Park in Berkshire, now owned by John Rigby's Themes International plc, was originally the brain-child of circus baron Billy Smart, and was opened in 1970 by Princess Margaret.

Billy Smart had already gained some experience with cetaceans in 1965, when 30 seemingly lost pilot whales were sighted swimming in the Thames. Always with an eye open for an unexpected opportunity, Smart, together with staff from Don Robinson's Flamingo Park, promptly mounted a catching expedition. But after five days and expenses of a thousand pounds, they were informed by the police that whale catching in the Thames was illegal. It apparently contravened the 1324 Royal Fish Law which states that all whales are the property of the Crown. In his 1982 book *Next Panda, Please,* intrepid vet David Taylor relates, in yet more incredible adventures, how he accompanied Garry Smart, grandson of the circus czar and one of the directors of Windsor, to Malta in an effort to save two baby pilot whales which had been languishing on a fishmonger's slab for three days. Taylor promptly patched up the animals and then had them put in a local swimming pool, while he and Smart went off to arrange passage for the rescued whales to Windsor. When they returned to the pool, however, they discovered that the animals were suffering from acute sunburn, apparently because the locals who were tending them concluded that they enjoyed the sun; they had even smeared their bodies with suntan lotion. The whales promptly developed infected blisters and soon died.

Billy Smart's first dolphins arrived from the USA in the summer of 1969, caught off Florida by Jerry Mitchell and the ever-present Reg Bloom. In 1977 a financially ailing Billy Smart, also beset by family squabbles, sold out to Don Robinson's Trident Television, and six years later Windsor once again changed hands, coming into the possession of Southbrook and City Holdings. The latest owner is entrepreneur John Rigby who purchased the park for £23 million in January 1989. In total, from its founding to the present day, at least 24 dolphins have known the pools of Windsor Safari Park, and at least 14 have died, ten during the six-year tenure of Trident Television. Such estimates however may once again be far off the mark, since Klinowska reports, apparently without sarcasm, that "in the changes of ownership, animal records at Windsor appear to have gone astray."

When the dolphin controversy first broke out with a vengeance in 1984, the managing director of Windsor Safari Park, Andrew Haworth-Booth, maintained that dolphinaria were constantly improving and gaining valuable experience in husbandry. Ten or fifteen years earlier, he was quoted as saying, there might have been a valid case for protests against animal welfare abuse. "There were quite a few cowboys around then. They would come along, dig a hole in a car park and stick a couple of dolphins in it. It's no wonder they didn't live very long. But people like that haven't stayed in the industry." If only that were true. Today, under the supervision of general manager and veteran dolphin dealer Terry Nutkins, Windsor has the most overcrowded pools in the UK. The main rectangular display pool, 26m long, 14m wide and 3.5m deep is shared by five adult bottlenose dolphins, two calves, and one killer whale owned by the world's largest animal dealing company, International Animal Exchange. One side of the pool is divided into four holding pens used to "store" the animals either during shows, training, behavioural problems, punishment, or maintenance. They measure just 2.6 x 3.5 x 1.5m deep. Doug Cartlidge, a former head trainer here, notes that "animals have been observed to be locked in pen areas, even when shows were completed and no training or any other activity was being carried out in the main pool area." In some cases, confining the dolphins to these minuscule holding pens was not an oversight on the part of the trainers, but a deliberate attempt to punish the animals. Writes Cartlidge: "I have been informed and shown documentation that animals have been disciplined for poor performances etc., by being locked away in pens. In addition, feed cuts have been regularly made as punishment."

During Margaret Klinowska's official enquiry on behalf of the government and taxpayer, all of the existing dolphinaria reported ambitious plans to modernise and improve their facilities. This was hardly astonishing, given the industry's acute defensiveness following several years of scathing publicity in the media and critical scrutiny by organisations such as Greenpeace and the RSPCA. But it was the style rather than the substance of their proposals which aroused curiosity. It was as though they had been tailor-made, not to conform to realities, but to appease and impress the government reviewer who, in her professional capacity, already harboured a certain degree of favouritism towards the concept of the captive dolphin — as long as their captivity could be justified in the name of science or education. The task of the industry was to convince Klinowska — and the public — that the industry's brutality was a thing of the past, and even then caused not by greed or the dolphins' inherent unsuitability for captivity, but simply by inexperience in animal husbandry. Predictably, euphemism and pretension once again reached cloud nine, with dolphinarium managers portraying themselves as the "curators" of "zoological aquaria", responsible establishments which promise to play a vital role in education, science and conservation. By appearing before her as compliant and reasonable, the soul of respectability, the dolphin circus hoped to pre-empt the harshest measures against the industry which Klinowska might have been obliged to recommend. All in all, it amounted to yet another disingenuous scene in the industry's kaleidoscope of illusion, even though, behind the Potemkin facade, those zoological aquaria are still no more than glorified amusement parks.

The masquerade of dolphinarium science was nowhere more evident than at Whipsnade Park, though Klinowska seems to have been well and truly dazzled by the illusion. "Whipsnade would like to build a large breeding complex," she enthused, "stocked with animals of appropriate age from the same wild social group, near the existing dolphinarium, retaining the old pool for performances." Mr Victor Manton seems to have been the author of this proposal. As "curator" of Whipsnade's Water Mammals Exhibit and employed in one capacity or another since the dolphinarium's founding, he is also a respected board member of the European Association of Aquatic Mammals (EAAM), and has been editor of the organisation's journal *Aquatic Mammals* since 1972. "I don't like commercial exploitation," Manton was quoted as saying when the dolphin controversy blew up in 1984. "I don't agree with making dolphins sing 'Happy Birthday' or dress up in funny clothes." He does however defend the keeping of dolphins in the name of science, and with a Nelsonian eye, conveniently claims that it cannot be proved conclusively that dolphins die prematurely in captivity. "No one knows how long a dolphin lives in the wild," he is quoted as saying. "The claims that some dolphins can live 40 years are inconclusive." Quoted by John May in the *Observer*, Manton declared: "We are not involved in commerce. We are part of a scientific and educational trust whose covenant is to introduce new and curious specimens to the general public. That is our major justification." Despite such self-esteem, the dolphin show at Whipsnade, prior to giving up the ghost in the summer of 1988, generally followed the same banal pattern as everywhere else, with as many "facts" thrown to the audience as dead fish to the dolphins.

Fearful that the dolphin import ban might be extended indefinitely, nearly all of the dolphinaria proposed the construction of "breeding and rearing areas" — knowing full well that if Klinowska wanted dolphin breeding she would also have to recommend lifting the import prohibition so that the establishments could first of all form viable breeding populations. Ostensibly to reduce pressure on wild populations, breeding could also be utilised — as it is today whenever a dolphin calf is born — to prove that the animals are happy in captivity. Perhaps, being a confirmed pragmatist, Klinowska believed that she should encourage the dolphin industry to reform itself, using carrot and stick. And yet is this really pragmatism, or merely vain hopes and sophistry? Dolphinaria are scientifically and educationally untenable and even Klinowska — though she has tried persistently — cannot squeeze a square peg into a round hole. Notwithstanding Pilleri's "inherent contradiction" of keeping in cramped conditions creatures accustomed to vast open spaces, the litany of continuing abuse, exploitation, and systematic deceit on the part of the industry must automatically disqualify it from any supposed role in education or science, which, in theory at least, should have some relation to honesty and truth. To pretend otherwise is to turn reality on its head, and indeed, during the government enquiry, this was the star turn of the dolphin circus.

Accusations of "conflict of interest" were heard repeatedly against Klinowska. Declared veteran conservationist Ian McPhail, European Co-ordinator of the International Fund for Animal Welfare: "From the very beginning it was professed by the government that the consultant of the investigation would be independent and impartial. Margaret Klinowska was eminently unsuited for this task. Almost her entire career has been dependent upon research on captive dolphins and she was therefore highly unlikely to come out in favour of meaningful restrictions or abolition, whatever the evidence in favour of such action. We protested to Waldegrave over the choice, we said this loud and clear, but to no avail."

Once the enquiry was under way, it became increasingly evident that Klinowska was consistently evading the very terms of reference for which the review had been initiated in the first place, namely, *can the import and display of live cetaceans be justified in terms of education, science and captive breeding?* These parameters were arrived at expressly because of EEC Council Regulation 3626/82, which specifically forbids the import of dolphins and whales into member states for purely commercial purposes. Indeed, it must be stressed that Klinowska's attempts to improve the lot of cetaceans already held captive actually lay well beyond the jurisdiction of the Review. Yet by focussing much of her attention on mortality rates, optimum pool sizes and water management, the continuation of the dolphin industry, albeit under stricter controls, became a *fait accompli*. Thus, although Klinowska concluded that "it would be difficult to justify UK dolphinaria on educational, research or breeding grounds", with certain improvements, "such establishments *could* meet professional standards in all three areas and make significant contributions." This was despite the fact that the Review's consultant educationalists voiced grave doubts as to the educational value of such establishments. The Review attributed the following comments to one consultant: "The claim that a particular exhibition intended to promote and preserve commercial interests has specific and valuable educational spin-offs should be treated with caution. The crude and demeaning use of music in the Flamingo Land show together with its 'show biz' commentary exemplified... a lack of sensitivity to the status of wildlife and demeaned the relationship between humans and animals." Klinowska went on to admit that "the experts are concerned that the unnatural, anthropomorphic exhibition of animals as performers, may be merely showing the majority who witness the displays that the animals' existence is legitimated only by their ability to meet the demands for human entertainment. This is considered to be anti-educational." Not withstanding such expert testimony however, Klinowska concludes that "there seems to be no reason why professional education about the animals, their habitat and conservation cannot be provided by dolphinaria." But Klinowska is wrong, for one very simple reason, a reason that was quite lucidly expounded by one educationalist: "A *truly* educational experience of dolphinaria would be self-defeating, in that it would help children to realise that the importation, confinement, treatment and exploitation of dolphins and whales for the purpose of entertainment was against the natural order of things."

As it is, education in the dolphinarium is inevitably reduced to mere deception, a junk-food cocktail in which a few bland facts and figures are grudgingly blended into a circus-style concoction where dolphins wear straw-hats and sunglasses or have their teeth scrubbed with outsize toothbrushes. Take the show at Knowsley dolphinarium which was cited by Klinowska as a "representative example because it contains the widest range of information." The commentary, interspersed with the usual banal dolphin tricks, merely drags educational credibility into the realms of farce, a kind of latter-day *Pathe* Newsreel patriotic to the cause of the industry: "Sooty, our youngest member, is nine years old. She was featured on a TV series called *Animal Magic* with Terry Nutkins. Three years ago, Terry brought Sooty out of Japan, and at that time the Japanese fishermen were slaughtering the dolphins and if Sooty had not been rescued and brought into captivity, she would have been eaten as dolphin meat."

"The last straw was when they showed me — evidently with great pride — a dolphin which had been totally mutilated, a huge carving knife sticking out of its back" — Prof. Giorgio Pilleri. A dolphin under experimentation in Rene Guy Busnel's laboratory near Paris. (Giorgio Pilleri).

Klinowska brought the same standards of scientific methodology to bear when she recommended that scientific "research should be an integral part of the keeping of cetaceans". This was in spite of many submissions of evidence which supported the Pilleri view that the study of dolphins kept against their will in stressful, artificial conditions can only provide artificial scientific results. Furthermore, Klinowska never adequately explained how such envisaged in-depth scientific investigations could be fitted into an already hectic entertainment schedule, some establishments holding up to eight dolphin shows a day. Apart from the more innocuous forms of research proposed, focusing on such aspects as behaviour and feeding, Klinowska also hinted at more invasive studies. In discussing the potential impact of the Animals (Scientific Procedures) Bill, she stated that "such research animals must be kept in licensed premises and may be required to be destroyed by recognised humane procedures at the termination of an experiment." According to CITES transaction statistics, from 1980 to 1983 alone, 157 live cetaceans were traded between nations to satisfy the curiosities of science. Although some of these dolphins — their owners conveniently exploiting CITES loopholes — may well have become no more than circus animals, others undoubtedly ended their days in the nightmare of the laboratory tank and the specially designed strait-jackets which facilitate various forms and methods of vivisection. One need only recall the distinguished career of Prof. René Guy Busnel, who, in his Paris laboratories, gained a reputation for "cutting up dolphins like sausages", sacrificing at least ten animals every year in his obsessive and ultimately futile quest to learn the secrets of dolphin sonar. Rather more benignly perhaps, there was the Frankenstein named "Kuri", which science created at an aquarium in Kanagawa prefecture south of Tokyo. Proclaimed as "the world's only hybrid offspring of a whale and a dolphin", this engineered freak of nature was born in May 1985 to great acclaim by the crowds, only to die of pneumonia a few days later.

In the same extraordinary way in which she was able to ignore her own evidence, Klinowska also came out in favour of dolphinaria as potentially successful breeding establishments. Although conceding that "the breeding of cetaceans in captivity has not been particularly successful or reliable in any part of the world," she went on to portray the survival of three calves at Windsor as evidence of a significant improvement in husbandry. This was despite the fact that out of 24 known cetacean births in Britain — at least eight conceived in the wild before capture — 22 died either as miscarriages, stillbirths, premature births, or, within weeks, succumbed to disease or were drowned by the mothers. Furthermore, little or no credence was given to well-grounded scientific reports which concluded that to produce second generation animals with a minimum starting colony of a male and 12 females, it would cost millions — a sum that not even the richest dolphinarium in Europe could afford.

Lobbying Power

At centre stage of the dolphin circus' remarkable act of turning reality upside-down during the course of the government Review was the European Association of Aquatic Mammals (EAAM). Although regularly used as a password of respectability — even by distinguished member Margaret Klinowska — the EAAM is in fact scarcely more than a lobbying organisation for the dolphin industry. Over the years, the shrewder members of the Association have pushed for the adoption of universal guidelines to forestall government attempts to impose stricter ones, at the same time hoping that the more disreputable dealers and showmen will be put out of business, if only because they invariably cast their grotesque shadow over the entire industry. The EAAM's *Standards for Establishments Housing Bottlenose Dolphins*, for instance, recommends minimum pool dimensions and offers suggestions on hygiene, feeding and health. Klinowska did, in part, recommend the adoption of those EAAM guidelines. Much to the chagrin of the Association however, Klinowska, to her credit, did not quite grant the wish-list they had so fervently hoped she would. Complained a bitter Mike Riddell, secretary of the EAAM, upon learning that the educational content of the shows would have to be drastically improved: "It would seem wrong to oblige the average citizen to sit through a pedantic lecture with diagrams, charts etc. and forget the unforgettable experience of seeing, hearing and smelling another living creature, such as the dolphin or killer whale… This intellectual snobbery should not stop dolphinaria from continuing to bring science to the lay-man, without being turned into boring classrooms. One needs to look no further than his own Antibes Marineland to see just what ringmaster Riddell means. There, the orca whale spectacle is accompanied by blasting rock music while the combined dolphin and sea-lion show is probably the most anthropomorphic in the whole of Europe, the algae-stained pools, some with peeling blue paint, set against brightly coloured stage scenery depicting a nursery-rhyme village. The mischievous antics of the sea-lion, "Slicky", come complete with an affected piped oratory almost identical to a Disney cartoon character. This contrasts with the cool, impassive, military-style efficiency of the Marineland administration, with walkie-talkie equipped trainers and guards patrolling the grounds. Not that Marineland, founded by cigarillo baron Roland de la Poype, has entirely forgotten the call of conservation or science. In Marineland's glossy brochure it is written: "Our dolphins will not be harpooned and used as pet-food, and our seals will not be turned into expensive fur coats or fluffy toys, but others will. Splash, Kim, Chou-Chou, their brothers and kin, thank you for the interest you have shown towards their problems."

As "the only marine zoo in Europe", over the years Marineland has tried to maximise the species contained in its animal menagerie. Some years ago, Roland de la Poype became fascinated by scientific research which seemed to suggest that the Mediterranean bottlenose was more sensitive and intelligent than its Gulf of Mexico cousin, but Marineland's subsequent attempts to capture specimens in the straits between Malaga and Gibraltar went disastrously wrong. "It was an experiment," Roland de la Poype was later quoted as saying, "but we presumed that dolphins with higher intelligence would be more docile." Five dolphins were apparently captured without difficulty and were quickly transported to Malaga for an onward flight to Nice. At this point, the delicate animals went into a state of shock. They struggled and reared in their transportation slings, hit out violently with their flippers and gasped for breath. Trainer Martin Padley injected them with sedatives, but for one dolphin it was already too late; it had apparently already died from the sheer terror of the experience. When the surviving dolphins were at last put in one of Marineland's pools, they were so weak from the journey that they could barely stay afloat. Several days later, listlessly circling the pool, the animals still hadn't become adjusted to their new surroundings. After much hesitation, Marineland's management, fearing that they would soon have four dead dolphins on their hands as well as a major scandal, decided to return the animals to the sea. Whether they lived or died is open to question.

Today, the Marineland menagerie not only includes two killer whales and seven dolphins, but also two elephant seals, and various other species of phocid. As I relate in my book *The Monk Seal Conspiracy*, one of Mike Riddell's driving ambitions, supported by the French government and the EEC Commission, is to capture critically endangered Mediterranean monk seals, ostensibly for captive breeding, and put them on public display at Marineland. Although monk seals have never been known to breed successfully in captivity, the plan, if initiated, would seem to confer upon Marineland the much-coveted credibility of being a fully-fledged zoo, and not, as the neighbouring children's playground and "Aquasplash" seem to suggest, simply a glorified amusement park.

The EAAM's annual general meetings are itinerant circus-like affairs which, for each occasion, gather at a different dolphinarium or theme park, from Duisburg in Germany, to Loro Parque in Tenerife. They serve as a convenient rallying point for the industry, gathering together many of the European dolphin owners, dealers and trainers, as well as various scientists representing such esteemed institutions as the University of Cambridge, Münster University, St Hilda's College, Oxford, and the Max Planck Institute in Germany. Also much in evidence are the representatives of major European insurance brokerages which, for astronomical premiums, are still prepared to grant life insurance policies for whales and dolphins. The gatherings are completed by the dolphin owners themselves, such personalities as James Tiebor of Munich, European representative of the International Animal Exchange and manager of the Florida Dolphin Show, Wolfgang Gewalt, the intrepid dolphin catcher and director of Duisburg Zoo, dolphin dealer René Duss of the Ocean Life Company, Peter Bössenecker and his *Société Biologique des Caraibes*, Terry Nutkins of Windsor Safari Park, "government-approved" dolphin catching vet Jay Sweeney of Dolphin Services International, and the notorious Conny Gasser of Conny's Flipper Show in Switzerland. Besides the usual "compelling" scientific programme, "Get Together Party" and the "Guided Tour" through whichever dolphinarium or amusement park the conference is being held, "Business Meetings" are also a regular fixture. Although conference sessions are open to the public, these unofficial seances which invariably take place at the same time are strictly barred to both casual observers and associate members. Critics portray the organisation as a rogues' gallery and say that its main aim is to create a front of respectability for the dolphin trade whilst acting as a co-ordinating body for its business interests. One persistent complaint is that David Taylor's recent presidency of the EAAM and his involvement in all aspects of the industry, including the buying and selling of dolphins, gave rise to a potential conflict of interest since his main occupation — to care for the health and welfare of dolphins and whales in captivity — also includes the issuing of health certificates which are used as a kind of guarantee for sales purposes. Both Taylor and his associate Andrew Greenwood habitually deny any participation in the dolphin catching business. But in his 1985 article in *GEO*, German journalist Udo Tschimmel relates how their partner, Dr Martin Dinnes, applied in writing for a catching and export license for Mexican dolphins. Included in his letterhead, as part of the International Zoo Veterinary Group, were the names of Taylor and Greenwood. Tschimmel also contends that Taylor earns regular commissions from Lloyds whenever he brings them a new cetacean life-insurance policy, and receives additional fees by acting as an intermediary in purchases and sales from one dolphinarium to another.

Reached by telephone, David Taylor informed me that he would only consider answering written questions and only then if they were of a purely technical nature. "If on the other hand they have to do with personal, particular problems of clients, we won't divulge that any more than a doctor would reveal information about a patient because it's none of your business." High ethics indeed, until one realises that it is not the *patient's* privacy Taylor is respecting but that of the patient's owners. They of course have every reason to insist on confidentiality — to conceal the reason a captive whale is suffering from pernicious frostbite, for instance, or why a dolphin belonging to one of his Italian clients perished after being carted around in a circus-style travelling show.

An Anathema of Ethics

Controversy surrounding the EAAM effectively caused a split in the organisation in 1987, with the more objective scientists and conservationists, concerned that the EAAM had become increasingly dominated by the captive cetacean lobby, joining the newly formed European Cetacean Society. Founded by the respected Portuguese cetologist Paulo de Santos, its aims are to encourage the study and conservation of cetaceans in their natural habitat.

There can be little doubt that the Klinowska report was impressive in its in-depth research into the fate of individual dolphins held by UK dolphinaria since the early seventies, its damning evidence of animal welfare abuse and of the educational and scientific irrelevancy of such establishments. But when it came to results and recommendations, Klinowska revealed the anthropocentrism of today's reductionist approach to science, and its quantitative rather than qualitative judgements. It is thus that "pragmatism", a guiding principle of Klinowska's Review, and a favourite catchword of government, establishment science and the business world alike, becomes little more than an alibi for continued exploitation. Moral considerations are regarded almost as an anathema simply because, in Klinowska's words, "ethical beliefs cannot be quantified" by clinical scientific methodology. They are therefore conveniently dismissed. Indeed, although almost 250 pages long, the Klinowska report dedicates just two and a half pages to the subject of "Ethics", effectively revealing that this is in chronically short supply not only in modern science but also in the dolphin industry.

Besides studiously avoiding her terms of reference, it also came as a shock to conservationists that much of the impressive evidence compiled in the Klinowska report seemed to have no bearing on its ultimate conclusions. The juggling of statistics to "prove" that mortality rates of cetaceans in captivity are approximate to those of the animals in the wild was particularly galling since even Klinowska herself admitted that there were so many variables and inconsistencies involved — not least of all the refusal to include the numerous anonymous dolphins whose fate remained undiscovered — that such figures could not be reliable. But if that is indeed the case, why pass off impressive though inherently faulty algebraic equations as precise science? Declared Kieran Mulvaney, then director of the Whale and Dolphin Conservation Society: "Klinowska failed to make proper use of some submissions of evidence — including some data which seemed to show that the mortality rate of orcas, for example, was approximately ten times higher in captivity than in the wild. This would seem to provide a strong argument in favour of a complete ban on the keeping of cetaceans in captivity."

Klinowska however would not compromise on pool size. Following the publication of her report in July 1986, Secretary of State for the Environment William Waldegrave announced that Britain's six dolphinaria would face closure unless pool sizes were doubled, captive breeding programmes instituted, education radically improved, and scientific research co-ordinated. The industry had until November 1991 to implement these measures. Until then, imports of cetaceans would continue to be blocked. Pools for dolphins, the report concluded, should provide a minimum of 1000 cubic metres for up to five animals. No pool should be narrower than 7m or shallower than 3.5m, and at least a third of each pool should be at least 7m deep. For killer whales, pools should have a minimum volume of 20,000 cubic metres for up to five animals. No pool should be narrower than 15m or shallower than 7.5m, and at least a third of each pool should be at least 15m deep.

Such pronouncements came as a severe shock to the industry, which despite its attempts to woo Klinowska suddenly faced daunting expenditure in reconstruction. The shock also reverberated throughout Europe, with the fear that the recommendations might well set a precedent for legislation throughout EEC member states. Indeed, suddenly, after the rosy prognosis, the outlook seemed distinctly bleak. While some dolphinaria already met or exceeded the new volume requirements, none complied with the new depth recommendations. A fuming Andrew Haworth-Booth, then Managing Director of Windsor Safari Park, stated: "We consider the recommendations regarding volumes and depths for pools to be totally unrealistic. They far exceed those laid down by the European Association of Aquatic Mammals." Haworth-Booth's dismay was understandable, given the fact that Windsor would have to rip up its 3.5m deep combined dolphin and orca pool, make it deeper by another 3.5m and also construct a brand new whale pool. "We intend to make representations to the DoE's Steering Committee," said Haworth-Booth. He was not the only one. In what might be considered as part of the whole ritual, the Steering Committee was poised to water down Klinowska's already-diluted recommendations.

At first, animal welfare organisations had greeted the Klinowska report with barely concealed glee, not because it adequately addressed the plight of captive cetaceans, but because they felt confident that the stringent recommendations on pool size would force most of the dolphinaria out of business, in other words, a ban by any other name. This supposition seemed to be confirmed when Knowsley's dolphinarium closed down in 1987, followed by Whipsnade's pretentious "Order Cetacea" exhibit in the summer of 1988. With the animal welfarists busy counting their unhatched chickens, the Steering Committee was hard at work unravelling some of the threads of Klinowska's arguments, evidently paying more attention to business interests than the welfare of the captive cetaceans. The final result only tended to magnify the pro-industry aspects of Klinowska's recommendations, particularly the demonstrably spurious claim that dolphinaria can and should play a vital role in education and captive breeding. While the Report of the Steering Committee, published in August 1988, endorsed Klinowska's recommendations on minimum pool dimensions for dolphins, those for killer whales were drastically scaled down from 20,000 cubic metres to just 12,000 cubic metres. No reason was given beyond that of financial considerations for the industry. Furthermore, the Steering Group went on to state that "the welfare of captive animals in the UK is considered to be adequately covered by existing national legislation". This was despite repeated violations of the Zoo Licensing Act 1981, and continuing animal abuse — from keeping dolphins in solitary confinement, to tipping neat chemicals into the pool water. In considering the thorny issue of education, the Steering Committee, reacting to Klinowska's decidedly unscientific assertion that "there is a certain 'something'" in being close to a living wild animal which cannot be reproduced by any other means, concluded that education could be classified as the "less formal absorption of knowledge and experience due to the exposure to live animals". This alone would eventually qualify dolphinaria for exemption under EEC regulation 3626/82, even though surveys show that visitors are still coming away from the shows believing that dolphins are fish. Indeed, with the quite incredible and arbitrary assumption that "many of the concerns about the physical and mental welfare of the animals were... not well-founded," it would thus be business as usual for the dolphin circus once they had renovated their pools. Put in a nutshell, UK dolphinaria, to qualify for further supplies of their mortality-prone charges, would simply have to put on a better show of education, science and breeding.

ICELAND

In Reykjavik, there is Helgi Jonasson and his animal dealing company *Fauna*. Up until spring 1988, when his activities at last fell foul of public opinion and an international scandal blew up around him, he had been building up a lucrative and exclusive business trading in live orca whales. For fourteen years, Fauna had virtually cornered the European market, supplying animals to various marine circuses in Britain and continental Europe, including Windsor Safari Park, Conny Gasser's Flipper Show in Switzerland and even Mike Riddell's pretentious Antibes Marineland in the south of France. Jonasson would have the orcas captured off the Icelandic coast, and then, waiting for buyers, would store them temporarily at the bankrupt Saedyrasafnid Zoo where they were show-trained to boost their value on the international animal market. Indeed, according to 1988 statistics provided by Reykjavik's Marine Research Institute — which "regulates" the live orca trade with the Ministry of Fisheries — between 1975-1988, Iceland captured 84 orca whales, 19 of them destined for US and Canadian oceanaria. Between 1975-1988, live-capture permits provided to the director of the Saedyrasafnid Marine Zoo, Mr Jon Kr. Gunnarsson, and his successor at the institution, Helgi Jonasson of Fauna, represented 64 individuals. Most are now thought to be dead. In 1980 alone, several died of frostbite because the water in the zoo's pool was too shallow to accommodate them, and there was no roof to shelter them from the harshest winter winds; with sub-zero temperatures, the five whales' delicate skin became scored with painful cracks and fissures. Despite the resulting outcry, Fauna continued in its operations, with the tacit blessing of the Icelandic government which for many years has regarded all whales as just another "fish resource".

When a coalition of conservation groups opposed the application by Marine World Africa USA of Redwood City, California, to import two of Fauna's orcas for display, the response was swift and sharp. In a 14-page document attempting to refute the coalition's charges of cruelty and negligence in the Icelandic operation, the American oceanarium declared that only two whales had died of frostbite, not five. To support their contention and their import application, they submitted evidence by British celebrity vet David Taylor, who testified: "Nothing like this has ever been recorded before. As a result of what we have learned from the case, for the first time we feel it necessary to roof over the whale pool, a building feature that has hitherto been considered totally unnecessary for killer whales... Intensive therapy abolished secondary problems in the remaining three whales leaving them eating well (30 kg of fish each per day by 15 February) but with large areas of damaged, though painless skin... It was therefore decided that, with all medical treatment courses completed, the three whales should be set free again so that they could regain normal skin condition under free ranging conditions... Fortunately, we feel sure that in the light of what we know from this unique case and the lessons learned, no recurrence of this phenomenon is likely in future catching seasons."

But as Greenpeace remarked in its publication *Outlaw Whalers,* although Taylor's statement may have sounded convincing, a subsequent investigation in Iceland uncovered some troubling inconsistencies. A few days after the release of the ailing and unsellable whales, which, under the media spotlight, had become an increasingly intolerable burden to Fauna, a dead orca washed up on the beach not far from Saedryasafnid Zoo, its body covered with frostbite fissures. As "it is unlikely that the other two orcas fared any better," declared Greenpeace, "five probably died as previously reported. Obviously 'intensive therapy' had not been very effective."

By 1988, yet another four young whales were being kept under guard in the bankrupt zoo, awaiting either sale or a slow death in the fouled and

Celebrity vet David Taylor examining a severely frostbitten killer whale in 1980, captured by the notorious Saedyrasafnid zoo in Iceland. (Greenpeace.)

dimly-lit pool. Just half a year earlier, the whales had been swimming with their mothers in the open sea, together with the other family members of their tightly-knit pod. At Jonasson's behest, in October 1987 they were netted off the island's east coast in a secret operation mounted by the Reykjavik-registered vessel *Gudrun*, which enjoyed a virtual monopoly in the capture of live whales for the European market. Each of the ship's crew of ten was paid £1500 to catch the four orcas. Herring nets were used to separate the young whales from their mothers and they were then hoisted aboard in slings, their bodies kept wet until they reached shore, a journey of at least five hours. After landing on the east coast, there was an even more gruelling journey awaiting the abducted animals, a 20-hour drive by container truck to the sordid and dilapidated zoo at Hafnarfjördur near Reykjavik. In one previous catching operation, it is reported, a 5.5m orca was hoisted up from the water by its tail, still wrapped in the catch net. Although its back had been broken during capture it was nevertheless transported to Hafnarfjördur. Three weeks later, the Saedryasafnid zoo called in the local dentist who shot it.

After six months in captivity, the whales began to attract the attention of the world's press. Accompanied by their informants from the animal rights movement, some European journalists, sensing an animal abuse exclusive, tapped their generous expense accounts and flew up to Reykjavik. Outside the zoo, they were confronted by a faded killer whale with a wan smile, painted onto the squalid main building — a mute testament to the zoo's better days when weekend crowds in search of the spectacular had flocked to see its orca show. Together with the deserted animal enclosures, and the leaden overcast sky, it must have been a bleak sight. Once inside the oceanarium, that impression can only have been accentuated by the haunting, if somewhat eerie underwater calls of the four imprisoned whales. The sounds echoed plaintively through the deserted building, with its claustrophobically low asbestos roof and its six small and grimy windows which filtered the grey daylight.

Confronted by the journalists, Jonasson was unrepentant, even defiant. "I don't see anything wrong with selling killer whales," he was quoted as saying. "They should be harvested like any other fish species." He insisted that the whales were "happy and healthy", and "regularly examined by the state vet". Although they had already been up for sale for six months, he felt certain that he would have no trouble in finding buyers for them. He was simply holding out for the best price — at least £65,000 per animal. Their trainer, formerly of Sea World in San Diego, was Jeffrey Foster, alias Jim Jefferies, employed by Fauna to teach the whales circus tricks — the first one being to beg for food. The four orcas, christened Miss Piggy, Bubba, Stella and Wolfie were confined to a pool 40m long, 9m wide and 4.9m deep. A British newspaper, remarking that the whales measured between 3 - 5m, declared that this was "like keeping four adults in a furniture van for six months". The pool held only 2000 cubic metres of water, pumped in directly from the sea. By comparison, Klinowska recommends a minimum of 20,000 cubic metres of water for captive killer whales. Filtration equipment seemed to be barely functioning, with the water so murky with waste that the bottom of the pool was invisible, and a tide of scum coated the walls of the pool at water level. Judging by the overpowering smell of chlorine, chemical means alone were being employed in an effort to sterilise the water. When former zoo veterinarian Bill Jordan visited the orcas he declared that the pool was a breeding ground for bacteria and disease. "I was shocked at what I saw. The pool water is some of the worst I have seen. If the whales are kept there any longer in those conditions, they could die — there is a real danger of an outbreak of disease which would kill them all." Jordan, a consultant to Zoo Check and also a member of the British delegation to the International Whaling Commission, went on to state that the entire facility "is substandard in size and quality. It's too small and cramped and the whales were continuously circling. These whales are being sentenced to a slow death." The confinement was already causing behavioural problems between the two young males, with bite marks and scratches apparent on their bodies from fighting.

Several days later, notwithstanding protests from around the world, the four whales were sold off to Kamogawa Sea World in Japan, and consigned to a pool where several orcas had already recently perished. Then in November 1989, yet another four orcas, aged between one and five, were caught by Fauna, despite international protests. Two were later sold to Mike Riddell's Antibes Marineland to join the facility's two other orcas, whilst plans were being hatched to sell off the remaining pair to Japan.

GERMANY

Zoo-Agentur in Hohenstadt, West Germany, already in disgrace for its unscrupulous dealing in exotic species for the circus, zoo and pet trade, gained further notoriety in 1984. In the May edition of the *Geflügelbörse* it began advertising for sale an undisclosed number of rare Commerson dolphins from Patagonia, at a cost of DM 40,000 each, complete with what were claimed to be authentic CITES papers. *Zoo-Agentur* is owned by the international animal dealer Walter Sensen, who is described by one former dolphin trainer as a "tough and shadowy figure purely interested in profits". Reached by telephone, Sensen declared irritably: "We have a man in South America who offered us these dolphins and we're trying to find clients for them, but I'm not the right man for you to write about." Sensen then hung up, obviously refusing to answer any more questions concerning his involvement in the dolphin trade. As far as the Federal authorities are concerned, Sensen already seems to be virtually a *persona non grata* when it comes to importing endangered species, though this has hardly cramped his lucrative dealing activities. Declares an emphatic Dr Rainer Blanke, head of the Scientific Authority for CITES at the Ministry of Agriculture and Forestry: "This animal dealer will never obtain an import license to bring dolphins into Germany".

Dr Wolfgang Gewalt, the bearded and self-assured director of the Duisburg Zoo, considers himself to be a "pioneer" of keeping cetaceans in captivity, partly because he has been catching dolphins and whales since 1965, including rare Orinoco river dolphins.

Writing of his catching expedition to the Orinoco, Gewalt seems to display the same kind of sensitivity for local culture as he did for the lives of the dolphins he destroyed there. Styling himself as the intrepid, jungle-slashing explorer, and raising the suspense of his adventures notch by notch, he remarks that the natives' beliefs prohibit them from catching or hunting the river dolphins. Their reluctance, Gewalt explains, "seems to lie in legends... which speak of all kinds of secretive powers of *Inia geoffrensis*. It is said, for example, that whoever looks at a lamp fuelled with oil from an *Inia* will go blind." But, being the "rational, objective scientist" above such primitive superstition, the hunt for the Orinoco dolphins continued, led by an ironically myopic Gewalt. After days of frustration and fruitless waiting, he relates, finally an Orinoco dolphin was captured in shallow water. "River dolphin No. 1 is on board!" Gewalt exclaimed ecstatically. "One can almost bet on it: he who has once caught an Orinoco river dolphin will soon get a few more. The method is rather more sneaky than Christian. We bind our freshwater dolphin... with a towel around its tail and then anchor it in the middle of the river onto a vine." The dolphin then transmits "S.O.S. signals" with its ultrasound and "it is only a matter of time before the first dolphin approaches the 'scene of the accident'", with 2 or 3 others following behind. A net was then thrown across the river, and we are told that Gewalt managed to catch one of the dolphins in his own arms, which was immediately injected with sedatives and antibiotics. By the end of the expedition, two other dolphins, including a mother and calf had been captured using the same method.

His menagerie collection, which also includes Beluga whales and Commerson dolphins, as well as the habitual bottlenose, is regarded as one of the most exotic in Europe. "What is so special about these wonder-animals?" Gewalt is quoted as saying by journalist Udo Tschimmel. "It is just not understandable why they shouldn't be kept in a zoo." On the other hand, Gewalt's touchiness *is* understandable. His name hit the headlines in 1979, 1980 and 1984, when, as the result of three catching expeditions to the Magellan Straits of Patagonia, 14 out of 17 Commerson dolphins died. Furthermore, not only did his self-proclaimed "zoo" have no breeding success with its exotic cetaceans, but it also lost several of its inhabitants during those years due to disease and cramped conditions.

Following his 1984 expedition to Patagonia, Gewalt was even fined DM 4000 for contravening EEC import regulations. During the winter of 1983/84 Gewalt travelled to Cape Horn and caught six Commerson dolphins with the intention of bringing them to Duisburg. Of these six, only one survived the ordeal of capture and transportation, yet Gewalt, with typical disdain for such inconvenient details, imported it without any form of approval from the German authorities. According to Gewalt, the Duisburg Zoo did not set out to obtain its Commerson dolphins from a dealer in Chile, but "through our association with Sea World", in Santiago. "There were 4000 Jacobitas in the small area where we captured the four for Duisburg Zoo," Dr Gewalt told me — inexplicably reducing the number caught — "so we hardly endangered the species with our small operation. Okay, we did have traffic problems with them. The Chilean Air Force promised to airlift them for us, but at the last minute they backed out and other arrangements had to be made — which unfortunately caused many delays and included an unexpected stop-over in Santiago where the dolphins had to be put in a temporary holding pool, and it was very, very hot. In the end, all but one died. It's a pity, but it's not dramatic, despite the outcry in the press." He then added, almost as an afterthought: "I had hoped to obtain some females for the other three males I have here in Duisburg, but I ended up with three males. Such is life I suppose."

According to press reports at the time, the Commerson dolphins, a species discovered barely a century ago, died of stress-induced heart attacks and immune deficiency. Writing in *Das Tier*, Gewalt justified the death toll of the Jacobitas on the grounds that it was all part of the zoological learning process. "The problems we currently experience with some marine mammals, our grandfathers had with orang-utans or okapis, but we have learnt such a lot about these animals that we breed them now almost as domestic animals". Indeed, there seemed nothing at all to complain about, even in the breaking of the law, since Gewalt couldn't find time to fill out the necessary applications for an import permit, but merely informed the authorities after the event by phone, presenting them with a *fait accompli*. A sardonic Gewalt remarked that "even the government and the ministers became active because of our import of six Jacobitas". Indeed, according to the annoyed and embarrassed German CITES authority at the time, "the case will create waves". Ripples would probably have been a better word. Even though EEC regulations demand that smuggled species should be confiscated by the authorities, these rules were not applied in the case of Dr Gewalt. Explains Dr Rainer

Blanke: "That was a big problem for us. Only one of the Commerson dolphins was left alive and it was in bad condition -- and so the question was, what were we to do with it? We considered many different possibilities, including bringing the dolphin back to Chile, but we thought it doubtful that it could survive another journey. In the end we thought it best for the animal to stay in Duisburg, but we gave orders to Dr Gewalt to improve the dolphinarium's facilities, including making the pool bigger." But later, says Blanke, "Gewalt came with his lawyers and told us that there was a danger the dolphin might die from noise if they were forced to reconstruct the pool. We finally had to agree but made it clear that he would never legally import one of these dolphins again... I must confess that the fine was negligible."

Also in Germany, based in Munich, is the veteran American dealer James "Captain Jim" Tiebor, operator of the Florida Dolphin Show, which continues to provide a number of European amusement parks with dolphins. It was Tiebor who organised Europe's first itinerant dolphin and whale shows at fairs and carnivals, including those appallingly-primitive spectacles staged at the Munich Beer Festival. Apart from the ill-fated orca whale which he flew in to exhibit at the Beer Festival in 1971, Tiebor also supplied killer whales to other establishments including an individual leased to the distinguished Hagenbeck Zoo in 1981, for an annual rent reputed to have been in the region of a quarter of a million Deutschmarks. He also provided dolphin, sea-lion and parrot shows to various establishments, including Knie's Kinderzoo in Switzerland and Adriatic Sea World at Riccione in Italy. More recently, he has supplied dolphins under lease to Germany's giant Europa Park in Baden-Wurttemberg, to Heide-Park — at a price of 300,000 Deutschmarks per year for two animals — and Safaripark in Gänserndorf near Vienna. About the only remorse Tiebor can muster for the dead dolphins that brought him a fortune is his admission that "we finally realised that this wasn't okay. We had more sick animals and more losses than today." But, like most of his compatriots, Tiebor won't specify those losses simply because too much truth is bad for the make-believe business. He refuses to comment on his present business dealings, although it is known that he continues to sell his own dolphin shows to the highest bidder, has business connections with dolphinaria in Spain, is reputed to utilise non-EEC Austria as a conduit for dolphin supplies from South America, and is also the European representative of Ferndale's International Animal Exchange.

Based alternately in Germany, Italy, Spain and Mexico is the Ocean Life Company, owned by the Swiss dolphin dealer and showman René Duss, a former trainer for "Captain Jim" Tiebor. Other animals in his repertoire include sea-lions, fur seals, parrots and chimpanzees. According to reports of former trainers, Duss used to operate the dilapidated

Ocean World dolphinarium in Viareggio, near Pisa, but cut his losses when all five of his dolphins died of some mysterious illness which covered their bodies in pus-filled blisters. Rather than submit the carcasses to autopsy, it is alleged, Duss rapidly had them incinerated. Asked to comment on the fate of the Viareggio dolphins, Mr Duss said, "I know where you're leading to, and I don't like it. I'm not prepared to give any information over the telephone." However, when pressed further, the Swiss showman declared: "Like everyone else, we make mistakes, and we learn by our mistakes. I lost five dolphins at Viareggio, that is true. But autopsies were performed. The first dolphin that died was sent to the University of Pisa." Duss characterised the allegations as "an act of revenge by a disgruntled former employee". Asked to comment on why the five dolphins had been kept in such squalid conditions, he replied: "In our business nobody is an angel. When you first start out you don't make compromises. But I didn't just put the dolphins there to exploit them. We had no other possibility because our pool in Germany was broken."

In 1984, Duss obtained two dolphins from Peter Bössenecker, the owner of *Société Biologique des Caraibes*, a company which, until recently, was based in a caravan at a local zoo in Rhenen, Holland, and its South American dolphin-catching operations on one of the Caribbean Antilles islands. Earlier in the same year, Bössenecker had caught at least ten dolphins in Guatemala where, despite CITES controls, international export papers are still easily obtainable. Indeed, at this point, it is interesting to see in practice, just how the spirit of CITES is repeatedly violated, not only by the animal dealers themselves, but also those petty bureaucrats who process catching and export applications. A letter dated the 4 February 1983 from the Guatemalan Ministry of Agriculture refers to Peter Bössenecker's original request for permission to catch and export 20 *Tursiops truncatus.*

Bössenecker, then director of the Ouwehand dolphinarium in Rhenen, Holland, attached four testimonials in support of his application, as required by law. All attested to his impeccability of character and his competence as a dolphin catcher. But just where did these glowing references originate? Quite simply, Bössenecker's own clients within the dolphin industry. Testimonial No. 1, for example, comes from the *Koninklijke Maatschappij voor Dierkunde van Antwerpen*, Belgium. This respected institution, the Royal Zoological Society of Antwerp, confirms that Bössenecker is an experienced dolphin-catcher, and a member of the EAAM. As principal dolphin catcher for the *Société Biologique des Caraibes*, the letter continues, Bössenecker has already delivered many dolphins to "renowned zoos and dolphinaria", which are members of the EAAM. "Our Society received in 1977 three Guyana dolphins and in March four bottlenose dolphins which were caught by Bössenecker and which are still all very healthy." The testimonial was signed by Pieter De

Block, curator of the Royal Zoological Society's dolphinarium. Reference No. 2 comes from the Ouwehand Animal Park, Aquarium, Dolphin Show, and Caravan Site in Rhenen, Holland. "We are pleased to confirm that Mr. Bössenecker has been working for our dolphinarium for many years," the letter states. "Amongst others, he provided us with *Tursiops gilli, Tursiops truncatus* and *Sotalia guianensis*. All the animals he delivered were excellently provided and cared for, including during the flights from Japan, South America and the Mexican Gulf. Furthermore, we would continue to make use of the services of Mr Bössenecker, and we know from the annual symposiums of the EAAM that all its members like to make use of his knowledge and skill." The signature on this reference is unreadable.

The third testimonial originates from the Dolphinarium Harderwijk which also features an "underwater panorama", a sea-lion show, and a "Sea Mammals Scientific Research Department". It confirms that "Mr Bössenecker delivered dolphins — namely *Sotalia* — several times to the dolphinarium Harderwijk. Those deliveries were always accomplished to our complete satisfaction and we also hope to be able to use his services in the future." The letter was signed by the dolphinarium's director, F. B. den Herder. Last but not least, the fourth glowing character reference comes from the Nürnberg Tiergarten. It confirms that during a six-year period, "several, partly complicated and extensive animal deals" were conducted through Bössenecker who provided, "amongst others, bottlenose dolphins, Guyana dolphins, sea-cows and tapirs". Bössenecker, the testimonial continued, "proved during all transactions to be a reliable business partner, with whom cooperation was always trustful. As we discovered for ourselves in South America, Mr Bössenecker has acquired a considerable specialised knowledge about sea mammals, which stands him in very good stead for the catching and transport of those species. Mr. Bössenecker is also a member of the EAAM and regularly takes part in its meetings. We are convinced that Mr. Bössenecker has gained a great deal of experience during his far-ranging catching expeditions..." Signed, Dr Manfred Kraus, Director.

Evidently the CITES authority in Guatemala regarded such testimonials as more than sufficient to expedite Bössenecker's application. A subsequent document prepared by the Ministry of Agriculture states that in view of the favourable response of the Guatemalan Fisheries Directorate, and the Guatemalan Natural History Association to his application, Bössenecker and the *Société Biologique des Caraibes* would be entitled to catch 20 *Tursiops truncatus* in Atlantic waters. How many were actually caught is unknown, though ten were later exported to Europe.

René Duss had the intention of importing two of these animals for a new dolphinarium called Hansaland near Lübeck in Germany, which he then operated under a leasing arrangement together with his wife, Julia.

But when all ten dolphins arrived at Luxembourg airport, they were refused entry by customs authorities. They were then re-routed to Spain. It was on Sunday, 22 April at 3 a.m. that a small transport plane landed at Valencia airport with a cargo of bottlenose dolphins. Customs authorities had not been informed of their arrival and hence no arrangements had been made to receive them. Though they possessed no CITES import papers, the animals were nevertheless unloaded and taken into the customs building. The illegal import put customs officials in an unenviable predicament; it was obvious that the dolphins, after the long journey from Guatemala and the stop-over in Luxembourg, would soon die if they were not put into water. For humanitarian reasons they decided to waive existing rules, and the dolphins were granted temporary asylum in Spain, even though Spanish officials apparently harboured doubts as to the authenticity of the Guatemalan export permits. Even so, after hours of tangled discussion and argument, the dolphins were at last released from customs and were driven to two of the nearest dolphinaria, both in the province of Alicante, where they were stored in temporary holding pools. By this time, the long and arduous journey had taken its inevitable toll: one dolphin died the following day at René Duss' Safari Park in Vergel, while another died a few weeks later in Walter Moser's dolphinarium in Elche. Moser, yet another Swiss, used to own the company Sea Artist Enterprises in Rapperswil, and was contracted by Switzerland's famous Knie circus to arrange their dolphin shows — until the dolphins threatened Knie's hallowed image by dying.

Despite the mortalities in Spain, there were still enough surviving dolphins for Bössenecker to turn a modest profit on the ill-starred venture. While two were disposed of at a bargain-basement price to Walter Moser, four of the remaining Guatemalan dolphins were sold-off to a Bulgarian amusement park on the Black Sea, reflecting a new trend in the dolphin business to bypass more stringent regulations in western countries. That left Bössenecker with two dolphins with which to fulfil his contractual obligations to Duss. Ironically, these animals were actually replacements for yet another pair of dolphins purchased by the Ocean Life Company the previous year, but which died before the one-month warranty expired. As the two new Guatemalan dolphins passed automatically into Duss' ownership in Spain, Bössenecker considered his part of the contract satisfied Duss however desperately needed those dolphins in Hansaland, Germany. Despite the refusal of the German authorities to countenance the import, several months later it was discovered that two young dolphins had suddenly appeared at Hansaland. Customs officials, it was reported, suspected that Duss had smuggled the animals into Germany by private plane, quite prepared to face the insignificant penalties of the law and the negligible risk of confiscation.

Duss, reached by telephone, vigorously denied that the dolphins had been imported into Germany illegally. "To say that I smuggled two dolphins into Germany by private plane is absolutely slanderous," he asserted. "The official documentation is all in order. It is the press which have lied and have distorted things out of all proportion." Yet Duss consistently refused to divulge any information that might conceivably have served to dispel suspicions as to the identity and origin of the Hansaland dolphins. Indeed, the controversy surrounding the allegations of smuggling was destined to become more intense in the months that followed, with the German CITES authority announcing "a thorough investigation of the affair to be conducted by the Customs Police". Ultimately, that investigation simply petered out for lack of evidence. Explains Dr Rainer Blanke: "We never discovered where these dolphins came from. As far as we know ten arrived in Luxembourg, some of which were sent on to Spain. There was a suspicion that Duss smuggled two into Germany by private plane but the result of the Customs investigation was inconclusive." Indeed, it might well be surmised that inadequacy in the law and its application was at least partly to blame for the confusion. In 1988, Bössenecker's old haunt, the Ouwehand Zoo and dolphinarium in Rhenen, Holland, inexplicably attempted to reclaim one of the dolphins at Hansaland. In litigation with Duss, the zoo claimed that they were owed back-payments for the dolphin which had been provided on a rental basis to Hansaland; they also accused Duss of failing to return the dolphin once the contract had expired. Explained the director of Ouwehand: "We originally had a contract in 1983 to lease a dolphin to Duss temporarily — for ten months — until he could replace it with one of his own animals. The contract expired and it was shipped back to Rhenen. Then the same animal was rented to Duss again for eight months so it went back to Germany. It was supposed to be back by October 1984, but he didn't return the animal and he also stopped paying us."

The zoo, despite its previously glowing testimonials for Peter Bössenecker, had by this time parted company with the dolphin-dealing showman. "We are a scientific zoo and we now have no dealings with Bössenecker," declared Ouwehand's director. "We dislike this kind of animal dealing." Although the zoo won the first stage of its legal battle in the courts, Duss promptly appealed against the verdict. At the same time, although he was still under contract to provide dolphin shows to Hansaland for the 1989 season, Duss inexplicably failed to reappear. It was soon discovered that two dolphins were also missing, prompting renewed allegations of smuggling. This time, Duss had illegally made off with two dolphins to Spain — including the individual owned by Ouwehand Zoo. A veterinary official in the state of Schleswig-Holstein, where Hansaland is located, declared: "Because it was an internal movement within the EEC, no export permit was required, but what was necessary was a CITES document testifying that Duss is the legal owner of these dolphins. This export was therefore illegal because Duss absconded with a dolphin that was not his property."

Duss however, continues to insist that he is the legal owner of the dolphin, under the terms of a disputed agreement between himself and Ouwehand that the zoo provide him with a replacement animal for one which died before its warranty expired. "I think it was in 1985 that Peter Bössenecker sold us three dolphins which came through Luxembourg," Duss recalls. "One of the dolphins that arrived was a baby — I mean no more than a few months' old. It died in my arms one or two hours after it arrived. It was completely criminal dolphin selling. This is the reason that the Ouwehand Zoo got rid of Bössenecker — the catching, export and transport documents for these dolphins all had the name of Ouwehand on them. But the agreement was that if they couldn't provide us with a replacement dolphin, then under the terms of the guarantee the hired one would belong to us." Though conceding that the German courts failed to agree with his interpretation, Duss refuses to admit that he stole the dolphin — which he later sold in Spain — and accuses both Ouwehand and Bössenecker of deceit.

Apart from the three "scientifically-led" establishments — Gewalt's Duisburg, Hagenbeck's Tierpark in Hamburg, and the Tiergarten Nürnberg which is one of the few establishments to obtain its dolphins from Guyana — Germany also boasts six other dolphinaria which are regarded as purely commercially orientated, despite the usual haphazard educational disguise: Holiday Park, near Hassloch, Pfalz, with five dolphins in two small pools giving six shows a day to a million visitors a year; Phantasialand at Brühl near Cologne; Hansaland at Sierksdorf, on the Baltic Sea now operated by Edi van Stijn of Phantasialand fame; Heide-Park in Soltau; Europa Park, near Lahr in the Black Forest, and last but not least, the Allwetterzoo in Münster.

Sometimes, "education", "breeding" and "entertainment" in such establishments may go hand in hand. In his 1984 article in the German magazine *Natur*, Udo Tschimmel reports that during show time at Holiday Park, a soft voice from the loudspeaker announced: "In the Hassloch dolphinarium Germany's first dolphin baby was conceived and born. We are very proud of that, because it proves that our keeping of dolphins is exemplary." What they didn't say, Tschimmel wryly remarked, was that the calf died within just a few days of its "historic birth".

ITALY

Along an 8 kilometre stretch of a once-alluring Adriatic coastline, now desecrated by concrete block hotels, nightclubs, discotheques, bars and restaurants, the sea fouled with oil, pesticides, plastic and sewage, there are three of Italy's six dolphinaria, all vying for the summer season's explosive tourist trade. First of all, there is the Rimini Aquarium, its green-tiled dolphin pool somehow reminiscent of a public toilet in a *Motta* service station on the Italian autostrada. Indeed, one is expected to pay an entrance fee at both, but while the toilets are normally kept passably clean by the purgatory of those poor souls who must spend half their lives staring blankly at a bowl of 100 lira coins, at the Rimini Aquarium, peering through the little portholes which provide an underwater view into the murky depths of the pool, one can actually see dolphins swimming in their own excrement. Here, despite a seedy and moth-eaten museum of marine artifacts, the dolphin show is conducted with such garish and unbridled vulgarity that the only educational value that could possibly be ascribed to it would be an entirely inadvertent study of human egotism and ignorance.

The presenter of the show, a patronising and aggressive individual obviously plagued, like his own dolphins, by a complete repertoire of personal neuroses, nevertheless displayed not even the slightest empathy with the animals, but indeed seemed to regard them with barely-concealed scorn, encouraging them to jump to the highest limits of their endurance and, upon their return to the water, to deliberately send cascades of spray over the shrieking audience. Predictably, the holiday crowds who fill the coffers of the Rimini Aquarium show as much concern for the dolphin as a free-living species as they do about animal welfare. During my visit to the Aquarium in 1988, no one seemed to notice that one of the establishment's four dolphins, with open wounds under the flippers, was ailing and lethargic, refusing to take part in the spectacle. Presumably these must be the same dolphins — Speedy, Chico, Alpha and Beta — that were brought into the country in 1984 and 1987. What happened prior to 1984 is anybody's guess since it was only then that the Italian government began to register the imports of dolphins.

Another eight kilometres along the concrete coastline, one comes across the financially ailing Aquatic World in Cattolica, a victim not only of the rabid competition which exists between the three neighbouring dolphinaria, but also, to use the habitual and euphemistic phraseology of the industry, of "bad luck with dolphins". When two of Aquatic World's animals, including an Adriatic bottlenose, died after being attacked by an aggressive male called Clyde, it came up against the determination of the authorities in Rome to put a stop to the establishment's travelling shows during the off-season winter months with the Italian circus *Medrano*. Traditionally, these tours took them to Florence, Rome, Bologna and Nervi near Genoa. According to the trainer at Viareggio's Ocean World Aquarium, Rocky Colombo, another dolphin, called Bonny, died in 1987 in Nervi when leaves blew into the pool from a nearby railway embankment. "She was poisoned because the embankment had been treated with pesticides," explains Colombo. Left with only one dolphin, and desperate to import replacements, Aquatic World was forced to compromise. Says TRAFFIC's Pier Lorenzo Florio who was instrumental in having conditions imposed upon Cattolica: "These dolphins were carted around the country with an Italian circus during the winter months. Up until 1987, despite all our protests, they were still moving their dolphins, but they have now formally promised not to do so — in exchange for approval in obtaining two more as replacements for those that have died." Though Cattolica had requested permission from the Ministry of Merchant Marine in 1988 to capture and maintain two Adriatic dolphins, its application was denied following protests by WWF and TRAFFIC.

Sandwiched between the two aquariums of Rimini and Cattolica is Adriatic Sea World of Riccione, considered to be Italy's foremost dolphinarium. Operated by the warm and ebullient Leandro Stanzani, it is one of the very few establishments of its kind in the whole of Europe which does not seem to use "education" and "research" purely as a legal alibi to obtain dolphins for the familiar drudgery of crude entertainment. While his colleagues in the industry grudgingly fling a few meagre facts and figures at the audience during show time to qualify for exemption under EEC regulations which prohibit the importation of C1 species such as the bottlenose dolphin for purely commercial purposes, Stanzani actually seems to believe that dolphinaria can play a major role in education and research. With this aim in mind, Adriatic Sea World plays host to 150,000 school children every year, and it has produced video presentations, slides and lessons in association with WWF Italy. In the realm of research, Sea World organised the country's first ever symposium on cetaceans and it is now planning a similar, international gathering. It was also here that Milan's respected Centre for Cetacean Studies was born, an organisation that has now managed to create a network of nationwide contacts to facilitate the prompt and efficient rescue of dolphins and whales that have become stranded or trapped in fishing nets, operations which Stanzani himself has often joined personally.

But what sets Stanzani apart from his colleagues in the industry is something more subtle that is evident in his manner, a natural and heartfelt empathy for his dolphins. The ruthlessness so evident in other establishments is missing here. To begin with, there is none of that blaring rock, pop or circus-style brass band music which is normally used to set a show on its breakneck pace. Instead, the music is more classical in nature, producing a calm, dignified and inspiring atmosphere. Nor does it seem to matter if the dolphins' stunts sometimes go wrong, or take up a longer time than expected. Patience and inter-action, together with Stanzani's infectious compassion for his dolphins, seems to encourage the audience to take delight in the characters of the animals themselves rather than their feats of dressage. That is not to say that some of the stunts that the dolphins perform here are not as demeaning as anywhere else — particularly the dreary routine of the animals having their teeth brushed or being encouraged to wear outsize sunglasses, but Adriatic Sea World must be one of the very few dolphinaria which actually tries to demonstrate to the audience the echo-sounding capabilities of the dolphins. This is achieved by placing soft latex eyecups on one of the animals which is then encouraged to retrieve a sunken rubber ring that Stanzani has thrown across the 25m diameter pool. Critics might well point out that the dolphin is so accustomed to its featureless concrete prison that the successful accomplishment of this stunt is almost inevitable, and yet even if that is partially true some credit must be given to Stanzani and his colleagues for including this time-consuming feat in the dolphins' repertoire.

And yet despite all the care and attention that Adriatic Sea World has taken to improve the welfare of its animals and institute genuine research and educational programmes, one is still confronted by the central tenet of Prof. Giorgio Pilleri's objection to dolphinaria: the inherent contradiction of keeping animals accustomed to vast open spaces in confined, artificial conditions. Throughout its long history, there have been no dolphin births, and the animals seem to face the same hazards and health problems which afflict captive dolphins everywhere. During my own visit in the autumn of 1988, the single male dolphin, Bravo, had become seriously ill after swallowing a plastic ball that had become lodged in its gut. Unable to eat or digest, the animal was visibly weakening, and Stanzani had already summoned British vet David Taylor in a bid to save the dolphin's life. "We are trying different things," Stanzani said. "Our plan now is to use soft towels to keep the dolphin's mouth open and for two basketball players with very long arms to reach down and try to retrieve the ball. But it won't necessarily die. Maybe it just becomes a weak animal that can't be used in the show." Each visit by Taylor or his partner Andrew Greenwood would cost Adriatic Sea World at least $2000, Stanzani added. "Taylor and Greenwood only move because they are paid. It costs a lot because they have to travel by plane, quickly, and the first flight is always the most expensive. Then there's all the taxi fares and the hotel bills." Small wonder then that many dolphin owners can't afford the services of the world's most exclusive marine veterinary consultants.

Despite such carelessness in allowing a dolphin to play with show props without adequate supervision, Seaworld's reputation remains intact. What Stanzani has managed to achieve in putting his compatriots to shame is especially remarkable since it might be said that right in the beginning of his career, he "fell in with a bad crowd". It was the summer of 1973, recalls Stanzani. "I already had a good feeling for dolphins, from seeing them in the wild and in the shows. And here on this coast in summer all the young people tried to find some kind of job to make some money in their spare time. I was a student and I was looking for work. It was at that time that Conny Gasser got me interested in catching Adriatic dolphins." Co-ordinated with the "expert advice" of British vets Taylor and Greenwood, the Gasser plan was to have 25 Adriatic dolphins caught by local fishermen and stored pending sale in a seaside canal near Cesenatico. "A similar operation was mounted a year before by some Spanish people, I think. Everybody was saying to them, 'they're dying just because you don't know what to do,' and so it was thought if we came there with specialist people, this wouldn't happen. That's where Greenwood and Taylor came in." To give the animals "time to settle down", and to ensure that "maximum veterinary care could be given to individual animals" only four dolphins were to be caught per month. Instead of that, relates Stanzani, the fishermen caught all of the dolphins in ten days, and the facilities at Cesenatico were just not ready. His reluctance to specify the numbers of dolphins that subsequently died seems to confirm the worst. "I think the poor knowledge of the Adriatic dolphin and the bad attitude of the fishermen was the cause of this... let's say killing," he says with a wince. "Even Taylor and Greenwood who were involved in this capture operation didn't know anything about these dolphins. As well as the canal in Cesenatico, two small portable pools were also used. But the Adriatic dolphins are weaker than the Gulf of Mexico bottlenose dolphins. The American dolphins are used to shallower water, but these are used to 30-40m of water. So staying in an enclosed space, they suffered." That canal in Cesenatico eventually became the site of a municipal dolphinarium, and Stanzani recalls that "hypothetically-speaking, it could actually have been one of the best places, completely natural, with 300x50m of space, but the dolphins there started to die because of sewage contamination, and in the end those that survived were released back into the sea."

Despite his brush with the darker and dominant face of the dolphin industry, Stanzani still seems to hold an inordinate faith in what could best be described as the inalienable rights of science to further human knowledge, whatever the cost in animal suffering. "I don't know if I would try again to have Adriatic dolphins," he declares. "But if it's necessary to have research done on these animals, it will be necessary to have them back in captivity. I know that the first year is the worst. If they can get through the first year, then they are quite normal, although weaker. After this period, I think they are sweet animals. There is a difference in character. I always remember one of the Adriatic dolphins we had here for four years — she died a few years ago. They are not quieter, but they are much more involved in what you're doing. I would say they have more 'heart'." He concedes that there could well be a strong detrimental impact on a dolphin school by removing individuals that are part of a tightly-knit community, though he is candid enough to add that he knows "very little about dolphins in the wild". That is an admission that most dolphin owners prefer to keep to themselves.

Stanzani is also one of the very few dolphinarium operators to have the grace and courage to admit, in spite of fundamental disagreements, that Prof. Giorgio Pilleri's controversial work on captive dolphins is worthy of merit. "He is a nice man, and very knowledgeable," says Stanzani, "but I think he had the wrong experience with his own dolphins, and the ones in Duisburg Zoo in Germany. At that time the death rate was high, but we have learnt a great deal since then. What he says about the dolphin brain becoming smaller in captivity is nonsense, but part of his work is very valuable. I think dolphins *do* suffer from psychological problems. We can't say that they don't — but they may also have psychological problems in the wild. What we must try to do is to alleviate those problems. Our standards can't only be limited to the size of the pool — it's much more than that, the most important being a good rapport with the animals and how the group is composed. They must have their own social life — and in this way even our own attitude has changed. People were once coming here and saying, 'we would like to swim with the dolphins', and we would say, 'okay, do it'. And afterwards we realised that the pool is their home and so if you want to swim with them you have to ask *them*, not us. In other words, you must get to know the animals before, and build up some kind of rapport with them."

Nor does Stanzani deny that captive dolphins are susceptible to strain, anxiety and boredom, though the measures that can be taken to alleviate these all too common afflictions must, by implication, be as limited as their artificial environment. "Just like us," he says, "these animals suffer from stress and boredom, especially at the end of the summer. It's not that they're tired physically, but they're tired mentally because they always do the same things, and so we try to keep them interested by teaching them something different. These are the things that help to make their life happy."

Although the Italian dolphinaria, like those in every other EEC nation, must abide by ordinances which only approve imports for the purposes of research, education or captive breeding, that is where the law ends its protection, since domestic animal welfare legislation is virtually non-existent. There are no rules governing pool size, and no procedure whereby a member of the public, witnessing some form of animal abuse, could complain to the authorities and set an investigation in motion. "It is left only to common sense," laments Stanzani, and indeed, in numerous instances common sense in the Italian dolphinarium industry is sadly lacking.

Close to the shores of Lake Garda there is the Disney-style theme park called Gardaland, whose attractions, from Dracula's Castle and the Magic Mountain Roller-Coaster to the Rio Bravo, a Wild West Village replete

Probably the smallest dolphin pool still in existence in Europe, estimated at 8m in diameter; the Florida Dolphin Show at Gardaland in Italy. (Matthias Schnellmann.)

Probably the smallest dolphin pool still in existence in Europe, estimated at 8m in diameter; the Florida Dolphin Show at Gardaland in Italy. (Matthias Schnellmann.)

with Saloon-Pizzeria, act as a magnete for over 2 million people every year. Almost at the very centre of the park is the "Florida Dolphin show" operated by veteran Italian performer Franco Carrini and his son Oscar. "It is purely a circus-style show," declares TRAFFIC's Pier Lorenzo Florio contemptuously, and even Leandro Stanzani, who is normally too diplomatic to openly criticise his colleagues in the industry, declares that in this style of show, it is not so much the dolphins themselves which receive top billing but, with all the razzle-dazzle and exhibitionism of the circus, the sensation-hungry *Duo Carrini*. Young Oscar's star-turn is to be launched out of the water on the nose of one of the Show's two dolphins. Although this particular trick is also seen in many other dolphinaria, it is here where it seems most spectacular, quite simply because it is undoubtedly one of the smallest dolphin pools still in existence in Europe. A hand-me-down relic from the former owner of Adriatic Sea World in Riccione, it was constructed in 1962 with travelling shows in mind, and was sold off to Gardaland in 1973, complete with circus-style "big top". "Tiny top" would probably be a more accurate description however, since the circular pool which occupies the centre of the tent is no more than 8m in diameter, with an estimated depth of between 3 and 4m. There is no holding pool, and other standard equipment — apart from essential show props like toothbrush and rubber dingy — is either primitive or non-existent. Perhaps it is especially fitting then that the two dolphins here are named Romeo and Juliet, since their inevitable tragedy will be played out again and again before the unseeing crowds.

Italy's fifth dolphinarium is situated in the park known as Zoo Safari in Fasano, near Brindisi, its four dolphins, Sandy and Lola, Speedy and Cubie, provided under long-term lease by Switzerland's inimitable Conny Gasser. With all the hyperbole that is endemic to the circus world, on 17 November 1988, Matteo Colucci, owner of the Zoo Safari, announced that 15-year-old Lola had given birth to a calf, prompting the local press to proclaim it "a phenomenal event of world-wide interest". This is in spite of the fact that births of captive dolphins are by no means exceptional: only their survival into adulthood is. But Colucci was obviously flogging the media horse for all he was worth. The calf, he declared to the press, had been given the name of Katia "in honour of the soprano Katia Ricciarelli, who had expressed the desire to personally attend the nocturnal birth." Hopes of a similar media blitz in March the previous year were soon quashed when Cubie's newborn calf perished because the mother refused to push her child to the surface to take its first breath. "Normally, in the wild, other dolphins would assist in the birth," explains Florio, "but the people at Zoo Safari had no idea what to do to help the mother."

The squalid Ocean World Aquarium at the Lido Camaiore on the outskirts of Viareggio has been plagued by controversy for years, not only in terms of animal welfare abuse but also as a seemingly magnetic attraction for shady business dealings. In recent years, the dolphin shows have been provided by René Duss, who, conceded defeat at Viareggio when all of his animals suddenly succumbed to disease. In his wake came Bruno Lienhardt, dolphin-dealer *extraordinaire* who, as we shall discover later, eventually broke into the Aquarium in the dead of night and stole his own dolphins. Following this fiasco, the dolphinarium was taken over lock, stock and barrel by Umberto Riva, a member of the Riva circus dynasty. Since then, the scandals have not abated, but multiplied. Like many of Italy's dolphin showmen, *di Riva* — which inexplicably also boasts an office in Las Vegas, obtained its first three dolphins from the quasi state-run *Aguaria Nacional* in Cuba in 1987. Within weeks one female had died, leaving the dolphins Fidel and Malu as the sole occupants of the pool.

By this time, Riva had promoted the young American Rocky Colombo to the position of head dolphin trainer, having recently dismissed Giuseppe Cohen, formerly a hired hand at Riccione. "Cohen was a hopeless trainer," Colombo told me, "and bad news for the animals. I wouldn't like to see him go anywhere near a dolphin." One of the tricks presented at Viareggio, explained Colombo, was for the dolphins to lie on their backs at the edge of the stage and for the trainer, using a large show prop hammer, to gently tap one and then the other on the belly so that the animals would splash their tails in the water as though displaying a kind of knee-jerk reaction. The climax of the stunt is for the first dolphin to splash its tail at the precise moment that its companion is tapped. "I had just gone out for a short while during one of the training sessions," relates Colombo. "When I got back I saw that Cohen had really lost his temper or something and he was really thumping one of the dolphins with the hammer. I went up to him, shouting, 'what the fuck do you think you're doing?' Some time after I managed to persuade Riva to get rid of him, and he was sacked."

With endearing naivety, Colombo seemed to display inordinate faith in the goodwill of the Riva brothers. "Viareggio is not the best in the world, but this is my first big break," he explained. "I would rather be out there with the dolphins," he said, gesturing towards the sea, "working with them in the wild. I know they don't really like it to be in a pool." As he put Fidel and Malu through their paces, practising the repertoire of stunts for the new season, the two dolphins displayed an impressive degree of synchronisation — perhaps because they had only recently been captured, their uncanny communication abilities not yet impaired by their captivity. There can be little doubt that like Stanzani, Colombo too loves his dolphins, but as it is in human relationships, ambition can conflict with, and even ultimately corrupt that love. Asked whether there was any substance to the rumour that the Rivas were intent upon having the dolphins take part in a circus-style travelling show, Colombo replied: "The Rivas have big plans for the future including a completely new place where they'll need another four dolphins. And here the pool has to be completely reconstructed and that is the only reason why they wanted a permit for moving dolphins — not for a travelling show." But either Colombo was lying, or in the exuberance and naivety of his years, he was being deliberately misled.

With ambitious though tenaciously obscure plans for the future to exploit the summer tourist trade, Riva, much to the consternation of Pier Lorenzo Florio, had already submitted an application to import another pair of dolphins. "I was and I continue to be irrevocably opposed to any importation of dolphins by Riva," Florio declares adamantly. "The three original dolphins were imported under false pretences. Prior to granting the application, the CITES Scientific Authority demanded that Riva produce a scientific or educational justification for the import. It later transpired that Professor Romagnoli, director of the Institute of Veterinary Medicine at the University of Pisa, who is also one of the four members of the Scientific Authority, was tricked into giving his signature and approval for a spurious scientific study to be conducted at the dolphinarium to make it eligible for import approval. Professor Romagnoli now says that he must have signed this paper carelessly without even looking at it."

One of Florio's main objections to the original import was his suspicion that Riva, with its circus tradition, would be tempted to take the animals on tour. Indeed, it wasn't the first time that an Italian circus had made big plans for a travelling Flipper Show. Notwithstanding the EEC education or scientific clause, *Circo Medrano*, known as *Circo Italiano* when it tours abroad, had the gall to request permission to import two *Tursiops truncatus* in 1985 on the grounds that animal acts in the circus are inherently educational. The application was denied by the CITES Scientific Authority, though Medrano's garish billboard posters, so typical of Italian circus art, continued to depict a performing dolphin, even in 1988. As we have already seen, this was due to Medrano side-stepping the law by signing a lucrative business agreement with Cattolica's Aquatic World to provide show dolphins during the off-season winter months. Florio's suspicion of Riva's motives proved well-founded when, in December 1988, Fidel and Malu were transported to Livorno to perform in a Christmas show. There, Fidel died. Explains Rocky Colombo: "We were already having an emergency pool built at Livorno so we could move the dolphins temporarily while the Viareggio pool was being renovated. But the government told us not to move the dolphins anywhere. Then we started to have big problems. The pool was leaking badly and with the water loss we were also losing thousands of kilos of salt. This began to have a bad effect on the dolphins because however much salt we put in —

and the Rivas were spending a fortune on salt — we couldn't keep the salinity, the osmotic pressure high enough. Both of the dolphins began to suffer with badly peeling skin and ulcers over the eyes. We phoned David Taylor who told us we either had to get the salinity high enough immediately or we had to move the dolphins. So we decided to move them, and we didn't even have time to tell the government."

Despite such pleas of innocence, the fact remains that the dolphins were conveniently moved in time to appear at the pre-arranged Christmas show at Livorno. The elevated metal pool — apparently 10m in diameter and 4m deep — awaiting Fidel and Malu was contained in a circus-style big-top on the outskirts of the city, holding about a 100 people. Even though the dolphins were both ill, two Christmas shows were held there. "Then one morning I went to the pool and found Fidel dead," says Colombo. "The Greens and the environmentalists — they all said it was caused by stress because of taking the animals on the road, and afterwards we had demonstrations outside the gates. But David Taylor has said that it had nothing to do with stress. He supported us moving the dolphins. It was only a half an hour journey — there was no stress — not like Cattolica's travelling show which was on the road for five hours at a time."

Predictably, the Rivas are now exerting pressure on the government to allow replacement imports, arousing public sympathy for the plight of the lone female and condemning it as cruel to leave the animal on her own. "She needs a companion," insists Colombo, although he also concedes that it is hard for any trainer to present "a good show with a single dolphin." But for the moment at least, the authorities seem to be sticking to their guns, realising that they would have no legal means to prevent continued circus-style travelling shows by the Rivas. "I think they're being paid by the other dolphinaria who get as many dolphins as they want," Colombo complains bitterly. "They want to drive us out of business. Look at Riccione. They once had six or eight dolphins there. What happened to them? Why is no one asking that? Or Rimini or Cattolica. They complain about circus people being involved here, but those guys over there used to be lifeguards and beach bums!" Yet Colombo remains determinedly optimistic for the future, and with advice from colleagues in the industry in America he is compiling a scientific study proposal which he describes as "dynamite" but which he is keeping a closely guarded secret lest it be sabotaged by his competitors. Asked how scientific study could be compatible with a travelling circus, Colombo insists — once again — that the dolphins would not be moved. This is our long-term pool now," he says. "We won't go back to Viareggio any more." Florio on the other hand remains resolutely pessimistic regarding Riva's chances. "Now, after being tricked like this, the Scientific Authority is unlikely to grant Riva permission to import any more dolphins," he says. "Indeed, there has even been talk of revoking their license. In any event,

Professor Romagnoli of Pisa University has told me that only over the collective bodies of the Scientific Authority will this application be granted." Barring a case of smuggling, declares Florio, Riva will have to wait for the EEC to de-list the dolphins from Annex C1 to C2. "This case demonstrates precisely what will happen if that de-listing comes about," he warns. "The Scientific Authority will have little or no influence on further imports of dolphins, unable to impose even the most rudimentary conditions. Remember, prior to 1984 when the EEC regulations came into force, we did not even have import records for dolphins. It will completely clip our wings." Ironically, Rocky Colombo agrees. "Then they'll really have to worry," he gloats. "There'll be lots of parks with dolphins opening up here in Italy."

Not long afterwards, Riva once again took to the road, moving its sole surviving dolphin to the *Marina di Pisa*, 10km outside the city in the direction of Livorno. The circus is seeking permission to build a permanent pool here, and although building materials are in evidence around the site, the local authority, which is being besieged with vigorous protests by WWF Italy and other conservation groups, has yet to give its assent. For the time being, the dolphin Malu has been consigned to the swimming pool of the neighbouring bar/pizzeria.

SWITZERLAND

Although there are only two permanent dolphinaria in Switzerland today, there is more to the Swiss connection in the dolphin trade than meets the eye. Immune to more stringent EEC regulations on the trade in endangered species, Switzerland and its little neighbour Liechtenstein — well-known for their numbered bank accounts and bogus postbox companies — are also havens for two of the world's most infamous dolphin dealing enterprises, Conny Gasser's Flipper Show based in the canton of Thurgau, and Bruno Lienhardt's International Dolphin Show of Vaduz.

Although the country prides itself in having one of the most progressive animal welfare laws in Europe, the activities of Bruno Lienhardt and Conny Gasser are tolerated and even pampered by the Swiss authorities. Dr Peter Dollinger, head of the federal veterinary office's international traffic and animal welfare division, is, together with circus fan Dr Thomas Althaus, responsible for monitoring the Swiss dolphin trade's compliance with government regulations. Generally, however, the practical implementation of animal welfare ordinances rests with the cantonal authorities, and Dollinger admits that "these controls may not be too tight." Unless they receive their dolphins from the USA, owners "are not obliged to inform the authorities of every death but must keep records which should in theory be checked every year." In practice, however, the law evidently leaves much to be desired: a relative of Conny Gasser reports that "an inspector from the cantonal veterinary office does come over very occasionally, but only for a drink."

"Connyland as it used to be was a very bad establishment because of the standard of its facilities," Dollinger concedes. "There was also frequent transportation of dolphins which is now practically prohibited in Switzerland, although we can't prevent them from being taken abroad. However, up until 1 July 1975 when CITES became effective, we had no legal basis whatsoever to control such trade. The only means of controlling the international trade in live animals was animal health legislation and this doesn't apply to dolphins. It applies to just a few *taxa* which might transmit diseases either to man or to domestic livestock."

Despite the advent of CITES, Dollinger acknowledges that "it is difficult to keep track" of Switzerland's import-export cycle of dolphins, "but I can't believe there is any illegal trafficking in dolphins. Transportation is so complicated that to smuggle a dolphin over strictly-controlled borders is more or less impossible. Also, because of the great deal of work required to train dolphins, owners have a vested interest in retaining their animals and keeping them as healthy as possible." Although Conny Gasser was involved in regular import-export activities, "they were always the same animals," Dr Dollinger asserts, a view which clashes with the testimony of two of Gasser's former trainers, Ingrid Killer and Debbie Steele. Asked if official import documents support his contention, Dollinger quickly resorted to the standard refuge of the bureaucrat. "Because of Swiss legislation, you have no right whatsoever to obtain this information," he announced curtly. "What I have given you verbally is already too much in principle. Furthermore, the regulations do not require that dolphins' individual names be stated on official documents." When informed that evidence seemed to suggest that dolphin names are being transferred from dead ones to newly acquired ones, Dr Dollinger stated: "This happens all the time. These dolphins often have two names, one that's official and one that's for the public." The same blue-eyed explanation is echoed by Dr Margaret Klinowska who declared that this juggling of dolphin identities was simply due to the fact "that it is inconvenient and expensive to reprint guidebooks and other material every time animals change." Yet Conny Gasser, for example, insists that his dolphin "Flipper" has been with him for 15 years, despite the fact that "Flipper's" life actually spans at least three separate individuals. If Klinowska interprets this common practice of name-juggling so innocuously, then what unseen effect did this have on her mortality statistics upon which her conclusions were largely based?

As in most other countries, in practice Swiss regulations seem to serve the interests of the dolphin-owners rather than the dolphins themselves.

Furthermore, attempts to trace the fate of individual dolphins belonging to Conny Gasser and Bruno Lienhardt were hampered by the refusal of the cantonal veterinary hospital in Zürich to release autopsy reports without permission of the owners since dolphins are regarded as "private property" and in fact, almost as inanimate merchandise.

Knie's Kinderzoo

"A paradise for young and old" is how Circus Knie describes its children's zoo at Rapperswil, where the five times daily dolphin show is billed as the central attraction for 350,000 visitors every year. It was the Knie brothers who established, in 1965, mainland Europe's first commercial dolphin show — the prototype of today's dolphinarium. "Captain Jim" Tiebor, the industry's European pioneer, supplied a show for two seasons with a pair of Jerry Mitchell-caught dolphins called Skipper and Sindbad. Says Knie's public relations manager Chris Krenger: "We never had dolphins with the circus, but in '66 or '67, we used to have a travelling dolphin show. But the dolphins weren't ours, they were just presented in one of Knie's tents. In the end the Knie brothers decided against further travelling shows because transporting dolphins was too complicated and the pools were too small." He might also have added, "and the dolphins kept on dying."

So enthusiastic was the public response to this then unique form of entertainment that the Gebrüder Knie readily gave orders for a permanent dolphinarium to be built to replace Tiebor's small travelling pool. This was eventually opened to the public in 1970 with no less than seven dolphins on hand to entertain the crowds, but Tiebor's entrepreneurial spirit soon began to ail in provincial Rapperswil, especially since the dolphin entertainment industry was on the verge of becoming a worldwide gold rush. Knie therefore struck a deal with Tiebor's former partner, Walter Moser, who had established the company Sea Artist Enterprises to market his own travelling Flipper show. With Tiebor supplying dolphins from the USA, Moser remained under contract to Knie for several years until a spate of dolphin deaths caused by water pollution and careless handling threatened Knie's much-coveted image. With the advent of the Marine Mammal Act in 1972, dealer-showmen like Moser and Tiebor, having already learned the hard way that demand can outstrip supply even in a free market, began to experience greater constrictions in the dolphin pipeline, forcing them, in the jargon of high finance, to "rationalise" their activities. It was thus that Moser, having seen untold numbers of dolphins die in primitive travelling shows, moved to Spain in 1978. Says Rudolph Jäckle who worked for Sea Artist Enterprises: "Moser moved to Spain to build his own dolphinarium on the Costa Blanca. He moved out because he had bad luck with the dolphins, and with the trainers too." It was then that the Knie dynasty, seizing a lucrative opportunity, began organising its own shows with Jäckle as head trainer.

Today, Circus Knie normally acquires its dolphins through the International Animal Exchange, Ricky Borguss or Harvey L. Hamilton. Because it prefers to obtain its dolphins from the United States, it is also subject to the strict provisions of the Marine Mammal Act, which, in effect, stipulates that US dolphins be provided on permanent loan rather than outright sale. The Act prohibits trading, transport and even exchange of dolphins without US permission, and the restrictive nature of the law might explain why the more disreputable dolphinariums still prefer to acquire their animals from dealers in Third World nations — "no questions asked". According to Jäckle, dolphins provided under US law "are strictly recorded from the day the dolphin is taken out of the sea, until the day it dies." But despite its well-intentioned provisions, it would be tantamount to sophistry to suggest that the US Marine Mammal Act can in any way guarantee dolphin well-being or longevity in captivity, especially when it is used as a convenient alibi by dolphin establishments eager to win or maintain respectability. Knie is a case in point, particularly since it enjoys international respect. At home, it commands the same kind of reverence afforded to William Tell, or Switzerland's ubiquitous red and white flag, yet its cramped dolphin facility at the Children's Zoo at Rapperswil on the Lake of Zürich has been plagued with mortalities and behavioural problems.

It is the Federal Veterinary Office in Berne which is ultimately responsible for the dolphins at Knie, but theoretically a US inspector could be sent to Switzerland if allegations of maltreatment were substantiated. Depending on the inspector's findings, the "loan agreement" could even be revoked. Predictably, such a visit has never taken place, despite growing misgivings over Knie's dolphin keeping standards. In the case of a national institution such as Knie, with friends in high places, there are several prerogatives to be enjoyed, not least of all the fact that the Federal Veterinary Office is staffed by "realists" who also happen to be ardent fans of the circus or believe that keeping animals in captivity is the inalienable right of Man the "Alpha species". Under such circumstances it is perhaps understandable that any genuine concern over Knie's dolphin keeping is inevitably reduced to a whimper. Dr Peter Dollinger for instance, with diplomatic understatement, looks upon Knie "quite favourably in principle". But although he freely admits his dissatisfaction with the size of the Kinderzoo's dolphin pool, the Knie family maintains that they have never heard of any such complaint by the authorities. Knie's dolphin pool measures just 700 cubic metres, the bare minimum for the four dolphins that — notwithstanding deaths, premature replacements and temporary storage — it likes to maintain there on a permanent basis. As we shall see later, for half a year in 1988, five dolphins were confined to that minuscule concrete prison, with the full knowledge and encouragement of the Federal authorities. While admitting that the pool is suitable "for two animals" Rudolph Jäckle emphasises that "the size of the pool isn't really important to the animals if they fit nicely together. Alright, you must have your minimum standards but even if you give them a hundred metre pool they're still captive." The problem is, Knie's dolphins have rarely fitted nicely together unless one imagines sardines in a can, and this is something that both the Swiss and American authorities have known for years.

Of course, like all circuses and dolphinaria, Knie publicly preens itself on the standards of its animal husbandry, the skills and compassion of its trainers and keepers. Carefully nurtured for public consumption, once again the projected image does not always stand up to scrutiny, as evidenced by the beatings of the baby elephant Malayka in Knie's circus ring. Evidently dolphin husbandry at Knie has also left much to be desired. South African-born Rudolph Jäckle joined Knie as head dolphin trainer in 1978. Prior to that, he was an up-and-coming prodigy of the nascent dolphin business in South Africa, a protégé it seems, of Europe's terrible twins Tiebor and Moser. Reports speak of Jäckle's dusky dolphins dying while being carted around by truck to agricultural shows, from Johannesburg to Rhodesia. Jäckle was also heavily involved in dolphin catching until his endeavours caused a public outcry and provoked a temporary government ban. The *Cape Times* of 8 March 1976, takes up the story: "Horrified onlookers at Hout Bay beach yesterday watched trek fishermen as they dragged three dolphins, spurting blood from numerous injuries, from their nets to a commercial dolphin-training organisation."

Wrapped in a "blood-stained sheet", the newspaper continued, the dolphins were loaded into a van, surrounded by an angry crowd. "A blood-spattered Sea Fisheries inspector who helped with the loading of the animals told the *Cape Times* that the catch had 'complied with all departmental requirements.'" He confirmed that the men, led by Jäckle and his American assistant Ricky Borguss, had a permit to catch three dolphins, provided that they were over a metre in length and were not pregnant females. The newspaper reported that five of the dusky dolphins had been trapped in the fishermen's nets after being herded from a school which had been feeding in the Bay. Two were released after the dolphins began to panic. As the crowd surrounding them turned ugly, the men became increasingly desperate to finish the job, said the *Cape Times*: "'Hurry up,' a helper urged his mates in Afrikaans. 'The people are getting angry.' One man, incensed by the struggles of the bleeding animals, held up his hand and appealed: 'Are you all going to stand here and let these people get away with it?'"

"The van left immediately after the animals were loaded, leaving a trail of blood. A doctor and his family, driving behind the vehicle, later told the *Cape Times* that the blood trail lasted 'all the way to Constantia Nek and then only stopped because the van was going downhill.'" The newspaper went on to say that the operation was being organised by the only person in the Peninsula with a permit to catch dolphins, the professional trainer Mr Rudolph Jäckle. He was to supply the animals to a Swiss dolphinarium — presumably Knie's Kinderzoo in Rapperswil. At this time, Jäckle was already a veteran dolphin-catcher, having supplied, during a period of eight years, over thirty of the animals to European dolphinaria via the Tiebor-Moser twins.

About an hour after capture, while they were still in the back of the van, two of the dolphins died of shock. Jäckle then made plans to catch replacements to join the last surviving dusky dolphin — cynically called "Solitaire" — which had been put in temporary storage in a 7-meter diameter outdoor tank at his base in the Strand. But he evidently didn't count on the public outrage which greeted news of his activities at Hout Bay, which included petitions to the government to prohibit all dolphin catches in the area, and angry letters and phone calls to local newspapers and politicians. Within two days, a blanket ban on the catching, transporting and keeping of dolphins had been ordered by the national government pending an inquiry into the deaths of the Hout Bay dolphins. All outstanding permits were promptly cancelled, leaving the dolphin catcher and his Swiss client somewhat in the lurch. None too popular with the locals and hounded by the press, Jäckle confessed to the *Cape Times* that the capture had been "badly handled" but said that he had been forced to rush because of the ugly mood of the onlookers. One man, declared Jäckle, had even threatened to throw him into the net and hold him underwater — and all this while he had been trying to calm the three dolphins which had just been brought ashore. "Usually I talk to the dolphins," Jäckle was quoted as saying, "take them into shallow water, run my hands over them and soothe them so that they stop struggling... If they don't struggle I can take them away but if they are panicking too much I make a practice of letting them go. I have handled more than 35 dolphins without a death."

Mrs Susan Jäckle seemed more defiant, and was not above trashing her compatriots in the dolphin business to boost the Jäckle reputation: "Compare our record with that of the Port Elisabeth oceanarium which has lost up to 40 dolphins since they began operating," she declared. Her husband, however, evidently reeling from the government's temporary ban on dolphin-catching, seemed more apologetic. "It was a mistake," he confessed, "I should have returned them to the sea."

In 1984, Knie imported two new dolphins, George and Angel, to replace two which had perished. One, a female aged nine years named Star, died from a chronic lung infection, and a male called Stormy aged 23 years succumbed to a heart attack. Jäckle became typically vague and reticent when discussing the deaths of the dolphins in his care. When pressed, however, he admitted that a newborn dolphin had also died, which inadvertently shed light on the demise of Stormy. "One of the females gave birth in March 1984 I think," Jäckle recounted. "I don't know when it was born, it must have been in the middle of the night, and there was something wrong with it — the mother didn't want it, and wouldn't let it nurse." Although this was the third death of a newborn dolphin at Knie, Jäckle disputes Prof. Pilleri's assertion that dolphins refuse to give birth and rear their young successfully in captivity. He also fervently denies the allegations of one of my sources, who reported that the male became so agitated that "Jäckle panicked and gave the dolphin horse sedatives" which in turn induced a coronary thrombosis. However, Knie's head trainer did admit that the female dolphin was "being bothered all the time" by the male, and that they had to be separated. "But I don't want to say that the male got into such a state that he had a heart attack because of that — I don't know!"

When asked about the intelligence of dolphins, Jäckle's response also shed light on the allegation that dolphins are purposely underfed so that during show-time a fish becomes a prize for every successfully completed trick. "If you feed him what he needs then he's so naughty and so full of energy that he's like a guy who gets his money anyway, so why should he work?"

Asked to comment on the findings of Prof. Pilleri's scientific research, Jäckle said: "I read his report. I argued with the man but he's made up his mind and that's his business. He has some points where I must admit that he's right. But he's always negative. The thing is, his words are taken more seriously because he's a professor and I'm only a bloody dolphin trainer. And even though we trainers have the most experience with dolphins, we're rarely if ever consulted. But what annoys me about Pilleri is that he doesn't even want to talk with us. He says that dolphins in captivity are losing their communication. I've told him, come to Rapperswil and stick your bloody head in the water — and you'll hear how they communicate. But no, he's tried it all in Duisburg, he says. I say, we are *not* in Duisburg, Duisburg has a very bad reputation and I don't want to be associated with it. If Pilleri was more constructive in his criticisms — not saying that dolphins in captivity are like people in concentration camps — then we could really do something to improve the facilities. Perhaps he should shift his attention to what's happening to dolphins in the sea. That is terrifying. I can tell you, it's unbelievable what they do to the dolphins, especially in South Africa. It's very fashionable to be against zoos and dolphinariums now — but if the slaughter goes on in the wild like it is, then eventually these are the only places where you'll ever be able to see a dolphin." But ironically, Jäckle and Pilleri do seem to agree on one point, and that is that the best form of dolphinarium — and the rarest — is the one which has direct access to the sea, such as those in Panama, Hawaii and Florida where the dolphins are kept in natural fenced-off lagoons. "The dolphins are much happier there," admits Jäckle. "I don't know if you can fool them making the pool look like the sea — there's always a wall." To emphasise his point, Jäckle recalled that while he was in Florida preparing to collect George and Angel, "one morning I went down there and those two buggers were behind the fence. They used to jump into the channel and then out to sea, but they always came back to eat." They probably didn't realise they'd end up at Knie's glorified bathtub at Rapperswil.

The same could probably be said for the dolphins Amit and Reut which were imported from Israel's Tel Aviv dolphinarium in 1986, again under Marine Mammal Act permits. Within two days Amit had died of cardiac failure. But by this time, the goings-on at Knie were beginning to arouse the suspicion of the National Marine Fisheries Service (NMFS), the government body which administers the Marine Mammal Act. This became apparent after the Knie brothers applied for a permit to capture and maintain two more dolphins from the Florida west coast in October 1986. According to Ann D. Terbush, chief of the Permit Division of NMFS's Office of Protected Resources, "in reviewing the application... the Marine Mammal Commission noted that a number of dolphin deaths which occurred at the applicant's facility between May 1984 and April 1986 appear, in large part, to have been related to social behavioural problems." Knie was invited to "consult with experts" in an effort to rectify the problem, and then submit a report on the results for review. By September 1988, however, the application had been returned because of what was termed "inadequate response to the Marine Mammal Commission's concern regarding possible past behavioural problems among Knie's animals." This included rumours that one dolphin became so aggressive in captivity that even its trainer couldn't go safely into the water with it any more. In an eventual compromise hammered out with the NMFS, Knie agreed that Whipsnade's Victor Manton should initiate a study to determine the cause of the Rapperswil dolphins' behavioural problems. Wryly, Doug Cartlidge notes that "this was the man who wanted to solve Samson's suicidal behaviour as he repeatedly charged the underwater viewing windows, by using a net to push him away!" As expected, Victor Manton obligingly provided Rapperswil with a clean bill of health. Says Cartlidge: "The Marine Mammal Protection Act regulations were very easy to 'get around' and still are. It's the same with the Zoo Licensing Act in the UK. So called 'independent inspectors' are often those with vested interests in the industry."

By January 1989, Rudolph Jäckle had cut his losses and set sail for America to seek his fortune, joining-up with the dolphin-dealing team at Dolphins Plus Inc. in Florida, run by his old pal Ricky Borguss.

Conny's Flipper Show

Like the Gebrüder Knie, the Gasser family has a long and chequered tradition within the circus world. Conny Gasser and his wife, Gerda, are former trapeze artists who went by the name of *The Flying Tongas*, travelling the globe from circus to circus for a good ten years. But by the early seventies the risk that the high-flying act was posing to their health had become too great and, taking a final bow, they set about plotting their future careers in animal dressage. Yet it was only after seeing a dolphin show in Florida that Conny and Gerda joined the gold-rush, eventually travelling with their tent and Flipper Show around half the world. "Wherever we performed with our dolphins, soon permanent dolphinaria were built," reminisces Conny, more out of vanity than any shred of accuracy.

Until a few years ago the dilapidated Royal Circus, founded by Conny's father Ludwig in 1955, and now operated by his brother Bruno, had its winter base at Lipperswil in the eastern canton of Thurgau. Very much a family affair, Conny, Gerda, and their son Robbie and daughter Nadja, are all personally involved in animal training programmes with sea-lions and dolphins. "We were born in the circus," Conny Gasser relates proudly. "My father, my grandfather and even my great- grandfather had a circus. And today we're really international, with sea-lion acts that have become famous all over the world, even in Australia. My son has had his sea-lion show in New York, Las Vegas, Monaco and Paris. Our other sea-lion acts have gone to the Circus Krone in Germany and the Scala night club in Barcelona." Gasser's greatest pride however is his sparkling dolphinarium and pleasure park *Connyland*, which opened to the public in 1985 and which now dominates the tiny village of Lipperswil. It is surprising how a little glass and chrome can, with such apparent ease, erase a squalid past and confer an air of respectability upon an enterprise still rooted in the merciless exploitation of animals.

> *"Only once did I hear of Andrew (Greenwood) letting his hair down, when he went to treat some animals for the high-class Gasser's dolphin show in Switzerland. After a hard day catching, blood-sampling, and vaccinating a group of dolphins, Andrew went with Conny Gasser, a good friend of ours, and some of the staff to a little weinstube famed for its home-made pear liqueur. The beverage must have possessed remarkable properties, for I was amazed to hear how Andrew had delighted the assembled company by listening through his stethoscope, for what I know not, to the buttocks of a buxom Swiss barmaid."*
> — David Taylor, *Zoo Vet*, 1976

In the 1970s, Conny Gasser's Travelling Flipper Show, originally known as the Miami Dolphin Show, was based in a collection of circus caravans in an open field at Lipperswil. Like many of his European cronies, Gasser obtained his first two dolphins, Flipper and Lady, from Jerry Mitchell's notorious Marine Productions International Corporation in Florida. During 1971, with Peter Moses as head trainer, the dolphins were taken on tour to Austria, Britain's giant Belle Vue amusement park in Manchester then owned by the Trust House Forte hotel chain, and even to Israel. Appearing in a pool just eight metres in diameter and two metres in depth in a circus tent holding a spellbound audience of 1500 people, their star-turn was to jump through a blazing hoop. The following year Lady died in Germany, but was quickly replaced by Lady (No. 2).

In January 1973, Debbie Steele arrived from her native England to take up employment as an assistant trainer at the Flipper Show's winter base at Lipperswil. "We went into this old wooden barn, pushed open the door and there was one tank — almost like a child's swimming pool — with two dolphins inside. Further in, there was another pool cut into the floor with two other dolphins inside. The water was stagnant and dark green. I was shocked. When I asked to see the fish preparation room, Mr Gasser pointed to a box of fish on the muddy floor with an old tap dripping onto it. In the middle of the night someone came banging on my caravan door shouting, 'a dolphin's dead!' And that's how I started with Gasser."

Until quite recently, the barn that Debbie Steele refers to could still be seen at Lipperswil, but no one apart from Gasser presumably knows how many dolphins actually died in those pools which were five times smaller than today's minimum legal standards. That barn has now been replaced by Gasser's new three million franc dolphinarium, restaurant and "discotheque with underwater panorama". Gone are the jumble of caravans, replaced by theme-park attractions such as merry-go-rounds, a miniature railway, a "Moonwalk", a "Las Vegas Magic Show", a few menagerie animals, and soon to come, elephant seals and a "Wild Water" run. To complete the respectable image and emphasise its "educational value", specially arranged school visits to the dolphinarium take place on a regular basis. This is Connyland today, reflecting just how kind dolphins have been to Gasser and his bank balance.

After going on tour to Siegen and Koblenz in Germany in March 1973, Debbie Steele flew out to Tokyo to join Gasser's two other trainers, Ingrid Killer and Peter Moses, who were managing one of the Swiss dolphin dealer's most lucrative ventures — a travelling show through the Far East under conditions it would be just too kind to call "primitive". With the dolphins Flipper and Lady (No. 2), the show travelled through the Philippines, Taiwan, Japan, Korea and Indonesia, while a similar dolphin menagerie toured South Africa. Moses was already an experienced dolphin handler by this time, having started work with Gasser in 1971 after a three year stint with "Captain Jim's" Florida Dolphin Show, first as a show-speaker and fish-cutter at Tiebor's act in Riccione and then, in 1969, as a jack of all trades at his winter quarters in Munich. His first assignment for Gasser was to travel to America to collect the Swiss impresario's first two dolphins — Flipper (originally called Mr Bingo) and Lady — from the legendary Jerry Mitchell in the Florida Keys.

"All of the dolphins that Ingrid, Peter and I knew are now dead," Debbie Steele told me. "The dolphins were transported regularly using trucks, trains and buses, but in the travelling show in the Far East they were literally put on anything that moved, even open trucks. When you put a dolphin on a stretcher, sometimes they panic and try to get out and so you have this special kind of strait-jacket which you tape-up so they can't move. The record transport time for a dolphin to be taken from Switzerland to the Far East was 120 hours, but this wasn't exceptional. Even from Belgium to Manila via Hong Kong with few delays it took us about 28 hours to transport the dolphin Didi. And of course you can't put them in the water immediately. You have to put the water in the pool gradually, and hold them because they're temporarily paralysed, and some remain in shock for days."

"We can honestly say that the conditions in the Far East were the worst you can imagine, the worst we had ever seen," said Debbie Steele. Gasser, shrugging off any responsibility for the travelling show apart from reaping profits and finding replacement dolphins, had simply rented out the whole caboodle — dolphins, trainers and equipment — to Butz Promotions, a company based in Munich. When Lady (No. 2) died in Surabaya, Indonesia, apparently of pneumonia, it was later replaced by the dolphin Didi. "But for two months we only had Flipper to do the shows," recalls Ingrid Killer. "And Flipper was terribly upset about Lady No. 2's death. After two weeks he went mad with grief and tried to kill himself by banging his head and nose against the walls of the pool."

In fact Lady No. 2's death may have been virtually inevitable. Gasser had purchased the dolphin from Windsor Safari Park in the UK, then owned by Don Robinson's Trident Television. According to former dolphin and whale trainer Doug Cartlidge, who was present during the sale of the dolphin: "Gasser was desperate for dolphins when he came over to Windsor — that can be the only explanation for him wanting to buy the dolphin, unless he didn't know about its long history of illness. It had a chronic cough and it had been on medication a long time." Debbie Steele: "During the seventies, the sale of sick dolphins happened regularly, and this is what happened to Lady No. 2. The dolphin was sold to Conny Gasser with one month's warranty. Afterwards, it was sent out to the Far East. But the problem was that because of the health certificate, Gasser didn't continue the medication, and by the time we knew how seriously ill Lady was, it was already much too late."

Peter Moses with Flipper during Conny Gasser's Far East Tour.

Preparations for dolphin-transport during Conny Gasser's Far East Tour, the collapsible pool erected at the airport slowly being drained of water...

The dolphin is lifted onto the stretcher by Sigward Glotzbach (right) and Moses (centre)...

Flipper being prepared for transportation.

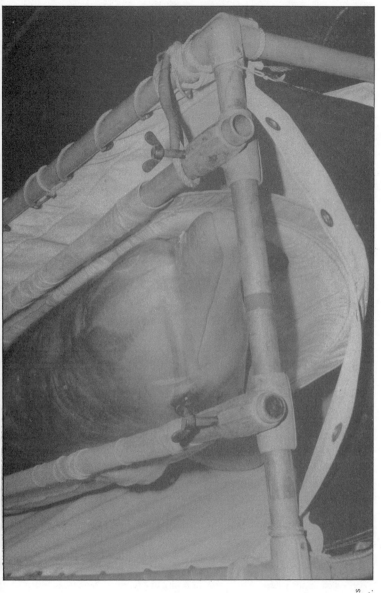

The dolphin Flipper in its
stretcher.

Careless transportation was also threatening the dolphins — a problem that continues to frustrate the dolphin entertainment industry. "When Didi arrived in the Far East her wounds were terrible," Peter Moses told me. "I've never seen anything like it, and because of the climate and conditions, they took a long time to heal." But at least Flipper, with a new companion, began to calm down again.

Mr Sigward Glotzbach was the agent for Butz Promotions in the Far East. Each show was sold to local sponsors, such as banks, garages, cigarette and ice-cream manufacturers. Some speculators would even market their own brands of Flipper ice-cream or Flipper cigarettes. "The problem with this arrangement," says Debbie Steele, "was that to obtain fresh water, ice to cool the water down, salt, fish, chemicals and medicine, we had to battle with three different sets of people and more often than not we wouldn't get these supplies unless we bought them ourselves."

In Jakarta, it was estimated that the sponsors were raking in up to 20,000 dollars a day and in Taiwan even more, with 10,000 people for each show, six shows a day. But according to Ingrid Killer, when Butz realized how much the local sponsors were making, he raised the price and lost all interest in the welfare of the dolphins. "He sold the shows to anyone who could pay his price and with no exaggeration they turned out to be real mafia types, gangsters. Glotzbach left at this point because he couldn't agree with Butz's methods. And so suddenly we had no one left to provide us with supplies. It was a constant battle to get anything from the new sponsors. They even refused to give us fresh water for two weeks because it meant buying tons of salt again. When the water finally arrived it was brown, filthy. Some of the trucks they brought it in had tried to cheat us by filling up from the sewers."

Back in Switzerland, co-ordinating his many other business ventures, Conny Gasser was reaping huge profits from the Far East Show — according to Ingrid Killer, at least Sfr. 5000 a week. But he was also learning that dolphins, as a "perishable commodity" are a high risk investment, notwithstanding their "two-a-penny" price in the Keys. In a letter sent to Ingrid Killer and Peter Moses in Taiwan in February 1973, Gasser complains: "I was in England and bought two dolphins... During the time I was in hospital, both dolphins died, so again I have only two left. It's enough to make you vomit. I lost a lot of money and I can't get any dolphins from anywhere. The whole of Asia can't repair this damage." But in fact the shows in the Far East proved so successful financially that Gasser and other European dealers soon sent out other teams, including Keith Franklin of Queen's International Dolphins. Indeed, it seems more likely that Gasser was attempting to ward off pay rises for his Far East trainers, and also unexpected bills for clean water, fresh fish, and repair of water purification pumps.

In his 1976 book *Zoo Vet*, David Taylor recounts how he was summoned to Bandung in the hill country of Java where he found two ailing dolphins in a portable plastic swimming pool, one suffering from hepatitis. Though Taylor declines to identify the show, this was Keith Franklin's Far East Flipper circus, and it was here in Bandung that, two days before Taylor's visit, several spectators were crushed to death as the crowds pushed and fought each other to enter the already packed arena. "The water was brown and contained a high concentration of particles; it looked for all the world like oxtail soup but smelled like rotten fish," wrote Taylor. He concluded: "To dolphins the Far East recently has been like Devil's Island to French convicts; once arrived there they rarely return alive."

Being "desperate" for dolphins seems to have been a perennial problem not only for Gasser, but other dealers as well. According to Moses, after Franklin lost all of his dolphins in the Far East, he and Conny Gasser made arrangements to capture dolphins in Mexico. A few years later, with Leandro Stanzani, the out-of-work lad who later went on to become director of Adriatic Sea World in Riccione, Gasser mounted that ambitious operation to catch Adriatic dolphins at Cesenatico, north of Rimini, "where twelve dolphins died during capture and transportation." Documents reveal that another six Adriatic dolphins were transported to Queen's International Dolphins in Britain. In the Swiss newspaper *Tages Anzeiger* in June 1974, Gasser is quoted as saying that although the restrictions of the US Marine Mammal Act had forced European dolphinaria to look to the Mediterranean for their supplies, "those animals are much more sensitive and are probably not so well suited for dressage." Following the Italian capture, says Moses, Franklin made a deal with Bruno Lienhardt to capture dolphins in Mexico. Franklin was desperate to replace his dolphins which had perished in the Far East, and Lienhardt, having lost a small fortune at Safariland in Germany because his dolphins were on strike and refusing to perform to the Easter holiday crowds, was also keen on getting in replacements. Upon capture, several dolphins were transported to Safariland, and, via Franklin's Margate dolphinarium at the Queen's Hotel, to Flamingo Park in Yorkshire. "Gasser was sold two of these dolphins," says Moses. And indeed, from the Klinowska report, we can see that it was late 1976 or early the following year that two dolphins, named Baby and Speedy, were imported from Mexico. They were re-exported to Gasser late in 1978. Baby is probably long dead and Speedy (if indeed it is not actually Speedy No. 2 or 3) is still alive and on long-term loan to the dolphinarium in Fasano, Italy.

A second travelling show in the Far East mounted by Conny Gasser was abruptly cancelled when one of the dolphins died in Manila. It was then that Ingrid Killer baulked at going any further with Flipper, Didi and Butz Promotions. "After Indonesia they wanted us to go to Saigon," she said, "but I promised myself that I'd bring Flipper back alive to Switzerland."

In 1974, Gasser put on shows at his Lipperswil winter-quarters with Flipper, Didi, Skipper and a new dolphin called "Lady" — this time No. 3. No doubt it was deemed important to maintain the happy-dolphin illusion to the Swiss public, Gasser's home crowd, but 1974 turned out to be a bad year for image. When the four dolphins suddenly became ill with blood poisoning and Flipper died, the remaining shows had to be abruptly cancelled. Within days, two more dolphins had died, and the only one that could be saved was Skipper. With the media spotlight upon them, there followed a desperate effort to save face. This rapidly degenerated into farce when an anonymous saboteur was accused of deliberately poisoning the animals. According to a front page headline in the tabloid *Blick*, "Three 'Flippers' Died Painfully: Owner Suspects Poison Attack!" According to that report the dolphins had suffered in agony with kidney and intestinal bleeding. But "Conny Gasser didn't spare any costs to save his darlings," the paper reassured its gullible readers. "He had vets from London and Germany flown in. Thanks to this at least 'Skipper' survived." As a precautionary measure, *Blick* added, "Gasser brought a charge at the police station against unknown assailants." But there was a second, perhaps more likely explanation for the poisoning. Says Debbie Steele: "From what Ingrid and I knew of the situation, it was chlorine reacting with the new synthetic rubber solution and paint of the tank which produced some kind of toxin."

Shortly afterwards, Flipper No. 2 appeared on the scene, but was already ailing by the end of that year. To compensate for his streak of bad luck, Gasser sent out his revamped travelling Flipper Show to tour Switzerland again, this time with four new dolphins called Sonny, Blacky, Poco and Chico. A newspaper report at the time declares: "For three weeks now the 25 vehicles of 'Conny's Flipper Show' are no longer on the road. Because three of his four dolphins became mysteriously ill, Gasser had to stop his tour and return to his winter quarters in Lipperswil. Sonny and Blacky suffer from a skin fungus and Poco from an infection. Only Chico seems to be still okay. 'Suddenly they didn't want to jump any more,' explains Gasser. 'Of course I could have continued with forced training. But it is better for the animals if they have some peace now.'"

Only relatively recently has Gasser decided to abandon his travelling dolphin shows — partly to preserve the new respectable image of Connyland at the urging of his wife, and partly due to a tightening legal noose. "It's now too difficult to transport them," Conny Gasser told me. "We have good boxes and everything but there are so many problems to go through customs." According to Willem Wijnstekers at the EEC, even as recently as 1984, Conny Gasser, apparently having a couple of "spare" dolphins, was refused permission for a travelling show through Holland.

Though this reflected a new seriousness on the part of the authorities in EEC member states to clamp down on the most blatant forms of commercial exploitation of dolphins, a repeat of the Far East show always remains a distinct and ominous possibility.

Even today, Gasser cannot admit to any flaw in the tarnished illusion. When I spoke to him at Connyland, shortly before its gala opening in 1985, he declared: "We're circus people. We know about animals. We've been working with lions, tigers, elephants, horses, seals and dolphins for years. We keep the animals like children. My wife won't even allow a mouse to be killed up there around the circus caravans — she'd rather train them!" Gasser went on to inform me that Flipper had been in his possession "for 12 or 14 years," and that "he never had a day's illness in his life." Can Mr Gasser be referring to the Flipper which was imported in 1971 and which died four years later in 1974? Or was he referring to Flipper No.2, who by September 1973 was already ailing? "I still have the same dolphins," Gasser asserted. "Of course I lost one or two but I also lost my father and my grandfather, and so this is quite normal."

Citing the case of Flipper, he claimed that his dolphins, "insured at Lloyds at very high premiums", can live to a ripe old age in captivity. "They can last for a good 20 - 25 years," Gasser told me. "They have a much easier life than in the wild where they have to fight for survival — with sharks attacking them and ship's propellers injuring them — I'd like to live like that — just opening their mouths to catch their food. My dolphins have doctors here and first class food from Holland. They're happy here — you can see it in their eyes and the way they play. When I get a wild dolphin the eyes are blank, dull, far away, but when you start to work with them, you can see how their eyes open up, how they watch you, become bright and clever."

In his pre-Connyland days, Gasser even had an orca whale languishing in one of his minuscule concrete pools at "Flipperswil". Purchased originally from Helgi Jonasson's Fauna in Iceland, the effects of rabid speculation upon an intelligent living being seem to have gone entirely unnoticed. "You're lucky if you can get a killer whale for $100,000," Gasser said. "For three years I had one here at Lipperswil but we had no permit then to build this place so I had to sell him to South America. But now I'm interested to get one back here again."

But what of Prof. Giorgio Pilleri's allegations against the dolphin industry? "He is the worst of all!" Gasser exclaimed heatedly. "He had a tiny pool in the cellar, no filtration, no daylight — the poor animals, Ganges dolphins — didn't get any light and every month one died. They were swimming around in their own shit, and he even implanted cables in their brains. And now he starts to complain about us, but it was him who lost the dolphins!" But what of the specific allegation that dolphins in captivity suffer psychological problems? "Of course the dolphins got crazy in a pool like that! They couldn't even turn in the tank. But look at these animals here — they're not crazy!" A liberal sweep of the arm, to draw my attention to the generous expanse of Connyland's new circular pool, stopped just before the holding tank. Here, sometimes two and sometimes four of Bruno Lienhardt's dolphins were being "stored" temporarily, their skin gashed under the flippers, the animals hardly able to turn. They were being confined there purely for economic reasons: Gasser was afraid that Lienhardt would come to him demanding part of the spoils in show receipts if they were allowed in the main pool. Predictably, the federal authorities under Dollinger and Althaus did nothing, and so in the end, the dolphins languished in that glorified bath tub for three years. Nor did Gasser care to mention that just two weeks earlier, one female dolphin had perished after being savagely attacked by other dolphins in the pool — an unknown phenomenon in the wild, but becoming increasingly common in the tense artificial environment of the dolphinarium where a sophisticated dolphin society is reduced to a primitive pecking order.

When I first visited Connyland in late 1984, the four million franc dolphinarium, self-service restaurant and bar/discotheque with underwater panorama was nearing completion. The idea of a discotheque with a dolphin pool seen through plate glass was already generating controversy. According to Prof. Giorgio Pilleri, it was a "perversion of the highest degree", particularly since the windows and concrete walls of the pool would conduct the music and vibrations directly into the water, perhaps causing acute distress to the dolphins which are particularly sensitive to sound. Moreover, the badly insulated water-pumps were contributing to this underwater noise pollution. Although federal veterinary officer Peter Dollinger, attempting to assuage critics, reported that "it may not be permitted to have loud music and flashing lights", it wasn't long before Gasser's discotheque was hosting live rock and pop bands until 3 a.m. Gasser, however, protests that his dolphins "love to jump and dance to the music! Of course not the whole night through, but they have plenty of time to relax."

Conny Gasser designed the new dolphinarium with the co-operation of David Taylor — or so he claims. "We have a fantastic system," Gasser enthused with evident pride in his achievement. "In three hours we can change the water in the entire pool — one and a half million litres of water, and there's automatic chlorination, automatic pH and higher salinity than in the sea — but this is good for the dolphins' skin." Although Gasser believes that all this makes Connyland "one of the most modern dolphinaria in Europe," the physical well-being of the dolphins there did not seem to confirm that view. Apart from Lienhardt's ailing dolphins Nemo, Girl, Missy and Leo with the infected wounds and gashes under their flippers — injuries received during careless transportation —

James Tiebor, Heidi Bader and Bruno Lienhardt, photographed at the opening of Conny Gasser's Connyland in 1985. (Urs Möckli.)

there were also Gasser's own dolphins Sandy and Lola, one of which was refusing to eat, its eyes swollen and half-closed.

Though Conny Gasser repeated his claim to have lost only two dolphins since 1971, even newspaper reports mention three dolphins dying at Lipperswil in 1973 alone. Also, his statement in 1985 that "I have a dolphin here who's been with me for 14 years," seems highly implausible since his first dolphins, imported in 1971, are both dead. Flipper's longevity for instance actually spans at least three separate individuals — a juggling of identities intended to deceive the public. Indeed, since 1971, Gasser has owned at least 36 dolphins, of which 24 have died or cannot be accounted for. It is known that two dolphins were sold to an amusement park in Holland and another two to a dolphinarium in the Far East, that four dolphins are currently held on long-term loan at Fasano, Italy, and another four at Connyland, but this still leaves unaccounted for, Lady No. 1, 2 and 3, Flipper No. 1 and 2, Didi, an unnamed dolphin which died in Manila, Skipper which apparently managed to survive the 1973 winter in Lipperswil when three others died, Bonnie and Clyde imported from Britain in 1980, and Sonny, Blacky, Poco and Chico who were reported to be ill in the summer of 1974. There is also the uncertain fate of Gasser's orca whale which was sold to an amusement park in Argentina.

Furthermore, according to the Klinowska Report, Gasser also obtained the following dolphins from the UK: Pebbles and Sonny Boy bought from Franklin and Holloway in 1972 — both of which are reported to have died in Switzerland in 1977 — Cleo purchased from Morecambe in 1977 (perhaps the unnamed dolphin that died in Manila?) and Baby, Speedy (No. 1) and Windy purchased from Don Robinson's Flamingo Park in 1978. Strangely enough — though anything is possible in the dolphin industry — Klinowska speculates that the already ailing animal that Gasser purchased from Windsor in 1972 with a David Taylor health certificate, and which died a year later in Surabaya, Indonesia as Lady (No. 2), was actually a male dolphin called Flipper! Last, but not least, Klinowska cites two anonymous dolphins purchased from the UK by Gasser early in 1973 which died within two months. These are just some of the dolphins once under Gasser's care that have simply disappeared, thus earning him the title, even in far away England and America, of "Conveyor Belt Gasser" — the dolphins would be alive at one end and dead at the other.

The Strange Case of Bruno "Houdini" Lienhardt

"We all try to be clean, but he's a black sheep. Whenever Lienhardt's around there's trouble and everyone would like to see him put out of business."
— Conny Gasser

During his 18 years in the business, Bruno Lienhardt of Einsiedeln, Switzerland, has gained the dubious distinction of being one of the world's most notorious dolphin dealers. Although a razor-sharp entrepreneur, Lienhardt could also be likened to an outstanding circus showman, a Houdini-like character who has been able to extricate himself, entirely unscathed, from one animal abuse scandal after another. He obtained his first two dolphins in 1971 from Walter Moser's Sea Artist Enterprises which was then under contract to supply a Flipper show to the "National Circus" of the *Gebrüder Knie*. By October 1984, Lienhardt's International Dolphin Show was described by the French newspaper *Libération* as one of Europe's leading specialists in the capture of dolphins, sharing that privileged position with Peter Bössenecker's *Société Biologique des Caraïbes*.

Debbie Steele, Ingrid Killer and Peter Moses have all worked for the IDS at one time or another. Parting company with Gasser after the cruel fiasco of the Far East, it was out of the frying pan and into the fire for Ingrid and Peter as they agreed to take care of three dolphins in a Lienhardt show at the Bois de Boulogne in Paris, in 1974. Moses later went on to catch dolphins for Lienhardt in Taiwan. For Debbie Steele, recruitment into the Lienhardt ranks occurred unexpectedly in 1982 when the boss himself personally appointed her head trainer of an IDS dolphin show at the giant Walibi amusement park in Wavre, Belgium, 22 km from Brussels. "By this time," says Steele, "Lienhardt must have been raking in a fortune. He had dolphins at the Moulin Rouge, at Viareggio in Italy, at Safariland in Germany and Walibi in Belgium."

When she arrived to take up her position as head trainer at Walibi, Debbie Steele was again confronted by crude and shabby facilities. "The water was like pea soup and two out of the three filters weren't working. The temperature was 6 degrees and it should have been between 19 and 24 degrees. Both dolphins, Boy and Missy, were very ill. They'd been fed on mackerel all the time they were in captivity and one had stomach ulcers and the other had mackerel poisoning. The mackerel had been kept in the freezer for fourteen months and you should only keep it for three. We managed to nurse them back to health but when I complained very strongly to Lienhardt about the bad fish, and insisted on buying proper food for them, he told me it cost too much money. Eventually — just six months after I started — he told me to pack my bags and get out. Ten days after I left I heard that Boy had died of a hernia because they'd lifted the jumps another metre."

The company operations of the IDS are based at Bruno Lienhardt's house in Einsiedeln, Switzerland. Officially though, it has its home in Vaduz, Liechtenstein, yet this is little more than a convenient postbox company, up until 1987 run by the *Fundationsanstalt Vaduz* of Dr Peter Marxer who acted as a paper-director of the IDS. After a row blew up over contracts, the IDS shifted to another postbox company in Vaduz run by Dr Horst Marxer. Such disputes over money and contracts have been a regular and somewhat tedious feature of almost every Lienhardt venture, from the time he stole his own dolphins in Italy, to the occasion when he abandoned his animals in a hotel swimming pool in Cairo. Although the son of a respected family doctor in Einsiedeln, it was not long before Bruno became the black sheep of the Lienhardt family, a ne'er-do-well who eventually squandered his parents' estate. Bruno had a fascination for the glamour of the "good life" and when he had money, he liked to show it off to friends and acquaintances, talking and spending big. He never wasted any love on the animals, not even those that provided for him. People who have known him paint a picture of a man both ruthless and dangerous. Debbie Steele: "About 40 to 45 years of age. Looks like a typical Swiss farmer, gnome-like, with ruddy cheeks and a red nose. But as some people have discovered to their great cost, you should never cross him." Ingrid Killer: "Lienhardt shouldn't be allowed anywhere near dolphins. He's just not fit to keep them. He has no feelings at all for any animal. He's a real businessman and he doesn't care how many dolphins he loses."

Moulin Rouge

For what it is worth, Bruno Lienhardt made his name — and much of his fortune too — by renting dolphins to the *Bal du Moulin Rouge* on Boulevard Clichy for fourteen years. It was at this romantic Paris hot-spot that the IDS dolphins appeared in the celebrated striptease revue *Girls, Girls, Girls* — "a unique and highly popular attraction", according to Lienhardt's former girlfriend and confidant, Heidi Bader. Below the plush drapings and opulent stage settings of the Moulin Rouge, in the establishment's squalid and murky cellar, three IDS dolphins — one as an emergency stand-in — were kept on hand, confined to a lift-up tank measuring just 4 x 5m. At the climax of the show, and evidently to rapturous applause, the half-starved animals would suddenly be elevated onto the stage, where, attracted by the scent of fresh fish, they would leap out of the water and rip away the showgirl's bra.

Lienhardt, however, denies that the only way of achieving a consistent success in the act was by under-feeding the dolphins, insisting, as most wild animal tamers are prone to do, that all that is required is a measure of firmness and the hand of loving kindness. Although mounting criticism finally forced the closure of the revue in 1984, many dolphins are thought to have died in the cramped and primitive conditions. At this time Lienhardt owned at least ten known dolphins which are almost certainly all dead today: Boy, Kiki, Tiny, Speedy, Missy, Zoe, Jelly, Jilly, Bobby and an animal called Nobody. Debbie Steele, working for Lienhardt in Belgium during this time, relates how she had to deliver a replacement dolphin to the Moulin Rouge: "It was in 1981, I think, while I was head trainer at Walibi. I spent two days in Paris and then came back to Belgium. The dolphin's name was Kiki, a small female, only about four or five years old. She was incredibly highly-strung and she hated being touched and hated being transported. She was going mad in the back of the van, jumping right out of the stretcher. I had to hold her down for the whole trip because they wanted to tranquillise her with valium — but I would never use tranquillisers on a dolphin." Despite the show's success with the Moulin Rouge's clientele, there were also numerous complaints. When Greenpeace sued the police prefecture for failing to take action against the illegally small tanks in which the dolphins were being kept, the management promptly dropped the revue.

By this time in 1984, one dolphin had died of pneumonia, another was ailing and the French authorities, already accused of callousness and incompetence, did nothing to help their bruised image when the official veterinary officer referred to the dolphins rather contemptuously as "those fishes". Invoices from the IDS show that each dolphin was rented to the Moulin Rouge for 5000 Deutschmarks per month. Heidi Bader, Lienhardt's jilted girlfriend and former personal secretary, tensed when questioned about the welfare of the Moulin Rouge dolphins. "We never had any problems with the dolphins," she told me defiantly. "They were always healthy and were exchanged for others regularly. These would then be given rests in the south of France or somewhere warm and sunny." So not one dolphin died at the Moulin Rouge? "One did become sick with pneumonia." And did it die? "Yes, it did," she admitted reluctantly. After further questioning, Bader, an employee of the bank *Schweizerische Kredit Anstalt* in Zürich, but still a fellow-director of the IDS in Liechtenstein, finally lost her temper, declaring that during those fourteen years, "if one dolphin died it would be replaced by another one." The replacements usually came from Central America, captured during one of Lienhardt's many expeditions to Mexico and Guatemala. "Mr Lienhardt has been catching dolphins in Mexico for many years," Bader told me. "Within the statutes of the company, Mr Lienhardt has reserved the right to capture dolphins. The local fishermen usually know where to find them and they use their nets to capture them." An untrained dolphin, she said, will bring up to $20,000, "and a trained one more than double that, sometimes even reaching $80,000."

The 14-year long saga of the Moulin Rouge dolphins explains why many less flamboyant dealers have learned to despise Lienhardt. It is not only a question of image, but also of profit. Take the attitude of Mike Riddell, self-styled "curator" of Antibes Marineland. Riddell grouses that it was Lienhardt's activities at the Paris strip-tease revue which provoked the French government to impose rigorous and costly new restrictions on dolphinaria — and indeed, these are still known in France as the *Moulin Rouge Standards*. Introduced in 1981, they required performance pools to have a surface area of at least 800 square metres and a depth equal to one and a half times the average length of the species. They also obliged owners to cold-brand their dolphins for identification purposes. "Bruno Lienhardt should be shot," growls Riddell, "he's giving the whole industry a bad name." Hardly mute criticism perhaps, but as secretary of the EAAM, a lobbying group that has invested much time and effort into inflating the industry's image as a caring, scientific, educational trust, the shrewd, military-style governor of Antibes Marineland realises only too well that Bruno Lienhardt has become a loose cannon. What Riddell doesn't mention in his tirade against his former associate, is that it has taken eighteen years for the top echelons of the industry to condemn Lienhardt's activities. Hardly a word was muttered in protest before investigative journalists began to publish the lurid details of Lienhardt's abuse of dolphins. More importantly, such denunciations are designed expressly for public consumption, a kind of last resort which must somehow emphasise the inherent distinction between the reputable and disreputable dolphin dealer. There is at least one major flaw in this argument: without the continuing support of the mainstream of the industry, Lienhardt could not possibly survive. Indeed, he would have sunk without trace years ago.

By the time the striptease revue was axed, there was only one dolphin left at the Moulin Rouge, a small female called Niki. In frail health, she was transported to Walibi to join two of Lienhardt's other dolphins, Missy and Leo. All three were then imported into Switzerland on 9 October 1984 to join another pair of IDS dolphins, Girl and Nemo, being held temporarily at Connyland.

The Taiwan Massacre

Although raking in profits from Paris, Bruno Lienhardt soon came to realise that such amounts would pale into insignificance compared to what could be earned from mounting an ambitious dolphin catch. Bringing in thirty dolphins to Europe might net him over half a million dollars. He shared some of this dream with Heinz Pelzer, owner-manager of Safariland in Gross-Gerau near Frankfurt, also known as *Pelzer Tier und Freizeitpark*. At this time, Pelzer was on exceedingly friendly terms with the dolphin industry's black sheep, enjoying cosy business dealings which included sharing the spoils of previous dolphin catches — the result of Lienhardt forays into Mexico — and also Safariland's own lucrative IDS Flipper show, managed by the company's chief trainer Peter Moses.

It was early in 1980 that, having drummed up orders for dolphins in Europe and wishing to replenish his own dwindling supply, Lienhardt decided to mount an operation to capture *Aduncus* bottlenose dolphins in Taiwan, eventually seconding Moses to be responsible for the transportation of the animals. The first phase of the catch was organised in association with the French scientist Prof. René Guy Busnel, a Lienhardt client who was attempting to buy up to twenty dolphins for NATO-connected scientific research on the military application of dolphin sonar. Now retired to Fontainebleau, Busnel was then director of the *Laboratoire d'Acoustique Animale* at the *Ecole Pratique des Hautes Etudes* in Jouy-en-Josas near Paris. The Taiwan capture was viewed with such importance by Busnel and Lienhardt that both men were on hand to oversee the operation.

According to Moses, "at least sixty dolphins died during or as a result of the Taiwan operation." The animals were caught at the Penghu islands, lying off the eastern shores of Taiwan. During misty weather, relates Moses, shoals of squid often drift towards the northern coasts of the islands, followed by schools of feeding dolphins. Twice during January and February, local fishermen were paid to take their boats out through the reefs and then chase the dolphins towards the island. By yelling and banging bamboo sticks against their boats to herd the animals, they were able to trap them in a small channel in the reefs which was then sealed off with nets. The dolphins were subsequently lifted out of the water and transported on open trucks to the harbour city of Makung where they

Divers of the China Diving Enterprise struggle with an aduncus bottlenose dolphin during Bruno Lienhardt's disastrous dolphin catching operation in Taiwan in 1980.

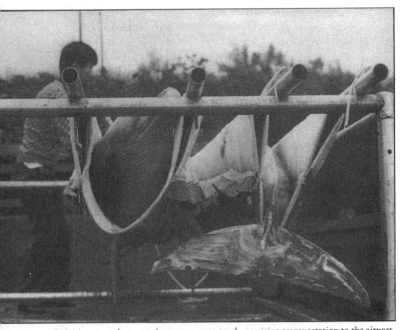

Dolphins secured on stretchers on an open truck, awaiting transportation to the airport.

were stored in temporary holding pens in the bay.

When about thirty dolphins died during this first phase of the catch, an incensed Lienhardt ordered further attempts, summoning Moses from Safariland to co-ordinate the operation and arrange transportation of the surviving dolphins. The animals being kept in the pens, however, soon began to die in the filthy waters of Makung harbour. When Moses arrived he discovered that "there were only twelve dolphins left alive in the pens," and that the "project was so badly organised" that, in the absence of his boss who had already beaten a hasty retreat, he felt obliged to take command of it himself. He set about making unusually comprehensive check-lists on each and every dolphin that was caught.

Under Lienhardt's orders, the IDS had procured the services of the China Diving Enterprise in Taipei — a company which had previously organised another disastrous dolphin catch for Hong Kong's Ocean Park. With the assistance of the China Diving Enterprise, another 18 dolphins were put into the five temporary holding pens in the bay. China Diving's President, Steve S. Shieh, "guaranteed that there will be no injuries" and "no cruelty" to the dolphins. Although this statement was written after at least forty dolphins had been fatally maimed, it provided Lienhardt and Busnel with a comforting alibi in their dealings with the authorities. During this second phase, a minimum of eight dolphins died before transportation, including a calf. With ropes around their tails they were dragged ashore and, muddy and blood-stained, were discarded.

In March, while the dolphins were still in the holding pens, Moses' records reveal that one dolphin — evidently pushed beyond the limits of endurance — attacked the divers, and that all of the animals were then given valium regularly. Via telephone and telex, Prof. René Guy Busnel was providing veterinary advice to Moses directly from Paris. Indeed, they stayed in close contact throughout the operation, as evidenced by the following telex dispatched to the professor on 4 March: "Animals are looking good; vitamins and minerals are given carefully; fish not the best, but still usable; yesterday caught 15 new animals, total of dolphins now 27." From Paris, Busnel was also playing a key role in arranging transport, repeatedly assuring Moses that cargo flights were being booked and confirmed to take the animals to Europe.

In a hastily arranged meeting on 15 March in Taipei, Busnel informed Moses that transport for the dolphins had been arranged for 31 March, all of the 22 animals to be flown in one batch. They also reviewed the health and general status of the animals, with the professor advising Moses on worm, antibiotic, hormone, vitamin, mineral and sedative treatments. Returning to Makung the following day, Moses discovered that dolphin no. 14 was dead and that the divers had taken it out of the pens but had discarded it nearby, letting it sink into the murky waters of the harbour. Moses notes that he complained bitterly about the possibility of infection

The director of the China Diving Enterprise, Steve S. Shieh, posing with a young captured dolphin.

but "they just nod their heads and don't show any understanding of what I mean, one of them saying, 'We've done this since the very first time we caught dolphins here.'" Moses then learnt that the transport scheduled for 31 March had been cancelled, a turn of events which once again illustrated the incompetence that plagued the entire operation. He was left to care for the dolphins as best he could, beset by inadequate veterinary care and difficulty in obtaining essential supplies, and even having to contend with a consignment of rotting fish intended as food for the dolphins. He notes in his reports that several of the dolphins had begun to suffer from pus-filled blisters despite regular injections of antibiotics. Still hearing no news from Paris or Switzerland, Moses, increasingly anxious and distraught, contacted Danzas airfreight on his own initiative, only to be told that the cargo flight could not be booked until the necessary funds had been received from Lienhardt. It was not until two weeks later that he finally obtained confirmation of the flight: a Boeing 707 bound for Frankfurt on 27 April.

On 26 April the surviving 22 dolphins were hoisted out of the water on stretchers and placed on open trucks to await transportation to the airstrip on the outskirts of Makung. With "four or five for each load", the dolphins were subsequently put aboard light aircraft bound for Taiwan's international airport. Steve S. Shieh's China Diving Enterprise was paid $22,264 for those dolphins. But the following day, on 27 April, one dolphin died in the freight area. In his notebook, Moses wrote that "suddenly the dolphin reared up and died, apparently because of sheer terror caused by aeroplane noise." Documents state that the original consignee was to have been the "bassin du dauphin" of the *Zoo Marines*, an amusement park operated by Willy Stone in Perpignan, the Pyrenees, France, which Lienhardt was apparently renting at the time. For legal and economic reasons, however, this was changed to Heinz Pelzer's Safariland at Gross-Gerau in Germany. Bruno Lienhardt was charged 275,000 Deutschmarks for transportation of the dolphins to Germany by Danzas airfreight. Incredibly, as though they had been manufactured by one of the island's cheap industries, the customs papers for the 22 live dolphins declared that they had been "produced in Taiwan".

According to an article entitled "Penghu's Jet Set Dolphins" in *Vista*, a Taipei newspaper, "Prof. R. G. Busnel awaited their arrival in Frankfurt." But soon there were no dolphins left alive for the scientist and predictably, hearing of the debacle, Bruno Lienhardt had once again conveniently disappeared. Upon their arrival in Germany, the 21 remaining dolphins were transported to Safariland, but on the 28 April, a still-nursing calf perished and a day later his mother also died. Eight of the remaining dolphins were sent to Walibi in Belgium, Holiday Park in Hassloch, Germany, and to two other dolphinaria in Saarland and Luxembourg. Within two days of arrival at Neunkirchen, Saar, two more dolphins

With ropes around their tails the dead dolphins were dragged ashore and, muddy and blood-stained, were discarded.

died, and of all the dolphins transported from Taiwan to Europe, says Moses, "not one has survived." Shocked by the disaster in Taiwan, Moses then retired permanently from the dolphin business.

Reached by telephone, Heinz Pelzer, whose name appears as consignee on several Taiwan documents, denied any involvement in the IDS catch. He also insisted that he had severed his connections with Safariland, selling out to a Herr Kinzler in November 1984, and subsequently giving up his managerial role. "There have been no dolphins at Safariland since 1982, when the dolphinarium was destroyed by a heavy storm," Pelzer declared. When it came to Lienhardt's Taiwan dolphin catch, Pelzer was quick to assert his innocence. "We were not involved at all," he told me. "Only afterwards, when the dolphins arrived, did we give Mr Lienhardt the possibility of storing them in our place." Pelzer went on: "We never had our own dolphins. We used to rent the whole show as a package from Lienhardt, Walter Moser or René Duss." Asked how many dolphins arrived at Safariland from Taiwan, Pelzer replied, "in all about 20 for sure. To my knowledge not one is alive today."

The Scientific Loophole

According to Moses, the Taiwan operation was arranged so that the authorities would assume that the dolphins were to be used purely for scientific research, a ploy that perhaps portends an inauspicious fate for EEC regulations which stipulate that dolphins may only be imported for educational or scientific purposes. A more ominous development, however, would be a kind of marriage of convenience between unscrupulous traders and scientists to obtain dolphins, a precedent set by the Taiwan operation.

When I attempted to obtain further information on the Taiwan massacre from the IDS, Heidi Bader responded by saying that the operation "was not arranged by Mr Lienhardt but by a professor in Paris who wanted the dolphins for scientific research." Bruno Lienhardt himself was not prepared to comment on the issue. Reached by telephone, Prof. René Guy Busnel's first reaction was to claim that he was "only giving advice" to Lienhardt for the dolphin catch. Upon further questioning however, he admitted that he was attempting to obtain dolphins for scientific research but said that he had received no dolphins from Taiwan "because they all died, I don't know how many." And in what seems to be a strange warp of scientific logic, Prof. Busnel declared that the dolphins "died because of polluted water in Makung harbour, not because of capture." Although admitting that capture necessitated the animals being stored in holding pens in the harbour, the professor insisted that "you can't capture and transport dolphins immediately because first they must be kept in these pens to domesticate them." He therefore concluded that the death of so many dolphins "is quite normal." When questioned as to whether he was aware that Lienhardt was using his name for official purposes so that the export and import of the dolphins would be categorised as being for "scientific purposes" even though they were actually destined for a number of amusement parks in Europe, Busnel replied testily that "you know nothing about this subject. Everywhere, in the USA, South Africa, Singapore, Europe, dolphinaria are engaged in valid and valuable scientific research."

NATO and the US Navy

Asked what kind of research his 20 Taiwan dolphins were to have been used for, Busnel replied: "For sonar research. I have been working for 25 years on this subject at the Institute in Paris and at the dolphinarium and research station in Antibes. NATO funded our experiments in the Mediterranean and the Atlantic, and we also worked in the USA and Denmark." Rather vaguely, Busnel recalls that during those years "about ten dolphins every year" were used for scientific research. When asked if this included terminal vivisection experiments, Busnel rapidly terminated the interview.

According to a spokesperson at NATO's scientific section in Brussels, Prof. Busnel "was awarded a research grant by NATO's Scientific Committee in 1979," and "such research grants are usually in the region of one million Belgian francs." The grant was for "an advanced research workshop" which in 1980, resulted in a 1000-page tome entitled *Animal Sonar Systems*, co-edited by Busnel and published as part of NATO's Advanced Science Institute series by Plenum Press.

In addition to his association with NATO, Busnel and his colleagues also worked closely with the US Navy's Marine Mammal Program, based at the Naval Missile Center and Naval Ocean Systems Center in San Diego, California. The Marine Mammal Program is devoted to the military application of dolphin research and has even trained dolphins as "living torpedoes" to attack enemy divers. In this day and age of increased sensibilities over animal welfare, the 1987 Pentagon budget authorised "the taking of not more than 25 marine mammals each year for national defense purposes". But it is difficult to tell whether the capture of more dolphins, whales and seals could be hidden in highly-classified military budgets. The *Advanced Marine Biological Systems Project* (AMBS), which administers the exploitation of marine mammals in the US Navy, was allocated $5.4 million in 1986 — and this only for the unclassified section of the budget, the tip of the iceberg.

Animals Go to War

> *"'You asked me once,' said O'Brien: 'what was in Room 101.*
> *I told you that you knew the answer already. Everyone knows*
> *it. The thing that is in Room 101 is the worst thing in the*
> *world.'"*
> — George Orwell, *Nineteen Eighty-Four.*

As the saying goes, "what the eye doesn't see, the heart doesn't grieve over", and this, together with official censorship, is probably the reason why little is ever said or written about the military exploitation of animals, undoubtedly one of the most perverted of all human activities, too terrible even for the best public relations experts to prettify or euphemise. Indeed, for well over a million animals every year, World War III has already begun. Rhesus monkeys are shot in the head and eyes at point blank range to compare the effectiveness of Russian versus American bullets; others are burned and blinded with lasers in "Star Wars" research. Dolphins are studiously dissected to perfect military sonar. Horses, sheep, dogs, cats, mice and rats are dosed with chemical and germ warfare agents both for the limitless refining of these weapons and to test cures and antidotes which, by the very nature of the vertical arms race, are eternally elusive.

Then there are the simian pilots of the US Air Command — 4000 of which were destined to die in one research establishment alone in a quarter of a century of mindlessly repetitive experiments. These victims were "trained" — with the judicious use of electric shocks — to fly aircraft simulators through take-off, aerial refuelling and either tree-top or high-altitude bombing runs. To discover whether airmen, in the event of war, could cope with the debilitating symptoms of flying through deadly radiation bursts and fall-out clouds contaminating the atmosphere, the monkeys were irradiated, and, fighting terrible sickness on one hand, and electrocution on the other, were once again sent on their doomsday bombing mission to Moscow.

It is in experiments such as these, utilising creatures that have never known the meaning of war, that scientists the world over are engaged in the most intricate planning imaginable for Armageddon. On a deeper level, this kind of research not only reflects the excesses of utilitarianism as a dogma which has run amok, but also science's chronic blindness towards spiritual and ethical values. Indeed, the exploitation of animals in laboratories is still firmly rooted in the archaic and mechanistic principles that were expounded by the earliest patriarchs of vivisection, men like René Descartes, who believed that animals were inanimate objects that must be "strictly considered as machines," and Claude Bernard, the nineteenth century French physiologist who declared that he could "act upon living bodies as upon inanimate objects." In much the same way, even the closest of our fellow species which are conscripted into fatal military service every year are also reduced to mere statistics, and "scientific models". The dry and impassive statistics so grudgingly produced by the military establishment actually provide a convenient curtain against a litany of individual suffering.

The ritual justifications for military experiments on animals bear more than a passing resemblance to Orwell's drab and fearful world of *Nineteen Eighty-Four*, where hypocrisy has been tuned to a fine art, and where, governed by Big Brother and the paranoia of power, doublespeak is the order of the day — "War is Peace, Freedom is Slavery, Ignorance is Strength." It is thus that military vivisection is justified as being "strictly for the purposes of defence" — although animals are also routinely killed in the development of obviously offensive weapons systems; that the secrecy surrounding such experiments is for the protection of "national security" — but also to save the public from "emotional prejudices" and "sentimentality"; and that while animals are utilised precisely because of their alleged physiological and psychological resemblance to humans, "anthropomorphic judgements" which might accidentally confer upon them some shred of fundamental rights and dignity must be avoided at all costs.

From chariot horses in the ancient world, to Hannibal's merciless exploitation of elephants to cross the Alps and confront the Roman Empire, animals have played a fundamental role in the long and murky history of human warfare. But it was not until the twentieth century that the military use of animals became distinctly sinister and bizarre. During the Second World War, the American army used kamikaze "tankdogs" to blow up German panzers. In their book *A Higher Form of Killing*, Robert Harris and Jeremy Paxman describe how the dogs were taken away from their mothers as soon as they were weaned, and were only given food under the bellies of tanks. Once on the battlefield, the dogs were held on the verge of starvation, with explosives and a tall triggering antenna strapped to their backs. As the German panzers approached, the hungry animals were released. Running instinctively under the enemy tanks searching for food, the antenna would scrape along the metal belly, detonating the explosives and thus destroying both tank and dog.

Even more imaginative plans were laid by the American OSS, the forerunner of the CIA, report Harris and Paxman. One of these focussed on the instinctive fear of cats for water and their legendary ability to always land on their feet. The OSS scientists thus reasoned that a bomb could be attached to the cat which would then be strapped under a fighter plane. When dive-bombing Nazi warships, the cat would be released and in the animal's desperation to avoid water, it would almost certainly guide the bomb onto enemy decks. Experiments with the flying cats, however, proved rather less than successful since the animals became unconscious long before the ship far below them presented an ideal place to land. Over the following years, millions of animals were to become victims of World War III. The justification was as simple as ABC, that acronym of the kindergarten, representing the first steps of knowledge, also applied with unintended cynicism to atomic, bacteriological and chemical weapons.

But it is in the USA, which gave the world its first monkey head transplant, that military experiments seem most grotesque. By the early 1960s, the military scientists had shifted their unquenchable curiosity to the cetaceans, both as a research tool and a war machine. The US Navy launched its secret dolphin project in 1960, trying to discover whether the sleek physiology of the animals could be applied to the design of submarines, underwater missiles and torpedoes. The programme however was soon growing by leaps and bounds, encompassing distinctly more sinister research. This included the training of dolphins to attach explosives and electronic eavesdropping devices on enemy ships and submarines, and helping Navy divers recover lost, expensive weapons from the ocean floor. By 1965, it became obvious that the USA was facing stiff competition from the USSR, raising the spectre, according to the CIA, of "a dolphin gap". According to US intelligence reports, the Soviet dolphin project involves five Black Sea research stations, including small bioacoustics laboratories and a dolphinarium. The Russian programme, the CIA fretted, "could enable the Soviets to evaluate the potential benefits of developing acoustic jamming countermeasures to US Navy dolphin programs..." In the 1981 issue of US Naval Institute Proceedings, Lt. Commander Douglas R. Burnett, an admiralty attorney, discussed the issue of combat-dolphin escalation between the superpowers. "There may be no choice except to destroy dolphins," he warned, "or any marine mammal representing a similar threat."

But are the animals trained or brainwashed to become killers? Ironically, it was the neurophysiologist and "New Age Guru" Dr John Lilly who first perfected a technique of implanting electrodes into the brains of unanaesthetised animals to stimulate the "pain and pleasure sectors" of the mind. After butchering monkeys by the dozen at the National Institute of Mental Health, Lilly concluded that judicious manipulation of these brain areas could inspire joy and well-being, or pain, anger and fear. Indeed, by using the electrodes to deliver reward or punishment stimuli, the animal could be entirely subordinated to human will. The ingenious Lilly then turned his attention to dolphins, under the pretext of wishing to "communicate" with these intelligent and highly perceptive creatures. To insert electrodes into the brains of the fully-conscious animals, holes were made in the skull with a sharp instrument and a carpenter's hammer. According to Prof. Giorgio Pilleri, "the dolphin was held down but tried to jump up at every blow — not because of the pain, but because of the unbearable noise produced by the hammering."

Indeed, many of Lilly's dolphins suffered an agonising death. "Despite disappointment and sadness," he announced, "we had to go on with our research: our responsibilities lie with finding the truth." It was not until years later however that a repentant Lilly finally stumbled across that apparently elusive truth. After suffering drug addiction and a mental breakdown, he characterised his research in an entirely different light: "I was running a concentration camp for my friends."

But predictably, perhaps, the practical applications of such research were not lost upon the US military and intelligence services, which had promptly ordered Lilly to provide full demonstrations of his work. Not long afterwards, the Sandia Corporation, under government contract to design a small and easily portable nuclear bomb, presented its experimental delivery system: a mule, controlled by a sun compass and brain electrodes. Although crossing mountainous country and difficult terrain, the mule was kept on a perfectly straight course by the feelings of punishment or reward that the electrodes delivered into its brain.

Judging from the testimony of former trainers in the CIA and US Navy, similar, though perhaps less invasive "brainwashing" techniques have been employed using cetaceans since the early 1970s. One former and disillusioned trainer, the neurophysiologist Dr Michael Greenwood, revealed that the US Navy had trained orcas to carry and deliver explosives. Most frightening of all, he declared, the animal, capable of towing a weight of up to 7 tons for several miles, has been taught to carry nuclear warheads to enemy shores. Stopping a nuclear killer whale on such a mission would be virtually impossible, he added.

By 1972, the US Navy had deployed a top-secret team of "warrior porpoises" in Vietnam, part of its "Swimmer Nullification Program", yet another Orwellian code name for killing. For at least a year, these experimental dolphins were utilised to protect strategic Vietnamese harbours against infiltration by enemy frogmen. According to Dr James Fitzgerald, pioneer in dolphin research for the CIA and US Navy, after detecting an intruding diver, the animals were trained to pull off his face mask and flippers, tear the air-supply tubes, and finally "capture him for interrogation." In fact the dolphins serving in Vietnam seem to have been considerably less benign. Indeed, it was the increasingly sordid exploitation of cetaceans by the US military which began to provoke repulsion amongst its own dolphin trainers. Several resigned in disgust, and experienced few qualms about betraying at least some of the military's secrets to the public. According to Dr Michael Greenwood, the Navy's dolphins had also been taught to kill, with knives attached to their flippers and snouts. Worse was to come however, when dolphins were equipped with large hypodermic syringes loaded with pressurised carbon dioxide. As the dolphin rammed an enemy frogman with the needle, the rapidly expanding gas would cause the victim to literally explode. Years later, it was revealed that the killer dolphins of Vietnam had actually been responsible for the deaths of 40 Vietcong divers, and accidentally, two American servicemen. As one former dolphin trainer for the CIA put it, "they can't tell the difference between a friend and an enemy." Indeed, perhaps the very concept of friend and deadly foe — a duality manifesting itself within the same species — is an alien concept to the dolphin.

Although the Navy conceded that it had been able to "program the dolphins and keep them under control for distances up to several miles," it strenuously denied allegations of brainwashing. Training however remained strictly secret, prompting Dr Farooq Hussain of the Department of Biophysics at King's College, University of London, to ask: "How is an animal which for centuries has only been recorded for its intelligence and friendliness towards man, now taught by one man to kill another? They must use electrical stimulation of the pain and pleasure centres of the brain in order to induce and reward aggressive behaviour. Of all the depraved and disgusting activities of which man seems capable, this one in particular must rank highly." By 1984, the *Washington Post* columnist Jack Anderson alleged that the military dolphins would soon be used clandestinely to mine Nicaraguan harbours. Attesting to the unsurpassed skills of the cetaceans in this area of warfare, former trainers declared that the dolphins could sow mines a hundred times faster than the Navy's most elite units of frogmen.

By October 1987, however, the role of the animals had been reversed, when six of the Navy's dolphins were deployed in the Persian Gulf to search for Iranian mines. According to the Pentagon, they would also be responsible for security patrols against potential saboteurs around the large barge off Farsi island which served as a floating base for helicopter gunships and more than 200 American servicemen. In spring 1989, Rick Trout, who worked as a Navy animal trainer between 1985-1988, revealed that the military's dolphins and seals had been starved as part of their training at the Naval Oceans Systems Center in San Diego, California, and even punched and kicked. Official documents show that 13 dolphins have died in Navy hands over the past three years, more than half suffering from starvation or stomach disorders. "My second day on the job I saw a sea-lion kicked in the head for refusing to eat," Trout testified. "I also saw a dolphin punched in the face." An "independent" government commission has confirmed some of Trout's allegations, yet predictably tame, its final recommendation was that the Navy should capture no more marine mammals until it has hired more veterinarians. It currently holds, trains or deploys at least 100 marine mammals, with one team of dolphins used to patrol the waters around Trident nuclear submarine bases in the states of Georgia, Connecticut and Washington. However, it is reported that significant numbers of dolphins and sea lions have been escaping from their military tormentors. According to local conservation officials, several sea lions recently turned up on the beaches of San Miguel island off the coast of Southern California, still wearing Navy equipment harnesses.

Apart from active service, dolphins are also recruited extensively as passive "models" for "invasive laboratory research". The mysteries of dolphin sonar, for example, have obsessed military scientists for at least twenty years for the simple reason that the species' innate abilities in echo-location, or "seeing with sound", far surpasses even the most advanced radar equipment in the arsenals of the great powers. Indeed, that obsession alone has resulted in several thousand dolphin deaths, and in the USA, an annual budget of at least one million dollars.

This was precisely how countless dolphins died in Prof. René Guy Busnel's laboratories, and it must be said that the Taiwan dolphins were probably more fortunate to perish during capture than to end at the *Laboratoire d'Acoustique Animale*. Prof. Giorgio Pilleri describes many of the French scientist's dolphin experiments as "horrific". Explaining why he cut short a working visit to the French laboratory, Pilleri explained: "The last straw was when they showed me — evidently with great pride — a dolphin which had been totally mutilated, a huge carving knife sticking out of its back. On top of that, in sending a greeting card to one of their colleagues abroad, this 'research team' all signed their names in dolphin blood."

Lienhardt Steals His Own Dolphins

Unfortunately for its already battered reputation, the IDS was involved in yet another scandal in 1984 which was splashed across the front page of Switzerland's tabloid rag, *Blick*. Two of Lienhardt's dolphins, Nemo and Leo, both originally from Guatemala and later to be abandoned in a hotel swimming pool in Cairo, were, for several years, rented out to the Ocean World Aquarium at the Lido Camaiore on the outskirts of Viareggio, Italy. At some point during 1984, a heated dispute broke out over contractual obligations, with Lienhardt alleging that he had "never seen a cent" of the 45 per cent of ticket sales he should have received, and the management of the Aquarium retorting that they had "never seen a lira" in compensation for food and care of the dolphins. "The dolphinarium itself may have been one of the best in Europe," contends Heidi Bader with unabashed gall, "but because of some kind of disagreement our dolphins were placed in the small holding tank. When Mr Lienhardt complained, the management told him that they had to be removed from the main pool because it required repair. However, no repairs were done and so Mr Lienhardt became suspicious and concerned about the fate of his animals." More likely however, was that Lienhardt had become concerned about the fate of his wallet. And so on the night of 14 November 1984, the IDS president and five helpers, intent upon "rescuing" the dolphins, broke into the Aquarium. Drugging two watchdogs with valium, they lifted the dolphins onto stretchers and carried them to a waiting car. "Six hours later we were in Switzerland — an hour before police blocked the border," Lienhardt boasted.

"When I demanded the return of the customs papers for the dolphins, the Italians refused to give them to me," the IDS president claimed later. But how was it that the dolphins could enter Switzerland without such papers? Quite simply because they are regarded as circus animals. Explains Dr Peter Dollinger of the Federal Veterinary Office in Berne: "The animals were declared at the Swiss border and we issued an import license for them. We did not request an Italian re-export certificate under CITES because there's a special provision in the Convention which provides for the transport of circus animals. And the animals concerned had CITES documents but issued in Belgium. For this reason we decided not to consider them as Italian animals."

At about the same time, Lienhardt also received temporary import papers for three other dolphins, Girl, Missy and Niki, veterans of IDS shows at Walibi and the Moulin Rouge. All five animals were subsequently placed in Conny Gasser's new dolphinarium at Lipperswil, though it would not be long before yet another wrangle over contracts and "gentlemen's agreements" would erupt. Lienhardt had promised both Gasser and the trusting Federal authorities that the dolphins would be in Switzerland for no more than three months. Declared Dr Peter Dollinger: "Lienhardt's dolphins were only accepted for temporary importation. They will be moved this year to a municipal dolphinarium which Mr Lienhardt will be leasing in the South of France." That was in 1985, but by 1988 the temporary dolphins were becoming embarrassingly permanent. Indeed, that dolphinarium — at Cap d'Agde — was entirely fictitious and, much to the embarrassment of the Federal Veterinary Office and the annoyance of Gasser, the "temporary" dolphins remained at Connyland for three years, during which time two — Niki and Missy — died. Says Debbie Steele: "Lienhardt's been talking about his dolphinarium in the south of France for years. According to him it's been under construction since 1981, and I think that's how he gets through half the laws. He applies for a temporary import for two dolphins and says, 'my new dolphinarium isn't quite ready yet'."

Complacent Bureaucracies

In recent years, increasingly critical media coverage has sometimes had the bizarre effect of government officials protecting the reputations of the dolphin dealers in order to vindicate their own professional credibility. Despite irrefutable evidence to the contrary, Dr Peter Dollinger, for example, asserts that "there are no dolphin dealers living in Switzerland, and I can't imagine there are any in Europe at all." While Prof. Giorgio

Pilleri is regarded as someone who "makes waves" and is therefore denigrated as a "so-called dolphin expert", Lienhardt's reputation on the other hand appears almost saintly. Asked whether Bruno Lienhardt — who describes himself as a "business manager" — is involved in the trade in dolphins, Dr Dollinger replied, "no, certainly not. He has purchased a few animals — apparently legally — but he's not dealing with them, he's performing." The term "apparently legally" may be regarded as a glossing over of the facts. Captured off Guatemala and Mexico, Girl and Nemo began their existence in captivity under a cloud of legal uncertainty, imported without permits into Belgium in 1981. Prior to 1984, when Belgium at last joined CITES, the country was notorious as a conduit for animal-dealing supplies destined for other European countries.

Dollinger seems to show the same kind of favouritism towards Conny Gasser. In 1985, he actively supported Gasser's application to the US authorities for permission to capture four additional dolphins for Connyland. The application, which Dollinger "reviewed and corrected where necessary" included false statements and diagrams regarding the size of the holding pool. The pool was both described and depicted as being "20 feet in length and 20 feet in width" which might just conceivably be accurate if one completes, with a vivid imagination, a narrow L-shaped tank into a square. The application also included the deceptive declaration that there had been "no mortalities" at Connyland — without mentioning that the complex had only just opened. Dollinger also saw fit to include a glossy magazine article praising the new dolphinarium. In fact, as I discovered from editorial staff at the magazine, the dolphins' infected wounds and gashes had been blotted out by an overzealous graphic artist for "aesthetic reasons". Furthermore, neither Gasser nor Dollinger saw fit to reveal any information about the tragic death of Lienhardt's dolphin Niki, which up until November 1984 was being cared for at *Connyland*.

Even by the middle of 1985, official records continued to reveal that the IDS owned five dolphins in Switzerland and it actually required a three-day investigation to discover the fate of Niki, the missing dolphin, a female aged only five years whose life appears to have been a sad one since the day Bruno Lienhardt had her captured off the coast of Mexico and confined her to a tank in the Moulin Rouge. The cantonal veterinary office in Frauenfeld is responsible for the implementation of animal welfare regulations at Connyland, yet incredibly their response to the apparent discrepancy was that "we don't know where the fifth dolphin is. You must ask Connyland. This is all the information we have." Predictably, the IDS denied its very existence, as did Connyland. Information on the fate of the fifth dolphin was finally received from an impeccable source who, for fear of repercussions, wished to remain anonymous. She revealed that the dolphin had died in November 1984 after catching pneumonia, partly as a result of "being torn to pieces by other dolphins in the pool at Connyland

— she was full of bites and gashes — something that hardly ever happens with dolphins unless there is great stress caused by their confinement." When finally confronted with details of the dolphin's death, Heidi Bader claimed that "it had always been a weak dolphin," but the truth of the matter is that she did not die of natural causes, perhaps explaining why Bruno Lienhardt refused permission for the autopsy report to be released. On 25 November 1984 her emaciated and mutilated body was driven to the cantonal veterinary hospital in Zürich whose pathologists declared that the dolphin was in appalling health, "suffering from acute fibrosis of the lung, acute dermatitis, and wounds caused by bites to the genital region". More mysterious however was that the autopsy specifically mentioned wounds on the dolphin's flippers, tail and nose "not consistent with an attack from another dolphin". The pathologist I spoke with was "not willing to speculate on the cause of those wounds".

Abandoned in Cairo and Vienna

Lienhardt's three surviving dolphins were rapidly becoming undesirables at Connyland, not to mention a particularly knotty predicament for the Federal Veterinary Office. Two of the animals, Leo and Nemo, had been consigned to a tiny holding tank because Conny Gasser feared that Lienhardt would charge him performance fees if he allowed them to join his own dolphins in the main pool. But evidently to avoid the illegality of overcrowding the holding tank, Gasser felt obliged to keep Lienhardt's third dolphin, Girl, in the main pool, where it joined in performances "of its own free will". Predictably, Lienhardt suspected that he was being cheated and after heated arguments broke out between the two dolphin dealers, an abashed Dr Peter Dollinger once again intervened, arranging temporary asylum for Leo and Nemo at Knie's Kinderzoo in Rapperswil. It was hardly an ideal solution, however. For six months, the animals shared the cramped pool with Knie's three American dolphins, resulting in a technical breach of space requirements under both under US and Swiss law. "We were glad to be rid of them," says Chris Krenger, Knie's public relations officer. "Our pool was too small for all of these animals. They didn't get along with our three dolphins and they disturbed the whole show."

By October 1988, Lienhardt was once again hitting the headlines, when it became apparent that his long-suffering dolphins, Nemo and Leo, had been abandoned in the swimming pool of the five star Hotel Meridien, situated on the banks of the river Nile in Cairo. For several months, no experienced trainer had been on hand to feed and care for the animals, and the hotel, which wanted to give its 35m diameter pool back to its guests, was becoming increasingly desperate to be rid of the animals. By comparison, the third surviving dolphin, Girl, had for six months been provided with decidedly down-market accommodation —

an unheated open-air pool just 12m in diameter at Safaripark in Gän-serndorf near Vienna. With winter weather imminent, the animal's life was threatened by freezing temperatures.

For once, the plight of the three dolphins lucidly revealed the inner workings of the cetacean entertainment industry, its greed, cynicism and callousness, this time with no convenient public relations veil. Bruno Lienhardt had abandoned his dolphins not because he suddenly had no money to feed them, but because they had become pawns in yet another bizarre legal wrangle over contracts. Gambling with the animals' failing health was simply part of Lienhardt's systematic plan to force the two establishments to meet his demands and pay up.

It was on 4 November 1987 that Nemo and Leo, together with two IDS sea lions, arrived at Cairo's Hotel Meridien, where they were put in the main swimming pool to entertain guests. Cutting costs, the dolphins had quite simply been put in the baggage hold of the aircraft bound for Cairo, and categorised as "unaccompanied freight". They arrived with wounds which, even a year later, had failed to heal. The opening ceremony for the show, with free champagne and canapes all round, was attended by the *crème de la crème* of Egyptian society, including the wife of President Hosni Mubarak. But all too soon the Meridien saw a successful publicity stunt turn into a public relations nightmare. "We were initially supposed to have a dolphin show for 18 months," hotel manager Edouard Speck told me, "but we cancelled the contract after only six months because the dolphins were not up to international show performance standards." No less than five IDS-employed trainers arrived on the scene to manage the show during those six months, declares Speck. "None of them seemed particularly competent either in training or caring for the animals. One of the sea-lions even died because it swallowed a plastic ball due to lack of supervision. The remaining sea-lion was confiscated and is now kept in Cairo zoo." By all accounts, as soon as the Meridien abrogated its agreement with the IDS, Lienhardt disappeared, leaving the dolphins to be fed and cared for by one of the Meridien's bellhops. Although a vet from Cairo zoo visited the animals once a week, he possessed no professional experi-ence in treating dolphins. "We had no news from Lienhardt for four months," declared Speck. "He showed up sometimes but never did any-thing about the dolphins." Indeed, Lienhardt apparently had other reasons to stay in the background: he was also being sought for non-pay-ment of a £3000 bill for air-freighting his two sea-lions from Germany to Cairo.

Although Meridien had already announced that it was in the process of taking court action to evict the dolphins, because of red-tape and a clog-ged judicial system the hotel was facing the prospect of having to wait "anything from one month to several years" before the case even came before a judge. "The most important thing for us is that these dolphins are out by next summer," declared Speck. "We lost the whole summer season this year. Not only was there no dolphin show but our guests were also prevented from using our main swimming pool." In their legal action, Meridien was claiming over £22,000 in lost admission fees to the hotel pool, compensation of over a thousand pounds a month for feeding the dolphins, and payment of a drinks bill of £3000 which Lienhardt had apparently run up in six months at the hotel bar. But lurking in the shadows, Lienhardt was steadfastly resisting any attempt to move or confiscate his dolphins. "Even though he has nowhere to put them," protested Speck, "he's still demanding a large sum of money from us in order to take them away." Indeed, Lienhardt was counter-suing the hotel for breach of contract, demanding £56,000 in lost earnings.

By this time several conservation organisations were hatching plans to rescue the dolphins held hostage in Cairo and Vienna, including Virginia McKenna's Zoo Check, Prince Sadruddin Aga Khan's Bellerive Foundation and TRAFFIC, a WWF-affiliated organisation which monitors the international trade in endangered species. When it was realised that the dolphin stranded in Vienna's Safaripark was threatened by sub-zero temperatures, Bellerive and TRAFFIC encouraged the authorities to confiscate the dolphin. "I'm somewhere between the devil and the deep blue sea," moaned Edwin Wiesinger, owner of Safaripark. "I've got this dolphin here and it costs me a lot of money every day to feed and care for. I know I won't get the money from Lienhardt but on the other hand if the dolphin should die because it's getting colder now and we've got it out in the open, for one thing the public will be onto me — 'why doesn't he take care of his animals' — and on the other hand Lienhardt will come and say, 'well this dolphin is worth $30,000 and you let it die.' I don't know what to do, and I don't know where to get hold of Lienhardt. The animal should have been out of our pool by the end of September. Now it's nearing the end of October and the animal is still here." Birgit Schacht of TRAFFIC in Vienna, however, remained distinctly unimpressed by Wiesinger's sudden scruples and pangs of contrition: "We have had very bad experiences with Safaripark. We know that on many occasions Wiesinger buys animals and then he has no money to feed them. He then takes out large advertisements in the newspapers to play on the public's sympathy to raise funds. He doesn't care well for the animals — they are kept under bad conditions." Indeed, it seemed as though Wiesinger was loathe to heat the pool to prevent it freezing over simply because of the costs involved. But within days of intervening in the case, TRAFFIC, under the expert guidance of Dr Daniel Slama, had forced Wiesinger to arrange some temporary comfort for the abandoned dolphin. "Safaripark is now heating the pool," Dr Slama declared. "If they stop they will be sued immediately for breaking Austria's animal welfare laws." And yet no one quite realised, at this juncture, just how complex and tangled the whole problem was to become. Edwin Wiesinger and Conny Gasser, it turned out, were *both* expecting imminent litigation with the IDS, and the reasons for these legal scuffles seemed to present the international dolphin trade in an even more grotesque light.

Safaripark had declined to pay Lienhardt for his dolphin show because "Girl", regarded by the IDS as "one of the best show trained dolphins in Europe, capable of over 30 different tricks", consistently refused to perform. "In the beginning it didn't work at all," complained Wiesinger. "It didn't even want to eat. This was simply the behaviour of a dolphin that hasn't been trained." To Lienhardt, there was only one explanation for this: Conny Gasser had obviously "switched dolphins," substituting one of his own poor quality animals for "Girl", the star of his travelling show. Predictably, Gasser vehemently denied the allegation that he had stolen Lienhardt's "Girl". And who would have imagined that Gasser, even when flustered, would parrot the sayings of Pilleri in order to substantiate his innocence? "A gregarious animal like that you can't put alone in a pool. Obviously it doesn't work because that is more or less like solitary confinement." Gasser also declared that he was counter-suing Lienhardt for the costs of maintaining the three dolphins at Connyland for three years, despite an agreement that they would only stay for three months pending transfer to the fictional dolphinarium at Cap d'Agde. With unabashed audacity Gasser also added that Lienhardt "is known the world over for using the animals to further his own interests. He realises that most people will take pity on a dolphin and feed it in his absence."

Despite repeated attempts, no response to this accusatory shooting spree was received either from Lienhardt, his fellow-directors of the IDS, or his lawyers in Zürich. Nor could any of them provide Lienhardt's current address or telephone number. First of all, I tried Dr Horst Marxer's postbox enterprise in Vaduz where the IDS is officially registered as a Liechtenstein company, enjoying tax concessions and much-favoured anonymity. Marxer and Heidi Bader share the dubious privilege of being on the board of directors of the IDS, which, as they have discovered through bitter experience, can become something of a burden when their boss falls victim of yet another legal dispute or media blitz. When asked to explain Lienhardt's conduct in abandoning his dolphins, a conspicuously nervous Dr Marxer replied: "I know nothing about these problems. I have had no contact with Mr Lienhardt for several weeks. Even though I am a member of the board of directors, it's not my mistake what's happening with these dolphins. I like animals too and I'm not very interested to be the big bad guy in the newspapers." Marxer, claiming as alibi the legal framework and code of ethics which govern the operations of any Liechtenstein postbox company, went on to insist that he had "nothing to do with the dolphins but only the management of the IDS. The IDS is a Liechtenstein company — it's registered here — and the law says there must be a Liechtenstein member on the board of directors."

From Lienhardt's lawyers in Zürich, *Prof. Giger & Dr Simmen*, came the terse statement that "we are not authorised to give any answers by telephone. Lienhardt contacts us once every few weeks but we don't know his exact whereabouts." However, the IDS's so-called "correspondence secretary", Hugo Kälin, under siege in Lienhardt's house in Einsiedeln, denied that his boss had "disappeared". Although guarded and reticent, Kälin confirmed that the IDS was in the process of taking legal action against Conny Gasser, claiming that his old comrade-in-arms, French dolphin vivisector Prof. René Guy Busnel, had provided evidence that the dolphin at Safaripark was not Girl. "This is definitely not Bruno Lienhardt's dolphin," insisted Kälin. "Gasser has deliberately given him the wrong dolphin. Bruno sent Professor Busnel photos of the flippers of the two dolphins — Girl and the one now in Vienna — and the Professor has replied that these are definitely two different dolphins. I know Mr Lienhardt very well and I can tell you that in this affair he's playing with open cards — no dirty business or anything like that." When asked why Lienhardt did not intervene to protect the dolphin against freezing temperatures in Vienna, Kalin replied tersely: "This is Gasser's problem because this is Gasser's dolphin. It must go back to Connyland — then there will be no risk to the animal. Gasser has to send the real dolphin — Girl — to Mr Lienhardt." Conny Gasser however, adamantly refused to accept the Vienna dolphin, and both the Swiss and German authorities made it known in early November that they would allow no Lienhardt-owned dolphins to be imported into their countries. According to Dr Slama of TRAFFIC, "the Austrian authorities will probably give Lienhardt a deadline of two weeks to sort out the problem. If the dolphin is still here then, it will be confiscated and sent to Nürnberg Zoo." Just before the confiscation deadline was reached however, Conny Gasser, despite previously resolute refusals to even contemplate the possibility, made it known that he would accept Lienhardt's dolphin after all. This turn of events was inexplicable, though one can probably surmise that it was due to some furtive back-room solution hammered out between their respective lawyers. The Vienna dolphin — whatever its true identity — was collected by truck from Safariland in November and driven off on its long journey back to Connyland.

In the meantime, events in Egypt were reaching a climax, with the world's media circus converging on the Hotel Meridien and almost producing greater worldwide publicity for the stranded dolphins than that afforded to the PLO's declaration in Algiers of the creation of an independent Palestinian state. Centre stage was claimed by Air France's Meridien Hotel which had orchestrated the pre-emptive media blitz to portray not only the dolphins but also themselves as the innocent victims of Lienhardt's latest escapade. For the sake of pragmatism and the international press corps' requirement to have only one villain per dispatch, almost nothing was said of the hotel's foolishness and avarice in ordering the dolphin show in the first place.

On 5 November, just as editors were beginning to consign updates on the story to filler paragraphs on the back page, Doug Cartlidge flew out to Egypt on a rescue mission on behalf of Zoo Check. The media's response was swift, with television crews even flying in from as far away as America and Japan. "Someone has got to take responsibility," Cartlidge declared. "These animals should be swimming in the sea where they belong, not in a featureless concrete tank." Zoo Check's objective — which set alarm bells ringing throughout the industry — was to gradually rehabilitate the dolphins and eventually release them into the Red Sea. That plan however was soon shelved by the sheer necessity of keeping the ailing dolphins alive. Cartlidge found Leo and Nemo aimlessly circling the pool, sickly and listless, subsisting on a diet of frozen Nile sardines. The pool, being designed for human bathers who do not normally eat and excrete when they swim, was becoming increasingly fouled due to poor filtration. The putrefying condition of the water aggravated the dolphins' wounds that had been sustained during transportation, and both were found to have ulcers of the cornea. According to some reports, the dolphins were only being provided with 3kg of fish per day, even though their average requirement is around 8kg. Perhaps, as the dolphins were no longer earning their keep, the Hotel was eager to cut costs?

Although nowhere to be found, evidently Bruno Lienhardt was hardly whiling away the time in Cairo, as evidenced by two intriguing telegrams intercepted from Saudi Arabia. One of these cables, originating from Jeddah and signed *Imad al Aboud* stated: "Attention Mr Bruno. Please refer to Mr Omar Bararman, Saudi Consulate, and Mr Omar will provide you with a visa for Saudi Arabia." A second telegram read: "Pool and facilities almost ready." With tension mounting, it appeared that a "contract" had been put out on Cartlidge's life should he attempt to have the dolphins removed from the Hotel Meridien. Abdul Nasser, the bellhop turned dolphin trainer, realised that Cartlidge was being constantly shadowed by a skulking and furtive individual known only as Mohammed. Making further enquiries, he discovered that a sum of 1000 Egyptian pounds had been offered to report on Cartlidge's activities. If it seemed as though the Zoo Check consultant would attempt to move the dolphins, Mohammed was to go to a Cairo circus and alert two "heavies" who would take care of him, possibly for good. As this information came to light, Mohammed was promptly apprehended by Hotel security, and was later detained by the police. Says Cartlidge: "The police told me I was a very important man in Egypt. They said it usually cost 400 to 500 pounds to kill a man there."

Meanwhile, the incandescent media spotlight also encouraged the dolphin industry's most devout hypocrites to crawl out of the woodwork. While Gasser, Wiesinger, and Lienhardt were all contending for the title of wronged animal lover of the year, the godfathers of the industry were holding midnight seances to plot an urgent and spectacular action in damage control. There were few qualms about throwing one of their own kind to the dogs. After all, Lienhardt's conduct had already proved expensive to the industry, not only in terms of bad publicity and the harsher laws that were introduced in France following the closure of the Moulin Rouge revue, but also in the IDS president's shameless habit of stinging his own business partners. The ongoing scandal in Cairo, splashed across the newspapers of the world, was viewed as a serious threat to the dolphin entertainment industry as a whole. On top of that, an upstart former whale and dolphin trainer, backed by a meddling organisation of bleeding hearts, was actually planning to release the dolphins into the wild. Although a similar operation had been mounted in 1987 by the American organisation ORCA, with a pair of dolphins being successfully released after seven years in captivity, worldwide media coverage of Leo and Nemo being given their freedom would be a precedent-setting event with damaging implications for the industry. It would prove to the public that captive dolphins can be re-introduced into the wild and survive, despite the industry's ritual denials. A major rescue operation was called for — as much for the industry's battered image as for the dolphins themselves — spearheaded by Mike Riddell of Antibes Marineland and celebrity vet David Taylor. Lienhardt would be branded as a black sheep, the disreputable exception which proves the irreproachable rule. It was thus that after seventeen years of silence regarding Lienhardt's conduct, Mike Riddell, as secretary of the EAAM, declared to the press that "most respectable dophinaria would like to see Lienhardt put out of business... We have worked hard to get rid of him from our proffession."

Furthermore, in a gesture of boundless compassion, Riddell offered sanctuary for the stranded dolphins: Marineland's "purpose-built hospital pool" would be readied to receive the animals and nurse them back to health. Its vet, none other than EAAM President David Taylor, would be dispatched to Cairo immediately to treat the ailing dolphins. Though the Riddell-Taylor brain-child was sure to steal the limelight on behalf of the dolphin industry and therefore play right into its hands, for Zoo Check there was no other option but to accept the ostensibly magnanimous offer.

Taylor's veterinary checks revealed that Nemo was near to death with pneumonia in the left lung and an intestinal infection contracted from eating rotten fish. Both dolphins were suffering from scars caused by careless transportation, and skin problems attributed to poor water quality. Tourists had also thrown potentially lethal objects into the pool, including bottles, knives, forks, coins, and even batteries. Taylor declared that it was the first time that the dolphins had been seen by a marine vet for seven years — though why they had not been examined at Connyland, where Taylor is actually a consultant vet, was not explained.

Lured by the imminent departure of his dolphins, Bruno Lienhardt made one of his rare cameo appearances at the Hotel Meridien, protesting his innocence to the assembled press corps. Interviewed by a *Sunday Times* reporter, he angrily refuted Meridien's accusations that Leo and Nemo were not up to international dressage standards, retorting that "the audiences loved the show." He also denied that he had abandoned the animals. "I was here more than 50 per cent of the time," he claimed. "Now I come every two days to look at my dolphins from the terrace, but I won't go close to the pool because I would be blamed if anything happened to the dolphins." Even the ugly, if sometimes ludicrous spectacle of the European dolphin dealers vying with each other for the role of "best animal lover" had not quite come to an end. Lienhardt went on to say that he originally decided to work with dolphins after seeing and becoming enthralled by the film *Flipper*. "The greatest pleasure I get," he solemnly declared, "is to see the expressions on the faces of the children when they watch the dolphins perform."

Following sustained international appeals to the Egyptian government, on 17 November Doug Cartlidge was informed by the Vice President that permission had been granted for the dolphins to leave the country. This decision had been reached not through confiscation which would have entailed time-consuming legal procedures, but via a "place of safety order" triggered by increasingly urgent humanitarian concerns for Leo and Nemo's deteriorating health. The dolphins would still belong to Lienhardt, but he would have to fight his way through the courts to reclaim them. An Air France cargo plane flying from Rwanda would be specially diverted to pick up the dolphins and transport them to Marseilles. By this time, the pool had been cordoned off because of the dolphins' new tendency to bite curious onlookers — even members of the press. Not surprisingly, it seemed as though they were well and truly fed up with their terrestrial brothers and sisters.

Leo and Nemo were flown out of Egypt on 24 November. Within hours of their departure, a Cairo court granted an injunction to prevent their removal from Egyptian soil but this was too late for Lienhardt, despite his irate protests that the dolphins had been "kidnapped". With the press suitably primed for the happy ending their editors so fervently desired, upon arrival at Marseilles, the dolphins were transferred to two waiting ambulances, and, with an escort of police outriders, were rushed to Antibes Marineland, an hour's drive away. After being nursed back to health in the "hospital pool", declared Riddell, Leo and Nemo would make the acquaintance of Marineland's own dolphins — five females and one male.

It is not the first time that Bruno "Houdini" Lienhardt has confounded predictions of his imminent demise in the dolphin business. Insisted his loyal comrade, Hugo Kälin, at the height of the Cairo and Vienna debacle: "I know that Mr. Lienhardt has places to put the dolphins — he's also planning a new dolphinarium but I don't know if I can comment on that." In any event, rumours within the industry suggested that the IDS president would soon embark on another dolphin-catching operation in Indonesia or Guatemala. Even David Taylor had to admit, perhaps as image-insurance for the future, that "unfortunately, I have a terrible feeling that this practice will not end, just move to countries less in the public eye." Back in the Cairo bars which he frequented, Lienhardt was even heard to boast that he already had other dolphins in his possession which he was having trained for his new show.

At Antibes, David Taylor declared: "We fully expect him to turn up any day with a lawyer or heavies, saying he wants his dolphins back. Lienhardt is bad news for dolphins and for the zoological world. The man is completely irresponsible." There was also the haunting possibility that Lienhardt would take legal measures to reclaim Nemo and Leo, and sure enough, several months later, it was learnt that Lienhardt had initiated court proceedings in France, not with the intention of shipping the animals to some new dolphinarium on the Persian Gulf, but to yet another hotel swimming pool in Saudi Arabia. Lienhardt's plans were blocked, however, when the dolphins were made a ward of court pending legal proceedings in Egypt. By April 1989, the IDS president was suing Marineland for £300,000 in damages as well as the return of the dolphins. Declared Mike Riddell: "He is trying to get the dolphins back, and is also claiming a share of the proceeds he says we will have made from having them here."

By aggressively resisting such moves, an ingenious Marineland was also jockeying for position in any future legal claim to the animals. Bill Travers, Zoo Check's co-founder, stated that the organisation welcomed Marineland's involvement, but regarded Leo and Nemo's stay at Antibes as only temporary. "Leo and Nemo have suffered enough," he said. "Let us make the final gesture and give them their liberty. We must give them a chance to be wild and free again." Suitable sites for their planned release were being investigated, the most favoured areas under consideration being along the northwest Atlantic coast of Spain. "We are opposed to dolphinaria," Travers continued. "We feel there is no justification for them as they exist at present. We would like to see them converted to rescue centres and do what Marineland is doing in this case — nursing sick animals back to health." No wonder then, that the industry had become alarmed at the prospects of a successful dolphin release, or that Mike Riddell had made it known that he would fight vigorously any attempt to wrest control of the dolphins away from Marineland. There were suddenly rumours that the "marine zoo" was desperate for male dolphins in order to consummate Roland de la Poype's age-old dream of whale-breeding, and after receiving a windfall in the form of two free dolphins worth in excess of $60,000, had no intention of letting them slip through his fingers.

Indeed, Leo and Nemo were never released into the wild. Instead, the ill-fated dolphins were destined to spend over a year in their "hospital pool" at Antibes, half the size of the hotel swimming pool they were actually rescued from. Complained Doug Cartlidge: "Chlorination was carried out by hand. I observed staff walking around the pool pouring chlorine from a watering can directly into the water. This is against all recommendations contained in the present standards for keeping cetacea... During my visit I noted and expressed concern over the hanging behaviour which is developing in Nemo, the animal just lying motionless in the water. Prolonged hanging is a sign of depression and boredom. In this concrete tomb, they are worse off than they were in Cairo. If I had known that they were going to spend a year in a 15 metre by 10 metre pool I would never have agreed to them going to Marineland." Though Cartlidge had arranged for the dolphins to be part of a rehabilitation and release programme in the USA, both Taylor and Riddell insisted that they were still too ill to travel, and that their presence in the hospital pool was essential to facilitate constant medical attention. They also rejected any idea of an independent vet inspecting the animals. A long journey would be "tantamount to murder", Riddell was quoted as saying.

VI. THE FINAL CURTAIN

*"The highest wisdom has but one science — the science of
the whole — the science explaining the whole creation and
man's place in it.*
— Leo Tolstoy, *War and Peace*

In September 1988, four animal rights campaigners were found guilty at
Lancaster Crown Court of what was described as "a totally irresponsible
plot" to liberate Rocky, the solitary captive of Morecambe Marineland.
The four, who expressed a wish to release Rocky into the sea as "an act of
mercy", had been observed running away from the dolphinarium in the
dead of night. They were later apprehended by police, and were found to
be in possession of a large net, ropes and a home-made stretcher. The two
alleged ringleaders of the plot were sentenced to six months' imprisonment suspended for two years and fined £500 each. The judge concluded
that Rocky had given pleasure to countless people without any apparent
harm to himself and was clearly treated and trained with affection and
kindness. Notwithstanding the dubious moral lecture by Her Honour
and the fact that the penalties meted out to the defendants were harsher
than those imposed upon traffickers in wildlife, the scheme to free the
dolphin was undoubtedly ill-planned and ill-conceived.

Over the years, there have been several other attempts to release dolphins into the wild, some spontaneous, some planned, but few that were
professionally organised. Rather conveniently, this has enabled the dolphin entertainment industry to portray the rehabilitation of captive cetaceans as unachievable and little more than a naive pipe dream of
"idealists" and "bleeding hearts". "From time to time," declares Prof.
Paul Schauenberger, "sensitive, sentimental individuals and groups
worry about the fate of dolphins in captivity and utter the wish to give
these intelligent mammals their freedom back. This is easier said than
done. One should be aware of the fact that this can, under certain circumstances, be a crime, to send a dolphin back into the open sea. It is
extraordinarily difficult, sometimes even impossible, to get a trained
bottlenose used again to a life in freedom... Dolphins that lost their way
during exercises with the US Navy or dolphins that were freed illegally
by goodwilled but unknowledgeable people met a terrible death in the
sea, in complete freedom."

Schauenberger provides no evidence for this claim, though certainly
some dolphins released from captivity through ill-conceived schemes
have perished upon their return to the wild. Yet as Doug Cartlidge points
out with respect to his planned release of Bruno Lienhardt's dolphins Leo

and Nemo, "it is not just a matter of dumping them in the sea. They will first of all have to gather their strength to fight infection and learn how to fend for themselves. It will be a gradual, carefully planned process." Nor would the release even be precedent-setting, Cartlidge insists: "Successful dolphin rehabilitation has been achieved on several occasions, most notably in 1987 in America when two Atlantic bottlenose dolphins, Joe and Rosie, were released by ORCA, the Oceanic Research and Communication Alliance."

These were the first dolphins ever to be released with the sanction and blessing of the US government, and their successful return to the wild proved even more remarkable since the animals had already been languishing in captivity for seven years, caught in 1980 for "communication research" by none other than Dr John Lilly and his Human Dolphin Foundation. Veteran dolphin handler Ric O'Barry — who caught and trained "Flipper", the star of the 1960s television show, and who defected from the captive dolphin industry after Flipper's death in 1969 — was hired to "untrain" the animals. He began by feeding them live fish, and instead of rewarding the dolphins when they performed, he would turn his back on them, effectively reversing the normal training programme. At the same time a sighting network was established, designed to keep track of the two dolphins and monitor their interactions with local dolphin schools following their release. In June 1987, Joe and Rosie were introduced into the Wassaw National Wildlife Refuge on the Georgia coast. A specially designed free-floating, portable holding pen was constructed for their gradual readaption to the natural environment. From the safety of the pen, the two dolphins could learn to catch their own fish, come into contact with wild dolphins, and reacquaint themselves with the ocean's myriad influences, sounds and rhythms. When Joe and Rosie began playing games with pieces of marsh grass which floated in their enclosure, the ORCA team knew that the time had come to let the dolphins go.

"That was a good sign," Project director Virginia Coyle declared later, "indicating they felt happy and comfortable" in their new habitat. Thus on 13 July 1987, the gate was opened, giving Joe and Rosie their first opportunity to return to freedom. After three quick trips in and out of the pen, ORCA reported, the pair swam towards a tidal creek about 3 kilometres from the release site, defying industry predictions that the dolphins would be loathe to leave behind them the comforts and security of captivity. Over the following weeks and months they were observed on several occasions, easily distinguished from their wild companions by the freeze brands on their dorsal fins. Rosie was spotted twice swimming with a local dolphin school, feeding near shrimp boats; Joe was observed surfing off a nearby beach, and later the pair were seen together again near fishing boats. As an exultant Virginia Coyle stated: "The result of such an effort could have far-reaching effects on both humans and dolphins... a catalyst for other humans and dolphins who seek the benefits of an open-gate relationship."

No one knows why, but almost every day for more than twenty years now, along a stretch of coral sands known as Monkey Mia in Western Australia, a local dolphin school has chosen to come into voluntary contact with human beings. It is, says Australia's cetacean protection organisation *Project Jonah*, "a dolphin lovers' paradise — there are no rules other than obvious self-imposed restraints necessary to maintain the friendship." There is also no technology, no feeding expenses, drugs or vitamins, no entrance fee, no compere and mindless spiel, no money-grabbing impresario, and above all, no walls. With public pressure continually mounting on the captive dolphin industry, it is perhaps conceivable that one day Monkey Mia will be looked upon as the prototype of the "dolphinarium" of the future, open sanctuaries where wild cetacea will voluntarily interact with human beings, genuinely fulfilling the callings of both education and science. As Prof. Giorgio Pilleri points out, "the only solution" to the present dilemma "is to establish reserves or large open-air parks for the dolphins. Although this would complicate research, the results would be far more rewarding."

The *Latest* Show on Earth

As for the circus menagerie, it has been said that more stringent laws in the future, coupled with a chronic scarcity of some exotic species, may eventually spell its extinction. But according to Dr Fred Kurt, it is precisely because circuses are facing this shortage that their existing animals are being made to suffer. Fearing an end to their supplies, he says, some circuses are literally working their animals to death. "Circus Krone in Germany, for instance, now has only old Asian elephants and all of them have open tuberculosis. This is because when circuses like Krone visit big cities such as Brussels or Berlin, the stables are often in small damp cellars where there is bad air, cold floors and no natural light." Kept under such conditions, elephants may also be afflicted by lameness of the trunk. "Because of the coldness of the stables and the permanent beatings," explains Kurt, "many elephants in Italian circuses can't even drink and eat with their trunks any more, or even lift them — they have to kneel down and be fed like a cow. And still these animals are used and re-used for animal shows."

Paradoxically, such desperate abuse may also represent the death-rattle of the circus menagerie and the "tradition" of the performing wild animal under the big top. Indeed, as an institution, the circus is already facing traumatic times, and having expended so much of its imagination and ingenuity on defending the menagerie by systematically deceiving the public, it appears that it has precious little left in reserve to help combat its inexorable decline. Says Kurt: "Almost every circus in the world — including such renowned ones as Knie — are now fighting for their survival. But they have no new ideas and no inspiration, only gimmicks and meagre variations of the traditional animal acts. They still don't realise that the end is already in sight for the performing wild animal in the circus. By means of television alone, people are beginning to understand the way in which these animals behave in the wild, and within ten or twenty years public opinion just won't tolerate the idea of them being trained to perform unnatural tricks in the ring." David Hancocks, director of the Arizona-Sonora Desert Museum, agrees: "The true image of wildlife is seriously and deliberately distorted in the circus. It is inevitable that eventually this will cause their downfall, as the groundswell of knowledge about ecology and ethology grows, and as the true conditions of animal life in the circus become known to more people. There is a new age of understanding and compassion on the horizon. It will not tolerate the abuses of the past."

Under siege from punitive taxation, competition from television, and changing social mores, the demoralised circus community still clings tenaciously to its ailing wild animals tradition with the ritual refrain that "a circus without animals is not a circus". For obvious reasons, they prefer to pretend that they're weathering the storm, presenting an upbeat yet increasingly brittle image to the public. Quoted in the *Sunday Times* January 1989, Malcolm Clay, secretary of the Association of Circus Proprietors, buoyantly declared: "Britain has more large circuses than at any time since the war. There are ten large touring companies, with a full complement of animals, and business is looking up. The public is moving back to traditional, live, family entertainment, and they want animals." Audience figures, however, do not seem to confirm such a rosy prognosis. Indeed, even Chris Krenger of Knie admits that, because of fierce competition in the entertainment industry and burgeoning costs, "many circuses are already struggling to survive financially." Foreseeing inevitably stricter laws imposed upon the menageries, he adds that "in 20 years the circus will probably only have some horses and ponies and maybe a camel or llama." Yet by the same token, the circus will inevitably resist such reforms for as long as it possibly can. As ethologist Dr Rolf Keller points out, change comes hard to such institutions steeped in their own lore and traditions. The old guard of Knie, for instance, like many venerable circus families, has been reluctant to relinquish the most exotic stars of their menagerie, despite the pressures of ethologists and public opinion. After all, in their lifetime the menagerie even featured Eskimoes and other curiosities from the world's tribal peoples.

It was in November 1988 that, at the invitation of Fredy Knie Snr, I attended a matinee performance of the Swiss National Circus in Locarno. Though the big top was packed with boisterous, excited children, to my utmost surprise most of the shouts, applause, cheers and whistles came not for the elephants of Louis Knie or the white tigers of John Campolongo, but the daring aerial acrobatics of the South African Ayak Brothers, and the extraordinary mime of Mummenschanz, expertly kneading their plasticine masks into numerous shapes and likenesses, including an elephant and rhino. It led me to believe that we may all be underestimating the children of today; they have changed while those who stage-manage the circus have stood still, bound by a strait-jacket of tradition. Ironically, this fear of breaking the mould, and this reluctance to utilise the imagination which once nurtured the very heart of the circus tradition, could ultimately spell the death of the circus as more than mere entertainment, but as an art form where humans can learn and present diverse and intricate skills. Nothwithstanding the current battle over animal rights, such an eventuality would be more than lamentable. Yet there may well be a solution. Circus impresarios in the U.K. habitually bemoan the fact that they receive no subsidies or any other form of support by central or local government, and enviously point to their East European counterparts who enjoy the privilege of state-run circus schools; to France which currently spends some 18 million francs annually on promoting the circus arts; to Italy where towns are required by law to provide travelling shows with sites and amenities. While such state aid does not currently discriminate against circuses with performing wild animals, it is high time that it did so. Indeed, instead of relying on laws steeped in political pragmatism rather than moral principle in a half-hearted effort to ensure animal welfare, governments would do better to recognise the groundswell of public opinion rising against such institutionalised abuse and, following the lead of Finland, impose an outright ban on the circus' menageries and their wild performing animals. To sweeten the pill, and to drive a wedge between animal tamer die-hards and those practising the genuine arts and skills of the circus, adequate government support should be forthcoming to establish circus schools, allowing re-training in other disciplines for former wild animal performers, and where necessary, tax concessions, grants to enable circuses to modernise their infrastructures and equipment, and special provisions for educating the children of itinerant performers.

Animal-free circuses would not, by any means, be precedent-setting. A unit of the Moscow State Circus, for example, enjoyed resounding success when it visited the UK in 1985 without animals. Similarly, for seventeen days in the summer of 1988, Jubilee Gardens on London's South Bank became a "Circus Village", hosting many of the world's new animal-free circus companies, with troupes from China, the USA, Spain, France and Britain. The event was billed as the "Circus of imagination, participation and spectacle: circus re-invented and re-energised — modern circus without performing animals." In his recently published book,

New Circus, Reg Bolton describes the phenomenon that is slowly but surely changing the face of one of the oldest of the performing arts: "New Circus tends to leave animals in peace and concentrate on the human endeavours of clowning and physical skills... All the traditional acts are there — acrobatics, wire-walking, juggling, trick cycling, trapeze, stilts and other displays of strength, balance and co-ordination... So circus is not dying, circus is alive and changing." Tongue in cheek, "New Circus" is also being portrayed as "The *Latest* Show On Earth".

Yet in instituting an outright ban on travelling menageries and performing circus animals, time will be required not only for circuses to comply and re-adapt themselves to the new regulations, but also to safeguard the future welfare of their existing animals. In this respect, carefully formulated provisions in the law would be required to prevent the deliberate killing of animals or their sale to unscrupulous dealers, and in this respect animal welfare organisations could play a pivotal role in monitoring the transition period, as well as finding homes or establishing refuges where the animals might live out their days in as natural an environment as possible. In many cases, birth control would be an unfortunate but essential ingredient of the plan. In other cases, partial rehabilitation might be attempted, following the example of Zoo Check's successful 1987 project where six tigers, rescued from the squalor of Cross Brothers' Circus in Kent, were provided with a home in 15 enclosed acres of tiger country in the Bannerghatta Wildlife Park, Bangalore, India. As Zoo Check founder Virginia McKenna admits, they will never be truly free after long years of confinement and doubts surrounding their parentage, but at least their new habitat allowed them to run and swim for the first time in their lives.

But although circuses are facing hard times, it would be premature to assume that the end is already in sight for the barred beast wagon and performing wild animal in the arena. Even though pressure is constantly increasing, it now appears that the circus, like its marine counterpart, is determined to flog the "conservation" and "education" horse for all it is worth. In this respect, the notion that the performing animal displays nothing but its own "natural behaviour" under the big top, and that an endangered species imprisoned for life in a beast wagon is actually being saved from inevitable extinction in the wild, is today being heard more often than ever before. Though such arguments are demonstrably spurious, having more relation to traditional circus mendacity and hyperbole than reality, it has often been said that a lie told regularly enough will eventually attain some semblance of credibility amongst a gullible public. Unfortunately, there is growing evidence to suggest that certain ethologists who have spent much of their education and careers studying animals in the artificial confines of the laboratory or model farm are aiding and abetting the circus in promoting this colourful fallacy. Should this trend continue, it is conceivable that some ethologists, to the shame of their science, may eventually give circuses a new lease on life.

A recently released report by the animal behaviourist Marthe Kiley-Worthington, *Animals in Circuses*, is a case in point. The repercussions of this study are potentially far-reaching, particularly since it was commissioned — to the tune of £10,000 — by the RSPCA, an organisation which has been vigorously opposed to the exploitation of wild animals in circuses for many years. The report revealed that in British circuses, lions and tigers are confined to their beast wagons for 90 per cent of the time, each animal occupying a space of between 0.17 and 0.45 cubic metres; that elephants are shackled for 60 per cent of the time and are only able to lie down with difficulty; that 40 per cent of the big cats have to be forced into the ring "by poking a broom handle into their wagon"; that bears spend more than a third of their time in abnormal activity such as pacing to and fro; that "Animals that persistently show a dislike of entering the ring and do not act up to the audience applause, or cannot get used to the performance with the noise, lights etc., are culled." Dr Kiley-Worthington's findings, however, appeared to have little bearing on her ultimate, pro-circus conclusions. Indeed, both circuses and dolphinaria were virtually provided with a clean bill of health, the ethologist arguing — albeit with greater recourse to subjective opinion than hard evidence — that circus animals actually benefit from learning tricks, that the endangered species of the beast wagon play an important role in conservation, and that the glittering shows have inherent educational value. Predictably, this provoked a veritable storm of controversy, with Kiley-Worthington threatening to sue the RSPCA if it dared to quote from her report without permission, and the charity accusing the scientist of adulterating her findings with an entirely subjective, pro-circus bias.

In the months of antagonism that followed, several full-page articles appeared in the British press which, while giving generous coverage to Dr Kiley-Worthington's supportive views of the circus, scarcely even touched on the actual findings of her study, nor the parameters under which it was conducted. Indeed, in this respect, it could be said that the very foundations of her research seem inherently flawed from an ecological point of view, since she chose to compare the circus animals' behaviour not — as might first appear logical — with their relatives in the wild, but merely with their counterparts in zoos and safari parks. Such profound subtleties escaped the press, however. Banner headlines declared: "Why Animal Lovers Can Still Be Circus Fans"; "Who Says It's Cruelty?" and "Circus Animals Benefit From Learning Those Tricks We All Thought Were So Humiliating". Inevitably, the Circus Proprietors Association (ACP) greeted both the report and its attendant publicity with barely concealed glee and promptly provided Dr Kiley-Worthington with additional funds to pursue her research and prepare her treatise for publication.

Also crowing over the report were the circuses themselves, with posters and ringmasters proudly proclaiming their scientifically approved clean bill of health to the visiting public. Outside the ticket caravan of Gerry Cottle's Circus, for example, a hand-written poster declared in bold lettering: "Latest RSPCA Survey Confirms NO Cruelty in British Circus. Circus Animals Benefit from Training, Says Dr Marthe Kiley-Worthington." Meanwhile, the ACP, citing the ethologist's most flattering conclusions, also petitioned the owners of the notorious Blackpool Tower Circus and its underground menagerie, urging them to cancel the forthcoming ban on performing animals there. But is it true to say that Dr Kiley-Worthington actually approves of the conditions in which the Tower Circus' animals are kept below ground in artificial light? "I said I would not mention circuses by name," she told me. "I was not going to be a spy organisation for the RSPCA — I'm a scientist. The circuses I think have to be patted on the back for letting me in at all knowing what the RSPCA policy was. I said I would not release individual circus names and I would not go into depth about the difficulties or problems or outrages of individual named circuses... I did work in Blackpool Tower and I don't think that it's worse than any other circus... there's plenty of places in zoos where animals are kept out of the light... I don't think Blackpool Tower Circus is to be banned unless you're going to ban a whole lot of other zoos and things... I don't think you get anywhere by banning things of that nature and you won't be able to do it anyway because public opinion has changed here now and it will not get through parliament — with or without me. It's a restriction on individual liberties."

And indeed, notwithstanding findings which actually serve to reaffirm the bleakness and deprivation that circus animals must suffer in captivity, there are a multitude of references in the report for the circus world to crow about. She writes, though without a shred of evidence to back up her claims: "Acts can enhance the natural behaviour and beauty of the animals, and encourage further respect and admiration of them as members of a species, and individuals... With appropriate music, props and proper presentation the act can be educational, entertaining and exciting." Reacting to criticism that circus animals are anthropomorphised, dressed up in human clothing and often portrayed as "clowns", Kiley-Worthington claims that this could actually encourage respect. She declares: "...it could be argued that presenting the animals as 'stupid' human beings shows them in a way that exercises our compassion and responsibility to them — as we must respond to children or handicapped human beings. It is a question of whether we believe that compassion for the underdog, or respect for a highly intelligent and able other being is most desirable to encourage in humans, and of most benefit to animals in the long run."

But in attempting to define "natural behaviour", Dr Kiley-Worthington apparently has to admit that at least some circus acts are distinctly alien to the animals' instincts. Is it something that an animal only does in the wild, she asks? If that is the case "we must include all dogs walking on leads, horses being ridden or pulling things, cows being milked, and so on since none of these behaviours are in the animals' natural repertoire." Still on the intellectual trapeze, she then asks whether behaviour which does not fall into the "natural" category is necessarily wrong anyway. She cites the example of elephants balancing on revolving spheres and points out that although there may be "coercion and fear" involved in training, it also involves admirable elephant-human trust and skills. It is therefore "debatable that only 'natural' behaviour should be performed by animals in circuses, if what we are after is increasing human respect, understanding and awareness of other animals as other intelligent, sentient, admirable beings." She concludes that "the dignity of the animal, and the wrongness of performing 'unnatural' acts by both domestic and wild animals in circuses and zoos are difficult concepts to define."

While voicing her dissatisfaction with conditions in which certain wild animals are kept in circuses, Dr Kiley-Worthington stresses her belief that little stands in the way of fundamental improvements. "The environment must be constructed to at least resemble the environment which the animal evolved to live in both in a physical and social sense," she declares, adding that "with a little innovative thinking" this can often be achieved. Once again, however, she provides no clues as to how the lion wagon can be made to resemble an endless expanse of savannah or dry thorn scrub, or for the snow leopard, the pure and ethereal wilderness of the Himalayas. Even so, the scientist even appears to suggest that circus animals can grow accustomed to their stress and deprivation: "Because of their past experience, lifestyle and training," she declares, "circus animals have become familiar with many things that inexperienced animals would find distressing. The same phenomenon is encountered in human beings where aborigines or bushmen who have never been to large cities find the traffic, noise and bustle initially terrifying, but become accustomed to it after a time, and indeed may even like it and become city people. This was amazingly illustrated by the recent popular film 'Crocodile Dundee'."

In another section of her report, Dr Kiley-Worthington voices her belief that the endangered species of the circus menagerie can even help the ecology of the planet, asserting that "It is nonsense to say that animals cannot play a role in conservation." Besides inferring that breeding in the beast wagon could contribute to the conservation of endangered species, she insists that performing animals have already helped to conserve their relatives in the wild. She writes: "It is the dolphins and other sea mammals demonstrating cognitive abilities that have sparked off world wide attention on their conservation. How better to demonstrate this, with them and other animals, than by showing how clever and able they are? Where else can this be done for the majority of people but in a circus?" But what is most ironic in Dr Kiley-Worthington's glowing praise of the dolphin exploitation industry is that her comments appear below a photograph of Circus Knie's dolphinarium in Switzerland, the very same establishment that even the American authorities criticised in 1987 for its spate of dolphin deaths caused by "social behavioural problems."

Perhaps most troubling of all, however, is Kiley-Worthington's attempt to alter the very status of the captive circus animal. She suggests — again with little evidence to support her views — that wild animals in captivity should no longer be regarded as wild at all, but as domesticated as any farm animal or family pet, thus removing their "special status", particularly the requirement that their environment should be as "natural" as possible. "There still remains the argument that wild animals are closely related to nature and must have all 'Natural'," she writes. "It is unnatural for the lion to be in an exercise cage or the ring and therefore by definition wrong. This of course depends on how one is to define Nature and natural."

Despite such intellectual obfuscation, information on animal instincts, genetic make-up, intelligence, behaviour in the wild and social customs was almost entirely ignored and therefore had no bearing upon the apparently arbitrary recommendation that "wild" captive animals should be downgraded to the "domestic" category. Indeed, it is all the more puzzling that this effort to reassess the "special status" of captive wild animals has come at a time when zoos are at last being obliged by legislation to provide their inmates with facilities deemed suitable for each species' unique behavioural requirements. The Kiley-Worthington hypothesis could also be challenged simply on the grounds of common sense. Dogs, for example, were first tamed during the Stone Age, and most farm animals too went through the process of domestication thousands of years ago. The innate wildness of the lion, chimpanzee, elephant, bear and rhino on the other hand — those typical stars of the circus menagerie and arena — remains virtually intact and one might suspect that even Dr. Kiley-Worthington herself would betray little hesitation if given the choice between stepping into a cage with a house cat or a circus leopard. Yet to Dr Kiley-Worthington and the particular brand of anthropocentrism which she espouses, civilisation will even teach the wild — suddenly domesticated — animal a sense of formal etiquette. She states: "Like pets, captive animals need to form emotional bonds, to be given rewards and even to be taught 'moral sense' of what is right and wrong."

At the core of such anthropocentrism is one of the most enduring follies of modern science — the notion that Life, with all of its myriad subtleties and interdependences, can be understood simply by breaking it down into separate component parts, in much the same way that an apprentice mechanic would disassemble his first motor-car. This mechanistic, fragmentary view of Creation is especially evident in ethological methodology, and given the fact that this particular branch of science is often linked to conservation, it is all the more ironic that its habit of systematic categorisation often amounts to an antithesis of ecology. The Kiley-Worthington report is no exception. In this case, not only are the animals artificially separated from their natural environment — by regarding them as no longer wild, but domesticated — and from the social customs which shaped their very existence as species and individuals, but their behaviour patterns in captivity are split relentlessly into convenient, though crudely over-simplified categories. Says a lecturer in veterinary science and former colleague of Marthe Kiley-Worthington: "This kind of fragmentation in ethology is becoming even worse. We're all joking about teaching Molecular Animal Husbandry — it's getting to that kind of state. If you go to an ethology lecture now it's all mathematics — the blackboards full of formulae. In trying so desperately to avoid emotion and anthropomorphism they go to the opposite extreme of anthropocentrism and the result is just another kind of bias."

Indeed, it must be said that many respected ethologists have already woken up to that fact, believing that the circus menagerie and dolphinarium has no place in an age characterised by a more profound ecological awareness. As the renowned animal behaviourist Dr Desmond Morris has declared recently: "I find circuses deeply offensive. We are just beginning to recognise animals as important in their own right. Circuses throw us back to the Middle Ages."

Though it may well be interpreted as being little more than another gimmick or public relations stunt, even some zoos are now alluding to the devastation that has been wreaked by the futile vanity of speciesism, where the human race is lord over all that it surveys, the master of all Creation. Amidst endless rows of cages holding animal curiosities from every corner of the globe, many of which are on the brink of extinction in the wild, visitors may come across a barred enclosure containing nothing but a full-length mirror and a large label reading *"The Most Dangerous Animal On Earth."* One might also add that despite its much-cherished, much-vaunted creed of freedom, the naked ape is actually the most imprisoned species of all, held captive by outmoded ideas and traditions, figments of superiority, and beneath this thin, brave veneer, a pitiful, haunting insignificance before the capriciousness of the universe and the unknown, spiralling away into eternity. For all the technological achievements of which it can boast, for all the art and culture that its civilisations have crafted, the human race has yet to learn, yet to practise, one childishly simple yet profound and immutable ecological truth.

As Albert Schweitzer declared: "Man can no longer live for himself alone. We must realise that all life is valuable and that we are united to all life. From this knowledge comes our spiritual relationship with the universe." Ecology, after all, is far more than mere science, more than the saving of individual species and habitats. In essence, it is an appreciation and understanding of the relationships, co-operation, and myriad interdependences of life's totality. Without that totality, without that diversity which the human race so strangely seems to regard as a threat akin to anarchism and chaos, we are all lost. The planetary ark is not merely a vessel that carries life through the great ebb and flow of the universe; it is actually *woven* from life itself. For every forest razed, every animal pushed overboard into oblivion, the ark lists a few degrees more, sinks a little deeper. Though the human hand that so jealously grasps the tiller seems supremely, even desperately confident in plotting some vague course towards some equally vague destiny, the ark, it could be said, is already foundering.

The barred menagerie and the dolphinarium, like the factory farm and the vivisection laboratory, represent a microcosm of our utilitarian relationship with the beings which give life to our planet ark. In hastening the demise of the beast wagon and the concrete dolphin pool, we are also hastening our return to Mother Earth; by breaking open the cages, we may also find release within ourselves; by resisting the temptation to play the role of a supreme technological god by keeping species on ice for a thousand years, we may uncover within ourselves a passion to save the wilderness instead and in so doing, re-discover the forgotten quintessence of the human identity, that ancient and mystical bond with the spirit of the planet that gave us birth.

BIBLIOGRAPHY

Adams, John L. Dolphinaria in Britain. Animals, January 1972 p. 10-13.

Anderson, Jack. A Fish Story in the Making Off Nicaragua. The Washington Post, 8 June 1984.

Anderson, Jack. Intrigue Deep Beneath the Briny Deep. The Washington Post, 7 May, 1981.

Arden-Clarke, Charlie. A review of Cetaceans in Captivity. Greenpeace, March 1984.

Atkinson, Rick. Scientists, in Pentagon's 'Sleaziest Job,' Rehearse World War III to Test Effects. International Herald Tribune, 13 June 1984.

Bookland, John; Hora, Cheryl; Carter, Nick. Injury, Damage to Health and Cruel Treatment - Present Conditions in the Shipment of Live Fauna. Environmental Investigation Agency, 1985. Pub. Animal Welfare Institute, Washington; Humane Society of the United States, Washington.

BUAV, British Union for the Abolition of Vivisection. The Military Abuse of Animals, BUAV, London, 1987.

Burton, John A; Sitwell, Nigel. The First Dolphin Pantomime. Animals. January 1972 p. 13-14.

Busnel, René Guy; Fish, James R, Editors. Animal Sonar Systems. NATO ASI (Advanced Science Institute), Plenum Press 1980.

Butcher, Lee. The Navy's Underwater Allies. Oceans, November 1981.

Canogar, Susi. Report on the Import of Eight Dolphins to Spain. August 1984. Greenpeace Spain.

Captive Animals Protection Society. Annual Report 1986-87.

Captive Animals Protection Society. Annual Report 1987-88.

Carter, Nick. The Adam Syndrome: Some Behavioural Observations on Homo Sapiens in Relation to Captive Animals for Display, in Particular Cetaceans. Investigations on Cetacea Vol. XVII 1985. Ed. G. Pilleri.

Cartlidge, Doug. A Survey of UK Dolphinaria 1988. Zoo Check; The Whale and Dolphin Conservation Society.

Collet, A. Review of the Live Capture Fisheries for Europe. LWC SC/35/SM 29. 1983.

Deimer, Petra. Das Buch der Wale. Wilhelm Heyne Verlag, Munich, 1988.

Dinner, Jeff. Military Madness. National Anti-Vivisection Society, USA, 1986.

Erni, Franz Xaver. Rolf Knie - Elefanten und Artisten. Benteli, Berne, 1987.

FAO. Cornell, L.H.; Asper, E. D. A Census of Captive Marine Mammals in North America. 1981. Mammals in the Seas, 3:137-50.

Greenpeace. Endangering Wildlife: How the European Community Encourages Trafficking in Endangered Species. 1987.

Greenpeace. Official Greenpeace Captive Cetacean Policy. February 1985.

Greenpeace. Outlaw Whalers. 1982.

Greenpeace. Small Cetacean Kills Around the World. Unregulated Whaling, 1983.

Greenpeace. Submission to government reviewers M. Klinowska and S. Brown, 1985.

Griffin, Donald R. Animal Thinking. Harvard University Press, 1984.

Grove, Noel. Wild Cargo: the Business of Smuggling Animals. National Geographic, March 1981.

Guirand, F. ; Pierre, A. V. Roman Mythology, Larousse Encyclopedia of Mythology. Paul Hamlyn. 1965.

Hancocks, David. Animals in Circuses. RSPCA. 1979.

Harris, Robert; Paxman, Jeremy. A Higher Form of Killing. Triad/Granada, 1983.

Hediger, Heini. Dressurversuche mit Delphinen. Zeitschrift für Tierpsychologie. Bd. 9, Heft 2 1952.

Hediger, Heini. Skizzen zu einer Tierpsychologie in Zoo und Zirkus. 1954.

Hughes, J. Donald. Early Greek and Roman Environmentalists. The Ecologist No.1. Jan-Feb 1981.

Hughes, J. Donald; Thirgood, J. V. Deforestation in Ancient Greece and Rome: A Cause for Collapse. The Ecologist Vol.12 No.5 1982.

Hume, C. W. The Status of Animals in the Christian Religion. Universities Federation for Animal Welfare.

Ings, Raymond. Circuses With Performing Animals - A Teacher's Perspective. RSPCA Today. Summer 1987.

Jackson, Peter. Finding Out About Elephants, Swissair Gazette 9/1987.

Johnson, William. Wenn Tiere denken (When Animals Think). Leben und Glauben, Berne, 28 October 1988.

Johnson, William. Tiere als Kanonenfutter (Animals As Cannon Fodder). Leben und Glauben, Berne, 22 April 1988.

Johnson, William. Die Zirkusmenagerie: Welt der Illusionen. Leben und Glauben, Berne, 20 May, 1988.

Johnson, William. Die Delphin-Mafia. Schweizer Illustrierte, Zürich, 10 June 1985

Johnson, William. Die Erde beherrschen? (Religion and Ecology). Leben und Glauben, Berne, 27 January 1989.

Johnson, William. The Monk Seal Conspiracy, Heretic Books, March 1988.

Jordan, Bill; Ormrod, Stefan. The Last Great Wild Beast Show. Constable, 1978.

Klinowska, Margaret; Brown, Susan. A Review of Dolphinaria. Department of the Environment, London, 1986.

Kurt, Fred. Arbeitselefanten - Helfer des Menschen. Swissair Gazette 9/ 1987.

Kurt, Fred. Das Elefantenbuch. Wie Asiens letzte Riesen leben. Rasch & Röhring, Hamburg 1986.

Kurt, Fred. Les Elephants et l'environnement. Swissair Gazette 9/1987.

Kurt, Fred. The Elephant in the China Shop. Swissair Gazette 9/1987.

Lilly, John C. The Scientist. Bantam Books, 1981.

Linehan, Edward J. The Trouble With Dolphins. National Geographic, April 1979.

Lovelock, J. E. Gaia - A New Look at Life on Earth. Oxford University Press, 1979.

Lubow, Robert E. The War Animals. Doubleday, New York, 1977.

Manser, Rodney N. Circus. Richford Enterprises, 1987.

May, John. The Zoo at Sunset. BBC Wildlife Magazine. March 1984.

McGreal, Shirley. Monkeys Go To War. Mainstream/Winter 1981.

McKenna, Virginia; Travers, Will; Wray, Jonathan. Ed. Beyond the Bars - The Zoo Dilemma. Thorsons Publishing Group, 1987.

Morris, Desmond. Must We Have Zoos? Life Atlantic Magazine, 9 December 1968.

Morris, Desmond. The Response of Animals to a Restricted Environment. Symp - Zool. Soc. Lond. Nr. 13 pp. 99-118. August 1964.

Mullan, Bob; Marvin, Garry. Zoo Culture. Weidenfeld & Nicolson, 1987.

Mulvaney, Kieran. Dolphinaria - Education or Exploitation? Sonar No. 1. Spring 1989. Journal of the Whale and Dolphin Conservation Society.

Mulvaney, Kieran. Dolphinaria in Britain - the Story of Nemo. Mainstream/Spring 1987, p 1.

Mulvaney, Kieran. Will Dolphinaria Take a Bow? New Scientist 7 August 1986, p 1.

Murray, Marian. Circus! From Rome to Ringling. Appleton-Century-Crofts, Inc. New York. 1956; Greenwood Press, Connecticut, 1973.

Oettermann, Stephan. Decline and Fall of an Imperishable Idea - The Elephant's Trail Through the Western World. Swissair Gazette 9/1987.

Ortiz, Roxanne Dunbar. Sitting Bull 1830-1890. Refugees. Number 44, August 1987. UNHCR.

Owen, Susan-Jane. Submission on the Issuing of a Permit to Napier Marineland for the Capture of Four Common Dolphins for "Breeding and Display." Greenpeace New Zealand Inc. October 1984.

Palmer, Martin; Nash, Ann; Hattingh, Ivan (Editors). Faith and Nature. Century Hutchinson/WWF.

Pilleri, Giorgio. "Animals on Display - Educational and Scientific Impact" - Comments on a Workshop Held at the John G. Shedd Aquarium, Chicago, Illinois. Investigations on Cetacea Vol XVI, 1984.

Pilleri, Giorgio. Cetaceans In Captivity. Brain Anatomy Institute, University of Berne, Switzerland. Investigations On Cetacea. G. Pilleri (Ed.) Vol. XV 1983.

Pilleri, Giorgio. Down With the Dolphin Zoos! Brain Anatomy Institute, University of Berne, Switzerland. Investigations On Cetacea. G. Pilleri (Ed.) Vol. XX 1987.

Robbins, Chris. Death Trail to the Pet Shop. Observer Colour Magazine. November 24 1974.

RSPCA. Animals in Circuses.

RSPCA. Submission of the Royal Society for the Prevention of Cruelty to Animals; To Dr Margaret Klinowska, Appointed Reviewer of the Case for the Import and Display of Live Cetaceans. 1985.

Ruesch, Hans. Slaughter of the Innocent. Bantam Books, 1978; Civitas Publications, 1983.

Sagan, Carl. The Dragons of Eden. Ballantine Books, New York, 1977.

Sarokin, David. Working Together to Mend This Wounded Planet. International Herald Tribune. 30 September 1988.

Schauenberger, Paul. Delphine und Schwertwale. Animan (Lausanne). Nr.2 1984.

Schul, Bill. The Psychic Power of Animals, Coronet Books, 1977.

Scullard, H. H. From the Gracchi To Nero. 1970. Methuen & Co Ltd.

Sharpe, Robert. The Horror of Room 101. Animals' Defender. January/February, 1981.

SIPRI. Warfare in a Fragile World. Taylor & Francis, London, 1980.

Smith, G. Entertaining Us To Death. Observer Colour Magazine, 23 September 1984 p. 5.

Taylor, David. Zoo Vet. George Allen & Unwin, 1976.

Tomilin, A.G. Wundertier Wal. 1974. MIR Moskau, Urania, Leibzig, Jena, Berlin.

Tschimmel, Udo. Flippern bis zum Todeskampf. GEO, Nr. 10/Oct. 1985.

Tschimmel, Udo. Leiden für die Show. Natur. Nr. 10/Oct. 1984

Tudge, Colin. Breeding by Numbers. New Scientist. 1 September 1988.

Wallace, Bruce. Conscription at Sea. Saturday Review of Sciences, 1973 1 (2) 44-45.

Wildlife Link Cetacean Group. Comments on 'A Review of Dolphinaria' by M. Klinowska and S. Brown, 1986. p. 17.

Williams, Heathcote. Whale Nation. Jonathan Cape, 1987.

Winfrey, Laurie Platt. The Unforgetable Elephant. Walker and Company, New York. 1980.

Woodford, M; Jordan, W. Report on a Visit to Tower Circus, Blackpool on 18th July 1986. Captive Animals Protection Society, 1986.

Ziesler, Günlter. Tigers - The Silent Hunter. World Magazine. August 1987.

Zoo Check Newsletter. Various Issues.

———— Being a Big "Fish" in a Little Pond. Mainstream. Vol. 18, No. 2, Spring 1987.

———— Dolphinaria. Report of the Steering Group. Department of the Environment, 1988.

———— King Pole. Circus Fans' Association of Great Britain. Various Issues.

———— Les dauphins du Moulin Rouge jouent les filles de l'air. Libération, 20 October 1984.

———— Newsletter - International Primate Protection League. Various Issues.

———— Report of a Workshop - "Animals on Display: Educational and Scientific Impact". American Association of Zoological Parks and Aquariums, 1984.

NETWORK

Australia

Project Jonah
672B Glenferrie Road
Hawthorn
Victoria 3122
Tel. (09) 819 2999

Belgium

Association Nationale des Societes
de Protection Animale (ANSPA)
BD Jules Graindor 5
1070 Brussels
Tel. (02) 524 2915

Denmark

Foreningen Til Dyrenes
Beskyttelse i Danmark
Alhambravej 18
1826 Copenhagen V
Tel. (01) 31 22 32 22

Federal Republic of Germany

Deutscher Tierschutzbund eV
Baumschulallee 15
5300 Bonn 1.
Tel. (0228) 63 10 05

Gesellschaft zum Schutz der
Meeressaugetiere eV (GSM)
Postfach 348
D-2000 Hamburg 55
Tel. (040) 86 87 74

France

Conseil National de la Protection
Animale (CNPA)
10 Place Leon Blum
75011 Paris.
Tel. (01) 4379 8776

Friends of Animals
16 rue Beaugrenelle
75015 Paris.
Tel. (01) 4577 5258

Robin des Bois
15 rue Ferdinand—Duval
75004 Paris.
Tel. (01) 4804 0936

Greece

Hellenic Animal Welfare Society
12 Pasteur Street
115 21 Athens
Tel. (01) 6435391—6444473

Iceland

Icelandic Whalefriends Society
Grettisgata 40b
101 Reykjavik
Tel. (01) 12014

Republic of Ireland

Irish Society for the Prevention
of Cruelty to Animals
1 Grand Canal Quay
Dublin 2
Tel. (01) 775922

Italy

Sra. Dinah Vescovo
Observer
Via Cimone 91, Appt. 1
00141 Rome
Tel. (06) 894761

Luxembourg

Ligue Nationale pour la
Protection des Animaux
33 rue Adolphe
1116 Luxembourg
Tel. 454535

Netherlands

Nederlandse Vereniging tot
Bescherming van Dieren
Bankstraat 100
2585 ES The Hague
Tel. (070) 423423

Portugal

Liga Portuguesa Dos Direitos
Do Animal
Av. Elias Garcia 172-1
1000 Lisbon
Tel. (01) 77 23 43

South Africa

The Dolphin Action and
Protection Group
PO Box 22227
Fish Hoek 7975
Tel. (021) 82-5845

Spain

Federacion Espanola de Sociedades
Protectoras de Animales y Plantas
Vico 21
08021 Barcelona
Tel. (03) 201 9615

Switzerland

Bellerive Foundation
PO Box 6
1211 Geneva 3
Tel. (022) 46 88 66

Schweizer Tierschutz
Zentralsekretariat
Birsfelderstrasse 45
CH-4052 Basel
Tel. (061) 311 21 10

United Kingdom

Animal Aid
7 Castle Street
Tonbridge
Kent TN9 1BH
Tel. (0732) 364546.

Captive Animals'
Protection Society
36 Braemore Court
Kingsway
Hove
East Sussex BN3 4FG.
Tel. (0273) 737756.

Care for the Wild
1 Ashfords
Horsham Road
Rusper
West Sussex RH12 4QX.
Tel. (0293) 871596.
Fax. (0293) 871022.

Eurogroup for Animal Welfare
Causeway
Horsham
West Sussex RH12 1HG
Tel. (0403) 64181

International Fund for
Animal Welfare
32 Boundary Road
St. John's Wood
London NW8 0JE.
Tel. (01) 624 3535.

IPPL UK
19-25 Argyll St.,
London W1V 2DU.
Tel. (01) 837 7227.

Royal Society for the Prevention
of Cruelty to Animals (RSPCA)
Causeway
Horsham
West Sussex
RH12 1HG.
Tel. 0403 64181.

TRAFFIC
c/o Conservation Monitoring Centre
219C Huntingdon Road
Cambridge CB3 0DL
Tel. (0223) 277314 / 277240.

Whale and Dolphin
Conservation Society
20 West Lea Road
Bath
Avon BA1 3RL.
Tel. (0225) 334511.
Fax. (0225) 480097.

World Society for the Protection
of Animals
106 Jermyn Street
London SW1Y 6EE.
Tel. (01) 839 3026.

Zoo Check
Cherry Tree Cottage
Coldharbour, Dorking
Surrey RH5 6HA
Tel. (0306) 712091.

United States

Coalition to Protect Animals
in Entertainment
c/o U.A.A.R
P.O. Box 2448
Riverside
California 92516.
Tel. (714) 682 7872.
Fax. (714) 784 4262.

IPPL
PO Drawer 776
Summerville
S.C. 29484
Tel. (0101) 803 871 2280

MONITOR
1506 19th Street N.W.
Washington D.C. 20036.
Tel. 202 - 234 65 76.
Fax. 202 - 234 65 77.

People for the Ethical
Treatment of Animals
(PETA)
P.O.Box 42516
Washington D.C. 20015.
(202) 726 0156

Performing Animal
Welfare Society (PAWS)
P.O. Box 842
Yalt
CA 95632.

Animal Protection Insitute
of America
PO Box 57006
Washington D.C. 20037.
Tel: 703-528 52 05

Humane Society of the U.S.
2100 L Street, N.W.
Washington DC 20005.
Tel. 202-452 1100

Also by William Johnson from Heretic Books:

THE MONK SEAL CONSPIRACY

A fascinating account of the author's own efforts as the head of an international project to save the Mediterranean monk seal, by creating a network of sanctuaries, centred on the Greek island of Samos. Once the special friend of the ancient Greeks, the monk seal's habitat has been under increasing threat, through urban growth, industrial poisons, mass tourism and overfishing.

The Monk Seal Conspiracy shockingly reveals the considerable obstacles Johnson was to come up against, with the project subject to increasing suspicion and harassment from the Greek security services, resulting in Johnson's eventual expulsion from the country. The author also attacks the complacency of the various conservation movements involved in the project, tantamount, he argues, to an endorsement of the monk seal's inevitable extinction.

"A sad and poignant account of the insanity of a world which allows such a delightful animal to become extinct" -- *Sunday Times*

"A passionately written and entertaining book... we need books like this to remind us how easy it is to believe that complacency is really pragmatism" -- *New Scientist*

ISBN 0 946097 23 2   208 pages
UK £4.95 / US $9.95 / AUS $14.95 / DM17.80